A HEART BLOWN OPEN

The Life

and Practice of Zen Master

Jun Po Denis Kelly Roshi

KEITH MARTIN-SMITH

DIVINE
ARTS

Published by DIVINE ARTS

DivineArtsMedia.com

An imprint of Michael Wiese Productions

12400 Ventura Blvd. #1111

Studio City, CA 91604

(818) 379-8799, (818) 986-3408 (FAX)

Cover design by Johnny Ink. www.johnnyink.com

Edited by David Wright

Book layout by William Morosi

Cover photo by Geraldine Overton

Printed by McNaughton & Gunn, Inc., Saline, Michigan

Manufactured in the United States of America

Library of Congress Cataloging-in-Publication Data

Martin-Smith, Keith.

 A heart blown open : the life and practice of Zen master Jun Po Denis Kelly Roshi / Keith Martin-Smith.

    p. cm.

ISBN 978-1-61125-008-4

1. Kelly, Jun Po Denis, 1942- 2. Zen Buddhists--United States--Biography. I. Title.

BQ968.E55M37 2012

294.3'927092--dc23

[B]

2011041193

Printed on Recycled Stock

MIX
Paper from responsible sources
FSC® C011935
FSC
www.fsc.org

"Written with extraordinary heart and skill, this book chronicles the making of an integral Zen master. Jun Po's life has been as unpredictable as it has been astounding. How many spiritual masters can speak of intense family abuse, life on the run, prison, fame and notoriety, hedonism, and monasticism as part of the journey to their awakening? Jun Po's dedication to exploring his own psychological shadows in light of his own awakening consciousness is *the* story of our times, for it is the integration of Eastern mystical wisdom with Western psychological insight. It is an absolute must-read for anyone with even a passing interest in human evolution and Keith Martin-Smith does a truly brilliant job of bringing it all together."

   — Ken Wilber, author of *Integral Spirituality*

"This is the legendary story of an inspiring teacher that mirrors the journey of many contemporary Western seekers. A flash of white light from psychedelic theophanies leads to a lifetime's pursuit of enlightenment under the Buddha dharma prayer flag."

   — Alex Grey, artist and author of *Transfigurations*, *Sacred Mirrors*,
     and *The Mission of Art*

"*A Heart Blown Open* is the real life saga of a true spiritual warrior. What is so fascinating about Jun Po Roshi's story is that it describes, at times with painful honesty, the challenges of warriorship in the strange new world of postmodernity, where Spirit is denied, all things are equal, and therefore real teachers are forced to find their own way. 'Mondo Zen,' the American Roshi's updated version of Japanese Buddhism, retains the immediacy and uncompromising fire of nonduality that too many Buddhist traditions seem to have lost in their translation from Eastern masters to Western teachers. This biography is a time capsule colorfully and poignantly conveying the powerful emergence and evolution of a cultural revolution from the inside out."

   — Andrew Cohen, founder EnlightenNext,
     author of *Evolutionary Enlightenment*

"This book provides a provocative window into the life of one of the more controversial Zen Masters of our generation, and will not fail to touch and inspire those who read it. Jun Po Roshi has lived a life of amazing fullness. Few have risen to such heights of notoriety and wealth in their youth and given back so much wisdom and service later in life. His greatest gift is his continuing effort to discover the best way to transmit the ancient wisdom of Zen in this 21st century."

   — Dennis Genpo Merzel, author of *Big Mind · Big Heart: Finding Your Way*

"This is a profoundly inspiring story about a rebel *with* a cause, Jun Po Roshi — a fiercely caring man who does not know what it means to give up. At one point in the book Jun Po has to own up to betrayal. Because of his status as a respected Zen master, Jun Po could have hidden behind the curtain like the Wizard of Oz. Instead he made a choice to tell the truth and risked destroying everything he had worked to create. Jun Po's life teaches us that it is never too late to regain our integrity and realize our true nature."

— Rich Tosi, Founding President, ManKind Project

"Jun Po Roshi's life is a powerful testament to the human capacity to go beyond fear. How rare is it that we risk our comfort, let alone our lives, to do what needs to be done? Jun Po's life and teaching seem to whisper, sometimes softly, sometimes with deafening force: to wake up, you have to risk it all."

— Vincent Horn, Chief Geek, *BuddhistGeeks.com*

"From the hills of San Francisco to the foothills of the Himalayas, Jun Po Roshi's life story is a mad rip through the jungles of Samsara. Brilliantly crafted by Martin-Smith, it left me by turns breathless, astonished, devastated, and finally redeemed right alongside Denis himself. I stayed up all night reading, not daring to put it down as jewel after brilliant jewel revealed themselves through the hero's journey that it really is. And it's our story, each of us... When that moment dawns in our lives and we're called through God's precious gift to take our seat, we need look no further than this modern day hero to show us how it's done."

— Robb Smith, former Chairman, Integral Life

"*A Heart Blown Open* is for *anyone* with an interest in Zen Buddhism, including those who are not Buddhist. Keith Martin-Smith's writing is so straightforward and engaging I felt as if Jun Po Roshi had knocked on my door and offered to tell me the story of his remarkable life. And in the process of hearing his story, my understanding of Zen was also deepened. The conversations about the role of emotions, especially anger, were the most insightful and powerful for me — they shone a new light on the immeasurable benefit the day-to-day practice of Zen can have in our lives."

— Gary McClain, PhD, author of *The Complete Idiot's Guide to Zen Living*

"Jun Po Roshi's teaching has a transcendent ring *and* gritty humor that speaks to decades of him surrendering every aspect of his life to more love and more truth. Whether I am meditating with Jun Po, or reading his book, or spending a couple of hours in the mountains with him, I receive the gift of the softness of him humbly owning his humanity and electric jolts as I am shown mine — tears from experiencing loss in this life and tears of hilarity from leaving no stone on a journey unturned. I love finding a teaching I know is being lived by the one teaching it."

— Decker Cunov, Founder, Authentic World

For Mom and Dad, who always encouraged and supported me in following my dreams....

TABLE OF CONTENTS

Acknowledgments . . . . *ix*

Author's Note . . . . *x*

Introduction . . . . *xii*

PART ONE *1*

    CHAPTER 1 — The End Is the Beginning *3*

    CHAPTER 2 — The Promise of the American Dream . . . *9*

    CHAPTER 3 — The American Dream, Perverted *25*

    CHAPTER 4 — Down the Rabbit Hole *41*

    CHAPTER 5 — An Institutional Man, Part I *61*

    CHAPTER 6 — A Fork in the Road *71*

PART TWO *83*

    CHAPTER 7 — The Making of a
    Counterculture Icon *85*

    CHAPTER 8 — Clear Light Windowpane LSD-25 . . . . *102*

    CHAPTER 9 — The Doors of Perception:
    When Reality Bends, and Breaks *114*

    CHAPTER 10 — The Age of the Guru *131*

    CHAPTER 11 — The Rise and Fall of the
    Order of the Golden Frog *167*

    CHAPTER 12 — On the Run *191*

    CHAPTER 13 — An Institutional Man, Part II *212*

PART THREE *231*

    CHAPTER 14 — Of Saints and Sinners *233*

    CHAPTER 15 — An Institutional Man, Part III *249*

    CHAPTER 16 — The Chains of the Past *268*

    CHAPTER 17 — The Great Liberators of Cancer,
    Bankruptcy, and Grief *286*

    CHAPTER 18 — Rebirth and Renewal *300*

About the Author *318*

On the Practice of Mondo Zen *319*

ACKNOWLEDGEMENTS

I WISH TO GIVE THANKS TO MARK FOR HELP WITH EDITing and for the inspiration that only an older brother can provide; to Madeleine for highly specific feedback on early drafts as well as her unwavering support; to Manny Otto who not only shared his editing expertise but also fought to get the book published and to keep a fire lit under my ass; to David Wright, whose keen eye and judgment as an editor were indispensable; to the entire FY Group in Boulder (Casey, Robert, Michael, Max, Pieter, Jason, William, Huy, Devon, Bryce, Joel, Marco, and Forest) who provided support and encouragement from the very beginning, including when I sold my house to finance this book; to Michael Wiese for believing in me; to Doshin M. J. Nelson Roshi for his clarity of insight and his help with fine-tuning the message of this book; to Ken Wilber for being willing to be the guy with all the arrows in his back; to the Laughing Goat coffee house for letting me use their establishment as an office, bathroom, and occasional place to buy coffee; and to Jun Po Roshi, who showed me what it looks like to walk the walk in your life. To all those others who have helped, prodded, and encouraged me and whose names I've forgotten to mention, I beg one thousand pardons. The bottom line is that this book could never have been written without the love and support of many, many people, and to all of you I offer a deep and humble bow of gratitude.

AUTHOR'S NOTE

JUN PO, THE SUBJECT OF THIS BOOK, AND I OFTEN HEAR the question, "Is this really a true story?" The answer is yes, but with a few caveats. For starters, some of the names had to be changed to protect the identities of people still living who had no interest in being a part of this story. Secondly, writing someone else's biography presents a creative challenge that must be carefully faced. Jun Po and I both wanted to craft an emotional, heartfelt book that would drop the reader into the scenes and settings of his life. For much of that life, his memory was vivid and accurate, and I had little more to do then report on what he told me. Yet some details of his youth, with the passage of half a century or more, had grown less vibrant and bright, and I didn't want to skip these important parts of his life or simply list what happened. The tapestry of characters and places, of feeling and touch, were vital to his story. In these areas, where his memory was less clear, I would take what he told me and work to fill in the details as best I could.

"What happened that day you went back to see Grace?" I said over the phone, referring to his ex-wife and his attempt at reconciliation, some forty years ago. "I don't have a sense of what happened."

"God," he breathed, "it was so long ago, so long ago." There was a long pause, and I could almost see his closed eyes straining to summon distant sights. "I don't remember the exact conversation, but I do remember how I felt. Let's see ... I rented a car to drive back to Wisconsin. Long drive. I had a friend meet me in Green Bay, and then went to see my folks."

For events like this, so long past and so far buried under the passage of time, I would create rough sketches of what happened and how he felt. Jun Po would read what I had written and offer corrections. My writing would jog his memory and the tapestry would come together.

That, at least, was our intention. While this is Jun Po's life, it is my book, and we did not always have the time to go through each and every part in excruciating detail. In some places I have presumed to speak for him and his insight based on our lengthy conversations, but this should not be considered the final word on his thoughts or feelings — ultimately, only Jun Po can speak for himself.

As I wrote this book I was challenged to set aside my beliefs about the way I thought the world worked, and to step into his life with beginner's mind. I had to suspend my disbelief and

my judgment about what was and was not possible. In the process I experienced what it was like to live inside of Jun Po's
amazing life, to evolve from getting through life to living one
of wonder, gratitude, and freedom.

I have come to see Jun Po's life as the Hero's Journey for the
twenty-first century, a tale full of sound and fury, signifying
nothing. And everything.

Keith Martin-Smith
Boulder, CO
Fall, 2011

INTRODUCTION

JUN PO DENIS KELLY ROSHI SITS ACROSS FROM ME ON a rainy morning in Massachusetts in 2009, a black hood draped over his head. We are on the enclosed porch of an old lake home, overlooking a small stand of trees and, as seen through an opening in the underbrush, water. We are both holding steaming cups of coffee, and even though it is late June our hands huddle around the cups for warmth.

Jun Po's eyes, intensely blue, stare past me at the distant memories I know he is conjuring, watching them take shape in his mind. We sit together, my digital recorder ready, notebook open with pen in hand; I wait in a measured silence as he searches for a place to begin.

Denis Kelly is tall and muscular with broad shoulders and a natural athleticism that defies his age, but his mass is now subdued, thoughtful, turned in on itself. When he places his coffee cup on the table, I notice the hands of a laborer; broad and sinewy muscles wrap across large bones. There are pleats in his cheeks and deep lines etched into the skin around his mouth. The scars from radiation treatments a few years before make a red arc across his neck, as if he's an old cowboy who somehow escaped the hangman's noose. His is a face accustomed to wearing serious expressions, and seems most at home with slightly narrowed eyes and downturned lips, despite the fact I know he is prone to sudden laughter and frequent smiles. His eyes are intelligent and measured and hold no fear or hesitation. Like the water outside the window they are clear, deep, and still. The dark hood comes away from his face, exposing large ears and a large nose and a large chin that, taken together, create a rugged handsomeness that harkens back to some dust bowl farmer stoically working his land.

His sixty-seven years show on his face, but his decades of daily yoga practice are hinted at in the deep masculinity and strength that emanates from his body. This is the first day of two weeks we are to spend together, two intensive weeks in which he will go over the events of his extraordinary life in extraordinary detail, being candid to the point of making me occasionally squirm in my chair. I will come to understand that any discomfort is mine alone to bear, for he long ago made peace with the demons and angels that gave him form and purpose.

"So," I say, "I suppose we should start at the beginning."

He considers for a long moment. When he finally speaks, his voice is a rumble, coming from somewhere deep in his belly, as if the story of his life will emanate from that place.

"Okay," he says, his eyes briefly engaging mine before they find some undefined point in the ether behind me. "We have to go back to northern Wisconsin, back in the dark ages, in 1942. I have to start in utero, because my story begins with that trauma. My mother and my father had Rh-negative blood problems, and an older brother died in the hospital immediately after birth; I was born prematurely seven months later, and I still have that taste in my body of being created and nurtured and destroyed all at once by my mother, which set up a very interesting psychological profile."

"Do you remember it?" I ask.

His head moves back and forth once. "No, but the feeling of that dichotomy — nurturing and destruction — is in my body. I didn't work that out until I was in my fifties, didn't understand that process. I could never quite crack the terror or intensity that was driving my basic narcissism. It was deeper than the trauma I had experienced in my youth..."

I take notes furiously, and Jun Po settles back into his chair, interlacing his large fingers and resting his hands across his lap.

"What's the first thing you remember?"

"Had to be nineteen forty-five or six," he says after a pause, "Father was just back from the war. Nasty alcoholic. I was lying in a pool of my own piss, my little fat baby boy hands stuck out in front of me. In the next room, there's an explosion of violence — screams and yelling, and I'm just trying to get away from it and have backed myself under a bed. I stare out between my hands, trying to make sense of just what the fuck is going on in the next room, and then," he snaps he fingers, "and then I'm gone, deep within the body in the most serene stillness you can imagine...."

I begin asking my questions: *What did the house look like? Was there dust under the bed? What happened next? How did you view your father at that age?*

His responses are calm and methodical, sometimes bordering on the lyrical. They are driven by the intensity that is this man, but there is little other emotion to animate them.

Over the next two weeks I will eventually become used to this. Jun Po's descriptions of his life are at times unbearably sad and poignant, but he never once falters in his story, never dabs a tear from the corner of his eye, never has a quivering voice, and never once expresses much beyond a stoic wonder and a wry sense of humor and irony. Far from being repressed or detached from his emotions, I realize as our days together pass that he has already spent more than two decades of his life deconstructing these impulses; many of these events, once problematic, have become old friends full of their own hard wisdom. He welcomes them as such, mostly without valuation, although in a few areas he is harsh — almost cruel — in his assessment of himself.

His life has been almost unimaginably full of different roles; world traveler, seeker of wisdom, ascetic, holder of vast wealth and power, lover of women, homeless mendicant, wanderer, fearless warrior, father and husband, spiritual adept, yogi, federal prisoner, family deserter, hedonist, Zen master. There are a dozen men that sit down with me every morning but they all exist within this man who has become Jun Po Roshi.

AT THE END OF THOSE TWO WEEKS TOGETHER, I HAD COME to know Jun Po quite intimately. I spent days reviewing my notes, and realized something profound: I had been handed a story far richer and more significant than I had previously imagined.

For this, I am, and will always be, deeply grateful.

PART ONE

"This old anvil laughs at many a broken hammer."

— *Carl Sandburg*

CHAPTER 1

THE END IS THE BEGINNING

DENIS KELLY WAS ABOUT TO COMMIT RITUAL SUICIDE. He was sitting on the spotless hardwood floor of a friend's beach house, each foot tucked onto the top thigh of the opposite leg in full lotus position. The house was nestled on a street overlooking the Pacific Ocean, only an hour or so from his flat in San Francisco. It was 1970, the height of the counterculture movement in the Bay Area, and Denis Kelly had just turned twenty-eight.

Kelly, as everyone knew him, was in the business of changing consciousness, and although he had never sought money or notoriety or the company of women, he wanted for none of those things. He wore fashionable clothes, lived in expensive homes, drove fine cars, ate and drank only the very best. He was on a first-name basis with members of the Grateful Dead and half a dozen other famous bands and knew many living outside of authority's established rules — ranging from the Buddhist philosopher Alan Watts to the founder of the Hell's Angels, Sonny Barger.

Like so many of his baby boomer generation, Denis Kelly was an idealist bent on changing the world, though his idealism had a distinctly different flair. The assassinations of President John. F. Kennedy in 1963 and his brother Senator Robert F. Kennedy in 1968 had galvanized most of those around him, but those two events had hardly registered in Kelly's consciousness. It wasn't that he was cynical, self-absorbed, or didn't care about the future of the country. He simply thought it futile to care for men he'd never met who were moving the country in a direction he figured was well short of where it really needed to go. Perhaps more to the point, Kelly wasn't the kind of guy that put faith in other people getting things right, in making the kinds of changes the world needed. He'd just as soon do it himself. It was necessary to have leaders, he knew, and it was good that men like JFK and RFK had risen to such prominence. Change, though, could only come from below, never *just* from above. The Kennedy brothers were a reflection of change, not a cause of it. They were murdered, yes, but the truth was that if the change they represented was actually part of a larger social movement that was going to have as deep an impact as so many hoped, there would be no shortage of people to take their place. With Richard Nixon in office, the United States deeply embroiled in Vietnam, and deep fissures emerging around race, gender, and social class (four college students had just been shot dead by National Guardsmen in Ohio), Kelly was suspicious of how much change the Kennedy boys would have been able to create *had* they lived. Kelly was doing his part to change the consciousness of the next generation of leaders, sowing the seeds of real change, he believed, that would ultimately flourish throughout all parts of American society once enough people had been turned onto a deeper reality. At the core of his being, Kelly didn't trust teachers, institutions, or authority figures. That meant that the only one left to trust was himself.

The house in which he sat was modest and modern, with hardwood floors and minimal decorations. In front of Kelly was a small makeshift shrine set up on a low, wood altar he had carried from his car. A statue of a sixteenth-century silver Tibetan Amitābha, or Buddha, faced him, its face forever cast in an expression of divine awareness. Fine ginkgo Aloeswood incense, imported directly from Japan, burned from a jade holder, its smoke curling languidly in ever-shifting patterns. To Kelly's right were some organic fruits, juices, and water, and he was sitting on an antique blue Persian prayer rug, a gift from a friend.

Outside the house the sun moved closer to the horizon, its light dancing off the ocean waves in undulating currents, the shimmering, otherworldly light then reflected onto the walls around him. Kelly was stripped to the waist, wearing only a pair of tight blue jeans, his body's leanness and flexibility the result of a disciplined physical practice. His brown hair was long and pulled back into a ponytail, showing off a prominent nose, cheekbones, and chin. His blue eyes were open, and Kelly began a deep, formal yogic breathing known as Pranayama, designed to clear the mind, settle the body, and open the energy currents between the two. He pulled out a wooden box the size of a pack of cigarettes and slid open its lid. Inside were a dozen tiny glass vials, and Kelly methodically poured their contents into the seventeenth-century, solid gold French chalice he owned.

It was time.

◯

THE LITTLE BOY'S HANDS WERE SPLAYED OUT IN FRONT of him, gripping the floor. Overhead the springs of the bed touched the top of his head. He peered past his own chubby fingers, looking through the gap between the bed and the hardwood floor, his instincts having taken him to a place where he might be safe from the madness in the next room. He felt the sickening thud of his heart against his ribs, itself a terrifying, otherworldly feeling. In this choked silence, breath came and went in ragged, uneven gasps, and tears slipped out of his eyes, dotting the floor around him and creating little craters of clean wood flooring in the thin layer of midwestern dust.

There was something warm around him, moving down the length of his body. His eyes were wide open, staring, as if trying to materialize a different reality than the one before him. He could see feet and ankles in the doorway of the adjacent room, and hear explosive noises coming from their direction. The words didn't make any sense to his young mind: "You're just a... you, all you do is drink and then come home... oh yeah you no good... this whole goddamn mess..." and on and on they went, nonsensical, insane, violent beyond measure.

The boy's existence until a few months before had been quiet and stable, with only a mother who nurtured and sang to him as if he were the only living soul in the world — the object of all her love and tenderness. Then this large man had appeared — who at first was tender, but slowly introduced an intensity and instability into the household. His mother now seldom held him and her soft song was heard even less.

His tiny body moved further under the bed until his bare feet came up against a baseboard and he could retreat no more. The insanity in the next room raged on with one sharp outburst overriding the next, the feet rushing this way and that, objects dropped explosively, chairs squalling out of place, doors banging open and closed. Hatred and love pushed together into an indistinguishable mess, something no child could possibly understand for the simple reason it did not make sense. Yellow urine, warm against his body, ran between his outstretched hands and threatened to move out from under the protective overhang of the bed, revealing his presence. He wiped at it frantically, listening as his parents threw such explosive tempers at one another it seemed a miracle the house didn't fall down around them. It did not make sense, it could not make sense, and choking down the tears and the violence that had come home with his father, the boy's heart broke open.

Lying on his belly in his urine, stuffed under a bed with a week's worth of dust and dirt, a strange stillness came to him. The fear and the contraction and the sense of a separate, terrified self fell away, and there was only a sense of pervasive peace, an overriding clarity, and an understanding that there was nothing to fear, an understanding that was beyond even fear. The toddler stopped fidgeting. His face relaxed from its spasm as he opened his eyes to see everything around him. There was no sense of fear, no sense of what should be, no sense that things were worse or better. There was awareness of his body and of a silence out of which everything arose. It was a peace deeper than anything his young mind associated with his mother's embrace or her breast, unbound to anything or anyone. It just *was*.

The violence in the other room finally consumed itself, leaving an exhausted peace in its wake. Denny crawled out from under the bed, soaked in urine, and stood, marveling at his hands, at his body, and the look and shape of the room, at the sounds of his mother down the hall and his father muttering outside. The feeling of deep peace faded slowly, like a dream, and the young boy was suddenly, acutely aware of how cold, how *awful*, his pants felt against his body. Suddenly afraid, ashamed, and sobbing, he ran on tiny bare feet to find his mother, who scooped him up, cooing into his ear, and helped him change into dry clothes. Against this ferocious man who had returned from the ravages of war, she had her ally.

Although the experience was gone, that sense of a peace deeper than anything he had ever known scored itself into the memory of the toddler, burned itself into the forming gray matter of his young brain, leaving a permanent marker for a sensation of stillness outside of time, space, or the sense of a separate self. For a few moments in early 1945, Denis Kelly had been utterly, radically free.

As he was dressed and fretted over by his mother, the safety and security she provided were but a shadow of what he had just experienced, and *mother* would never again comfort him quite the same way. A longing to return to that place of freedom outside of time and place and personhood was implanted, and Denis Kelly would spend half a lifetime attempting to recapture it and make it his own.

○

DENIS KELLY WAS CONCEIVED IN 1941, ONLY A FEW MONTHS before the Japanese attacked Pearl Harbor and killed thousands of Americans. As the Imperial Army rolled across Asia, the German war machine took control of much of Western Europe, quickly taking half the continent. France, ripped violently in thirds, had been effectively conquered, and it was an open question if England was strong enough to resist a full Nazi assault against her shores.

Denis' father was horrified at the thought of raising children in a world devoid of freedom, a world where the forces of tyranny and hatred could come to rule. What was the point of raising a family in a world consumed in conflict? How could one turn a blind eye to the war raging for the very soul of humanity, and risk watching ones grandchildren being born into bondage? Even though it meant leaving his family, he felt he was more valuable as a soldier than as a father. He would serve his family by serving his country, so he volunteered to enlist right after Denis was born.

William Robert Kelly had been raised on the ideals of the heroic soldier, and of war being a noble and dignified sacrifice that defined men in the best possible ways. He finished basic training in the Army Air Force and became a navigator, his ears ringing with words like *duty* and *honor*. He was deployed to India where he flew the Burma route to supply the British forces there. The Japanese were fierce and disciplined warriors, and heavy American causalities meant William Kelly served two tours of twenty-five combat missions in the Far East, fighting in the air and on the ground, before returning home to Green Bay, Wisconsin, to reunite with a wife and sons he barely knew. He had served honorably and fought with passion and valor, but in the end had been just one man among the tens of millions who were fighting and dying.

William came back to the safety of midwestern America a changed man. Deep lines were etched into his still-young forehead and jaw. While he appeared cool-headed and disciplined to his friends, they also felt heat just under the surface, like live coals buried under cool gray ash. At home, his wife was witness to his insomnia, wandering mind, and nightmares that brought him out of a sound sleep with a scream caught in his throat, sweating and wide-eyed.

Alcohol offered its cursed, temporary relief, but in the long run only created more fissures that ran deeper into the fire. When sober, William Kelly was a good Midwesterner who bore his demons stoically and silently, but when drunk a different man was free to emerge, one who on occasion would speak of the bodies of Allied airmen crucified and gutted at the hands of the Japanese, or of the desecrated corpses of American POWs, starved and mutilated. And with a humorless smile he would allude to the revenge wreaked on any Japanese soldier unfortunate enough to be captured by his ground unit, far from a commander's eyes.

The cultural conditioning of Green Bay, Wisconsin, was especially unforgiving to those broken soldiers who reminded them of a war they would prefer to forget. Abusive relationships must be tolerated and managed, marriage was always for life with no exceptions, babies were always born no matter how young the mother or who the father might be, a woman's place was behind her husband, and children were managed with the rod and the back of the hand to maintain the discipline of the home. It was a hard but ordered world. It made sense, and everyone knew his and her place within it. The nails that dared stand up above the board were systematically and relentlessly pounded back into place.

Bill Kelly was a working-class man who had large features and a larger personality to animate them. Like all the Kelly men he was tall and muscular — six feet and innately athletic and strong. His mixed-blood Cherokee heritage was strongly hinted at in his rough but handsome features, while long hands and tan skin kept no secret of a living made more by brawn than brains. He drank, worked, and lived hard, convinced that life simply did not offer the chance to slow down. A plain dresser, he was nevertheless always put together and neat with clothes pressed and clean. He spoke with an erudition that belied his minimal schooling, and he was far cleverer then he let on. He and his wife won dozens of swing dance competitions in town, and they loved to go out on a Saturday night to twirl, dance, and socialize into the wee hours of the morning.

Always in motion, he seemed to only settle down when drunk; otherwise, he was working, fishing, hunting, dancing, attending church, or otherwise busily engaged with life. It was as if his own energy would consume him from within if he dared stop for even a moment.

Denis' father slowly lost all discipline to his alcoholism and the demons it was feeding. The abuse he inflicted on his own children grew more disproportionate and unpredictable. The smallest transgression, like being a minute late for dinner, could lead to a vicious beating, while other more serious matters were laughed off. When Denis was caught stealing a car for a joy ride at the age of twelve, all his father said to the sheriff was, "Boys will be boys." Denis wasn't so much as grounded. Yet Michael, Denis' younger brother, was beaten unconscious just a few years later for a lesser infraction of the home's undefined code of conduct.

Denis grew up hating his father's violence and unpredictability, and was long a man before he was able to see a more complicated truth. As he watched his friends return from Vietnam, corrupted, distorted, and broken by their experiences, he saw shades of his own upbringing. He saw the true madness of the world and of boys sent to fight impossible battles at the whim of politicians. The poor and the disempowered bore the brunt of war always, and were too often discarded when they returned — left to fight their own battles with only their families to bear witness to how they suffered. His father had managed as best he knew how, never once striking out in malice, but only in ignorance, confusion, and a pain that knew no boundaries or restraints, a pain that would eventually consume those closest to him.

CHAPTER 2

THE PROMISE OF THE AMERICAN DREAM

THERE IS NOTHING LIKE FALLING IN LOVE AT THE AGE OF five. The girl of his very first affection was a striking redhead, who at nearly six years of age seemed impossibly soft, intelligent, and desirable. Her blue eyes seemed to hold the mysteries of the universe, while her small face captured all the potential for happiness that Denis thought could exist.

Denis wanted to share his love of her, and so he set about creating the perfect gift. An ancient bottle, small in form, was unearthed from the back yard and washed clean of dirt. It was then filled with several different kinds of his mother's perfume. Into this elixir of love he placed a treasure of almost unimaginable value: an ant he had found on the kitchen floor, carefully captured and entombed in the bottle. A more appropriate gift he could not imagine. It was the perfect fusion of her love, smelling nice, with his — bugs, stuff found in the dirt, and potions. She accepted his gift with much kindness and warmth but a small amount of confusion. To consummate their newly acknowledged love, Denis took her back to her house where he proceeded to take off all her clothes. He then stripped as well, and the 5-year-olds stood looking at each other. He could not help but notice that her parts were, at least from the waist down, different from his parts — a potentially important fact. He resigned to find out if all girls were missing parts or just this particular one.

After a few minutes Denis' finely tuned fear of authority overwhelmed his sense of wonder, and he carefully dressed himself. Her underwear went into his back pocket as a keepsake, and then he attempted to dress her with the remaining clothes. This transgression of her virtue might have gone unnoticed except that, being five, he had no idea how to put her clothes back on properly, and she wasn't much help. He did a pretty good job, he thought, good enough that he, at least, couldn't tell the difference. Denis left the house and stood blinking in the sun. Leaving his love seemed out of the question, but he couldn't wait in the house either, so he decided to play in her yard as innocently as he could.

Her father, who had a much better idea how to dress women after removing their clothes, came home from work and noted with curiosity the red-faced Kelly boy playing in his yard. Going inside he found his daughter with her shirt on backwards, her skirt inside out, and missing her panties. While far from the sharpest mind in town, he nevertheless put two and two together and chased Denis down, catching him by the shirt and dragged him into the house. Denis' father was called, and Denis was directed to wait on the outside stoop. Denis' shame was overwhelmed with the fear of what his father might do to him. Trembling and occasionally breaking into tears, he waited on the outside steps with his head buried between his legs.

His father, tall and muscular and in his work clothes, showed up twenty minutes later, his face copper-colored from the Midwestern summer sun. Bill Kelly walked by and, to Denis' astonishment, tousled his hair affectionately with a big hand as he ascended the stairs. Raised voices came from inside. When his father emerged from the house, he said gruffly, "Come on, boy." He led Denis to the car, going so far as to open his door. When they entered the house his father told him to sit down.

"Listen up, Denny, and listen closely." His father knelt down, looking him in the eye. He smelled of sweat and work, but there was no hint of the acrid smell that Denis had learned could sometimes make his father violent. "When you undress a girl, be sure to put everything back where you found it. Understand?"

Denis nodded. "Yes sir."

"Just like you found. Leave no trace, boy."

"Yes sir."

"You're life will be a lot easier if you live by that simple rule." His father smiled, winking at him. "Leave no trace. Got it?"

Denis nodded. "Yes sir," he repeated.

"Good boy. Now go and play."

Leave no trace is a central part of Zen and of Jun Po Denis Kelly's own teachings, where students are instructed to always leave their room, their community, their meditation cushion, and the world at large in better condition than they found it. It is also seemingly relevant when dressing girls.

As Denis neared puberty, there was a change at the top of his Catholic school, a position known as "the vicar." The headmaster had been a young priest who had given Denis his First Communion. Whenever Denis got into trouble and was sent to the office, the young priest would talk to him like an old friend. There were never lectures or shaming or talk of the Bible and God's will. He was a radical in 1952 in Wisconsin for he was advocating things like emotional connections with children, creating respect instead of demanding it, and other ideas that were thirty years ahead of their time.

It was rumored the young headmaster had been sent to Green Bay as punishment for inappropriate behavior — which could mean anything from screwing boys to advocating on their behalf. The Church up until very recently wasn't very good at making those sorts of critical distinctions. But whatever had landed him in Green Bay became a problem again, for the priest was ordered to an even more miserable climate and far-flung community somewhere in the frigid wastelands of North Dakota.

The headmaster's replacement could not have been more his opposite. Father Jonathan Michael Geiger was an old Jesuit priest who harkened back to another era. Father Geiger had a head of snowy white hair, as full and lustrous as a man a quarter his age, a great flaring nose packed with white hairs erupting from the nostrils, a ruby red face colored by frustration, scotch, or both, and blue eyes that were as cold and sharp as the Midwestern winter sky.

Father Geiger smelled of dusty boxes and unused attic spaces, and he always wore clothing that was clean, heavily starched, and meticulously pressed. The world for him was a simple one: everything that felt good, smelled good, looked good, or seemed good, was, in all likelihood, a sin.

Life in the Kelly household was stubbornly consistent month to month, with a slow downward spiral only visible from the view afforded by adulthood. In 1942, the year Denis was born, the family grew much of its own food and had its own chickens. When Bill Kelly first came back from the war, he and his wife went out dancing most weekends, had a vibrant social life, were great dressers with modest but well-kept wardrobes, and were able to manage their three boys without tremendous strain. He was president of the local VFW (Veterans of Foreign Wars), used to go on retreats with the parish head, and loved to have priests over to the house for dinner (where he would inevitably get them drunk).

As the years slid by, though, the family moved further and further into suburbia, relying on the new supermarkets to provide their food and the new ideas about the American Dream to feed their souls. As the Forties drifted by, Bill's drinking began to interfere with his social life and the weekly dancing, for gradually he came to prefer smoky pubs and the company of work and war buddies to socials and dancing with his wife. His drinking routine changed as well. When the boys were young he mainly drank on weekends, but as the children grew he would often swing by the bar on his way home from work and then head back to it once dinner was finished.

Starting when Denis was ten years old, a new ritual was formed that would be repeated every single Saturday for years to come. Denis came down for breakfast to find his father, freshly bathed and shaved, sitting at the kitchen table, his big hands closed into fists, the smell of soap and aftershave heavy in the room. His face was stern and accusatory, and he told Denis to sit by uttering that single, declarative word. A few minutes later the oldest Kelly boy, Patrick, tumbled downstairs, followed by the youngest, Michael. They spilled into the kitchen, stopping short when they saw their father sitting, motionless, eyes hard and purposeful.

"Sit," he commanded again.

The boys took seats around the table, eyes wide, stealing glances at one another to see who the guilty party might be.

"You boys think you're real smart, don't you? Getting away with just about everything under the sun, and I only catch you half the time, if that." Bill stood. "This household will not lose order. It will not become undisciplined, and you boys *will* respect authority. Now *line up*." He pointed to an open spot in the kitchen, and the three boys lined up shoulder to shoulder. They were afraid to make eye contact, for no boy wanted his brothers or their father to see the terror in his eyes.

Bill Kelly's heavy leather belt slid off his waist with a kind of hiss, and was placed on the kitchen table.

"This," he said, "is for all the things you did and got away with." He took up the belt. "Turn around," he said, and all three did. Michael began to whimper, although he fought heroically to hold in his tears. Denis felt tears coming to his eyes, yet when the belt slashed his buttocks, he stiffened. "Fuck you, old man," he thought.

DENIS MADE HIS WAY HOME FROM SCHOOL ONE SPRING afternoon. The sun felt warm against his skin, and in the flowerbeds he passed the heads of flowers were just breaking through the dirt. The naked trees had small buds forming on their branches. Everywhere life seemed to be stirring just below the surface of the brown and bruised Wisconsin landscape.

Feeling the lightness and airiness of spring, he was busily humming to himself as he rode his bike into the yard, ditching it and deftly hopping onto his feet in a single motion. He came up the back stairs of the house two at a time, slung his backpack off a shoulder, and opened the kitchen door. He was going to throw his backpack in his room and head right back outside to properly enjoy such a day.

The kitchen door opened inward, and Denis stepped lightly inside. He briefly noticed a lurking shape to his right, just inside the door, but he was struck behind the ear and knocked to the ground before he had time to turn. His face squarely impacted onto the linoleum, and his backpack went sprawling under the kitchen table. Even though Denis was still just a boy, he was quickly learning to use his fists on the streets of Green Bay, and spun onto his back, ready to defend himself. His father leaned into view.

"Shit," he slurred, opening his fists, "I thought you were Patrick." Denis wiped the blood off his mouth and nose, briefly looking at the smear of red across the skin of his hand. His father, unsteady on his feet, considered his bleeding son lying at his feet, now propped up on an elbow.

"Well," he said, turning and taking a perch by the back door once again, "That's for whatever you did and got away with."

Denis picked himself up, fetched his backpack, and dumped it on his bed. He left the house through the front door, mounted his bicycle and rode through the streets of Green Bay, trying to find Patrick so he could warn him. The beauty and warmth of the spring day were forgotten, and he rode frantically to all the haunts where he might expect to find his brother. As the dinner hour approached, he gave up and at last turned for home.

Patrick and Michael were sitting at the table when Denis came in, and he noted the bruised lip on his older brother, along with that distant, defiant light in his eyes. Patrick looked at Denis, and winked.

Their father, now very drunk, ate in stony silence. After he finished, he rose and grabbed his coat.

"Back later," he announced, heading out the door without so much as a glance back.

The tension went out of the room with him.

"Nice face," Patrick taunted.

"Nice lip," Denis retorted.

"Easy boys," their mother said. "Be nice. Now, who wants some dessert?"

"Father," Denis argued one afternoon, raising his hand in religion class.

"Yes, Mr. Kelly," Father Geiger responded, turning from the blackboard.

"I still don't understand why kissing a girl is a sin." This objection was, it should be noted, apropos to nothing being taught that day.

"The Bible and God's word are clear, my boy," Father Geiger answered, rising to the bait. "You *must* resist temptation until you are married; to do otherwise is to risk eternal damnation, shut away from God and from all that is good and just."

The problem was that at 12 the god testosterone had arrived and all Denis could think of was kissing girls. He woke up thinking about kissing girls. He went to bed thinking about kissing girls. And it occupied the majority of his day in-between. He wondered what it would feel like to touch a girl's soft lips with his own, to feel the tip of her tongue, what her hair might feel like across his neck, how the small of her back would contract under his hand. He was not only certain to commit this sin as soon as the opportunity presented itself, he was *determined* to commit this sin.

He was fairly certain that Father Geiger was wrong, but the classroom was full of the very girls he hoped to kiss. And they all stared at Father Geiger wide-eyed, as if God might snatch them to hell just for looking at a boy. Father Geiger was, in a word, ruining Denis' chances, and so deconstructing his argument was simply a matter of practical and self-involved necessity.

"But where," Denis followed, "in the Bible does it say that kissing is a sin? Or holding hands? Or just necking?" This last statement elicited nervous laughter from the classroom. "I mean, you say it's a sin, but you don't say *why*."

"Because," the priest answered, "it leads your young mind and your young hands to do things that *are* explicitly forbidden in the Bible."

"So God will send me to hell *forever* if I kiss a girl? I mean, *forever*?"

"Yes, Mr. Kelly."

Denis considered the many ways he might argue his point, but it seemed easier to express his opinion in decidedly less theological terms.

"*Bullshit*," he said. The word landed like a neutron bomb, that Cold War invention that was designed to obliterate people with a powerful blast of radiation while leaving buildings standing. The class went deadly silent. No one moved, and more than half of the room stopped breathing. Father Geiger's blue eyes blinked several times in quick succession, but his body, like the rest of the room, was otherwise immobile. The clock marked a few long seconds off, *tock tock tock*. And then, in the span of a second, so much color rushed into the old priest's face that Denis thought he might have uttered a magical, fatal word.

"*What*," Father Geiger stammered, "What? *What did you say*? What did you *just* say?" His tone was righteous, indignant.

"I said, 'I think it's bullshit'," Denis repeated, speaking slowly and clearly and very loudly. The classroom broke from its stunned silence into fits of nervous laughter.

"Get out, Mr. Kelly," Father Geiger commanded, pointing an old and crooked finger toward the door. "Get out, and go straight home."

"Sure," Denis said lightly, "Happy to." He hopped to his feet and headed for the door.

Father Geiger was an educated man. By most measurements he was a brilliant one as well. He thought the previous young priest far too liberal, far too soft to be teaching anything in an age when the Soviets, the Communists, the atheists, and other enemies of God were gathering strength all over the world. The time for liberalism and a soft touch was most certainly past.

"I will call your father at work," Father Geiger added, watching Denis' arrogant expression evaporate as he faltered at the door. "To make sure he knows what happened, and that he's there to greet you when you arrive home." Father Geiger was himself the product of a father who's heavy hand was often felt across his own face, and he could spot the boys whose fathers were prepared to do whatever it took to break their spirits that they might be productive members of society. Denis hesitated at the door, torn between the urge to apologize and the pride of continuing to walk out of the classroom, even knowing what was coming his way. He was getting thrown out of school for being insubordinate, and his ex-military father was going to get called at work and asked to meet his son at home. That meant someone would come and get him at work. Embarrass him. Make him lose money. Inconvenience him by forcing him to drive all the way home in the middle of the day. For cursing. At a priest.

Denis met Father Geiger's gaze, but when he saw the old priest smile cruelly, he quickly turned and walked out the door. *Fuck him. Fuck both of them. Let him beat me to death.*

Denis hopped on his bike and headed to the rail yard, hoping a solution might present itself there, but the massive, lumbering freight cars gave him no ideas or inspirations on how to mount them. He rode out to the main drag in Green Bay, and watching the cars roll past considered ditching his bike and hitchhiking, but to where and to what end he could not imagine. So, reluctantly, he turned for home.

Denis came in through the back door and, sure enough, his father was there, waiting for him. Bill was in need of a haircut, with the hair a little longer in the back and on the sides than usual. Its deep black had, of late, gone gray at the sides. As Denis walked through the door, shoulders raised defensively, he saw his father's sharp and focused eyes, intensely blue, shift to him.

Father and son looked at one other for a long moment.

"So what happened," his father asked, sounding almost amused.

Denis cleared his throat. He knew his father would get impatient if he backed away from the question.

"Father Geiger said that kissing girls was a moral sin and I told him it was bullshit."

"A *mortal* sin," his father corrected.

"What?"

"Not a *moral* sin. A *mortal* sin. As in one that will risk your immortal soul. So he threw you out of school for saying it was bullshit that kissing a girl would land you in hell? Do I have that correct?"

"Yes sir." Denis waited, wondering if the belt would slide out of its loops. But his father only shook his head.

"What's bullshit is him throwing you out of school for that. Come on, Denny," he said, standing.

"Where, Papa?" His father's gentle annoyance and overall good spirits suggesting the day was about to take an unexpected turn.

"Back to school. Gotta get that priest in line. He thinks me or your mother are going to come home and watch you boys every time you do something stupid, he's got another think coming. Isn't any way he shoulda sent you home. For Christ's sake. What else he got to do but teach kids? Man doesn't even have a real job or real responsibilities."

His father drove him back to school.

"Where are you supposed to be?"

"Social studies," Denis replied.

"You know where to go?"

"Yes sir."

"Then go. Where's that priest likely to be?"

"Maybe his office? Right over there," Denis said, pointing. His father walked straight there, and pushed through the door without knocking.

Father Geiger never sent him home again.

○

THE LAST NIGHT BILL KELLY RAISED A HAND AGAINST HIS children was one warm spring night in 1956. Denis initially had tried to insulate himself from the household violence, but the wanton nature of the abuse, combined with the ritualistic Saturday beatings, gradually but steadily worked itself into every fiber of his being. Even though he was the most skillful at avoiding his father's outbursts, he still was sometimes struck, thrown down the cellar stairs, or randomly had his legs kicked out from under him. His distrust of authority festered, and Denis pushed his rage further from his conscious mind. It took more and more of his mental energy to hold it there, and he was most terrified of losing himself to it. School fights, often vicious and bloody, offered an outlet and had the added effect of creating a reputation for him as a kid best left alone.

Denis rode his bike home from a friend's house, feeling the coldness of the air interrupted with delicious pockets of spring warmth, like eddies in the Wisconsin lakes. His thoughts were returning again and again to Grace, a raven-headed beauty who had managed to completely win his heart without so much as a kiss. He thought of the elegance of her long fingers, of the arch of her back, of the way her hair draped her shoulders, of the coolness of her eyes contrasted with the paleness of her skin. All that was wrong with the world seemed to float away at the thought of her, the problems of his life suspended like a balloon high above his head and only tethered by a tiny string she seemed to be inviting him to release. He casually discarded his bike in the yard, dismounting with an easy hop. Humming happily to himself, he climbed the kitchen stairs and entered a quiet house. The sun was nearly set outside, and the only light was what came in weakly through the windows. He had been excused from dinner that evening, and it seemed that someone had cleared the dishes and placed them in their rack to dry. Denis's feet caused the floor to creak and moan as he crossed it, and he paused when he noticed the cellar door was ajar.

"That's odd," he said to himself, since his mother was very particular about the house and especially about things like open doors to the cellar. Patrick, most inclined to leave messes behind, was gone, off to seminary in an attempt to run from the madness of his home and, it would turn out, from his own homosexuality.

"Hello?" he called down the darkened stairs, and no one answered. He went to close it, but something made him linger. Michael should have been home, and Michael was seldom quiet. He listened more intensely, then fingered the switch for the downstairs fixture. A pool of light pushed the darkness back to the edges of the basement and Denis went down the stairs.

Near the water heater was the heap of his brother, weeping. Denis ran to him and turned him onto his back, and saw where his father's belt had left marks across his brother's legs. Bill Kelly was careful to never leave evidence in places where it could be seen. Denis stood over his brother for a long moment, taking in an untied right shoelace, a left pant leg raised halfway to the knee, a tousled shirt, and a baseball cap lying a few feet away. Rage had done this to his brother, rage and uncontrollable violence, and Denis felt something deep inside of him go dark as the last piece of his childhood was snuffed out. Denis gently helped Michael up the stairs and to the bathroom to wash his face. He got him into bed, where Michael slid into an uneasy sleep, murmuring in his dreams.

Denis took his father's single-shot 20-gauge shotgun out of the closet, moving slowly and deliberately. He took the gun apart and cleaned it thoroughly, the way his father had taught him, his mind a blank slate. His breath came in and out of his body in steady, regular intervals, and it occurred to him at one point that he could feel the muscles of his diaphragm engage with each breath, then relax to accept the next.

His breath became that of a larger being, a curious sensation, and his mind was utterly at peace. No thoughts came or went; there was only a deep awareness of what he was doing and the sensual feel of the gun's cold metal to his touch.

A single shell was slid into the breech and two more shells were laid on the bed, ready to be picked up and held once he heard his father enter the house. With the shotgun across his lap, he waited patiently, neither dreading nor anticipating what had to be done.

In some ways his father was amazingly predictable. He had gone to work that day and from work to the bar, where he got drunk. He came home and ate dinner, drinking more. Michael had somehow angered him and was beaten unconscious. Bill Kelly then left to drink some more, after which he would come home and pick a fight with their mother. His father and mother would scream at each other for fifteen minutes downstairs before his father would pass out and the house would go tiredly quiet.

Once his father was passed out in bed, Denis was going to sneak down the stairs to his parent's bedroom, enter silently, and fire a single shotgun blast into his sleeping father's temple, with the two other shells held between the fingers of his left hand, just in case something went awry. His father, after all, was big and fast, and Denis had learned from experience it was never wise to underestimate him, even if he was sleeping.

Denis was no more concerned about this turn of events than a Dust Bowl farmer who had decided the family dog had gone rabid and had to be put down for its own good and for the good of the family. Such was the way of things. Denis sat on the bed, listening to the gentle sounds of his little brother breathing steadily. He heard the kitchen door open rudely downstairs, banging into the wall and rattling the glass in the panes. Uncertain steps followed, walking heavily and tiredly across the floor and through the house, weaving into his parent's bedroom. There was the sound of urine going into a toilet, then a sink running. Raised voices followed, his father's voice thick and undisciplined, his mother's terse and low. The disordered footfalls then went out of the bedroom and meandered down the hallway and back again. Slowly a bruised silence returned, and the house settled.

Denis rose from the bed, making his way down the stairs in his stockinged feet, until he stood in front of his parents' closed door, the shotgun held in his right hand, finger across the trigger. Reaching out with his left, he turned the knob and silently pushed the door open. His father's life would soon be over, but his brothers and sisters and mother would live on without worrying about the rabid dog biting them ever again. Whatever might happen to him for killing his father was not even considered.

Denis moved through the darkened doorway, raising the loaded shotgun as he crossed the threshold. To his surprise, the bed was empty and still made, and so he pushed the door open further, stepping fully inside, hoping his father might be standing somewhere in the room.

His mother sat in a chair by the window, her body bathed in the softness of the light filtering in from the streets outside. She turned and saw her second oldest son standing in the doorway of her bedroom, a shotgun in his hands, finger on the trigger. Their eyes met across the room, but she did not stand, speak, or move. She merely looked at him. Denis brought the muzzle of the gun to the floor, popping open the breech as he did so. Without a word he turned and left, pulling the door shut.

He went back to his room and, still in a surreal space of calmness, took the gun apart and cleaned it as if it had been fired. He then reassembled it, put the shells neatly back in their box, and climbed into bed. That night he slept without dreams. He did not awaken when his father came back home.

The incident was never spoken of, but afterward his father never again, no matter how drunk or angry, struck his children. This was not out of fear of Denis, but out of some kind of respect that his son was willing to take such definitive and resolute action. Bill Kelly's post-traumatic stress would find expression through emotional violence and cruelty, but his hands had been stilled.

DENIS AND FATHER GEIGER MADE PEACE AT LONG LAST.
Denis was less and less interested in school and more and
more interested in getting out of his house forever, by whatever means necessary. That meant he was less inclined to
argue in class and more inclined to simply not show up.

The summer was closing in, and Denis was planning on
working the entire summer to earn and save as much money
as he could. He knew what he had to do in life, and accepted
it without regret or resentment. At sixteen, he was financially
self-sufficient, which he'd been since he was ten years old.
He arranged and delivered flowers for a local flower shop,
delivered newspapers, sold knives to his classmates at a handy
profit, and took any opportunity for work that arose.

In his heart he felt nothing of the light and love of God;
he felt nothing for the man they called the Savior, Jesus; he
believed in nothing except the power of his own two hands
and of his mind to create the reality that would best serve him.

He knew that Father Geiger, for all his faults, was a deeply
learned man who spoke half a dozen languages and held two
advanced degrees. The old priest had lived all over the world,
seeing more of life than most people ever dreamed. He figured
Father Geiger must have a more sophisticated understanding
of what God was really all about, that he might be privy to two
kinds of truths: the one he told the sheep of his congregation
— high school-educated men and women who only needed to
be told what to think, not why — and the real version of the
truth, saved for those who could handle a broader understanding of things. Denis knew *what* the old priest believed; he
wanted to know *how* it was he believed it. Was there some missing, magical piece?

Kelly knocked on the door of the headmaster's office.

"Come in, come in," he heard through the door.

"Mr. Kelly," Father Geiger said, sitting behind his modest
desk in the headmaster's office. "Have a seat. How can I
help you?" The room was cramped and stuffy, and smelled
intensely of age and isolation. Heavy drapes were drawn
across the windows, keeping out views of the sun-soaked fields
of Green Bay, now exploding into a lively green. A single bulb
burned intensely over their heads, casting harsh shadows
downward. Books lined two walls, mostly out-of-print and
esoteric works whose authors had long turned to dust.

Denis leaned back in his chair and the young man and the
old one assessed one another. Denis neither needed nor wanted
the priest's approval. He only sought wisdom. For his part,
Father Geiger knew Denis would not finish high school. Even
though Father Geiger was certain of his verdict for Denis Kelly,
he did have a respect for the young man, whose blue eyes often
blazed with passion and determination and energy, even if they
were nearly always blinded by ignorance and lack of discipline.

"Okay, so I get it," Denis began. "The Virgin Birth. Rising
from the dead. Walking on water. Appearing forty days after
his death as an apparition to the Apostles. Bringing a dead

man back to life. Water to wine. All that stuff. It's like it's all, I dunno... all fictions that like, deepen faith, but they can't be real."

Father Geiger sat forward, the great tufts of white nostril hair coming more clearly into view. He folded his hands neatly in front of him. Denis noticed the priest's shirt was so stiffly starched it could probably be stood erect in the corner without a man to animate it.

"Is there a question in there, Mr. Kelly?" Father Geiger asked, arching his bushy white eyebrows. "Or are you simply informing me of your opinion?"

"I'm saying I know that stuff is bullshit, Father."

Father Geiger, unbothered, shrugged his shoulders. "Profanity doesn't make your points more salient, Mr. Kelly, just less convincing."

"It's like the idea of Hell. You teach that your God will condemn a man or woman eternally for a finite sin. That's beyond unfair — even humans have more compassion than that!"

"God's ways are not man's," Father Geiger responded diplomatically. "It is not our place to judge Him, but rather our place to accept His divine judgment. He has given us due warning, after all."

Denis's lips pressed together until they were white, and his fierce blue eyes sought the priest's. "I know *what* you believe, Father. I know you believe in all the stuff you teach." Tears came to Denis's eyes, surprising the old priest. "I want to know *how* you believe it. I know people like my parents need to be told *what* to do, *what* to think, *what* to believe. But you're the one telling them what to do. How do *you* believe in this stuff? It's so transparently," his limited vocabulary deserted him, "well, *bullshit*."

Father Geiger's face softened as he saw the young man's passion so clearly. He leaned back in his chair, bringing his hands together under his nose. The knuckles were swollen with arthritis, and the nails a little too long and distinctly yellow. "Those things you mention — Christ rising, His divinity, His coming back to the Apostles — these things are foundational to Christianity. The Council of Nicaea, in 325 of the Year of our Lord, determined the parameters of our faith: Credo in unum Deum, Patrem omnipoténtem, factórem cæli et terræ...." He paused, then smiled, "You never did study your Latin, Mr. Kelly."

Denis's face flushed.

"It's okay. I know your path is not one of erudition. It's the Nicene Creed: 'We believe in one God, the Father Almighty, Maker of Heaven and Earth and of all things visible and invisible....' You know the English version, yes?"

"Sure," Denis said, "but that's just a creed. It's just a bunch of words. All the miracles and water-into-wine and Son-of-God stuff." Denis leaned forward, elbows on the desk. "*How* do you believe it, Father?"

"Faith." The word dropped between them almost before Denis's voice had gone quiet. Father Geiger's eyes were kind, but hard.

"So you believe in the whole thing?"

"Yes, Mr. Kelly, I do."

"The miracles and the walking on water and the raising the dead and the bodily, uh, ascent into Heaven?"

"Yes." The priest smiled, not unkindly.

"So *how* do you have faith?" Denis repeated, exasperated. "I mean, you're really educated. You've seen the world. So how do you have faith?"

"Faith comes from grace," Father Geiger answered, again without a moment's hesitation, his answer bearing the weight of immutable stone.

"Grace?" Denis mirrored, stunned. "*Grace*? But... but... but how do you find grace, then?"

"Through the mercy of God," Father Geiger stated concretely.

Denis's face turned red, sensing the cul-de-sac of an argument into which he was being lead. "But what's faith without experience?" Denis protested. "What's faith without knowing it's true, in your own experience? I mean, isn't it experience that makes the difference between belief and, uh...."

"Knowledge?" Father Geiger offered.

"Yeah," Denis said.

"We are not given that luxury in our faith, Mr. Kelly. The Bible is quite clear: there is no room for interpretation. 'No one comes to the Father except through me.' John 14:6. It is faith, and faith alone, that will lead you from darkness to light. Your thinking mind," he tapped on his skull for emphasis, "fools and tricks you. Believe me. But faith shines like a light in the heart. Throw your doubt into your faith and you will find the grace to stand stronger than you've ever imagined. You think my argument circular, but I assure you it is not. You can, Mr. Kelly, be fed to the lions in front of your Roman captors, or be crucified for following your Lord Savior, or have your limbs torn from your body and not suffer or feel the least bit of fear. That," he said, his voice rising and his eyes boring into Denis, "is the product of faith, of grace, and of the mercy of God. It has nothing to do with knowledge."

Denis sat in a stunned silence. "I'm sorry, Father," he said, standing. "I don't mean this with any disrespect, but that doesn't sound like a very good way to live. I need more than faith. I need evidence."

"Yes, evidence," Father Geiger agreed quickly.

Denis hesitated.

"Evidence is indeed valuable. The theory of evolution, for instance, is very compelling. Yes, Mr. Kelly, I am not so ignorant as you might think. Evidence for evolution will help refine and reform our religion, it is true. Science, and the evidence it uses, can do a great many things, as can the mechanistic philosophy that puts man, not God, at the center of things. But neither science nor rational philosophy can bring you comfort in the night. You will find that your hands and your head provide you with little in life when things really matter." Denis, whose own hands were becoming as large and powerful as his father's, closed and opened them unconsciously. "They seem your greatest gifts right now, but without your heart you will be lost to darkness." Father Geiger's blue eyes were deeply alive, and Denis was struck by both their passion and the insanity of what they proposed.

"Make no mistake, Mr. Kelly: Without faith, without your heart, you *will* be lost to the darkness."

Denis nodded, then moved toward the door. "Thank you, Father."

Father Geiger nodded at him, then looked down at the open book on his desk, taking a pen up in his right hand and starting to work.

Denis lingered, but the old priest did not look back up. He left the headmaster's office and walked through an empty school, smelling spring flowing in through the open windows. The world, Denis realized, was mad. No one had any idea what they were doing; his parents stumbled and struggled through parenthood and their own lives; priests and nuns mirrored beliefs taught to them, but had no more an understanding of God than a parrot had of its empty phrases. Everyone everywhere was asleep, and those who pretended to hold answers held nothing but empty beliefs and tired stories as transparently improbable as a child's. Education did not translate into wisdom, or even to understanding. Someone could be incredibly bright and very well educated but utterly clueless. Intelligence and education had nothing to do with how much you actually saw around you. It would take Denis fifty years to unravel this mystery, starting when he first heard of the Integral philosopher Ken Wilber. This experience with Father Geiger, though, cemented his distrust of authority and of authoritative institutions, which only seemed to perpetuate ignorance, dependence, and patriarchy.

GRACE AND DENIS HAD, IN THE MANNER ONLY TEENAGERS can, the most serious of love affairs. When Grace was fifteen, she went to visit family out of state and, in the way that rumors are spread and multiply like viruses in small towns, an elaborate tale grew and morphed in the halls of the school concerning her disappearance. Each time the story came into the hands of another, it grew more lurid and fantastic in its details, until Grace's reputation was somewhere slightly south of a street prostitute.

Denis's feelings about Grace were not well concealed, and the rumors only came to him through his own friends, who informed Denis apologetically that the girl of his affections was now known as Greasy Grace.

A few days later, at lunch, one of the boys a year ahead of Denis stopped him in the cafeteria. "Hey, Duck Butt," the boy, named Michael, sneered, referring to Denis's haircut. He was thick in the neck and had small eyes that were dull and flat. His table of four friends all eagerly leaned forward, grinning cruelly. "Your dolly's real loose, I hear. Hear she fucked the whole football team and got knocked up. Hadda be shipped off to her relatives so they could knock some sense into her!"

"And knock that baby out!" one of the other boys chimed in. They all roared with laughter.

Denis stopped walking, and turned to face them. He held the lunch tray so tightly it was trembling. "You'll wanna watch that mouth, Mike," Denis warned.

"Oh," Michael taunted, "you gonna razz my berries, Kelly?" Kelly was the school-yard name Denis had acquired in his first few years attending classes. It seemed to better fit the hardening shell he was developing, and he had encouraged the rechristening. Now, only his family and close childhood friends called him by his given name.

He stood up, his doughy frame easily a third heavier than Kelly's. "Come on, tough guy." He opened his arms, exposing his chest. "Take a shot. Razz my berries!"

His three friends — Donald, Henry, and Gordon — bristled in their seats.

"What's a-matter, Kelly?" Donald, a short and muscular boy with a plume of black hair, called. "You porkin' Greasy Grace too? You and the whole football team? No wonder you're so sore about it!"

"I'll come after you, too, Donnie," Kelly threatened.

"Ooo," Donald replied in mock concern, "you and what army, Kelly? Huh?" He stood up as well, and Henry and Gordon joined them.

Kelly met each of their eyes deliberately. "See you guys around, then," he said, turning.

"See ya, Duck Butt!" Michael said.

"Bye, Nosebleed!" Donald called.

"Why don't you come by the Passion Pit tonight, tough guy?" Henry joined in. "Since you're too yellow to do anything here!"

Kelly went to his table with his friends, who wanted to conspire with him to wreak vengeance on Kelly's impugned honor. Kelly listened to his friends' impassioned pleas silently, and after ten minutes, when he was certain his voice would not be shaking with emotion, he said only, "I'll handle it, boys. Thanks, though."

The complicated truth of the Kelly household was that while Bill Kelly was inexcusably violent against his children, he also gave his boys the confidence of how to fight and win.

That meant that each child received formal boxing lessons from their father about how to jab, hook, and connect with a body blow, complemented with street-smart lessons on how to apply these techniques in the real world. This included how to take a hit and not lose your senses, how to strike an opponent repeatedly and viciously until he fell to the ground, and why no man surrendered so long as there was breath in his body.

Michael got it first. He lived closest to Kelly's own house, and the big eleventh grader had an alcoholic mother and a mostly absent father. Kelly knew the boy's parents were never home before five, and so he stopped by the house on his way home from school. Kelly's bike went into a nearby shrub, out of sight. Michael lived in a rundown shack of a home, a windblown ranch whose turquoise paint was coming off in large swaths. The yard was a tangle of dirt and weeds. Kelly ascended the steps, peeling and creaking wooden planks nearly worn to the breaking point, and knocked on the door. A moment later it swung open on creaking hinges.

"*Kelly*?" Michael managed to get out before Kelly's fist landed squarely on the left side of his nose, knocking him sideways into the doorframe.

"I'll razz your goddamn berry," Kelly shouted. The boy, unwisely, attempted to counterattack, but Kelly landed four more punches, all on the face, before Michael even thought to put his hands up to protect himself. The last punch caught him just behind the ear, next to the jaw, and he dropped to his knees. His watery eyes, the same dull brown as his hair, looked up helplessly. His lip was bleeding, as was his nose.

"Call her Greasy Grace again, and I'll kill you," hissed Kelly. "We clear?"

Michael nodded dumbly, but Kelly knew the battle had only just begun. He had to get at least one of the other boys before the next school day, so that they would be afraid of him and not team up in the bathroom or in the parking lot. He managed to get a hold of Donald after dinner, out by the railroad tracks where he knew the boy hung out. Kelly waited and picked him off as Donald rode his bike in. Donald was tougher than Michael but couldn't match Kelly's speed or his anger, and after the two exchanged a few glancing blows, Kelly landed a punch squarely on the boy's lips, bursting them. He followed it with a quick flurry of punches and, when Donald fell to the dirt and covered his face, kicks to the body.

He made the same threat: Call her Greasy Grace again, and I'll kill you. Donald, like Michael, nodded his bloodied head.

Kelly sought the two other boys, but was unable to find them. He had taken out the biggest and the toughest of the foursome, and sure enough neither boy came to school the next day, no doubt embarrassed to show their bruised faces when Kelly's was free of any marks. Kelly heard that both had mysteriously "fallen" off their bikes and banged their heads, and the taunting of Grace ground to a halt.

CHAPTER 3

THE AMERICAN DREAM, PERVERTED

GRACE RETURNED A MONTH LATER, AND IN THE PRESENCE of the actual girl the last rumors about her slowly withered and died. When Denis finally made love to her, his first time, it seemed to him he saw directly into her soul. Unlike so many stories of losing virginity, there was no awkwardness, no fumbling around each other's bodies. They took off their clothes and Grace mounted him solidly and demandingly, wrapping her arms around his back and pressing herself into his chest. Their eyes remained locked as both came to orgasm, and Denis was transported into that nameless peace of his childhood, that magical place where there was no subject or object, no time, no need, no Denis Kelly looking out on the world. There was only Perfection, arising in every moment.

He felt Grace's breasts pressed magically into his chest, smelled the light musk of her body, and in her embrace the pain and confusion of life softened and became more bearable. He was no longer alone, with the full weight of indifference of the world pressing in on him from all sides. He had an ally.

In the winter of Denis's sophomore year of high school, Grace became pregnant. He had managed to save a small amount of money, and bought Grace a tiny engagement ring. Although she was sixteen years old and a sophomore, she accepted. In 1957, marriage at such an age was not unheard of — his own mother, after all, had given birth to the oldest Kelly boy, Patrick, when she was seventeen — so with the blessings of both their parents, Grace and Denis set in motion everything necessary to bind their lives together.

Denis, intent on getting his own home, took to working two jobs, logging more than sixty hours a week. Part of the time he worked for his future father-in-law's maintenance and window-cleaning business, and after a few months had enough money to put a deposit on a modest ranch home in the center of town.

Towards the end of her first trimester, Grace went to see the doctor. Denis waited nervously in the waiting room. An hour ticked by. Grace finally emerged, tears streaming down her cheeks, and ran out the door.

Denis jumped to his feet. "Mr. Kelly," the doctor said gravely, leaning out from his office door. "May I speak to you? Your fiancée will be fine for a moment."

Kelly reluctantly followed the doctor into his office. The man had a stout, red face, and he ran a hand through graying hair. He bid Kelly to sit, and took his own seat behind a large desk, pushing his eyeglasses up. He opened up Grace's file and tapped it a few times with a pen.

His brown eyes flickered up. "Your fiancée, Mr. Kelly, is not pregnant."

Kelly stared back, uncomprehending.

"What?" he managed.

"Not pregnant," the doctor repeated, his eyes holding Kelly's.

"But," Kelly challenged, "how can she *not* be pregnant?"

The doctor nodded sympathetically. He tilted his head to the large medical book on the nearby shelf. "It is called *hysterical pregnancy*, Mr. Kelly. It's the darnedest thing I've ever seen, I can tell you that."

"But she isn't hysterical," Kelly countered, growing angry. "Not ever. Grace is cool as a cucumber. Doc, come on! She's got no period. She's pregnant!"

The doctor nodded. "I know it's confusing, Mr. Kelly. The only thing I can figure is that she wants to be pregnant so badly she tricked herself into thinking she was. Now listen here, Mr. Kelly. What that girl needs is *rest* and *relaxation*. The symptoms of her pregnancy will likely fade pretty quickly now that we know she isn't pregnant. Take this," he handed Denis a bottle, "for her nerves. It'll help to calm her. Have her take two of those pills a day, one in the morning and one in the evening, until she's no longer showing signs. Till she acts herself again." He stood up and came around the desk, placing an arm on Kelly's shoulder. "I'm sure she's crying in the car. You'd best go after her."

Kelly walked outside and, through the bug-splattered window, saw his fiancée with her head in her hands, her shoulders shuddering. He opened the driver's door quietly, slipping into his seat.

"You," Grace said through her sobs, "were only going to... going to... marry me because you thought I was pregnant, right? It's off now, I know. You're off the hook." She looked, with red and swollen eyes, out the passenger side window, tears heavy across her cheeks.

"No," Kelly said, laughing without humor. "Grace, I'm not going anywhere. I'm going to marry you because I love you, and we're going to get you pregnant for real, believe me!"

She turned her head toward him, looking down at the shifter. Her bloodshot eyes tentatively met his. "You mean...." Her lips began to tremble. "You... you still wanna get married?"

"Of course." Kelly reached out and took her hand. "It's you and me, baby. You and me against the world, right? I want you to be a part of my life forever and ever. I love you!"

"Oh, Denis," she sobbed, leaning across the car and allowing herself to be taken into his arms.

They were married not long after, and Grace conceived within a few weeks of their marriage, before Kelly had turned seventeen. She was overcome with joy, and at first Kelly shared the love and satisfaction his wife felt. Their first few months together were filled with the giddy delight of newlyweds; exploring sexual intimacy, learning each other's secrets and pleasures, and sinking fully into the culture of Green Bay. The hysterical pregnancy was never brought up, and they told their friends and family the first baby had been lost to a miscarriage.

As the months wore on and the baby grew in her belly, she grew increasingly distant in ways that confounded him. All of the exteriors were the same — Grace stayed at home, they ate dinner together, made love, but it was as if the part of her that he had fallen in love with had died. She remained physically present, but her eyes were often elsewhere, and whatever access he once had to her soul was gone.

Kelly complained to his co-workers that Grace was acting "weird" and "distant," the only words that came close to describing something that seemed much more serious and dangerous. His friends, many of them young fathers themselves, smirked at his complaints. "Pregnancy does weird things to women, Kelly," was a common theme, and his concerns were dismissed as bordering on the paranoid.

As Grace entered her third trimester, Kelly found that the world outside was growing harder and colder. She still let him have her body whenever he desired, but her soul was locked away, and the horrible feeling of loneliness crept into his days.

"Grace," Kelly said one Sunday afternoon, sitting at the kitchen table as the early morning sunlight filtered in through the window, "I need to talk to you." It was warm outside and she was dressed in loose-fitting pants and a tank-top, her belly protruding. One of her small hands rested there, protectively, while the other one was wrapped around a glass of orange juice.

She smiled. She was often glowing and radiant and breathtakingly beautiful, her skin and eyes vital and strong. Kelly's face contorted. "I ... I ... " he tried. Expressing emotional truths was not something his family had taught; emotions were explosive, dangerous things not to be trusted, and most certainly not to be expressed unless with peers late in the evening under the dimming effect of alcohol. Still, he pushed. "I've lost a connection with you," he finally said, putting it between them.

"Oh Denis," she laughed, "You're the father of our baby! What are you talking about? I love you." Grace's smile touched him briefly, but his face only contorted further. He knew she loved him, of course, and he loved her, but how was he to express what he had on his mind? Men, he had been taught, *did* things. Women *felt* things, and he felt the shame of not being man enough to simply go on with his life.

He tried again. "Something's different," he said at last. "Between us. Something's lost."

Grace's smile faltered, then fell. She looked suddenly hard, and the radiance of her being came to shine on him in the most unpleasant way. "I don't understand." Her words were sharp. "We've created a child. I've never felt so full of love, so full period. I've never been so happy." The hand on the orange juice retracted and joined her other hand on her belly as if to protect the baby from its father. Denis looked at her, across the table, as far away from him as a stranger who had wandered in from the outside. Her brow was creased, and her expression seemed to shame him for even bringing up the fact that he was somehow, in any way, not completely satisfied, not as overcome with joy as she.

"Grace, it's like you're not in your body anymore," he said, latching on to the most obvious, most physical thing. "When we have sex, it's like you're just... just not there."

She just shook her head, her expression clouding. "Can't you not be selfish *for just a few months*? Is that possible? It's not enough that I let you make love to me? I have to do it in some way that you like as well?" He felt his ears begin to burn, and fought to keep his head from dropping. His throat closed. She walked out of the kitchen, leaving him sitting in a ball of contracted energy.

"It'll change once she gives birth, Denny," his mother, who was pregnant with the last of the Kelly children, reassured him a week later. "The first one is a strange experience for a woman." Rosa nodded with the assurance of a woman about to give birth to her ninth child. Her gentle smiled suggested that *these things happen*.

Reassured, he threw himself that much harder into work and play, moving constantly just like his father did, not daring to slow down for a moment. When he finally put himself in bed next to his pregnant wife at the end of the day, he was so exhausted that he immediately fell into a deep sleep with no dreams able to rise to the surface. Getting up early, he attacked the next day with the same vigor, and in this way the months fell away. Grace grew ever bigger, and the summer gave way to fall and then an early winter.

His daughter, a pink, perfect baby they named Christine, was born without complication, and Denis felt, upon seeing her, an explosion of love and tenderness that knew no boundaries or language. At eighteen he was a father, his formal education having stopped two years before. Even though he was now long out of school, as he held his infant daughter against his chest, feeling her tiny heartbeat, he thought of Father Geiger's words: *without your heart, you will be lost to the darkness.* How could the old priest have been so wrong about so many things, and so right about a few others?

For a time, the hectic pace of Kelly's life diminished. He thought of his daughter in nearly every moment of every day, and rushed home after work for the chance to hold her, to see her feed against his wife's breast, to feel her tiny fingers wrap themselves around his calloused pinky, to watch her learn to smile and to laugh. The weeks bled into months, and Christine grew larger and more verbal and more precious to him.

Yet Grace's predicted return to him and to intimacy did not happen. Nearly four months after the birth of their daughter, Grace still had not opened up to him, and Kelly fell back into the pattern of hard work and harder drinking, nineteen hours of daily distraction that sent him to bed in a fit of exhaustion, muting the growing fire within. When he wasn't exhausted, he sometimes looked at Grace with eyes full of sensual longing and raw masculine power. She would meet his eyes with ones that no longer seemed to belong to him.

Some part of Kelly was growing harder and hotter, driven by a fire within that was threatening to consume him. Kelly felt as distant and indifferent to Grace as the stars that twinkled enigmatically light years away, afire but adrift in the coldness of space millions of miles from anything else.

He came home early one afternoon. He pushed through the back kitchen door, and heard frantic motion coming from the bedroom. Grace, who was supposed to be working at the women's shoe store downtown, called out.

"Hey!"

"Hey baby," he replied tiredly, "I'm home."

"Hey," Grace called, "You're home early!" She came around the corner in a skirt and tank top, hair askew and feet bare. There was sweat dotting her forehead, and her smile seemed forced and a little too bright.

"Hey, Kenneth — where are you?" Grace called out. Then, to Kelly: "I was just showing him our house."

"What?" Kelly managed, and a man came around the corner wearing a suit and holding a large briefcase. "Good afternoon, Kelly," the man said crisply, offering his free hand. "Good to see you again." Kenneth, a woman's shoe salesmen who worked with Grace, was also sweating a great deal.

Kelly looked at the two of them, and Grace turned to get a glass of water from the sink.

A terribly awkward silence came over the kitchen. Grace fumbled at the sink, and Kenneth straightened his tie, looked intensely at the art hanging from the walls, straightened his tie again, and cleared his throat while shifting from one foot to the other.

He at last looked at Kelly's feet. "You look like an eleven, am I correct?"

Kelly was looking at the back of his wife, where he could see sweat was beginning to darken the fabric at the small of her back.

"An eleven?" the man repeated, crisply.

"What's that?"

"Your shoe size."

"Oh, yeah."

"Thought so." Kenneth swallowed audibly. "Well, Grace, it was nice of you to show me the place I've heard so much about. But I should really get back to the store." He shook Kelly's hand again. "Let me know when you're in the market for a new pair. Of shoes. Could probably get you a discount," he said, not making eye contact. He let himself out, and although Kelly didn't know for certain, and never asked what had happened, one thing was clear: Grace was sharing a level of intimacy with Kenneth that she was not sharing with him.

Kelly followed the man out, and walking past him went straight to the corner bar.

Kelly's decision not to return to high school was confirmed when he committed to working two jobs to support his new family. During the daylight hours he was employed as a cheese cook for L. D. Schreiber & Co., while nights he pumped gas at a Shell station with another man, David. Kelly didn't much care for David, who was married to a young and incredibly beautiful woman but was busy having an affair with a four-teen-year-old schoolgirl. David sometimes claimed to be working when he wanted to see his very young lover, and asked Kelly to "cover" for him were his wife, Maurice, to call. Kelly hated doing this, and did a poor job of it when she would call.

"Look, Kelly," Maurice said late one night, not sounding very upset, "I know he's having an affair. You can stop lying to me." Kelly was all too happy to be let off the hook.

"You know?" he asked.

"Sure. I'm getting too old for David," she laughed, a little bitterly. "I'm almost twenty-one, after all."

They started talking on the phone on the nights David was "working," and found that their marriages were remarkably similar. Both of them had spouses that were having affairs, neither one felt a sense of connection or love anymore, and they both had an intense skin hunger in their young bodies.

When they met for the first time, Kelly was struck by Maurice's beauty. Tall and slender, she had long black hair and piercing eyes as well as the finest breasts he had ever seen — breasts that, as they made love for the first time, she was adamant he not touch.

"You're not serious," Kelly said, sliding a hand up her belly toward a breast. His hand was met with hers.

"I am absolutely serious," she said, and clearly was. "*No touching the tits.*"

Since he had permission to touch all of her other parts, he figured it was a compromise he could live with.

The thick armor that shielded him from the world was only opened when he was with a woman willing to expose some part of herself, aside from merely her body. For Maurice it was the shame and the danger of having their affair discovered, two things she was unable to hide from Kelly. It was only in these moments, now only experienced with Maurice, where his raw and emotional core could move toward the surface. Maurice allowed him to feel that his armor wasn't permanent, that it could be set aside even if only for a few hours at a time.

Kelly's friends were hard-drinking men whose vision was no broader than the next paycheck and the next happy hour. The larger community of Green Bay celebrated the confines of this kind of conformity in every way. At eighteen, he felt old and used-up, as if his best years were long behind him and all that remained was the daily grind of an unsatisfied life. His wife clearly had no interest in him and was likely having an affair with at least one other man; he too had strayed outside of his marriage vows, and the two of them now looked at one another like two roommates who had long grown tired of their mutual antics. He was miserable in his own home, miserable in his job, miserable in his life. For the second time in his life he sought help from his father for the simple reason he had no other man to whom he could turn.

Kelly came to the new ranch house, a few miles from the airport, where his family had moved. There were still five young children, ranging from a newborn to middle school, that Bill and Rosa Kelly were raising. He found his dad sitting in the kitchen, legs sprawled under the table. His father's face, clean-shaven, was smudged with exhaustion and intoxication. The darkness his father carried was heavy across his face, contempt weighing on his expression.

Bill Kelly looked at his son, so defiant and so powerful, standing before him with his strength and will nearly extinguished. It tore at him to see, and had he been sober he might have expressed compassion and understanding, and maybe even offered a helping hand. But he was not sober. Through the haze of intoxication and contempt, he saw a high school dropout and broken young father, a boy who didn't yet understand that the best you could do in life was manage the pain and disappointment and hang onto the few moments of happiness that might float your way.

"So it's like this, dad," Kelly was saying, sipping his drink, looking at the hulking mass across from him. "Grace just isn't interested in me anymore. I mean, I haven't connected with her in eleven months. Eleven fucking months. Mom says it's normal, but I dunno ...."

"You have a lot to learn about women," his father stated slowly, enunciating the words around his intoxication.

"Yeah," Kelly said, "no shit. So enlighten me."

His father leaned forward on his big forearms. "You ready for what I have to say, son? You man enough?"

Kelly raised his eyebrows, his own large hands pulling themselves unconsciously into fists. The muscles of his neck were suddenly active, their long, sinewy bands standing out under the flesh. His jaw locked itself into place as his breathing became faster and shallower.

"You want to stay here, in this town, you listen to me," his father stated. He waited a long moment, letting the silence gather behind his words.

"You need to rape her."

Kelly stared back, his body rigid and throat closed.

"That'll break 'er," his father continued, either not noticing the reaction to his words or not caring. "She wants to act like a whore, you treat her like one. *Rape her,*" he repeated.

Kelly felt fire spreading into his chest and stomach, and he unclenched his jaw just enough to utter a single, tense word: *"Stop."*

"Jesus Christ, you simple sonofabitch, *rape her,*" his father nearly shouted, shaking his head and leaning into Kelly.

Kelly felt his exquisitely constructed armor wrap itself tightly around him. His large laborer hands, conditioned by years of work, coiled so tightly that their knuckles, choked of blood, glared white. He stared at his father, at the cramped, ruined kitchen, at the neat clothes covering his father's bronzed body, at the cracked floors and cracked walls and cracked dishes drying next to the sink. The father noted the son's fists, and Bill Kelly stepped into that rage as only a man hoping to end his own suffering might do.

"You might have to rape Grace *repeatedly,*" he slurred, "until she gets it through her *thick Russian skull.*" Kelly exploded out of his chair, lunging toward his father with the intention of killing him where he sat. At the very last possible second his fist changed course and instead of hitting his father moved through the kitchen wall, smashing two layers of plaster and emerging in the living room. Kelly withdrew his shattered fist back through the wall, cradling it against his chest. He hated his father, hated his life; he hated everything he saw and touched and tasted, but most of all he hated himself.

Bill Kelly sipped his drink, not having so much as shifted in his chair at the spectacular display, and made no comment on the fist-sized hole in the kitchen wall. Without a word Kelly lurched out of the kitchen and into the night.

On the long walk home a story began to form in his mind. It looped over and over again, taking him with it, its truth seemingly undeniable: *Not even strong enough to punch a wall without breaking your hand. Not even man enough to hit your father who taunts you, that for so long beat your brothers. Not able to get your own wife to want you so she fucks another man. And you're too weak to remain faithful. Cowardly selfish adulterer. Useless at everything you do, as a son, as a father, as a husband. Uselessness. Worthless-piece-of-shit. You get exactly what you deserve.* And the story looped again and again and again. He choked on his shame and his rage, and stumbled to a local bar instead of to the continuing humiliation of home. There, amid the smoke and the churlish men, he drank himself into oblivion.

TWO WEEKS LATER KELLY WAS STANDING OVER THE CRIB of his daughter, looking at the sleeping child and unable to feel a connection to her or to anything around him. He moved to the tiny kitchen and sat, staring at the wall, letting a few drinks pass through his lips. The kitchen light over his head seemed harsh, making everything gray and ghoulish and not quite of this world.

In their cramped den, Christine began to cry from her crib. Kelly remained immobile, waiting for Grace to scoop up their daughter and comfort her. Christine cried louder in long, piercing wails that seemed to stab him somewhere behind the eyes. A minute passed, and still the baby cried. Kelly sat and stewed and raged in his kitchen chair. Everyone took and no one gave, and after working six days a week for what seemed like decades, he didn't even have a moment's peace to brood in his own kitchen. Veins stood out against the muscles of his forearms as his breathing turned shallow. Christine grew quiet, gathering herself, and erupted in a fresh frenzy.

Kelly burst from his chair and stormed the den. He glowered at the infant girl's bright pink face. "Be quiet!" he commanded, and his violence caused Christine's skin to morph from pink to bright red. She wailed louder.

"I said *be quiet!*" he thundered, picking her up roughly. She screamed as loud as her six-month-old lungs could manage, and Kelly struck her on her diapered rear end with his calloused hand. With those solid veins pressing against the muscles of his neck and forearms, he held her away from his body. Her tiny eyes, squeezed shut, opened and their exquisite translucency stopped him. He suddenly saw the fear and terror in his infant daughter's face, wrapped in a spark of divine energy. He flew into a profound stillness, and saw a man in a dirty white tank top and denim pants, barefooted, clutching a little girl as if she were the key to all of his misery, his self-contraction, his self-hatred. In a flash he was looking out from a face that had gone suddenly soft. He nearly dropped Christine, but managed to place her carefully back in the crib.

"I'm sorry," he mumbled, "I'm so sorry ... so sorry ... so sorry ...." His rage consumed itself like an explosion that burns the oxygen out of a room, leaving Kelly with nothing to breathe. His legs gave out from under him, and he pushed away from the crib. *I just hit my daughter* his mind repeated. *Worthless. Monster. Unworthy.*

"*Who the fuck am I?*" he whispered, wanting to tear off his skin, wanting everything to just stop and release him from the grip of his suffering and never-ending misery. He vaguely sensed Grace in the room, shouting, but her words seemed distant and alien. Rising, he stumbled through the house and into the yard, then wandered down the streets until he reached the downtown of Green Bay, his large, tear-stained face and leering eyes causing anyone who saw him to move far out of his path. He clawed at his body, wanting more than anything to just stop *feeling*.

A bus made its way down the main thoroughfare of Green Bay. He gauged the driver's likely reaction time and stepped into its path, closing his eyes. The mirror of the bus grazed his nose, and the wind and the noise of the engine and the squealing of tires rushed past. You crazy sonofabitch! he heard yelled into the night. When he at last opened his eyes, he found himself standing in a deserted street under the soft glow of sodium lamps. He was alone.

Without a goodbye, without so much as packing a suitcase, he was gone. He found himself on the streets of Milwaukee, wild-haired and wandering, having abandoned his wife and infant daughter and parents and younger siblings, along with his job and his belongings and everything he owned except for his car. He found menial work, a flophouse in which to sleep and shower, and slinked back into the world a hundred miles from his home.

In his heart, Kelly knew that he left his wife and daughter to save them from becoming part of his nightmare. Had he stayed in Green Bay, the abusive alcoholic within him would have been free to emerge, to turn his life into an expression of his own misery and neutered rage.

In the late hours of the night, when all the world seemed safely asleep, his mind would often turn to the little girl growing up without her daddy, and of a wife forced to make her own way in the world. He hated the man who had done this, who had run, who had so little integrity and respect for his own family. Pulled in two directions, he was a man at war with himself, for he understood in his heart why he had to leave yet hated himself for having done it. Stay and be damned, leave and be damned, Kelly was tormented by the past and torn apart by the present.

KELLY PASSED SIX MONTHS IN MILWAUKEE AS A SKILLED laborer, only slowly returning to himself. From there he moved to Chicago, where he augmented his income by hustling pool in the evenings. The nights were spent in smoky and dimly lit bars and pool halls, and Kelly came to know well the more colorful and less respectable characters living on the downside of society. In an ironic twist, it was his own father who had taught him the art of the pool hustle, taking the teenage Denis Kelly to pool halls to fine-hone his skills with the stick and with those foolish enough to bet on the game.

Just out of his teens, Kelly had become tall, handsome, and deeply athletic, and he was regaining his confidence and his extroversion. At Tony's Bar on the South Side, amid the steaming sewer grates, flashing neon signs, cobbled alleyways, and overfilled Dumpsters, Kelly found a kind of home. Local, street level Italian-American mafia figures drank at Tony's, and Kelly would hustle their money at pool while charming them not to knock his teeth out afterward.

Kelly and a man named Lou Cerone became particularly tight. Lou was a minor mob enforcer for a larger family, and as such he was always in the action, shaking businesses down, checking up on operations, handing off bribes to local beat cops, and enforcing the mob's businesses in a hundred other places. In his late twenties, Lou was a slab of a man whose slicked hair, olive skin, barrel-chest, deep-set eyes, and crushed nose made him almost a caricature. He loved to wear suits tailored after the Rat Pack — mohair, single-breasted jackets with a low-slung button, usually silver-gray or black, with a white collared shirt with double buttons on the cuff. His suits were always tailored perfectly to his less-than-perfect body. Lou would remove his silk tie when he arrived at the bar, leaving it slung across the back of his bar stool.

Lou could be funny and sincere, but his violent temper was always and obviously just below the falsely tranquil surface of his personality. His brown eyes were intelligent but predacious, and shined with the light of a man who had no fear of brutality. They were not the eyes of a psychopath who enjoyed violence for its own sake, but rather of a man who would do whatever necessary to get the job done. Lou had already served time in federal prison for assault and attempted murder, and his refusal to roll on anyone had led to a promotion to a kind of lieutenant — a man with men under him, jobs to hand out, and power.

Four months after moving to Chicago, on a warm spring night, Kelly suckered Lou into a game of pool and then led him on. Kelly had four balls on the table and Lou one.

"Care to make it interestin', Kelly?" Lou teased.

"When I'm getting my ass beat like this?"

"A real man'd go double or nuthin'," Lou challenged.

Kelly pretended to think about it. "All right, Lou. Twenty it is."

Five shots later, the game was over, and Kelly put out his hand for the money.

"You little fuck," Lou said thickly, looking up at the thin but muscular Kelly. "Don't nobody hustle me."

Kelly smiled at him. "Hate to tell you this, Lou. But I just *did*."

"Smartass Irish fuck," Lou snarled, all bark and no bite, at least when it came to Kelly. He threw the pool stick down on the table. A crumpled twenty-dollar bill followed.

"Choke on it, you fucking mick."

"I'll buy you a beer," Kelly offered, patting him on his thick shoulder. "A cheap one."

Kelly was nothing like the bare-knuckle bruisers who frequented the bar, and yet he was utterly at home in their rough company. Maybe it was because they always spoke what they felt, maybe it was because they seemed fearless, or maybe it was because they never asked questions or seemed to judge one's

past. At the end of the day, Kelly saw them as more in control
of their lives than the softer elements of society, where control
was coveted but so transparently illusory. Even a small timer
like Lou had more than a dozen of Chicago's finest on his
payroll, and he knew all the local businesses because he was
the one who shook them down. Whatever the reason, Kelly
was drawn to their world.

Kelly took a seat at the bar and Lou, in his pressed mohair
suit, sat next to him.

They were served their drinks. Kelly, like his father, drank
brandy and cognac, but while his father had settled for the
cheapest brands, Kelly only drank the finest.

"Hey Tony," Lou said to the bartender and owner. "Fuck
off for a minute, huh?" The bartender smiled and did as he
was told, moving to the far end of the bar where he cleaned
glasses with a rag. "Listen," Lou said, looking around conspiratorially, "my driver — he ain't with me no more."

Kelly raised his eyebrows, but Lou just shrugged.

"Happens sometimes, you know? So I need a driver. You
ain't family, and you're Irish as fuck, but you're okay. I can
tell. I know you need cash. Whaddya say you come and work
for me?"

"You serious?" Kelly was delighted.

"Fuckin' A," Lou said, downing his beer, "don't ever fuck
around 'bout business. You start tomorrow. Come by this
address." He slid a card to Kelly and finished his beer in a
tremendous chug.

"Okay."

You got a piece?" Lou asked Kelly.

"A gun?"

Lou just looked at him.

"Yeah," Kelly said, sheepishly. "I got a 20-gauge break-
action shotgun." He had brought the gun with which he had
nearly killed his father.

"Fucking micks," Lou muttered to no one. "You know
they make handguns these days, don't you? You can't carry
no fucking shotgun round town." He shook his head. "Go to
Bobby G. over on fifth. He owns the pawnshop next to the
newsstand. Tell him Lou sent you, and tell him to cut it down.
Don't let him charge you nothin', neither. He owes me."

The next day Kelly took the gun, as instructed, and, as
requested, Bobby G. sawed a good ten inches off the barrel.
He also put beautiful nickel plates on its sides, plus threw in a
soft-leather harness so Kelly could carry it comfortably under
his coat.

This wasn't so Kelly could be one more armed bodyguard.
Lou had people for that. It was just so Kelly could discreetly
move the shotgun to and from the car, where it was kept, loaded,
under the seat. Kelly's job was very simple: Drive Lou where he
wanted to go, keep his eyes open for any cops or dark sedans
with suited men, keep an eye on the exits of the buildings Lou
went into, and never, ever, ever ask any questions. Ever.

Lou would disappear into all manner of places, from white-collar high rises at noon to crumbling row homes in the middle of the night. Sometimes Lou would go in with a team of other mobsters, sometimes by himself, but Kelly's job was to open Lou's door when he got in and out and otherwise to stay with the car at all times. For six months Kelly made his living doing this, and he slowly came clean with Lou about his family, his background, him hometown, and his infant daughter and wife back in Green Bay. Lou was a good listener, and his love of Kelly was genuine and deep.

Lou wasn't training him to do anything else — in fact, Kelly was kept so in the dark that he knew less about Lou's business as his driver than he had as his pool buddy — but he was certain he was being groomed for a more important position. And the money was good, it was an easy job, and the prospects of being taken care of by "The Family" were shaping up.

A few times Lou pressed into Kelly. "What you doing working with stiffs like me? You got a good brain. Don't talk like no mobster. Got a good heart. You ain't a killer, Kelly, and believe me that's a compliment."

But the young Denis Kelly would dismiss Lou's observations. He wanted to be one of them.

After another six months went by, Lou told Kelly he was in trouble with the mob, and that his life was in danger. He didn't elaborate, and Kelly was trained to not ask any questions. For safety, Lou spent the night at Kelly's apartment. Kelly's room in the flophouse was lit mostly by the neon light outside the window. Kelly fell asleep in his small bedroom, with Lou stretched out on the couch, handgun still hanging in the holster around his torso. Kelly awoke the next morning with the sun shining through the stained curtains. The apartment was empty and quiet. Kelly got up and stretched. He peeked out onto the couch and saw it empty before something else hit him: the apartment wasn't just empty of Lou, it was empty of *everything*. His closet door was open, divulging nothing but coat hangers; the new two-hundred dollar suits Kelly had bought were gone, along with all his other clothes. A radio and record player were missing, along with a lamp, a clock, and his LPs.

How the fuck was I robbed with an armed Mafia guy on my couch, Kelly wondered, astounded. It was then he spotted his wallet, car keys, and shotgun sitting neatly on a tabletop, underneath a hand-scrawled note.

"Kelly — Took your shit just to show you how little you know about people. You don't belong in this business. Get out now while you can. Don't serve time like I did, don't make money doing the dumb shit I do. Your a better man than all that. Maybe you don't see it but I do and I know people. Don't come near me neither. If I ever see you again or if you come for your shit I'll kill you."

The note was unsigned. Kelly had nothing except a wallet, a shotgun, and a small amount of cash. Lou had taken everything else. Kelly, in shock, put the shotgun into its harness under his overcoat, and went down the stairs of the flophouse and out into the street. He stopped in the middle of the avenue, until a car blew its horn, jarring him to take a staggering step to the sidewalk. His Ford Fairlane 500 was parked right out front of the apartment building where he had left it, but Lou had stolen all four wheels and tires off the car and left it sitting on four concrete blocks.

Tears of anger, shame, and humiliation ran down his face. In a rage, he ran to the filthy Chicago River, tossing the shotgun into its still waters with a tremendous heave. He never set foot in Tony's again or ran into Lou or any of the family members. He found better paying work doing heating pipe installation, and in a few months was able to move into an actual apartment with a roommate, taking a small step toward a better life.

Years later he saw the truth of what had happened; Lou, a murderer and brute had also been some kind of angel. In his own crude way, Lou saw a light inside of Kelly that was rare and utterly out of place with street-level crooks like himself, and he had done the most compassionate thing he could. He cast Kelly out rather than watch him be perverted by the violence and brutality of mafia life.

"I'll kill you," Lou had threatened in the letter, and he meant it not in cruelty but with as much love and compassion as his world would allow. Love, it seemed, sometimes acted strangely.

MONTHS LATER KELLY WAS WORKING AS A CONTRACTOR, installing a heating system in a frozen shell of a house in sub-zero weather. There was an irony about his job. He would show up at a mostly finished construction site and, with the inside temperature well below freezing, install a heating system and get it running. As soon as it worked, he would be off to another partially finished home, again working in freezing temperatures to install and get a heater operational, and then leave for another property.

On his last day in Chicago, it was bitterly, unreasonably cold — twenty below zero with a stiff and constant wind howling out of the north. His fingers and legs had gone half numb before lunch. He finished one house on the South Side and readied his tools to go into the next property to start the same kind of job all over again. He lugged them down exposed stairs that looked like broken ribs, and tossed his tools into the passenger seat. The sun was low in the sky, and its warmth and light seemed incapable of piercing heavy winter clouds that crowded the city's skyline. All the world seemed gray and quiet and frozen into stillness.

Kelly blew into freezing hands, wiggling his fingers to try and get warmth into them. The shell of the house loomed over him, and he took the unfinished stairs wearily back up.

He stood on the landing, looking down at his beat-up car, the gray sky, and the naked trees that looked as dead as the wood they were using to build the house. It occurred to him that he had no idea who he was, no idea what he was doing, no idea how he was managing to animate his body day after day. A deep misery seemed to radiate from his bones, a misery that called him back to all the mistakes he had made. No longer driven by passion and without a purpose for his life, he was adrift aimlessly, living day-to-day and paycheck-to-paycheck, dead to a world that had gone dead to him.

He went in to his young boss Jamie — a stubbly, cigarette-smoking man who looked like an ex-boxer, big and bruised and intense.

"Jamie," he said, "we gotta talk."

Jamie's face was turned away from Kelly, his crew cut looking shabby and in need of a trim from the rear. "What's up, Kelly?"

"I gotta get outta here."

Jamie turned. "Fuck me." He knew Kelly to be a hard-working, no-bullshit kind of guy. "Okay, Kelly. Go. See ya tomorrow." Jamie turned back around.

"No, man. I gotta get outta here. Outta Chicago. I gotta get someplace warm."

Jamie turned again, mouthing his cigarette thoughtfully, the inhaled smoke coming out of his nostrils. He looked harder at Kelly's face, naked and nearly desperate.

"What the fuck you talkin' about, Kelly? *Now*?"

"Yeah," Kelly said. "Can you pay me, right now?"

"What the ...? You fuckin' pullin' my leg or what?"

Denis didn't try and hide the emotion from his boss. "Listen, man, I just realized I'm out of my fucking mind. It's twenty-fucking below outside. The goddamn wind never stops, not ever. This is insane. I'm going somewhere warm, today. I need to start over. And brother, I need to do it *right now*." Kelly's intensity landed somewhere between fierce rage and utter, tearful collapse.

Although Jamie was young, he had seen more than his fair share of hardship, leaving two ex-wives and three children in his wake. He knew a thing or two about the desire to start over and to just tuck tail and bolt. Because of this, he didn't need Kelly to explain it to him, didn't need to question the impulse, and felt no need to change Kelly's mind. Kelly wanted a fresh start. Fucking A.

"Fuck, man." Jamie pulled out his wallet, thumbing through some twenties. "Can't pay you the full amount, Kelly. Can give you what I got. Not even half your salary."

"That's fine. I'll take it."

Jamie held it out. The fingers of his black gloves were cut out, the skin pale against the fabric. "Where you going, man?"

Kelly thought a moment. "Florida or California. I'll decide once I get in the car." He offered his hand, and Jamie took it.

"Fuck. You *are* serious," Jamie said, and Kelly just squeezed his hand harder, put the cash in his wallet, and headed for the door. Jamie looked after him, feeling the deep tug of envy seeing a man who could, after what seemed like five minutes of thought, move halfway across the country to start over.

"Good luck, fella," Jamie called, and he meant it.

Kelly looked back once, waved, then took the stairs two at a time down to his car.

He first went to the flat he was renting, packed his things, and loaded them into the trunk of his Fairlane. The car started reluctantly in the deep cold, and Kelly let the engine idle while he warmed his hands. He knew a couple in Los Angeles, his former lover Maurice and her pedophile husband David. It wasn't much, but it was someone. He didn't know a soul in Florida, so L.A. it was. He eased the Fairlane into first gear and was soon heading west; by nightfall he was two-hundred miles outside of the city, a smile on his face cautiously emerging in the glow of the car's dials.

Kelly made it to L.A. without incident and moved into Maurice and David's garage, sleeping on a cot between the front of their car and the wall. It was far from romantic, but it was warm even at night, and it would do until he got back on his feet. His nights were filled with the smells of gasoline, oil, and radiator fluid, and his days with searching for work.

He took a job as a steeplejack, a dangerous but relatively high-paying job. L.A. was bright and big and weird, and even though the winter weather was nice, Kelly could not find a rhythm to the city. It was a disorganized, shallow place whose eddies and social currents confused and irritated him. He hated where he was living, hated the work, hated his boss, and eventually hated the entire city itself. So he worked and he saved and he slept on his cot crammed between the chrome bumper of a 1958 Buick and an unpainted wall.

Kelly made a few trips to San Francisco. He loved everything about the city. There was a misty atmosphere there that made it seem a universe away from the hot and dry air of L.A. The people were more eccentric, the fashions more extreme, the architecture more beautiful, and the nightlife more interesting. Lying on his cot at night, he imagined himself walking that city's steep streets, and resolved that as soon as he could afford it, San Francisco would become home. Three months later, he packed his few modest belongings into his car, thanked David and Maurice, and left L.A. for good, never to return.

CHAPTER 4

DOWN THE RABBIT HOLE

IN THE LATE SPRING 1962, NOT LONG AFTER HIS TWENTIETH birthday, Denis Kelly moved into a residential club in the heart of San Francisco, a kind of youth hostel where one could live cheaply month to month. Located on the corner of Bush and Pine streets, it was a well-run and modest place that was clean but inexpensive. This was at the very beginning of the counterculture movement, and the boundaries of conventionality were being pushed on from every direction in San Francisco.

Kelly met a man named Marty at a gathering not long after he had moved. The two of them hit it off quickly. Marty was a few years older than Kelly and had lived in San Francisco for a number of years already. He was well acquainted with the social scene, the party scene, and even the spiritual scene. Of Portuguese descent, Marty had a copper-colored complexion, thick and wavy black hair, and piercing blue eyes.

As the two men chatted at the party, two people asked if they were brothers. When a third person asked, Marty looked Kelly over more critically. Although Kelly was Irish and fair skinned, he had spent a great deal of time outdoors and was deeply tanned. With a similar complexion and build, it was easy to see why people thought they were related.

"You're six-two?" Marty asked.

Kelly nodded.

"Size forty-four jacket?"

Another nod.

"Eleven shoes?"

Nod.

"Inseam thirty-four?"

"Yup."

Marty laughed. "You're the same size as me, exactly." Marty's rough good looks were very in vogue in 1962, and he was often compared to actor Steve McQueen.

"You know what I can do for you?" Marty asked, smiling to reveal white teeth.

Kelly shook his head.

"Listen, man, I model some clothes for this real groovy chick named Silvia. She's a Chinawoman, a stone fox, and a designer. Works with that black fashion designer, the feminist chick, Dorothy somebody or another. Anyway, Silvia makes men's suits and has me model them. Always says she wished she had another man my size so she could put on more interesting fashion shows."

Kelly was intrigued. "What's it pay?"

Marty's smile widened. "There's more to life than money, Kelly." He put his hand on Kelly's shoulder. "Those threads you're wearing, man, they ain't so fab, you know? You look like a man who works with his hands every day."

"I do work with my hands every day," Kelly said, defensively.

"And good for you, my friend. Somebody's got to do it, and it sure as shit ain't gonna be me. But my point is you can work with your hands all you like. You just don't gotta look like you do." Marty offered a thousand-dollar smile. "You dig?"

Kelly nodded.

"So listen, man. Silvia lets her models keep the clothes they model, and she works with other designers too who 'pay' the same thing." He looked at Kelly's worn jeans and workman's top. "In six months, you'll have a closet of handmade clothing, custom tailored to your body." Marty pointed his thumbs at himself. He was wearing a woolen double-breasted suit, charcoal gray, with a silk tie. He took off his coat and offered it, and Kelly slipped it on. It fit him perfectly.

"It's yours," Marty said.

"I can't," Kelly protested, "It's too nice! And I just met you!"

Marty, though, just shook his head. "Take it. Looks boss on you."

"You sure," Kelly asked, smiling sheepishly.

"Don't sweat it, daddy-o." He lit up a joint, offering it to Kelly, who had never smoked pot before. He took a big puff, feeling the fine wool against the skin of his arms. He liked San Francisco. A lot.

Once again Kelly took a job as a steeplejack, but was determined to learn the secret of Marty's life, a life that seemed easy, fun, full, and unburdened with things like an honest day's labor.

"How's the steeplejacking?" Marty asked Kelly on the way to one of their modeling gigs a few weeks later.

"It's okay," Kelly said. "Pay's good."

Marty glanced over. His arm was out the window, and his thick hair, dark and wavy, was blowing. "I used to be a longshoreman," he said, referring to the highly coveted union jobs working the docks, where men made great money and received amazing pensions.

"Holy shit," Kelly said, "And you gave *that* up? Great pay, great bennies, great retirement?"

Marty glanced over, smiling. They came to a traffic light, and he pulled a small bag of cocaine out of his pocket, taking a scoop with a key.

"Bump?" he asked Kelly after snorting it.

Kelly shrugged, not knowing what a bump was, but he took the bag and imitated what he saw Marty do.

"I gave it up because a monkey can make a living with his hands," Marty said, sniffling. "It takes a man to make a living with his wits." He laughed.

"Where's your money come from?" Kelly asked. He touched his nose and cheek. "Fuck, my face is half-numb! Is that normal?"

"Good shit, that's why." Marty commented. "And it's normal. I get my money from lots of places. Mostly these days it's from dating older women. You know, older broads who got divorced in their thirties and don't want to hit the scene without a fella on their arm. So I take them out, show them a good time, and they pick up the tab for all the cool, first-class shit I take 'em to. For a little extra, I'll take 'em home and show 'em a good time there, too."

Kelly laughed, shaking his head. "You're a gone cat, man. You're telling me you're a *gigolo*?"

Marty grinned.

"That doesn't bother you?" Kelly asked. "I mean, making your money that way?"

Marty laughed. "Kelly, I drive a new car, live in a primo place, and don't ever get up before noon. What bothers you, man, is those ideals and attitudes of the Midwest. A hard day's labor is a good day's pay and all that bullshit. Fools work for their money, man."

They rode in silence a bit.

"What do you do?" Kelly asked at last.

"Me? I get my money to work for me. We'll talk about that later. But only fools put their money in banks. I got lots of primo shit you can invest in. A whole shadow economy."

They drove in silence for a few blocks, Kelly's head swirling with cocaine and pot and new ideas.

"You said you're a Buddhist," Kelly asked, changing the subject. "What is that? Like worshipping the Buddha as God or something?"

"Buddhists don't believe in God," Marty informed him.

"They don't?"

"Nope. There's a Zen temple right over on Bush street in Japantown. The roshi there's a guy named Suzuki, a real character. It's mostly Japs that come to the center, but word of roshi is starting to spread."

"What's a roshi?"

"It's like a high-ranking person, a teacher and leader and whatnot. To become a roshi you have to complete all kinds of esoteric training in meditation and Buddhist philosophy and shit."

"What do you guys do?" Kelly asked.

Marty laughed, a deep, belly growl. "It's Buddhism. You sit and meditate, man."

"I know that, asshole," Kelly laughed. "I've *heard* of meditation, for fuck's sake. What kind of meditation?"

"What kind? Shit man," Marty said. "Are you serious? You don't know anything, do you?" He looked over at his new friend. "*Meditation*, man — concentration meditation. You sit down on a cushion and watch your breath. Get in touch with your true essence, man. Have you ever experienced true stillness, a place bigger than your ego, bigger than everything you know? A peace and a bliss that comes to you and sweeps you away with it, man?" Marty flicked his cigarette out the window.

Kelly looked over again, feeling the hairs on his arms come to standing. "Actually yeah, I have. Since I was a kid."

"No shit, man," Marty said, unruffled. "A natural. Just my luck. Well, you'd love it then. You learn to get in touch with that shit, and learn to train your mind the way some people train their bodies. It's intense, man, and Suzuki is just off the boat from Japan. He's the real deal. He gives incredible talks about the Dharma."

"Dharma?"

"Just a fancy word for the formal teachings of Buddhism."

Denis looked out the window. "And you're telling me they don't believe in any god?"

"Not only in no god," Marty smiled, "But also in no theory. No philosophy. No truth, man. They teach how to get beyond those concepts, to the freedom that lies outside of your ordinary mind."

"They teach ... the philosophy of no philosophy?"

"Bingo."

"That doesn't make any sense, you realize," Kelly observed.

Marty smiled at him. "I know, buddy, I know. It's some crazy shit!" He lit another joint and passed it over. "See what Suzuki has to say. Challenge him, man. You'll like what you get in response. Here we are," Marty said, parking the car on the street. They were at a small bar and restaurant that was hosting the fashion show. Kelly finished the joint but, as was always the case, felt nothing from it. It would take another dozen attempts to get high.

"Don't forget food and booze are on the house for the models tonight," Marty noted. "And keep an eye out for those middle-aged ladies, man. We got no need to shag ass outta here after the show, so you should try a hand at them. Some of 'em are thick as five-dollar malts, but some are pretty interesting, really. Their rings will tell you if they're loaded or not."

"Married woman?"

"Nah, man. The divorced ones still wear the rings so you don't think bad of 'em. Ain't the world a strange place? Come on!"

They went inside, and the fashion show went well. Afterwards, Kelly watched the dark-skinned Marty work the room, focusing on the older women. Kelly smiled to himself as he sipped a brandy. He loved Marty's enthusiasm and rebellious attitude, but being a gigolo wasn't in the cards for him. He would find a way to make money outside of the system without whoring himself out, and he was willing to bide his time to see what opportunities might appear.

A week later Marty and Kelly entered a modest meditation room, full of Japanese men and women. They sat on zafus — low meditation cushions — toward the back. Kelly was very intrigued to hear what this man, Suzuki Roshi, might say. After a few moments, a short and unassuming man came out from a backroom and began a two-hour lecture. It was Suzuki Roshi himself, and he spoke entirely in Japanese.

Afterwards Marty and Kelly got back into Kelly's car.

"So what did you think, man?" Marty asked.

Kelly shot him a look. "You giving me the fucking run-around or what, man?"

Marty laughed. "I'm not pulling your leg, Kelly!"

"Are you out of your fucking mind? He spoke in *Japanese* the entire time. I don't know if you know this or not, Marty, *but I don't speak Japanese*."

Marty, though, just laughed. "Nah. It ain't about the words, it's about the *transmission*, man. It's about the *energy*. You know what I'm sayin'?"

Kelly, though, just shook his head. "No, I don't know what you're saying. When he starts giving lectures in English, feel free to let me know. God, what a waste of time!"

Kelly was skeptical and reluctant to believe in anything without firsthand experience. There would be no leaps of faith in his life, and sitting and listening to a roshi speak in Japanese made as little sense as going back to church to listen to a Latin mass he couldn't understand.

Yet he would find himself back in that center again and again, drawn more to the quiet than to the lectures spoken in a foreign tongue. Even when Suzuki switched to English lectures some years later and the new San Francisco Zen Center opened, Kelly preferred the quiet transmission of the empty meditation hall to the busy sounds of spoken wisdom.

KELLY SPENT HIS NIGHTS AT A CORNER BAR, DRINKING cognac and honing his skills on the pool table. Michael was a regular there, and was a few years older than Kelly. He was the resident bar scholar and philosopher, and loved to talk about everything from the history of the Roman Empire to the problems with contemporary Christian theology, all the while downing a glass of whiskey, chain smoking, and popping amphetamines.

"You read Huxley's *Doors of Perception* yet?" Michael asked, directing the question to Kelly but saying it loudly enough to involve the group.

Kelly shook his head.

"That's the book that talks about trippin' on mushrooms, right?" a man named Dan chimed in.

Michael scowled at him. "It's revolutionary, and about a lot more than getting stoned." He turned to Kelly, but still spoke to the group. "Huxley — he's an Oxford-educated philosopher — details how taking mescaline over an afternoon changed his perception of art, philosophy, science, and the mystical sayings of the great sages — it opened his perception, you see." The barroom philosopher was holding court, and his riveting eyes and bronzed skin made it hard to look away. "It's about the strong desire in all humans to transcend themselves, and what struck Huxley was how similar his experiences were to the states described by Eastern mystics, you see. Groovy, right? It was like he opened up to the whole collective reality. And that harkens back to Jung, of course, and his ruminations on the Collective Unconscious, which takes us to Hermann Hesse, Lama Govinda, Wolfgang Pauli, and the whole pantheon of revolutionary thought...." Soon the entire group was involved in the conversation, talking about mysticism, evolution, Communism, and a thousand other topics that were compressed into an incomprehensible heap in 1962.

In only two months Kelly had changed so radically in his outlook that he was struggling to keep up with himself. It seemed like every day he met a new person who held some kind of amazing perception of the world, learned about a new kind of thought or a new revolutionary theory, or heard about someone making their way in the world in a way that he could scarcely have imagined. Life, which only six months before had seemed stale and tired and depressingly predictable, now seemed limited only by his imagination. Although he still made his living as a steeplejack, with each passing day he wondered how he too might break from the confines of conventional society, a society that seemed to do only one thing well: bind people to a slow death far removed from the intensity of life. He resented them — his parents, his church, his hometown, his wife — for *almost* breaking him. He resented them and the institutions that had brainwashed them and nearly brainwashed him.

He and Michael fancied themselves as modern day Robin Hoods, and over the next few months robbed Massengill Pharmaceuticals of half a million pills of Strawberry Explosion (an upper and downer combined in one pill, prescribed for epilepsy) and stole cash from insurance company lockboxes. They distributed the money and the drugs to their friends, and it seemed as though free love and giving freely were going to change the world.

ESCAPING THOUGHTS OF GRACE AND CHRISTINE, EVEN with all the noise and commotion of San Francisco, proved difficult. When out partying or shooting pool or running scams with Michael or Marty, he was able to forget and keep himself focused on only what was in front of him. But sitting on a meditation cushion, wandering the streets at night, or in the long hours spent alone when working, his thoughts wore a groove into his mind, a trail taken so frequently he soon could go nowhere but there.

The simple truth was that his daughter was growing up without him, and that he had left without a shred of honor or dignity. While the uppers and downers, the parties, the modeling, and the free love kept flowing his way, they eased his mind less and less. Despite all the noise and commotion, he was profoundly lonely, and he missed having his heart opened and the vulnerability that Grace had allowed him to experience. He had saved enough money to leave work for a few weeks, and it seemed time to return to Green Bay. He had changed; perhaps Grace had as well. Perhaps there would be something new to the town, something he might appreciate, something that might make him want to stay and raise his daughter there. Or Grace might find his stories of San Francisco intoxicating, and agree to move out there with Christine. He might yet be a good father and husband.

Kelly contacted a car service that allowed people to drive brand-new cars from city to city, moving them for buyers and dealerships. He was given a time and place to pick up a new Chevy, and began the drive as the sun went to ruin in the west. The austere intensity of the California and Nevada land turned blood red in Utah before giving way to the multicolor expanse of western Colorado. The new Chevy took the steep Rocky Mountain passes with ease. Through eastern Colorado, Nebraska, then Iowa, Kelly watched as the land molted from brown to green. The rolling hills of western Wisconsin saw the earth come alive with lush grasses, endless stretches of blue sky, and clear lakes.

Des Moines, Dubuque, Madison, and Oshkosh passed by, and his hometown drew nearer. He drove into the city limits, and steered through downtown Green Bay, seeing the low, hunched buildings squatting together as if to shelter themselves from the outside world. Compared to the beautiful streets of San Francisco, Green Bay felt contracted with an anxious sluggishness. Kelly let out a deep sigh. He dropped the Chevy off, and a friend loaned him a car.

He was nervous to see Grace again, and knocked on the door of their old house with sweat standing out across his forehead. She was wearing cut-off shorts and a T-shirt, her feet dirty and bare. Her body was as trim and muscular and perfect as it had ever been. Kelly felt his breath catch in his throat at the sight of her, and his heart started to race. She twirled a strand of hair between her fingers, smiling at him shyly through the screen door before pushing it open.

"Well, hey there, stranger," she said.

"Grace," he said, stepping into the kitchen. "You look fantastic."

"Thanks, Denis. God, it's good to see you. You look great yourself." They embraced, and she stepped back from him. "You look ... intense. Are you okay? And your hair! It's so long ...." She ran her hands through his hair, which was now below the collar.

He smiled at her. "Yeah, I'm okay. Just been trying to figure a few things out." He looked around the kitchen, and saw some dolls and teddy bears in a corner.

"I sent Christine over to my folks' house," Grace said, following his gaze. "I figured we needed to get to know each other again, and see where things stand before we bring her back into it."

They went to dinner that night, and each felt the pull of familiarity, the ease of being with someone you'd once known better than yourself. Kelly had forgotten the way her jaw turned upwards halfway to her ear, creating a striking angle, or how she would close her eyes when thinking and then open them looking off to the side, a smile blooming at the corners of her mouth. Her lips were tiny but full, and when nervous they pulled inward toward each other.

"I know I shut down to you, Denis," Grace was saying over dinner. "That I locked you out. It was just ... so hard for me."

"It's okay," Kelly said, "I had to figure some things out. I had to break some patterns, you know? I mean, I was on the path to becoming my father, and I couldn't let that happen."

"What's San Francisco like?" Grace asked.

Kelly told her first about his days in Chicago with Lou, and then about Marty and Michael in San Francisco.

"You work as a *model*?"

Kelly laughed. "Sort of. I mean, I *work* as a steeplejack. For the modeling, I get paid in clothes and food and booze, not in money, but it's allowed me to experience the crazy nightlife of the city. I mean, people there are amazing, Grace." He grew more excited, and leaned eagerly across the table. "People there question everything. I mean, everything. It's groovier than you can imagine. Who tells us that we should be married for life, or work a single job, or make a living the way society says we should? So many people I know there are carving out an entirely new existence, and they're into opening their minds. It's like we're breaking free of the chains of authority, Grace. People live in communes there where they share all the expenses collectively. Could you imagine such a thing in Green Bay?"

"Like Communism?"

"Sure," Kelly said, "I mean, who tells us that Communism is so bad? Our government, which has a lot of reasons to bullshit us about it. But people in San Francisco are more free; they love more deeply; they're not constrained by ideas, Grace, by fucking concepts they've been taught in school about how things are *supposed* to be! Do you see? How much more free would we have been if we'd been raised by a group of loving people instead of our crazy families and religion? A whole community of people dedicated to truth and love and freedom."

Grace smiled, a little stiffly, shrugging her shoulders. "It sounds like a lot to take in," she said cautiously. "How do you tell right from wrong? I mean, what keeps it all from turning to chaos?"

Kelly laughed. "That's just fear talking, Grace. It's one of the ways they control us. Fear. We don't live through fear out there. You're free to do what you want when you want, and no one tells you that it's wrong. I know girls who make their living as escorts, because they can make a couple grand a month."

"*Hookers*?" Her eyes went wide.

"Yeah, but they're not socially stigmatized there for doing it. It's all cool. They can live more freely doing that than being married to some *man*."

"By selling sex?" Grace looked down at her food. "That's some choice."

A silence came between them. "I mean, the one thing my dad taught me was work hard, and life turns out okay," she said. "I guess I just don't get all the noise coming from so many places these days." Her father, a Russian immigrant, spoke fluent Italian, and had made a comfortable living by hiring the Italian men interred during the Second World War to help and run his business.

"Things are calm here," Grace noted. "Green Bay doesn't have race riots and all. Why would you want to be in the middle of all that, all of that — " she considered the word for a moment, "noise?"

"There's no noise in Green Bay, Grace," Kelly flashed, "because they drove out anyone who might have made it! They drove the blacks outta town, killed or sectioned off all the Indians, controlled all the women, and pushed out anyone who challenged the way things are. San Francisco culture says that blacks can eat along side of whites, women can have their own destinies, Indians are free to follow their own language and customs, and men free to follow their hearts wherever they might lead."

They both sensed that something was off between them, that the time and separation had only increased the distance so that it now stretched before them as a chasm. They were like two dancers who could move effortlessly together but who were separated by the expanse of the dance floor. They both knew the steps, the timing, and how the other would respond, but couldn't remember how to touch. Kelly steered the conversation to more polite topics like their families and mutual friends, and after dinner took her home.

"Come on in," she said. Kelly followed her into the kitchen that had once been theirs.

She put her nose against the side of his neck. "You smell so good," she whispered, and Kelly felt passion stir in the pit of his belly. "You seem taller," Grace said, "or bigger somehow." She bit his neck, gently, and Kelly took a handful of her hair and pulled her head gently back, kissing her deeply. Soon they were standing in a pile of their clothing, and made love on the kitchen counter, on the floor and, finally, in the bedroom. He fell asleep with Grace wrapped around him. He awoke to

the sunlight coming in through the windows, and got out of
bed, dressing quietly. He kissed Grace as she lay sleeping.

"Hey baby," she murmured.

"I'm gotta get into town," Kelly said, "I'll talk to you later
today."

Over the next few days he saw his parents and younger siblings, the youngest of whom was Christine's age. He saw his
daughter, who didn't remember him. He visited his old haunts
and got drunk with his old buddies.

After only a week he felt a terrible gravity pulling him into
stagnation. He saw the repressed anger and violence in his old
friends' faces, in the hardness of their eyes, and in the way
they cursed and complained about the world, their wives, and
their children. Again and again Kelly's friends acted like they
knew who he *should* be, and ignored or mocked any part of him
that seemed bigger or wiser than the man who had left. He was
the nail daring to stick up above the heads of his peers, and it
didn't take long for people to try and knock him back where
he belonged. He nearly got into several fistfights arguing
about religion and politics, arguments that left him feeling
utterly misunderstood and deeply resentful.

By his second week home, he knew he could not stay. To
stay would be to drown, and he could think of no other way
out but to escape — get a car and beat a straight line back to
the West Coast. His friends in San Francisco were, like him,
breaking free of what *was* to create something not yet conceived or even understood. It was life on the frothy edge of
possibility where there were no rules that couldn't be deconstructed and rejected.

Toward the end of his second week, he asked Grace to sit
down at the kitchen table.

"Listen Grace," he began.

"I know, Denis," she said, surprising him.

"You know ... *what*?"

"That you can't stay. That you don't belong in Green Bay.
That you're moving back to California."

He nodded, unfolding his arms. "Come with me," he
offered, knowing she would refuse.

She shook her head. "What would I do there, Denis? Wait
tables? Work as a maid?" She leveled her gaze at him. "Be
an escort? Here I work for the jewelry store and make good
money. Everybody knows me. My family is here, and they support me in raising *our* daughter."

Kelly's ears burned at the mention of Christine. "I don't
want to leave the two of you," he pleaded.

"But you won't sacrifice for us," Grace observed. "You
won't stay. You'd make me — us — be the ones to sacrifice for
you."

Kelly dropped his head in shame.

"You're different," she charged, "harder. Do you know that
you hurt me when you make love to me?"

"I do? Why didn't you say something?" Kelly reached out across the table for her hand, but Grace pulled it away.

"You're so hard, so full of intensity. It's like you're stretched so thin you're going to burst into a thousand pieces. Look at yourself now," she said, taking his hand and putting it on his neck. "Do you feel that?"

His neck muscles felt like bone, not soft tissue, and the tension in his shoulders wrapped from the base of his neck all the way to his forehead.

"You talk about San Francisco like it's the greatest place on the planet, and you complain about Green Bay all the time. What's so bad about it here?" she asked.

"It's just ...." he began, but didn't exactly know what he wanted to say. "Green Bay's a symbol of everything that's wrong, not just in my life, but in the world as a whole." The words came slowly, but each one was spoken with a trembling concentration. "People here work their jobs, go to their churches, drink with their friends, complain about their government — they do what people do everywhere in this stupid fucking country. But Green Bay," he said the city's name like it was a curse, "it's completely backwards, it's fucking crazy, and I can't stand this goddamn town. I hate it."

Grace looked back, saying nothing, but color had risen to her cheeks.

Kelly took a moment to breathe, and let some of the tension leave his body with an exhale. "Grace," he said, almost pleading, "to stay here means I will stay exactly the same."

"Is that so terrible?" Grace exploded, slamming her hands on the table. "So terrible to be a responsible father and husband and citizen? So terrible to work an honest day's job and love your family? So terrible to be a patriot and a Christian and to pay your taxes?" She stood up. "Is that so *fucking* terrible?" she screamed.

"Don't!" Kelly warned. "Don't condemn me to be like them. I'm better than that!"

"You're so hard," Grace said, "So inflexible. So judgmental." She glared at him, eyes burning.

"I'd die here," Kelly whispered at last. "This town would kill everything that's good and decent in me. I didn't do right by you, Grace, not by a long way. I know I fucked up. I know I'm leaving you, again, but I don't know what else to do but to find my own way. I hope one day I can make it right, by both of you. You think I have a choice, but I don't. I don't have a choice."

"Don't have a choice," Grace whispered. "We all have a choice, Denis. You just don't want to live with yours."

HE LEFT WISCONSIN USING THE SAME CAR COMPANY HE had used to get there. This time he had a humongous 1962

Chrysler 300—a two-door monstrosity that was longer than most station wagons. Kelly got on the roads leading out of the city, screaming away from Green Bay as fast as the car would allow. His life and his future were in San Francisco. What it might be he had no idea, but that it would be his own and no one else's he was certain. He was angry, defiant, resentful, and his jaw clenched so tightly that he had to stop and buy some gum to give the energy somewhere to go.

Three hours later he stopped to eat and get gas in Skokie, Illinois, before pushing the Chrysler up the on-ramp toward the expressway. His eyes registered a young girl in a miniskirt standing on the side of the road, her thumb out. As Kelly zoomed past the beautiful apparition he nearly broke his own neck trying to keep his eyes on her. He jammed the Chrysler's brakes and it screeched to a halt. He reversed the quarter mile to the hitchhiker, lowering the passenger side window as she smiled in at him. She was a petite girl with long hair, barefooted, and had only a tiny bag hanging off her shoulder.

"Hey there," he said.

"Hi," she responded. She was maybe a hundred pounds of fair skin and blonde hair. "I'm hookin' to San Francisco," she said.

Kelly's smile was as big as his ears. "No shit," he responded. "That just happens to be where I'm heading. Hop in."

She did, throwing her tiny bag in the backseat and immediately putting her bare feet up on the enormous dashboard, wiggling her dirty toes and leaving footprints. Kelly looked from the bare feet to the small bag, which didn't look like it could possibly contain much of anything. "You have shoes?" he asked.

"I don't believe in shoes," she responded with a laugh. "Or in underwear. Or razors. They're all candy-ass. All part of a patriarchy trying to control us."

"Groovy. I'm Kelly," he said, offering his hand. She placed her tiny one in his.

"I'm Nadia, the Flower Tramp."

Kelly threw back his head and laughed. "Of course you are."

They moved quickly across the country, sometimes sleeping in hotels, sometimes in the car, sometimes in camping grounds. They screwed in the backseat, the front seat, on the hood, and sometimes in the dirt on the side of the road. Kelly's intensity was so strong he only slept a few hours a night at most, and he felt like an unseen force was driving him. When they reached Salt Lake City they spent the night on the outskirts in a seedy motel, and in the morning Kelly opened his wallet to find only a few one-dollar bills. It was, literally, all the money he had in the world.

"Fuck," he muttered, looking out the hotel window at the huge Chrysler. "We're outta money. And we're almost outta gas." He thought a moment. "Don't worry," he said, paternally, "There are probably lots of pool halls in Salt Lake City. We'll drive into town, and I'll spend the day hustling."

Nadia rolled her eyes. "Kelly, let me take care of it. I'll make four times what you do in a quarter the time." She winked at him.

"Listen. I don't want you to hook for the money," he said. "Just let me take care of it."

Nadia shook her head. "*Men*," she said with a grin.

Kelly went to several pool halls, but no one was really betting. He was winning, but winning so little that by the end of the day he had less than ten dollars. As he looked through the haze of cigarette smoke hanging over the hall, he suddenly had an intuition that his days of hustling pool were forever over. So he sold his beautiful, custom-made pool cue for forty dollars cash, a third of what it was worth. Forty dollars was plenty to get them from Salt Lake to San Francisco at a time when gas was thirty cents a gallon.

Kelly was back at the car at 9 p.m., and Nadia came bounding up, each skip causing her skirt to billow rhythmically. She threw her arms around him. "Hi!" she said, hanging off his neck. "How'd *you* do?"

"Okay," Kelly lied, but when she raised her eyebrows, he shrugged his shoulders. "Slow day. Not a lot of men betting. Made us enough to get to California if we watch where we spend money."

"Well, that's fab," she said, twirling around so that her skirt flew up around her. "You did pretty good for an old guy." She grinned, pulling a huge stack of money out of her purse and throwing it onto the hood.

"Holy shit," Kelly exclaimed. "How much is that?"

"Three-hundred-and-twelve dollars," she said, giggling.

"Did you hook? Sweetie, I told you, no hooking. We can always get money."

"You *men*. No, I didn't hook you flabby old gasbag. I told you I don't do that, *and* I told you to just relax. You should have just gone and gotten a beer and let me take care of us. I just went down to the financial district, and stopped every man in a suit I saw. I told them I was trying to get home, back to my parents. They were very generous!" She hopped into the car, leaning across the bench seat to call to him through the driver's side window. "Let's go Mr. Cat-has-his-tongue!"

Kelly stared through the car window at her, feeling his ears burning before he broke into a long, loud laugh. "Shit," he muttered.

Their next major stop was Reno, Nevada. Kelly was feeling lucky and was always a believer in "got a hunch, bet a bunch." So he did, on craps, through an entire afternoon. By the end of a single day he walked away from the table with four thousand dollars, a modest year's salary in those days.

A week later, they rolled into San Francisco. He dropped off the dirty and stained Chrysler 300 after paying the substantial late penalties in cash, and retrieved his own car. He took Nadia to the Haight. They parked the car and went up the stairs to a large, three-story Victorian.

"How do you guys afford this?" Kelly asked in wonder.

"It was abandoned," Nadia said, "We fixed it up and moved in. We squat."

They came into the large main room, and half a dozen male teenagers, their faces full of pimples, jumped to their feet. Kelly, a foot taller than the next tallest boy, was clearly an unwelcome intrusion.

"You're back," one round-faced young man shouted, getting off a broken, sagging couch to hug Nadia.

"I'm the matriarch," she informed Kelly, who smiled and nodded. That was no surprise to him.

"We missed you," the young man said, his eyes darting to Kelly and back to her. He hesitated, then furiously whispered, "Who's *this*?"

"This," Nadia said with a smile, doing a curtsy, "is *Superfuck*."

THE RESIDENTIAL HOUSE WHERE KELLY LIVED WAS CLEAN, neat, and cheap. As such, it was filled with plenty of honest and straight-nosed blue-collar workers, but also had its fair share of hippies, call girls, low-rent thieves, drug users, and social-rebel upstarts. Kelly flew through the Reno gambling money, spending it on drugs, women, drinks, clothes and anything else he desired. He was constrained by nothing and beholden to no one, and the nights would bleed into the days in a confusing haze. He had enough money to live for six or more months without working, and used his free time to indulge in every whim and fantasy. He thought of Grace in defiant, angry moments, and then the puff of a pipe or the downing of a few pills would scatter the memory into a diffuse mist.

Two months after he'd returned from Wisconsin, Kelly met Marty at his place. Kelly was wearing one of his handmade, tailored suits, and Marty answered the door in a mohair three-piece.

"Look at this fab fella," Marty quipped, clapping Kelly on the shoulder. "We've got invites to two of the hottest parties in town tonight with some of the foxiest broads in the city. It's gonna be something else."

Kelly grinned. "Car's out front," he said, "can't imagine why I ever would have left Green Bay."

Marty laughed. "Come on in, buddy. Got a treat for you."

Marty took off his jacket and rolled up his shirtsleeve. He tied a leather strap around his bicep, making the veins stand out rudely. He removed a glass vial with white powder from a drawer, filled the vial with water and shook it, then used a syringe to draw the milky liquid into its barrel.

"Okay," he said, sitting down, "Shoot me up. Watch my face, man, you'll love it."

"Shoot you up?" Kelly asked, feeling a tug of nervousness. "You do this before?"

"Sure," Marty said, "lots of times. Makes those Strawberry Explosions you pop seem like candy."

Kelly took the needle.

"You sure, Marty?"

"Is that the voice of Green Bay I hear?" Marty asked, flashing a smile. "Come on, Kelly — time's hustling, man. The rules don't apply anymore. I've shot up lots of times. Trust me."

Kelly nodded and, with hardly a wince, stuck the needle into Marty's vein. The two men locked eyes. "You ready?"

Marty nodded his head. "Do it."

Kelly pushed the plunger, then untied the leather strap. Marty's blue eyes immediately dilated, and his cheeks turned an explosive red. The muscles of his jaw grew tight, and then his eyelids pulled back to reveal the whole of his iris. "Holy fuck!" he yelled. Kelly pulled the needle out, and Marty exploded onto his feet, speaking so fast the words were hardly discernible. He hopped back and forth on his feet, his normally soft smile now hardened into a madman's leer.

Kelly rolled up his sleeve and tied the leather strap around his arm. The veins, large and faintly blue, stood out against his muscular forearms. Marty pulled another glass vial out and shook some water into it, then took the same needle that had just been used on him and pulled the white liquid into it.

Marty got close to Kelly's face, wanting to watch the effects of the drug. He jabbed the needle into Kelly's arm, and depressed the plunger. Nothing happened. They looked at each other, puzzled, and Kelly looked down and saw a golf ball-sized lump under his skin.

"Jesus, Marty, you missed the vein!"

"Shit," Marty replied. "Sorry, man. Here, let me try again."

"Hey," Kelly said. "Watch what you're doing, okay?"

"Hey man, it's all groovy," Marty gushed, flashing a smile. "Don't worry, daddy-o!" He filled the syringe a second time, and Kelly felt the vein pinch as the needle pierced it. Marty was in Kelly's face grinning, his eyes dancing. "Ready, cowboy?"

Kelly nodded. The plunger went down, a few grams flooded his bloodstream, and the leather strap was removed. "Holy fuck," Kelly breathed. "I think that was too much! *Fuuuck ....*" He jumped to his feet with the needle dangling out of his arm. Kelly's heart was pounding so hard he could hear the *thump thump thump* inside of his own head, and he felt his jaw muscles clenching tightly as his teeth ground together. His body felt like it was as strong and fast as a superhero's, and he imagined he might be able to lift a car off the ground if he wanted. The room was incredibly bright and active, and everything he saw or touched was sensual beyond compare.

"Okay man, let's go out," Kelly blurted as Marty, laughing, yanked the syringe free from his arm. They jumped into the convertible and raced through the streets of San Francisco, chain-smoking, laughing, and feeling invincible. The golf ball-sized lump in Kelly's arm slowly leeched into his body, keeping him high for nearly twelve straight hours.

The next few months of his life involved sex with strangers, drugs of every shape and kind, and parties that stretched out for days on end. The endless narcissism of his life was coming back to eat its own tail, and with only himself to believe in and care about, Kelly's world imploded.

Thoughts of Grace and Christine followed him like specters, always in his peripheral vision but dissolving when he looked directly at them. When he was in Green Bay for two weeks, he felt the weight of the city's collective repression weighing on him in a depressive fog, but San Francisco was the opposite extreme. With no structure, no judgments from his peers, and no rules to follow, all that was left was the absolute terror of his absolute freedom.

He locked himself in the room of his residential house with a case of brandy and a slew of pills — uppers, downers, and everything in between. His body was strong and vibrant and filled with tremendous innate vitality, but the depression was crushing. Booze and pills found their way into his system in prodigious amounts. Kelly wasn't even sure if he was trying to kill himself. All he really wanted was to stop thinking about things he could not find a way out of, and from feeling a shame and guilt that made him hate who he was. And yet even after days of bingeing, he always woke up, suspended in a purgatory of hangover and withdrawal and fiery depression. He would immediately begin popping pills and drinking again, hoping to break free of whatever had a hold on him, through death or through insight he no longer cared.

He awoke one morning sprawled across the floor where he had passed out, and lowered his head into his hands. When he looked up he saw for the first time the true squalor of his room. Overturned booze and pill bottles were everywhere, the room was filthy, and great mounds of trash and dirty clothes clogged most of the open surfaces. What was going on? Who was he? Who was he *really*? He was like a figment of divine imagination — imagined, impermanent, alive only at the fancy of something larger that he had no way to recognize or understand, a cosmic joke. Except he didn't believe in any kind of god, in a holy angel sent from heaven or an unholy boogieman sent to torment. He longed to believe in such fictions, wished himself able to find comfort in their endless naïveté, but he was utterly, completely alone.

Everywhere he looked he saw only shifting patterns, swirling currents of self-identity, changing emotions, and contradictory stories. On drugs he was one way, sober another, when tired or aroused or angry still other ways. There was no Denis Kelly in any real sense; he was a combination of stories, narratives, conditioning, and emotions swirling in a biochemical lump of flesh. When cut all away, a simple truth stood nakedly before him: he had no idea who he was. There was no God, no real Denis Kelly, nothing he could imagine or conceive of that would survive death.

He saw that he was an entirely conditioned being — conditioned by his biology, his culture, his upbringing, his conscious and unconscious reactions to his life. He was bound and trapped, an animal that responded to stimuli in predictable, set patterns, trapped inside a rotting prison that had no key.

He raised a glass of Hennessy to his lips, ready to attempt another escape, and an extraordinary thing happened. As the glass touched his lips his mind split in two, and some part of him looked out over the wrecked young man who sat, glass of cognac in hand on the floor of his filthy apartment, naked and shivering. It was the part of him that had emerged when he was just a toddler, that part of him that had no end and no beginning, no boundaries at all, that was not bound to time or place, had no personality, no needs, no desires, nothing to do but simply be. It was like the mind of God looking out of its own creation, seeing and feeling for this small speck of its creation. The small part of Denis Kelly that didn't believe in such nonsense raised a cacophony of objections, but the noise of his own mind didn't alter or diminish the experience of being one with the mind of God.

The realization created a schizophrenic split in him; part enlightened sage and part manic drug addict, Kelly began to laugh and cry as his identity rapidly shifted from one perspective to the other. He dressed and left his apartment, his shattered sanity reflected in a wild, too eager stare. He made his way through the city and to Golden Gate Park, where he was welcomed by other madmen. They too heard the voice of God, speaking in a voice too beautiful and too powerful for their sanity to contain.

In a week Kelly became filthy and emaciated, and had eyes that bulged from their sockets. Through the mile-wide gap in his sanity, the pure, undifferentiated Divine seeped through, and Kelly was taken into the very heart of Perfection. The realization, though, was too strong for him and had no context in which it would arise — it overwhelmed and repeatedly deconstructed his ego, leaving him unaware of and utterly dissociated from the world. He could have easily died in the park, for he no longer had any need to eat, talk, or pretend to have any socially defined identity at all. Death was nothing but a simple play of perspective. There was nothing to fear, and nothing at all to do but just be. Kelly lost any sense of place or of any externally defined reality. Day turned to night and back to day again in what was an endless cycle of perfection. Time lost all meaning and relevancy and he saw God in the smudged and broken faces of his homeless brothers and sisters.

One sunny San Francisco day Kelly was sleeping on his right side, and he woke to someone shaking him. As he rolled

DOWN THE RABBIT HOLE

onto his back, his face bright red on one side and pale on the other, he heard a voice calling a name that was at once familiar and foreign.

"Kelly?" A cold hand was on his shoulder, shaking him. "Kelly?" There was alarm in the tone. "*Kelly!* Wake up!" Blinking, he managed to sit. "Jesus," the voice said, "Look at you! What the hell happened? Were you mugged?" Kelly's eyes rolled down and he blinked in the fading light of the day. Standing above him, framed by a gorgeous blue sky, was the angelic face of Silvia Lui, the clothing designer for whom he and Marty worked in exchange for wardrobes.

"Baby," she said, kneeling, "you're filthy." Her nose wrinkled. "And you stink. And you're skin and bones! How long have you been sleeping outdoors?" Kelly said nothing, for he was unsure if Silvia was real or imagined, and of course for him there was no difference between real and imagined anyway. She shook him, hard. "Let's go," she commanded, "on your feet. *Now!* You're coming with me." Silently and without protest, he obeyed.

Silvia had always adored Kelly, and the two of them were good friends and occasional lovers. One of the odd things about her was she had a body temperature far below average, so she was always cold to the touch and, perhaps because of this, lived on what seemed to be a few morsels of food a day.

She slipped a cold hand around his waist and, with Kelly towering more than a foot above her, his body burning with fever and madness and divinity, guided him back to her apartment. She nursed him back to health over the next week, bathing and feeding him while filling Kelly's ears with her thoughts that he was bound for something bigger than a rudderless life amid the growing flotsam of a generation adrift. She let him cry when he had to, held space for the darkness, shame, and guilt that lashed at him, and encouraged the divine insight that was flowing so powerfully and so destructively through him. She made love to him and held him, paid for his hair to be cut and styled, gave him custom-made clothes to wear, and over a month, slowly brought him back to himself.

Kelly recovered his physical health, and his mind followed. The strong and stubborn man he had been returned, and by the third week in Silvia's care he was laughing at himself. His depression had been shattered, and a lightness of being had taken its place. Far from being afraid of losing his mind again, he felt like he was standing on more solid ground than ever before. Kelly informed Silvia he was ready to go back to the residential house, and she took him to dinner to celebrate his return to the world of the sane.

As they sipped chilled white wine, she smiled at her friend and lover.

"That was some ride you went on, Kelly," she said, not terribly rattled by what she had experienced caring for him. San Francisco in the early sixties, after all, saw its share of people going over the edge. Most found their way back, but some were lost forever. Kelly, at least, had returned from the abyss. "How are you feeling?"

Denis took a long sip of wine. "It's been really wild. The last few weeks have been like waking up from a dream." He smiled. "But I feel *good*, Silvia. I feel like myself again, only more grounded. You saved my life."

"Eh," she said dismissively.

"No," Kelly said, leaning in, "I mean it. You saved my life. It's like remembering a dream," he repeated. "It's all emotion and impressions, but nothing really concrete or real. How long was I in the park?"

"Not sure. I'd guess at least a week or more based on how skinny you were and," she smiled, "how stinky. Do you know what happened? Too many drugs or something?"

The waiter came, interrupting them, and took their orders.

"Right now," he said, "Even here, I can feel it."

"Feel what?"

"I'm not sure what to call it. Peaceful. Stillness."

"I can see it in your eyes," she said.

"See what?"

"Something. They're like wizard's eyes," she laughed. "They're all deep and mysterious."

Kelly smiled. "I think the drugs broke something open in me, but they did it by costing me my sanity, at least for a little while." Kelly shook his head. "Wow. I mean, that was true madness, Silvia. I was stark, raving mad!"

"No shit," she said with a laugh. "*I* found you. With your face sunburned on one side and pale and pasty on the other, you looked like some kind of deranged Scottish warrior."

Kelly laughed and nodded. "But all through that madness I had access to a peace like I've never known before." He took her hand in hers, and felt tears come to his eyes. "It was like I was completely insane and completely enlightened, at the same time. And it's right here, right *now*."

Silvia nodded. "That's not unheard of. I've read a lot of Carl Jung's work, and he had moments where he would literally go into the realm of the archetypes — walking around and talking to figments of his imagination as if they were real. Not actively imagining or anything, but actually walking to and touching archetypes. That's insanity in a sense, but look at what he did with it. Maybe you needed to break down to get yourself out of the way. The question is: what are you going to do now?"

"Right," Kelly said. "I don't want to go down that road again, I can tell you that. But I also don't want to live apart from this feeling I have now — where everything is slower and calmer and arises as it should, if that makes sense."

Silvia nodded. "So what now, Denis Kelly? Off to an ashram? Off to India? Maybe go to a monastery?"

Kelly laughed, shaking his head. "I'm not an institutional man, and I'm most definitely no monk."

Silvia grinned.

"Nothing so dramatic. I need to get a job and get out of that residential house. Too many temptations there. Get back into the world, get back on my feet, get sober, and get into something more stable. There's gotta be a teaching out there that can explain what happened to me, and teach me how to keep this insight and deepen it, without the madness."

Silvia sat back. "You mean a *teacher*, not a teaching, right?"

Kelly shook his head. "No. A teaching. I don't trust teachers. I might be the only guy in San Francisco not looking for a guru."

"Hmm," Silvia said.

"What?"

"Dangerous road, Kelly," she cautioned. "Just watch yourself. Some things you can't teach yourself."

"And," Kelly said, smiling back at her while giving her hand a squeeze, "some things can't be *taught*. Who taught Carl Jung?"

"Freud, but all of his most interesting work was done mostly by himself," she admitted.

Kelly sipped his wine. His eyes gleamed in the soft lights of the restaurant.

After that night, Kelly and Silvia's paths crossed less and less, and by the late sixties he had lost touch with her completely. In 1982 he went into a bank in San Francisco to withdraw cash and was astonished to see Silvia standing behind the counter in a conservative pantsuit working as a bank teller. Her hair, once magnificently long and as dark as a starless patch of the night sky, was short and graying. He looked at her for a long moment.

Kelly too was much changed from the days of a shaggy beard and shoulder-length hair, and only his eyes might have given some indication of the man Silvia had known so many years before. Yet their eyes never crossed, and Kelly did his banking and left. As he stepped out into the gorgeous California morning, he knew that some things were best left in the past, where their magic remained forever undisturbed by the disillusioning passage of time and the changing of perspectives. Silvia and Kelly's bond belonged in another era, in a different world whose time had come and gone.

Word came to him a few years later that Silvia lost a battle with cancer. He sat with the news of her passing, remembering how she had saved his life and his sanity, and felt the depth of sadness in a world where nothing could be held and where everything slid inexorably, and inevitably, to ruin.

CHAPTER 5

AN INSTITUTIONAL MAN, PART I

KELLY HAD BEEN AVOIDING THE DRAFT, AND EVENTUALLY was forced to turn himself in. He was sent to basic training and, thirteen weeks after it began, had become an outstanding soldier and the acting sergeant of his platoon. As basic training wound down, the company commander, Captain Wilson, called Kelly into his tiny office. Wilson was a thick-skulled man whose head was the same width as his ample neck. An undefined slab of muscle made up his torso, out of which two dense arms emerged. Wilson frequently chewed on a cigar, was short-tempered, and had the gritty resolve of an army man recently returned from war.

Wilson had Kelly's personnel jacket out and open on his desk, and it had nearly doubled in size.

"Acting Sergeant Kelly," he said.

"Sir!"

"Sit down."

"Yes sir!"

Wilson looked down at the papers in front of him before he leveled a gaze at Kelly. "Out of the two thousand men in this battalion going through basic training," Captain Wilson said, a hint of pride in his voice, "we select two as outstanding Basic Trainees of the Cycle. We automatically invite these two into Officer Candidate School." Captain Wilson chewed thoughtfully on his cigar for a moment. "You have been selected. Congratulations, son." He stood and offered a stout hand.

Kelly hesitated in the chair, then reluctantly stood. "*Sir?*" he managed.

The captain smiled, his hand still held in front of him. "An officer. We're going to send you to Officer Candidate School, maybe make a man of you yet. And it just might save your ass in Vietnam."

Kelly took the captain's hand. "Sir?" he repeated. "An officer?"

"As an officer, Kelly, you don't lead the charge. Even a draft dodger like you." Wilson's smile widened as he sat back down. "You've come a hell of a long way in just a few months. You should be proud of yourself."

Kelly's face hardened. "With respect, sir, I have no interest in being an officer. Sir."

Captain Wilson leaned back in his chair, bringing his hands together across his stomach. "You're going to turn down Officer Candidate School?" He laughed. "Kelly, not even you can be that stupid. Turn it down, and it means you go to war as a grunt. That means you are in the front line, getting your ass shot at. It means you're the one who steps on a fucking gook landmine, and comes back without legs or a cock. Why the fuck would you *not* become an officer? You're a high school dropout, are you not?"

Kelly nodded.

"So here's your chance to kick all us college-educated faggots right in the nuts." The captain glanced at Kelly's jacket. "I'll level with you Kelly. But you didn't hear it from me, and I'll deny it to my dying day." He paused. "First Lieutenants getting shot by their own troops is a real fucking problem in Nam. It's a fucked up place, I won't lie to you. Served two tours. I know. You're the kind of man who can control that kind of chaos. Got the balls to lead men into the heart of it and bring 'em back in one piece, to kick those gook fuckers where it hurts 'em the most, and to not get shot in the back by one of your own men."

"Permission to speak freely, sir."

"Fuck, Kelly." The captain leaned forward again. "You don't gotta pussy-foot around me, for fuck's sake. Say what's on your mind, soldier."

"I don't want to be in the army, sir," Kelly admitted. "I hate it here. I hate everything about it."

"Tell me something I don't know," the captain snarled. "One look at your jacket," he tapped Kelly's personnel folder, "tells me that much. What the fuck does not wanting to be here have to do with anything? That's why it's the draft. Most of the men here don't wanna be here. What you want — shit, son, what you want is what I want. To be drinking a beer after work and fucking a pretty little thing when I get home. Go fishing on weekends. Take a nice vacation at the shore. Maybe have a couple of kids even. Yeah. Pretty as a goddamn picture. Only we're at war and our job is to fight that war."

Kelly felt his jaw clench and his fists close. "Not going," he stated, feeling a red hot fire in the pit of his stomach. "Not going to Officer's Training School. I'm gonna get out of the army, sir, and back to my life. I'm nobody's bitch. No disrespect intended, sir."

"None taken, except for your goddamn stupidity. This is your one, best chance to avoid getting killed in the war. You'll be an officer, have a nice military pension when you get out, and have gone from a goddamn draft dodger and high school dropout to an officer in the army. Fuck, son, there's honor in that. There's dignity there. No one is asking you to serve in the army. You are being told to serve. Do your time, get out, and get back to your life."

"Are you ordering me to go, sir?"

The captain shook his head. "No. But don't be a fool, Kelly. You'll be interviewed tomorrow in front of a board of officers. You tell 'em what you want. Dismissed."

Kelly saluted and went back to the barracks where he lay on his bed, looking up at the curved ceiling. He had to take a stand, no matter what the cost.

"Acting Sergeant Denis Kelly," a grave voice called from inside the room at precisely 0830 hours the next morning, and Kelly entered a small room. Four officers sat bolt upright on folding metal chairs behind a rectangular desk facing Kelly. They were middle-aged Korean War combat veterans — career military men with crew cuts and trim bodies, whose chests hosted a colorful array of the army's highest citations: Distinguished Service Cross, Bronze Star, Purple Heart, Korean Defense Service, and a dozen others.

The army men smiled slightly at the sight of Kelly — tall, lean, athletic, impeccably presented, picture-perfect uniform, hard face, disciplined body, and all standing at rigid attention. They introduced themselves, and the colonel in charge took Kelly's personnel jacket out, opening it.

"You have been an outstanding addition to our army," the colonel began. He had jet-black hair greased into a bullet part on his left side. Large ears stood away from his face, and his eyes were exceptionally clear and focused. "You came here as a draft dodger, insubordinate, and dropout. You transformed yourself into one of the top two soldiers on the base. We are here today to offer you a tremendous honor. We are inviting you to attend Officer Candidate School so you can become an officer in the United States Army." The colonel paused, looking Kelly over from head to foot. Kelly had not moved or indicated anything at all.

"Well, soldier," the colonel asked, "what have you to say to that?"

"Permission to speak freely, *sir!*" Kelly barked.

"Of course," the colonel answered.

Kelly lowered his gaze, his eyes settling on the colonel's. "*Sir*, there are a lot of professions out there, *sir*. Banker, lawyer, doctor, and down through window washer, trashman, grave digger, U. S. Army Officer, *sir*." The army men raised their collective eyebrows. "At the very bottom of that list are the syphilitic whores on the streets of Calcutta." He paused, then cleared his throat. "*Sir*, I would rather be that syphilitic whore than an officer in your *fucking* army, *sir*." Kelly then snapped back to full attention, eyes off in the distance, his inward smile showing nowhere on his face.

The colonel blinked, twice, and his large ears turned a dull red. The other three men's faces were drawn. Kelly's personnel folder was closed. The colonel offered Kelly the cold smile of an executioner.

"So be it, *private first class*," he said. "So be it. Dis-*missed*."

Kelly spun on his heel and left the room formally. He burst into laughter as soon as he stepped out of the building, thinking that he had been just too clever for his own good. He was bragging about his speech to some friends at lunch when Captain Wilson found him.

"Kelly," Captain Wilson barked, leaning his large frame onto the table with both hands. "You simple sonofabitch. You think you can speak to a colonel that way and get away with it? I have orders to send you immediately to Radio Carrier Relay School at Fort Gordon, Georgia."

Kelly, chewing his food, felt his smile falter. The captain raised his eyebrows impatiently. Kelly's friends all stared, wide-eyed.

"What, *now*?"

"*Now!*" the captain snapped. "As in, on your feet *now*, soldier!"

Kelly stood at attention.

"The moment you finish that training, you're to be flown to Vietnam to begin service." The captain shook his head as they walked through the mess hall. "My orders are to put you on the first bus out tomorrow morning to Fort Gordon, Georgia. Go pack. An MP will be stationed outside of your barracks. Attempt to leave before the bus at 0600 and you will be arrested. Those are my orders."

Kelly was numb with shock, and he turned toward his barracks without thought. Captain Wilson put a hand on his shoulder. "Son, why the hell did you do something so stupid? This is classified, but you should know it. The average life expectancy of a Field Radio Operator is thirty-three days. But by the grace of God will you live to see your next birthday." He shook his head. "May God have mercy on your soul, Private Kelly."

Kelly thought he could be an arrogant prick and get away with it, but as he packed his bags, fighting back tears, he realized he was not bigger, stronger, or smarter than the system. He was only stupid enough to be thrown, by his own choice and his own condescension, under its wheels. The battle lines had been drawn and he would die on the wrong side of them.

Kelly was shipped to Radio Relay School at Fort Gordon, Georgia. Once there, he began to act intentionally erratic, and after a week was sent to "Mental Hygiene" to meet with the base psychiatrist, Lieutenant Lewis. Lewis was young and liberal and also angry that he was stuck in the army, so he was able to get Kelly to level with him. After a few weeks Lewis decided that Kelly did not belong in the army and that he would help get him an honorable discharge. So the psychiatrist lied, falsifying reports and saying that Kelly was homicidal, a first step toward an honorable unsuitable discharge from the U.S. Army.

The company commander of that base, Captain Salvaggio, was a short man in his early twenties, younger than Kelly, whose flattop haircut gave his head a distinctly square look. He was compact, with a body that seemed to have twice the density of most men's. Even though Kelly was nearly eight inches taller, Salvaggio had at least twenty pounds on him. He hated Kelly and the base psychiatrist for trying to beat his system.

He was determined to break Kelly to set an example of what happened if you tried to take on the army. Once Kelly was deemed homicidal, company commander Salvaggio had him banned from doing anything or from leaving the base, so that Kelly was forced to wander around, like a ghost, for months on end with nothing to do, no one to talk to, and nowhere to go. Every week Salvaggio called Kelly into his office to tell him his discharge papers had come through, and then would smile, "Oh, wait, that's just a Chinese food menu. Dismissed."

After two-and-a-half months of this purgatory, the psychiatrist upped the ante. If Kelly was suicidal, he would be able to apply for an immediate discharge. He prescribed Kelly sedatives and told him how many to take to make it look like a legitimate suicide attempt. Kelly took the pills and nearly died, and after his stomach had been pumped, woke up to the psychiatrist looking over him.

"We'll have your paperwork in a week," Lewis told Kelly with a smile. "Congratulations."

Kelly smiled. He had beaten the system after all.

Two days later, Kelly was eating at the mess hall when he spotted a soldier staring intently at him. The man wore military fatigues, jackboots, and a black tank-top. The muscles of his arms were thin but taut and gristly stubble covered a deeply tanned face. The man sat by himself, ignored by the platoon sergeants and other soldiers. When Kelly made eye contact, the man walked over, sitting down across from him. His eyes were covered with Ray-Ban aviator sunglasses.

"Hey there, killer," the man said in barely a whisper. Kelly didn't respond. He could smell the man's body odor, and pegged him to be in his late twenties, by far the oldest man in the mess hall. Most of the older, able-bodied men were off overseas, leaving the base largely run by fresh recruits. On the man's right shoulder was a tattoo of a blue arrowhead with a yellow sword and three lightning bolts running across it. Green Beret, Airborne Division. The man smiled at Kelly, his teeth yellow with black residue between them.

"I've seen your jacket, killer," the man murmured. "I've seen what you're capable of. *I know*." He removed his sunglasses. His eyes were blue-green, the pupils noticeably dilated. There was little sanity left in them.

"Who the fuck are you?" Kelly challenged.

"Name's Kadinsky. I'm just back from Nam, back from the greatest place on earth, brother."

Kadinsky pulled his service knife out of its sheath, moving it around in his hand as if it were a living part of his body. "I'm back here training these young pussies how to fight, teachin' hand-to-hand combat. But they gave me a special assignment this time. Yes sir. Private First Class Denis Kelly. Natural killer, they tell me. Just needs some motivation. Thinks he's one of those pussy faggot antiwar Commies." He cocked an eyebrow at Kelly. "You ain't no faggot, I can see that much. And you ain't crazy." He tapped his forehead, his eyes boring into Kelly. "I know suicidal. You ain't that. *Clever* is what you are. You and that shrink. Almost worked, too. Almost worked, except for one thing. You know what that one thing is?"

Kelly, wide-eyed, shook his head.

"You're a killer, that's what." Kadinsky cracked his neck. "Some people good at numbers. Some good at sellin' shit. Some at farming or driving trucks or making pop records. But you? You're a killer. I see it in those eyes. Heard how you nearly killed a fellow in your platoon with a footlocker. *I see you. Killer.*" He smiled, showing Kelly those yellow-and-black teeth. The knife danced along his fingers fluidly.

"You that kinda man. I see it. We can send a man like you into a village and you can stomp skulls and break balls until we get what we need. You got that in you. That's why they put me on you, Kelly. You and me; we're gonna get real close in the next week." He was leaning steadily in, so that now he was only about a foot from Kelly's face. "I'm gonna show you your true nature. I'm gonna show you the killer that lives inside of you, the killer that wants to fight. The killer that *needs* to fight. The killer that does what he was put here to do. I guess they'd tell ya it's for your country and God and all that shit, but the killer in you don't give a shit. He just wants to feel what it's like to take a life, wants to walk in among all them fresh recruits and have them look at ya as if you *are* God, you know?"

Kadinsky licked his cracked lips and sat back. He sheathed the knife.

Kelly got up, leaving his tray on the table. Kadinsky got up as well, putting his sunglasses back on. Kelly walked out of the mess hall, Kadinsky next to him. For three hours he followed Kelly everywhere he went, and he never once stopped talking. Twice he popped pills, the speed fueling his aggression and insanity. Suddenly he was gone, and Kelly left to himself. That feeling of having someone's hands around his throat was more intense now, and Kelly decided to run it off. Six miles later, he was sweating and twice as nervous. Kelly showered and climbed into his bottom bunk. Just as he was drifting off, he heard a voice at his ear.

"Hey there, killer." Kelly opened his eyes, and there was Kadinsky sitting on the floor. "Let me tell you about what it's like over there."

"Why don't you fuck off?" Kelly said.

"Fuck off?" Kadinsky's voice took on an edge. "Now that's not *polite*. I can put up with lots of things, *private*, but a lack of respect, well, that's likely to push a man like me to violence." Kelly looked briefly into Kadinsky's eyes before looking away, heart pounding.

"Maybe you want that, huh killer? To go at it with me. You'd put up a good fight, you would. Here's a gift." He placed a metal string on the bed. "For Charlie's ears. You can have this one. It's for you. I got five, full of 'em. The ears, cause they're cartilage, dry real nice. You can keep 'em for a couple a months before they start to drop off. One ear per kill, that's the rule — taking two is cheatin'." He laughed. "So you always just take the left one. That way everybody know you not cheatin'. You gotta see it. You gotta see those gook faces when you go into a village with five necklaces of gook ears 'round your neck. Holy crow do those little eyes bug outta their heads!" He laughed again. Kelly looked at the loop of wire.

"My third tour," he continued, talking continuously, "signed back up twice. That's how great it is." In the dim light, Kelly could see eyes that were too wide and blinked too infrequently. And they never, ever left Kelly's face. Kadinsky's service knife, strapped to his leg, glinted in the light, and his entire body was like a live wire, vibrating with deadly energy.

"Your file says you're a pacifist."

"That's right," Kelly said.

"Those peace faggots back here, they don't know shit. The world was built on violence, like it or not. The Romans burned and pillaged. They rubbed Carthage off the face of the planet. We here, we wiped out the Indians to make room for us. The Brits, shit, they've burned and pillaged the world over. Seems violent and unnecessary, but it is necessary, Kelly. It's only through the fire of violence that civilizations can spread. Men like you and me, we lay down the fire, we wipe out the heathens, we become the things we destroy to make a better world. I cut down those slope-headed cannibals. I cut the dicks off their dead bodies. I rape their women and shoot their little gook children and their crippled old people in the face." He cackled with laugher again. "I make 'em watch me do it, then I kill 'em for it. Sometimes let some of 'em go so they can spread the word. I string their ears around my neck. I bring terror and death everywhere I go. I *am* terror. I *am* death ...." Kadinsky's voice trembled a little. "They drop me and a bunch of my brothers — your brothers — behind enemy lines. We find the hot spots where Charlie is real active. And brother, we exterminate them like the cockroaches they are. Sometimes, all we gotta do is walk into a village, and the men will throw down their weapons and drop to their knees. Because they know. *We are death incarnate.* They know that once they seen our faces, it's too late ...."

For the next six hours Kadinsky sat next to Kelly, whispering his madness into the dark. An hour before wake-up call, Kadinsky disappeared, leaving Kelly to fall into a nightmarish sleep. By 0700 hours Kadinsky was back, still wearing the same clothes, still whispering his delirium into Kelly's ears, working to drive him insane, to break him, to make him submit. At his very best and very strongest, Kelly might have been able to wall this madman's insanity out of his mind, but he had spent months wandering the base alone, promised release only to have it taken away.

By their fourth day together, Kelly was dreaming of killing his company commander, of killing Kadinsky, of killing the psychiatrist Lieutenant Lewis, of killing himself. He had horrible waking fantasies of unimaginable violence, and found himself weeping for long stretches. Kadinsky was shadowing Kelly everywhere — from the shitter to the shower, always talking, always pushing. The few times Kelly turned toward him in violence, Kadinsky had smiled broadly, opening his arms as an invitation to the attack. "That's it, killer. That's what you want to do. Kill. Kill me. I understand, believe me. Give it a shot. Come on ...." Kelly knew, though, that was part of the plan — to get him to strike a superior officer — so he'd turn and walk, desperately, to get away. He couldn't fight, and he couldn't flee, and the madness grew stronger until Kelly started to lose track of fantasy and reality, of dreams and of wakefulness. He was simply in a nightmare that moved from waking to sleeping with no distinction.

Kadinsky vanished in the early morning on the sixth day, and Kelly lay in bed as the other soldiers fell out for inspection. He heard Kadinsky whispering again in his ear, and turning saw no one there. Just an empty barracks. Kelly smiled, then laughed, then started to cry, and his mind went utterly, completely blank, the same way it had on the night he went to kill his father. With that same purpose, he got out of bed. He shaved carefully, trimmed his own hair so it was inspection-ready, and polished his boots. He put on his uniform carefully and precisely, and Kelly then cleaned his M16 and reassembled it. He placed a full magazine into the weapon, affixed the bayonet to the barrel, and locked and loaded the gun. Standing by himself in the deserted barrack he called out, "Ten *hut!*" and stood at full attention, the gun pressed across his chest, his sanity broken. Tears streamed down both cheeks. Kelly then ran to Captain Sargotti's office.

Kelly pushed in. A grizzled old master sergeant, DeLoch, looked up from behind a desk normally occupied by a secretary. "Don't move," Kelly ordered, "don't you fucking move. This is between me and him."

Sargotti was reading papers as Kelly came in and stood at attention, his weapon once again across his chest, the safety now in the off position. It was an offense punishable by court martial and could have easily led to the dishonorable discharge that Captain Sargotti so desperately wanted to issue, but Kelly was far from caring. Tears streamed down both cheeks as he laughed. Sargotti froze in place, starring at Kelly with his watery eyes.

"So here's the thing," Kelly cackled as two more large tears came down his face, "you and me, we've been playing this game. A good game. And I'm here to tell you ... I'm here to tell you that you won, okay? *You won the game.* But I've lost track, sir, I've lost track of what's real and what isn't. I've lost track." A sob escaped between the words. "I want to share something with you: It's you and me now. There's no one else. You've won the game, sir, but it's not a game anymore. Don't you see? It was a game, but now it isn't. It's real. It's more real than anything, sir. All there is is you and me. That's it. In the whole fucking world, just you and me, sir." He began to sob and Captain Sargotti's eyes moved from Kelly's tear-stained face to the magazine sticking out of the M16.

"Private Kelly," Sargotti said, testing the waters, "you could go to jail for this."

Kelly laughed. "I know! That's why you've won the game. Don't you see, sir? You won. But it wouldn't end there, sir. One day I'd get out, and I'd finish this, sir. I'd finish it, because it's just you and me now, sir. Just you and me. You and me. I'll find you, you understand, no matter where you go, and finish this, because it's just you and me, sir ...."

"Okay, Kelly. Look at me. Look at me, private. Sit down. Let's talk."

Kelly sat, shoulders slumping, holding the M16 in a white-knuckle grip.

"I know you don't believe me," Sargotti said, "but I'm telling you: You're off the base tomorrow morning. That's it. With a general honorable unsuitable discharge 635-201. You think you've lost, but you've won."

Kelly shook his head, beginning to cry again. "Just more words, another fucking game. You keep saying that."

"Has nothing to do with me. That little suicide attempt convinced the higher-ups we needed to get rid of you. Lost a man last week to suicide. We were delaying him as well, and can't risk it."

The captain put both hands up, palms out. He nodded to Kelly's weapon. "*You're* playing a different game now, Kelly, one you're not in control of. The antiwar speeches you were giving in the mess hall everyday were cute. I thought sticking that madman on you was a nice counter-punch. I made my point. To you, and to the other men. It's enough. You got what you wanted. You paid for it, paid a high enough price that no one will even consider playing your little game on me ever again. Cost you, Kelly. And maybe that fucking kike shrink will get back in line after I tell him about this. His stubbornness almost cost two men their lives. He should have just let you go to war, where you belong. Fucking micks like you always itching to fight the wrong fucking battle, aren't you?"

Kelly looked at him, not knowing what he should do. His grip on the M16 was tightening and Sargotti noted the safety was off.

"Kelly, listen to me. Listen to me. Give me your eyes." Kelly had been looking at the captain's chest, imagining shoving the bayonet into it. His eyes met the captain's, and he saw an utterly sane and practical look coming back toward him.

"Now listen to me: I'm going to slowly pick up this phone and call. You're going to listen to me make that call. I'm going to have your papers sent over here, *now*. Private Kelly: Is it okay if I pick up the phone?"

Kelly looked dumbly back, not aware of the power shift in the room.

"May I make the call?"

Kelly nodded.

"You can see the signed release orders in fifteen minutes yourself." Sargotti made the call and ordered the discharge papers, giving the person on the other end all of Kelly's information. Clearly the sergeant in the other room had called the MPs because Sargotti had to speak at length into the phone that he was fine, that Kelly did not need to be arrested, that no breach of the rules had occurred, and that under absolutely no circumstances were MPs to be sent. He hung up the phone.

"So you heard it with your own ears, Private Kelly. Now you do what you want. You can sit there and relax until your papers come. You can go back to the barracks and pack. But tomorrow morning, you *will* be escorted off the base, and you will be forbidden to ever set foot on an army base ever again. That much I guaran-fucking-tee you."

"Kadinsky ...." Kelly began.

"Kadinsky's teaching hand-to-hand combat the rest of the week. He won't come within a hundred feet of you. You're dismissed, private. Up to you if you want to see those papers with your own eyes."

Outside, Kelly removed the bayonet from the gun, then the magazine, which had not a single bullet in it. He went back to the barracks and lay in his bed, not knowing what to do, what to believe, or who he was.

The next morning he was standing outside the gates of Fort Gordon, discharge papers in hand, duffle bag underfoot, with two MPs staring at him through the gates with hands on their weapons. He had been dismissed five months and twenty-seven days into his service.

Kelly got on the bus to take him downtown. At the bus station he booked a ticket for Milwaukee, Wisconsin. He was a wreck of a man; his thoughts wandered, his attention fled easily, and he was frequently overcome with panic and fear. He had beaten the system, but it had very nearly cost him his life.

CHAPTER 6

A FORK IN THE ROAD

KELLY GOT INTO MILWAUKEE AND CALLED IN SOME OLD favors with friends he knew from his Green Bay days. He got a good job working as a skilled laborer and found a modest apartment which he shared with a roommate. The routine of working, saving, shooting pool, and casually drinking brought him a sense of normalcy. Three months after settling, he had enough money to loan one of the men he worked with, Carl, two-hundred dollars. A week later Carl had vanished, leaving the job and no one with any idea where he might have gone. Kelly was furious. He worked hard for his money, and two-hundred bucks was a significant sum. After a few days of searching, he came across Carl's sister's phone number, and figured that was as good a place to start as any.

When Kelly called, a woman's deep voice answered.

"Hello?" it breathed.

"Uh," Kelly fumbled, distracted by its sheer sexiness, "Uh, hi."

"Hello," the woman's voice repeated, a notch deeper.

"You don't know me," Kelly stumbled, "not yet. That is, I used to work with your brother. I loaned him two-hundred dollars. He quit and now I can't find him anywhere. I'd like to get my loan back from him. Do you have a forwarding address or phone number?"

There was a long silence.

"I'm not going to crack his skull or anything," Kelly added with a laugh. "I just need to talk to him. Find out when he can pay me back. Make sure he knows that I expect him to. That's all."

"Sure," she replied, "I hear you. My silence wasn't that I was worried you'd hurt him, just that I'm not surprised to get this kind of call. They come more frequently than I'd care to admit. You sound like a nice enough fellow. But you're going to have to get in line. He owes *me* money. I can give you a number that I have, for what good it will do you."

"Well, I'd really appreciate it. My name is Denis. Denis Kelly."

"Well it's nice to meet you, Denis Kelly. My name is Cheryl."

A strange telephone romance began between them. Kelly talked to Cheryl three or four times a week, and they shared incredibly intimate details about themselves. He told her all about his flight from Wisconsin, his crazy experiences on the West Coast, and his time in the army. She talked about a loveless relationship to a minor mafioso in Milwaukee, and her love for her two daughters. She was of Italian descent, worked as a fashion model when there was work and waited tables at night. They had an easy and fast chemistry, completely understood one other, and agreed to never ruin their connection by meeting in-person.

The weeks passed, Kelly worked his dead-end job, and he found himself looking forward more and more to the times when he and Cheryl would speak. It seemed ridiculous to him that someone that sounded so beautiful, so dark, and so deeply feminine should be kept confined within a telephone's headset. And so he set about finding her, against his word and without her knowledge.

Milwaukee, while not a huge town, was big enough that it took some time to figure out where Cheryl worked. Kelly asked strategic questions separated by a day or two so that she would not deduce he was slowly narrowing the potential places of employment. At last he was reasonably certain he had the neighborhood and the restaurant's name, more than enough. He knew she worked weekends, and so he slipped into a busy Italian restaurant on a Friday night, sliding up to a beautiful bar, feeling his heart pound in his throat.

He had fallen in love with her, and he was both terrified and excited to meet her face-to-face. Kelly took a seat and ordered a brandy. He watched the waitresses come up to their station to place drink orders, nervously listening to their voices when they spoke.

A pencil-thin woman approached. She was five-feet-ten, with black hair infused with red, gray, and white highlights. Her almond-colored eyes were full and round in an angular face, and they emanated a sadness that made Kelly's heart feel like it might break. He heard her sigh as she put her drink order down, and thought his heart might break open at the sound. His hands were trembling. When she did speak to the bartender it was in a voice too low to hear. Those full, sad eyes looked to him, twice, narrowing the second time in suspicion.

Kelly finished his brandy and fled. The next night, Saturday, was even busier than Friday, and Kelly again nervously took his seat at the bar. Not the kind of man who was shy approaching women, he found himself unable to muster the nerve to speak to her. When she would approach the bar he would look down, feeling her eyes move across his profile. He was prepared to leave without saying a word for the second night in a row when a voice spoke beside him.

"I thought we had agreed to never meet," he heard.

Kelly felt his face flush. "I know," he blurted, heart pounding. "We did. I'm sorry. I couldn't help myself." Her almond eyes held Kelly's without wavering. She leaned sideways into the bar, allowing Kelly's eyes to sweep her. Her nipples pushed against her shirt, and her figure tapered dramatically at the waist before opening again at the hip. With her thin eyebrows, elfin ears, and prominent lips, he knew at once that had she not been bound to Milwaukee because of her children, she could easily have been a full-time fashion model.

"You shouldn't have come," Cheryl was saying when Kelly's attention returned. "For one, I'm busy. More to the point, I'm also involved with the Fratachelli family."

The spell of Cheryl was momentarily broken. "Bruno?" Kelly exclaimed, "*Bruno*? Are you serious? He's a gorilla! A good-looking and chiseled gorilla, yes, but a gorilla nonetheless."

Cheryl's lips pursed, seemingly caught between a smirk and a frown. "Why don't you tell me what you really think, but this time don't spare my feelings."

"I don't mean to be rude," he apologized, unable to keep from laughing. "It's just — I mean, look at you — you're smart, gorgeous, worldly, witty — he barely walks upright."

Her lips gave up on the frown, and she smiled. "His family makes my life a lot easier," she noted with a shrug, "and my daughters' lives as well."

"I could make your life a lot easier," Kelly countered, "while also treating you the way you deserve."

"You shouldn't have come," Cheryl said, cutting him off. "There's nothing we can do aside from talking on the phone. There's no need to torture yourself."

"Right," Kelly said. He noted no part of her seemed to believe her own words. "So," he said, "unless you ask me to leave, I'm going to sit here and wait for you to finish your shift. Then I'm going to take you to the riverfront, where we'll walk along the water, holding hands, and get to know each other even better than we already do. And then," Kelly swallowed, "I'm going to kiss you."

Cheryl stared at him for a long moment. The drink order she put in with the bartender had been sitting at the end of the bar for over a minute. She glanced at the drinks and then back over her shoulder at her tables.

"I should be done by ten," she noted curtly, picking up the tray of drinks and disappearing into the restaurant without giving him a second look.

They became lovers and quickly fell in love. A month after their first meeting in the restaurant, Kelly was playing pool with a group of work buddies on a busy Friday night. Two Italian men dressed in custom-made suits approached Kelly.

"Game's over," the skinny one said, pushing the eight ball into a pocket. The other man, a thick-necked bear of a fellow, nodded. "Come on outside," he said to Kelly. "We need to talk."

"Be right back, boys," Kelly said to his friends, and the three men stepped into a back alleyway.

The skinny one spoke again. His face was pock-marked with acne scars with lips so thin they barely covered his narrow, uneven teeth. A large nose hooked prominently over his mouth, and his eyes, tiny pits, were set far into his head. "Most people don't step into an alleyway with us so willingly," he noted. "You're either brave or stupid is my guess, not that it matters."

"Maybe a little of both," he admitted.

"So," the skinny man continued, "You got a thing goin' with Cheryl. We're here to tell you that Bruno doesn't like it too much, and it's time you broke off your ... engagement." He spoke slowly and with a sincerity befitting a professor. The bigger man, his face lost in his jowls, nodded.

"I get it," Kelly said, "the brains and the brawn." He winked and smiled, hooking a thumb at the bigger man. The two enforcers looked at one another, then back at Kelly. "Look fellas," Kelly said, "I know Bruno. I don't mean any disrespect, but you've gotta be kidding me. He sends muscle down here to tell me to stop seeing a woman he obviously can't control? Come on. He couldn't come and tell me that to my face? Pretty boy like him?"

"He feels *especially strongly* about the situation," the skinny man said emphatically. "He thought that me and my colleague here might impress the seriousness of his feelings upon you a little better than he might."

"All the more reason," Kelly noted. "Look, fellas. I'm not a violent guy. I'm not stupid enough to threaten or disrespect him or you guys. But I'd tell him to fuck off, to his face." Kelly smiled, knowing he was skating on thin ice. "Cheryl makes up her own mind who she wants to be with, no? Do me a favor, and tell Bruno to man up. Maybe he should find a woman he *can* control." Kelly smiled again. "No disrespect intended," he repeated, putting his palms up. "I hear you guys. I'm just sayin' I'd respect it a lot more if it came from Bruno's mouth. His Papa would agree, I think." Kelly knew the reputation of the family's patriarch.

This time the big guy with the jowls shrugged and smiled.

"Okay, tough guy," he wheezed through his broken nose. "We'll let the old man know what you said. Exactly what you said. You want to say anything else, wise guy?"

"Yeah," Kelly said. "You guys look like a million fucking bucks. Where'd you get those suits?"

The two goons reported back to Bruno's dad, who apparently threw his head back and laughed about how Kelly had talked about his son. The men came back to the pool hall a week later, and the skinny one whispered in Kelly's ear, "Okay. She's all yours. No hard feelin's." And that was the end of it.

Kelly spent a long, miserable winter working and saving money. In the springtime he let Cheryl know that he was again leaving for San Francisco, in all likelihood never to return to the Midwest. She promised to join him, and in a few months, did exactly that. They lived in a Victorian flat within the city limits. Cheryl came to Kelly one night, her face streaked with tears, after only a few weeks.

"I can't, Denis. I can't stay anymore," she sobbed. "I miss my girls so much. I miss them so much."

"Okay," he said, "Okay. So go and get them. Bring them back. There's plenty of room for them here. I'm making good money now and we can raise your girls easily. School districts are good in this neighborhood and the girls will love the energy here."

"Mark will never give them up," Cheryl said, referring to the girls' father. "He's so well connected. And that stint I did in rehab a year ago gave him a lot of ammunition with the court."

"Marry me," Kelly said, impulsively.

"You're sweet," she said.

"I'm serious," Kelly pressed. "Marry me. Tomorrow. We'll get up, go to the courthouse, and get married. I've got a solid history of employment and a clean record. Even have an honorable discharge from the U.S. Army." He smiled and winked. "Then you go back to Milwaukee and use my résumé in addition to yours to make your case. Married to a stable and working man in San Francisco, a house for the girls, good schools. You take that fucker Mark to court and get your daughters back. You call me when you're ready, and I'll drive out and pick the three of you up."

Cheryl was now looking him intently in the eye. "You're completely serious, aren't you?"

Kelly dropped to a knee. "Does this help convince you?"

"You're fucking crazy," she gushed, throwing her arms around him. "I love you so much," she sobbed. "Yes, yes! I'll marry you!"

The next morning they filed for a marriage license and were married in the afternoon. Cheryl — now Mrs. Cheryl Kelly — flew back to Milwaukee to get her daughters.

Cheryl left at the beginning of the summer of 1967, a time when San Francisco was on the edge of a cataclysmic transformation. The old institutions where crumbling under the force and power of the counterculture, and new institutions had not yet formed to take their place. There was a sense of living evolution everywhere, and of the youth of the city creating the future from the ruins of the present. It was an exhilarating time to be alive. In the midst of it Denis Kelly had returned to his old strength, confidence, and sense of purpose.

While Cheryl was away, they talked on the phone a few nights a week. He loved to hear the deepness of her voice and the acerbic wit that she brought to bear on her world. Kelly, always generous with his resources, sent her money so she could live, and when he would get off the phone he could feel the depth of his love. He was dimly aware that there was a part of him that lived safely behind a wall — he had given Cheryl access to his heart and his dreams, but had kept a larger part of himself safely out of view. He loved her, and he loved women in general, but trusting them too much was a different story. He was like a gambler who always had a secret stash of money — Kelly might seem all-in, but was always careful to have a little of himself hidden out of sight, just in case.

○

ONE MORNING WHILE EATING BREAKFAST AND DRINKING his morning coffee he saw an ad in the paper asking for a *combustion engineer*, with good pay and benefits. Even though he had no idea what a combustion engineer was, he figured it was worth a call.

"Hello, this is Bill Matheson," a man's voice said.

"Hi, Mr. Matheson. My name is Denis Kelly. I'm looking at this ad you posted. I've heard of combustion, I've heard of an engineer, but I've never heard of a combustion engineer. What is that?"

"Well," Matheson said, sounding fatherly, his drawl as slow and patient as if he had all day to chat, "a combustion engineer, you see, he works with all manner of flame application in an industrial setting. Magnesium meltdown furnaces, industrial ovens of any kind ... pretty much anything you can think of involving industrial combustion, and we do it."

Kelly thought a moment. "Well, sir," he said, "I'm not an engineer, but I have extensive experience working with flame, from pipe fitting to heating and air conditioning to acetylene application to welding. Done pipe-fitting, worked with all kinda flame application, and I've worked on just about everything under the sun."

"Hmm," Matheson said, "Well, you sound like a nice enough fella. Why don't you come in today, and we'll see what you know and what you can do. I was looking for an engineer, but I'd be just as happy to train a smart, motivated fella. And the engineers don't have practical experience, which you do have."

Mr. Matheson was an avuncular man who looked every bit as kind as he sounded. He wore thick, black-framed eyeglasses, carried a small army of pens in his white shirt pocket, and was utterly devoid of any hair whatsoever. His pink skin and plump body meant he looked like some kind of human— hairless vole experiment gone horribly wrong. "Well," he said, after he and Kelly had talked for an hour or so, "you have the mind of an engineer, that much is sure. And you're outgoing, which is even better. We're as much a sales organization as a technical one — gotta get new clients all the time. You seem like you'd be able to work on both sides of the counter, as it were."

"Yes sir," Kelly said, smiling, "I do believe I would."

"Okay, then," Matheson said, offering his hand. "How soon can you start?"

Kelly started at an incredible salary — an engineer's — and was given a company car and more freedom than was reasonable.

Kelly found the best means of breaking into the "straight" world as he was likely to find, one that he enjoyed and that seemed to offer tremendous upward mobility. Each of the four men who worked for Mr. Matheson's company was a partner, meaning that they shared the company's privately-held stock and got dividends each quarter. Kelly was sure that within a year he would be a partner as well, and be well on his way to an upper-middle class lifestyle.

As the summer of 1967 wore on, the 25-year-old Kelly found himself with a fantastic job, a great circle of friends, and a deepening interest in the counterculture.

Kelly and Cheryl talked less and less while she was away, and when they did talk she seemed strung-out and distracted. Whenever he pressed her, she assured him that she was fine and that she was just a little hung over from too much wine. She made excuses about not being able to see her daughters, and, instead of being gone for weeks, was gone for months. When she at last came back to San Francisco, it was mid-summer and she no longer expressed much interest in her girls at all.

Kelly drove to the airport, parked his car, and walked up to the gates where her plane was set to arrive and sat on a bench. With his legs crossed, he was flipping through *Life* magazine when he saw the plane taxi up. Flowers sat in the seat next to him, and when Cheryl at last came down the off-ramp Kelly felt the familiar pounding of his heart in his throat.

She was wearing tight jeans, boots, and a light coat. Her hair was long and partially covered her face, and, even though it was evening, she wore large sunglasses. Cheryl offered a weak smile, and took the flowers from him.

"Aw," she said quietly, "that's sweet." Kelly threw his arms around her and immediately felt how emaciated she was. His hands pressed against her ribs.

"Hey sweetie," Kelly said, standing back. He took off her sunglasses, and saw that her eyes were clouded and distant, with dark circles running under each one.

"Oh baby," he said, "what's happened to you?"

"Oh," Cheryl said, "things got complicated back home." She nestled her nose into Kelly's neck. "Do you have any PMA on you?"

Kelly shook his head, pushing her back from him. "I don't touch that stuff, Cheryl. You know that. It's dangerous. And deadly."

Cheryl, her eyes dark and lost, looked blankly back. "That's just because people don't know how to chill on it. I don't try to fly off buildings." She laughed, but Kelly just shook his head. Cheryl had some substance abuse problems in her past, and she was clearly and obviously strung out.

Cheryl had gone back to Milwaukee to get custody of her daughters, but in so doing she had fallen in with her old circle of friends. That circle had come across a new drug, para-Methoxyamphetamine, that combined speed with hallucinogenics. It was particularly nasty because the meth-amphetamines in it gave the user a great deal of strength and certainty and narcissistic confidence, while its hallucinogenic compounds decreased self-awareness, impulse control, and the ability to apprehend reality. This led many of its users to not only getting addicted but to also attempting stunts that would cost them their lives. On the streets it was known as Doctor Death for a simple reason: It killed you.

"Let's get some food in you," Kelly said, taking her hand. "Something wholesome, okay? Then we'll go back to the house, and unpack your stuff, maybe draw a bath." She nodded, helplessly, and Kelly picked up her suitcase.

"I love you, baby," she said, collapsing into him.

Kelly nodded back, and sighed.

"Come on, Cheryl. We need to get you straightened out."

Over the first few weeks they were back together, he was able to help her wean herself off of the heavy use of PMA and get her life back into focus. But her strength and her resolve were tied to his, so that whenever Kelly was gone for too long of a stretch, Cheryl would end up strung out on PMA again, and he would have to work with her to get her off and detoxi-fied all over again. She wasn't working, so Kelly put her on a strict budget to prevent her from using any extra money to buy PMA.

That inaccessible part of himself felt safe and justified behind its walls, and while he was saddened and hurt to see Cheryl losing herself to addiction, he also knew that his life was heading exactly where he wanted it to. He would help Cheryl, would give her the money and the resources and the love and support he could, but if she chose to sink into addic-tion for good, she would sink alone.

KELLY WAS VERY DISCRIMINATING IN THE DRUGS HE USED. He bought only the finest marijuana, the purest LSD, and the best mescaline. As 1967 wore on, Kelly developed a reputa-tion among his friends as a connoisseur of fine drugs, and they asked him with increasing frequency to get them things as well. Marty made a wry observation one day when they were out at lunch.

"So," he said, "the federal government has made acid, along with pot, a Schedule 1 narcotic. You get busted you're gonna do big time in a federal fun house."

"Yeah, well," Kelly said, "me and about a million other people in the city."

"But you're getting dope for your friends, dope," Marty said, smiling. "That means you're dealing. And you're not even padding the prices or selling enough to cover your bail. Your buddies get caught and roll on you, and you go down.

Don't you think it might be a good idea to have enough money for bail and a nice lawyer?"

Kelly stopped chewing for a moment. "You gotta point."

"Goddamn right I got a point. Shit, man, you should pad the price. Five or ten percent should be enough to keep you covered, and you'll still be getting people great deals, right?"

"Yeah."

"Now," Marty said, smiling, "I still expect you to get *my* grass at cost, but fuck the rest of 'em."

Kelly began adding a small service charge. He put the extra money in a shoebox stashed away in the house. The amount of money in that box grew over a few months until when he sat down and counted it he realized he had almost two thousand dollars in there — almost a quarter of his yearly salary. He was amazed at how fast and effortlessly the money had grown.

At the end of the summer of 1967, Kelly met a classically-trained concert pianist named Bobby Grades. Grades ran a commune of about a hundred hippies, living in three connected Victorian row homes in Haight-Ashbury.

One day Bobby approached Kelly.

"Listen, man," he said, "we've got a lot of people getting shit from a lotta different people in this commune. All kinds of shit, man. I don't like the heat that might come from all those different folks asking around. Plus, they mostly get shit product. I know your reputation as a guy who gets good stuff. Would you be willing to provide for our commune? I mean everything? Can you handle that much? I'll put together a list every week, you get it, and we'll pay you when you deliver."

"Supplying one hundred people on a weekly basis?" he asked, laughing. "Are you serious?"

"Hey, man," Bobby said, "I've got tours and composition to worry about. Don't have time to screw around with drugs, man." He smiled. "Takin' 'em, sure. But I hate arranging to buy 'em. You're a good guy, Kelly. Come on — it'll be a nice chunk of change for you every week."

"I think I can swing that," Kelly said cautiously. "Have to check with some resources before I can commit to it, but I'll swing by in a couple of days and let you know."

Within a month Kelly was making an extra thousand dollars a month on top of his salary of one thousand a month, entirely in cash. Kelly finally opened a number of safety deposit boxes through friends he trusted, in several different banks where he stored the money. Eventually, Kelly would have hundreds of thousands of dollars stored in these safety deposit boxes, kept under the names of the many people he considered friends.

A month later, on a Monday morning in late 1967, Kelly got dressed after being up partying for most of the weekend.

"Shit," he groaned to himself, climbing into the car at 8:50 a.m. "Fucking Monday." Halfway to work he noticed himself in the rearview mirror. He had forgotten to shave. That was bad. Black stubble clung to his face in uneven patches. And he had forgotten to brush his hair, which looked long and wild in the mirror.

"That's not going to go over well," he said out loud. He'd have to stop by a drug store to buy a brush and razor. At the next intersection, he noticed his sport coat was chaffing his armpits, and was horrified to look down and see he had somehow forgotten to put on a shirt. He saw black chest hair, a few necklaces, and his own belly. That was worse.

"For fuck's sake," he muttered, and at that moment realized he was wearing slacks but no shoes or socks. That was really, really bad. He pulled over and rubbed his face between his hands, then turned around and went back home.

"Mr. Matheson," he said into the phone.

"Hey there, Denis!" Matheson said back.

"Hey. Listen, I'm not going to make it in today. I'll be in tomorrow, but we need to talk."

"Everything okay, son?" Matheson asked, concerned.

"Yeah, everything's fine. I'll explain it tomorrow."

He spent that night walking the city, thinking about where his life was and where it was going. He was twenty-five years-old. He knew he could no longer straddle two worlds. The engineer-in-training needed his sleep and a regular schedule. The truth was, though, that Kelly was making his yearly salary by selling drugs, something that took him about four hours of work a week. His wife was a PMA addict, and all his friends were deeply immersed in the counterculture. Everything in his life was pushing him in a single direction.

Kelly drove to work the next day, not having slept, and sat down with Mr. Matheson.

"So what's up, son?" Mr. Matheson said, obviously concerned. "You don't look so good."

Kelly nodded. "I'm sure I don't. Mr. Matheson, it's like this …." Kelly took a deep breath. He had always believed in telling the truth over bullshitting people, and his experience told him time and time again that if you were honest with people, they almost always rose to meet you in that place of integrity, no matter how hard or ugly the truth might be.

"It's like this, sir. I'm deeply involved in the drug trade, where I'm making about my salary already in cash — and that's just on the side. I can't keep doing both, and if I stay here, I'm gonna screw up this job and lose your respect."

He let out a breath of air.

"I want you to know how much you mean to me, and how much it means to me that you took a leap of faith to train someone like me. The fact you believed in me means more than I can express."

Matheson leaned back in his chair, and nodded. "I tell you, Denis. These drugs today — you just watch yourself. In my day there wasn't so much temptation. Things were so much easier. I pity you kids today, mainly because I can't blame you for making the choice you're making." He sighed. "I'll be sorry to lose you. If you ever come back to your senses," he said, his tone far less judgmental than the words themselves, "you have your job here. So long as it's my company. You'll be missed, son. And for God's sake, be careful out there."

"Yes sir. Thank you, sir, for everything."

Kelly drove home, feeling the freedom of having made his choice. He would never again work in a normal world of nine-to-five jobs, corporate meetings, and steady paychecks. For better or worse, his path was now clear.

PART TWO

"The unexamined life is not worth living, but the unlived life is not worth examining."

— *Unknown*

CHAPTER 7

THE MAKING OF A COUNTERCULTURE ICON

B Y THE SUMMER OF 1968 KELLY WAS WELL KNOWN AS A dealer of integrity and ingenuity. He was making nearly twice his old salary, entirely in cash. He had dozens of friends, access to all the best parties in the city, and lived an increasingly extravagant lifestyle. He was simultaneously pursuing spiritual inquiry and hedonism, utterly unable to tell the difference between the two.

His spiritual pursuits meant that he was spending more and more time practicing sitting meditation at the San Francisco Zen Center, studying under Suzuki Roshi, and trying to find whatever it was that LSD seemed to give him so effortlessly: peace and a sense of self beyond the finite, small ego. Kelly passionately believed that LSD was the key to a new spirituality, one that could transform the esoteric spiritual path and make it accessible to everyone. No more would people have to sit in pews or an audience and listen to self-proclaimed teachers talking about their insight into God or spirit or Enlightened Mind. LSD enabled everyone to have that experience. It was the great leveler that allowed anyone to experience the mind of God for his or herself. It would undermine the authority he distrusted so much, no matter if it came from a pope or a Tibetan lama. Both claimed to have special access to God or spirit, and both demanded supplication to their so-called wisdom. Kelly rejected such hierarchy, and he liked nothing more than to give people LSD and watch them "pop." This usually meant they would have some kind of deeply spiritual experience, one that he would then use to explain to them how such insight was the birthright of all humans, not just an elite few. Paradoxically, more and more people began to circle around Kelly, feeding off his certainty, his charisma, his insight, and his multitude of strongly held opinions.

Kelly was still drawn to meditation. From 1970 on, he always held open meditations at his home. The discipline and austerity of Zen was also deeply appealing, and he loved its extreme embrace of agnosticism that made God or angels or hell or morality all empty concepts and traps for the ego. Meditation, which Kelly took to easily and naturally, allowed him to experience the insights, sober, that he gained by taking LSD.

In June of 1968, Kelly was at a party in the Haight district. He was sitting on an outside porch by himself, listening to the sounds of the party rage inside. It was early evening and he was sober. Two men joined him, one squat and ponytailed, the other thin, bearded, and wearing glasses. Both were about his age, mid-twenties.

The guy with the ponytail leaned onto the railing next to Kelly.

"So, you're Kelly," he stated.

"One and the same," Kelly replied after a pause.

"I'm Russell," the man offered. He hooked a finger toward the bearded fellow. "That's Larry." The other man nodded.

Kelly looked back out off the porch. "So what do you want, Russell?"

"Well, we know of your reputation," Russell said, gruff and forward, almost confrontational. "We've heard about you now through at least a dozen people. You're known and trusted. You got a good word on the street."

"I work hard to ensure that's the case," Kelly said.

"Well, we're in the same kind of business, sort of," Russell said.

"What business is that?"

"We manufacture and sell meth."

"Can't help you," Kelly said immediately, thinking of Cheryl. "I don't touch that shit. Don't sell it, don't make it, and won't get it for you. Not for a long time. Fucks people up."

"We know," Larry chimed in, softly. "We *hate* making it. That's why we're here. We want to start making LSD."

"He speaks," Kelly said, turning to Larry. "LSD, huh? Well, there's a big market for LSD, sure. Sunshine's got the market cornered," he said, referring to the Brotherhood of Eternal Love. "But there's plenty of room for more. And they don't mind the competition. They believe it's about opening hearts and minds."

Kelly looked from Larry to Russell. "So what do you want from me?"

"We needed base and capital, for starters. We figured we'd make it, and you'd sell it," Larry said. "Seems like a no-brainer."

"You guys make LSD before?"

Larry turned red and lowered his head. Russell cleared his throat.

"Fellas?" Kelly asked.

"No," Larry admitted.

"But you know how?"

"I think so," Larry responded. "But I'm not certain."

"He's a chemist," Russell said defensively. "*And* he's brilliant. We have the equipment and the lab. He'll figure it out, no problem. We just needed a reason to try. Someone who could sell it if we made it. Someone who is connected, so we don't have to stand on goddamn street corners selling acid."

"You know how this would work?" Kelly asked.

Russell stared back, expressionless. Larry shrugged his shoulders.

"Okay. Let's say this was a go, and you guys were going to make LSD. We have to get the base, ergotamine tartrate. It's not only expensive, but it has to come in from South America. You guys know how to do that?" They both shook their heads. "You know how to get it through customs, or how to get it in such a way you don't automatically tip off the Feds and have half a dozen agents following you to your lab?" Both men again shook their heads. "You guys got fifty K sitting around?" Larry and Russell exchanged a look. "I didn't think so. So I get investors. They put up the money. I arrange to get the base, and buy us our raw materials. You make a run of acid, and I sell it through my connections. The investors get their money back, plus thirty percent, compounded monthly, so we want to pay them back fast. You fuck up your run and we owe those people their investment back, plus the interest — compounding monthly. You know what that means?"

"Don't fuck up," Russell said.

Kelly nodded. "After the investors are paid off, the three of us split the profits three ways."

"Deal," Russell said.

"But," Kelly said, "we have a bigger problem than the money: If I'm going to put my neck on the line, I need to know you guys can make quality LSD. So I'll ask you again: Do you guys know how to make LSD?"

"Sure," Russell said, "Don't even worry about it."

Larry lowered his head. "I think I can."

"Jesus, Larry," Kelly said, "At least lie to me."

Larry's face turned red. "I can't do that, either."

Kelly laughed. "So you're a moralist drug maker?" He clapped Larry on the shoulder. "So am I, boys, so am I. I've been thinking a lot about LSD. I think it just might change the world."

Larry cocked an eyebrow at him, smiling slyly and shaking his head. "Me and Russell don't want to change the world. We just wanna get rich."

"Without hurting people," Russell added.

Kelly just smiled. "Let me think about it, okay? Ask around a bit. See what the market's like. You guys can start by figuring out how and where you're going to set up a lab, and maybe learn how you're actually going to make the product. One of you guys got a phone number?"

Kelly, Russell, and Larry had, in a single conversation, laid the groundwork for what would become the Order of the Golden Frog, an LSD family that by 1972 would be grossing more than two million annually.

Kelly was sitting at home in his Victorian flat, running numbers on the business plan he had developed. He heard Cheryl in the bathroom, making strange noises, and got up.

"Hey baby," he called, "You okay?"

She came out of the bathroom wearing nothing but panties. Even after a year of living together, her beauty still took his breath away. She was thin, but her hips curved outwards in a perfect hourglass, complemented by slim breasts that contrasted sharply with the visible line of her ribs. Her hair was its usual rainbow of colors, hiding eyes that were murky and unfocused. Walking into the lights of the kitchen, she looked both upset and delighted.

"What am I going to do with these?" she said, pulling her lips away from her teeth.

Kelly saw red lips, straight teeth, and a pink tongue. "With … what?" he asked.

"*These!*" She pointed at her incisors. "They're fucking three inches long now! I look like a vampire queen or something!" Cheryl ran her fingers along the non-existent teeth.

Kelly rubbed his face with both hands. "Sit down, Cheryl," he said. She did. "Baby, those teeth grow big when you're doing way too much PMA. It's called 'Dr. Death' for a reason."

"I'm not doing PMA, baby," she lied.

Kelly shook his head. "It's not good for you. And those teeth," he nodded at the teeth she thought she had, "will fall out as soon as you stop taking that stuff and get sober."

"Really?"

"Really."

"They'll fall out?"

"As soon as you get sober. Where are you even getting this stuff? I know you don't have any money of your own."

She shrugged, rubbing her teeth self-consciously.

"Look," Kelly said, "I know I've been busy lately." He pulled Cheryl into his lap. "But I want to make it up to you. Why don't we spend some time together, like the old days? I'll go sober, too, so we can help each other. I have to meet Russell and Larry on Thursday, but after that I'm free and clear for a stretch, and we should take a little vacation. Maybe head to the islands."

"Aw, Denis," she cooed, "You're so kind to me. Let's do that."

He took her by the hand, and waited until her soft eyes finally found his and held them. "I'm serious, Cheryl. You — we — need to get sober. It's important. We'll go to the islands, but we're not going to take anything with us. I'm going to pack your bags to make sure. It'll be a fresh start."

"Okay," she said, breaking eye contact. "Okay. We'll do it together, baby. Like you said."

"Good," he said, "Let me make us some food."

But when Kelly rolled over in bed later that night, Cheryl was gone and the house empty. He didn't see her for several days, and when he did she looked worse and more strung out than ever. She wasn't home that Thursday, and didn't return until after the weekend. The trip and its promised sobriety and return to normalcy were forgotten.

Larry and Russell showed up at Kelly's house three weeks after their first meeting on the porch. It was after nightfall, and they came into Kelly's kitchen in a conspiratorial cloud. Russell was dressed the same way he had been when Kelly met him — blue jeans, a T-shirt, and a jean jacket, with a cup of coffee in one hand, a cigarette burning in the other. His hair was pulled into a messy ponytail, and a week's worth of stubble clung to his compact face. Larry was wearing khaki slacks and a white-collared shirt, his beard neatly trimmed and hair impeccably combed.

"You look like you stepped off a billboard ad for Marlboro," Kelly noted to Russell.

"Except he's too fucking short," Larry added with a smile.

"Yeah, like you're one to talk," Russell shot back, cocking an eyebrow. "I'm short and *pretty*, at least. You're just short."

The three men sat down at the kitchen table. Kelly opened three beers as Russell ground out his cigarette and, a few seconds later, lit another. He was nervous. Larry placed a container full of a black tarry substance on the table.

"That's LSD?" Kelly asked.

"We didn't refine it yet," Larry apologized. "Refining's a pain in the ass and time consuming, and if I fucked up there's not much point to it. This is the crude stuff. If it's any good, I'll refine it."

"Well, how did it go?" Kelly asked.

Larry and Russell exchanged a look.

"We don't know," Larry admitted.

"How are we going to find out?" Kelly asked.

"We have to eat some," Russell responded. "Or find someone willing to eat some for us."

"So you're telling me that you performed some hocus pocus in the lab, and came up with this black, tarry shit, and the only way for us to know if it's any good is to eat it?"

"Larry thought I should give some to Blackberry," Russell said, smiling.

"Who's Blackberry?" Kelly asked.

"His dog," Larry said.

"Don't give it to the goddamn dog," Kelly laughed, taking some of it and cutting it into thirds. "Here's to us." He popped his third into his mouth.

"You want to test it *now*?" Larry asked, checking his watch.

Kelly chewed, swallowed, and smiled, raising his eyebrows for a response.

Three hours later Kelly grabbed his car keys to his two-seater Sunbeam Alpine sportster. "Come on," he roared, and the three of them piled in. Larry sat on the hump in the back with his knees pulled to his chest, peering between Kelly and Russell. They had spent the last two hours watching Kelly's kitchen dissolve, touching faces with God, laughing, crying, and holding each other. It turned out that Larry was worried it wouldn't work, so he doubled the concentration.

THE MAKING OF A COUNTERCULTURE ICON

They flew across the city of San Francisco in Kelly's car, tearing out of the city, over the Golden Gate Bridge, and toward Mount Tamalpais at over one hundred miles-per-hour. They hiked under moonlight and found a cliff overlooking the valley. Each man was reborn, parallel universes opened up, and time ate itself. When the sun finally came they piled back into the car and drove back to the city, laughing the entire way.

While they were tripping, the name "Clearlight" floated back to them across the hills of California. When they began production of LSD a few weeks later, Kelly sold it as Clearlight LSD. He promised users that they would indeed see the clear light of their own mind.

By the winter of 1968, manufacturing LSD had become a full-blown business for Kelly, Larry, and Russell. They invested in a laboratory that had real security — cameras, state-of-the-art locks, and fire suppression systems. Kelly was frequently on planes to other states and to other countries, wearing custom-built vests that allowed ten-K packets to be seamlessly tucked throughout them. This was long before security checkpoints at airports and he paid people to fly back with several kilos of lysergic acid base either in briefcases or as part of their checked luggage. Business started to boom, and they weren't able to keep up with the demand. Based on Kelly's reputation, they began taking advance orders, and people were willing to wait weeks to get the Clearlight LSD they had paid for up-front.

The drug business was dangerous business, however, and the three men decided they all needed to create aliases to offer themselves at least a small degree of anonymity. They also got fake passports and IDs in case they needed to leave the country.

"What names should we take," Russell said one afternoon in the lab.

"Dunno," Kelly said.

"I think," Russell said, smiling, "it should be something cool. *Outlaws*."

Kelly smiled. "Whatcha got in mind?"

Russell started to grin. "I'll be *Jesse*. Jesse James. Seems perfect."

Kelly laughed. "Boy, how long have you been waiting for that? Okay. Well, didn't Jesse have an older brother?"

"Frank," Larry said.

"Frank," Kelly said, nodding. "So if you're Jesse James, then I'm Frank James, *little* brother."

"Frank and Jesse, huh?" Russell nodded, "Yeah, kinda like the sound of that."

"Whaddya think, Larry?" Jesse asked, turning. "Dillinger?"

"Too elegant," Larry said.

"Billy the Kid?"

"Too notorious," Larry said.

"He's so pretty," Kelly commented. "And so sweet. How about Pretty Boy Floyd, the gorgeous bank robber and bandit?"

"Yeah," Jesse said. "Pretty Boy, Frank, and Jesse. Fuck, man, it's perfect. Larry?"

"Pretty Boy," Larry said, grinning. "Pretty Boy. Yeah, I think that's it."

○

LYSERGIC ACID DIETHYLAMIDE, KNOWN AS LSD, WAS FIRST synthesized on November 16th, 1938, by the Swiss chemist Dr. Albert Hofmann. As part of a grant looking for medicinal ergot alkaloid derivatives, Hofmann was working with a naturally occurring fungus called *ergot*. This fungus sometimes got into the grains used to make rye breads, and people knew for centuries this would cause a temporary condition called "ergotism," which included hallucinations as one of its symptoms.

It was known because of this that ergot was a powerful fungus that could penetrate the blood-brain barrier, and so it was studied extensively in the lab. Through the nineteen-twenties and thirties many useful compounds were extracted from it, synthesized, and then used by medical science for treatment of various disorders. Lysergic acid diethylamide, the 25th lysergic acid derivative Dr. Hofmann synthesized, was developed because he thought it might help stimulate circulation and be useful to physicians. The research on LSD-25, as it was known, went nowhere. Hoffman abandoned it shortly after discovering it in 1938. In 1943, though, he decided to re-synthesize LSD-25 for further study, curious to see if he could use some new techniques he had learned to find a more useful application for the substance. While working, he became dizzy and had to stop what he was doing. He went home and had some mild hallucinations as he lay in bed trying to sleep. Ever the good and thorough scientist, Hoffman deduced that the stimulation had come from a small amount of LSD-25 landing on his skin.

Three days later Hoffman decided to intentionally ingest the substance orally to see what might happen. This isn't as reckless as it might seem — he had been working with this substance for nearly a decade, and was already well aware of its toxicity. Based on what he had already learned, he knew there was virtually no chance that he could be poisoned or harmed in any way — LSD-25 was nearly non-toxic, and he would have to ingest an absurdly high amount to raise toxicity levels into even the mild range.

It was the curious state of mind the small amount of LSD-25 caused that had piqued Hoffman's curiosity. He estimated that 250 micrograms would be sufficient to put him over the threshold, based on his experiments with other ergot alkaloids (it should be noted that the threshold is closer to twenty micrograms, meaning Hoffman took fifteen times more than he thought necessary to get just "over the threshold" and induce an altered state). He ingested the substance and noticed an almost immediate, extreme reaction. First, he lost language and the ability to speak intelligently — no small thing for a Swiss PhD. Unable to talk, and unsure what to do, he famously rode his bicycle back home to see if something there might settle him. But the "symptoms" grew worse, and at home Hoffman worried that he had somehow poisoned himself. Although having trouble speaking, he was able to remember that milk was an effective antidote to alkaline poisonings, and so he asked a neighbor for some. A doctor was called to tend to the strangely behaving scientist, but he found nothing physically wrong with Hoffman aside from dilated pupils. Hoffman reported later that at various times he experienced the sensation that he was possessed by a demon, that his neighbor was a witch, and that his furniture was threatening him. As he started to come down, Hoffman feared he was going to lose his sanity permanently. His doctor sent him to bed, not knowing what else could be done. Hoffman said that as the night wore on, his fear slowly turned to joy and happiness, and that his hallucinations took on a more pleasing form. He noted that sound was transformed into intense visuals, so that a passing car would create a brilliant kaleidoscope of color behind his eyes.

He eventually fell asleep, and awoke in the morning feeling refreshed and otherwise normal. The only effect he noted was that his garden seemed to make his senses feel much more vibrant and alive and that he had far greater sensitivity to them. This persisted for about twenty-four hours. Then Hoffman returned to "normal," no worse, it would seem, for the experience. He was the first human to "trip" on LSD-25, and he wrote copiously about his experience. Laboratories all over the world began to synthesize the drug and test it themselves, on animals and on human subjects.

Within five years, LSD was introduced legally in the U.S. through Sandoz Laboratories. It was marketed as a psychiatric cure for just about every affliction. A lot of Sandoz marketing materials were nothing but marketing buzz with no evidence to back up their optimistic claims. However, some research would indeed end up demonstrating remarkable results. Dr. Humphrey Osmond gave LSD to an Alcoholics Anonymous group that had very high rates of recidivism. After a year of LSD-based psychotherapy, fifty percent had been alcohol-free, a success rate never duplicated by any other means to this day. Other studies on other conditions were less convincing, especially for diseases now known to have a strong genetic component, such as schizophrenia. But LSD was studied exhaustively for three decades and found to be a very powerful and very effective clinical tool for a host of mental afflictions and disorders. From 1950 until 1965, LSD and other hallucinogens were the subject of over 1,000 scientific papers, dozens of books, six major international conferences by scientists and physicians, and prescribed to over 40,000 patients the world over. It is likely this would have continued if not for some famous troublemakers who brought these drugs forcefully and threateningly into the mainstream.

Aldous Huxley, the renowned British intellectual and author of *Brave New World*, was introduced to LSD by his friend, Dr. Humphry Osmond (who had treated the members of AA). Huxley used mescaline, another psychedelic, on himself, and it had an utterly transforming effect on his mind and his spirit. His landmark book, *The Doors of Perception*, published in 1954, described how the experiences he had on mescaline closely mimicked the writings and, arguably, the experiences of some of the world's greatest mystics. The book was a serious work of philosophy, and taken seriously by scores of intellectuals. Huxley was no dope-head — he was an Oxford scholar from a deeply respected family of intellectuals, and he was already a famous novelist and philosopher in his own right. To have someone of his pedigree and prominence writing so seriously about the transformative potential of substances like LSD bolstered the perception of the drug as something worthy of serious study. Huxley was adamant that these drugs not be used recreationally, but instead be used only for intellectual and spiritual pursuits. It was exactly the kind of thing that Denis Kelly had in mind when he first began experimenting with hallucinogenics only ten years after the publication of *The Doors of Perception*.

Huxley, being interviewed in the *Paris Review* in 1960, had this to say:

> *Interviewer*: Would the drug give more help to the lyric poet than the novelist?
>
> *Huxley*: Well, the poet would certainly get an extraordinary view of life which he wouldn't have had in any other way, and this might help him a great deal. But you see (and this is the most significant thing about the experience), during the experience you're really not interested in doing anything practical — even writing lyric poetry. If you were having a love affair with a woman, would you be interested in writing about it? Of course not. And during the experience you're not particularly in words, because the experience transcends words and is quite inexpressible in terms of words. So the whole notion of conceptualizing what is happening seems very silly. After the event, it seems to me quite possible that it might be of great assistance: people would see the universe around them in a very different way and would be inspired, possibly, to write about it.
>
> *Interviewer*: Here this afternoon, as in your book, *The Doors of Perception*, you've been talking chiefly about the visual

experience under the drug, and about painting. Is there
any similar gain in psychological insight?

Huxley: Yes, I think there is. While one is under the drug
one has penetrating insights into the people around
one, and also into one's own life. Many people get tremendous recalls of buried material. A process which
may take six years of psychoanalysis happens in an hour
— and considerably cheaper! And the experience can be
very liberating and widening in other ways. It shows that
the world one habitually lives in is merely a creation of
this conventional, closely conditioned being which one
is, and that there are quite other kinds of worlds outside. It's a very salutary thing to realize that the rather
dull universe in which most of us spend most of our
time is not the only universe there is. I think it's healthy
that people should have this experience.

LSD would have most likely remained largely outside of
the mainstream had it not been for Timothy Leary and Richard Alpert, who some blame for directly causing the mistaken
perception that the drug is dangerous to the minds of those
who take it. Leary did not share Huxley's strong belief that the
drug should be used primarily for expansion of consciousness; he felt that such expansion was an inevitable by-product
of taking it, and one need not coach or place expectations on
those taking the drug.

Of course, the problem with this was that up until the early
1960s, LSD was primarily used by people looking to expand
their consciousness, free psychological demons under the
care of professionals, or free their artistic and creative ener-
gies. It was, in other words, largely used in a structured way
by knowing participants. Remember, this was a drug that was
prescribed often, was being studied in controlled experiments
all over the United States and the world, was being written
about by the most accomplished intellectuals of the day, and
was leading to powerful breakthroughs for a large number
of the patients undergoing LSD therapy. It was also perfectly
legal to make, consume, and sell, and had no stigma associated with it.

Dr. Timothy Leary, a psychology professor at Harvard,
began to do LSD research in earnest in the early 1960s and
would change all of that. He believed that LSD could alter
behavior in dramatic and hugely beneficial ways. He conducted some groundbreaking experiments, including
one using hallucinogenic mushrooms on state prisoners,
where they then claimed that ninety percent of the participants did not become repeat offenders. This study was later
largely refuted due to a likely innocent statistical mistake,
but at the time the results galvanized Leary and his follow-
ers into action. He became an increasingly vocal proponent
of LSD use, was adept at manipulating the media to provide
exhaustive coverage of his every move, and he did some very

controversial things such as giving the drug to his graduate students at Harvard.

It turned out that he was less adept at managing the fallout from his actions. The wealthy blue blood parents of his Harvard students, connected to all the structures of power at the time, were not amused that this renegade professor was offering their children a drug that was reputedly so powerful — and possibly dangerous. It certainly led many people to a radical change in their beliefs, which was very threatening to many parents and leaders of institutions. Fear, about what LSD could do to people and to the larger society, began to set in. Pressure began to mount to dismiss Leary and his protégé, Richard Alpert (who would later become the deeply respected spiritual teacher and leader Ram Dass). Leary and Alpert were fired from Harvard in 1963, further cementing their fame. Both used the media coverage to convert themselves into counterculture icons.

With private funding, Alpert and Leary set up a "laboratory" in New York State known as Millhouse. There they could study LSD without the burdens of a school oversight committee. But things quickly got out of hand, and their "science" began looking far more like acid parties, even to sympathetic observers. The amount of research being done was questionable, the media attention was intense, and the images of young men and women floating around the property in a free-love atmosphere alarmed many who saw the broadcasts. Leary was utterly at home in the chaos he was creating, but Alpert began to have reservations. Alpert believed strongly that LSD could transform society, but also felt something was missing, and not quite right, about Millhouse. So he left the United States for India in 1967 to see if he could find a larger, deeper understanding of what LSD had shown him. He met and trained with the spiritual master Maharaji, and two years later returned as Ram Dass, transformed through the fire of meditative discipline and true spiritual insight not bound to any external substance.

Given the high degree of publicity LSD was getting, in part through Alpert and Leary, the U.S. government banned the use, manufacture, or sale of LSD in 1968, a ban still in effect to this day. That ban, it should be noted, had virtually no science to back it up. LSD had been clinically proven to be non-habit forming, non-toxic, and in fact left no noticeable trace of itself in the brain or other parts of the body, even when consumed in copious amounts. Things like "flashbacks" have no basis in biology, for LSD-25 is entirely out of the body in a matter of hours. The old stories of LSD being "stored" in spinal fluid are just that — stories — most of which were part of the anti-LSD propaganda put out by the U.S. government in the 1960s and 70s.

While Kelly was very much getting into the LSD scene, he was also very much getting into the Buddhism scene. If the goal in Christianity is to be saved (for some) or to see Christ Consciousness/know—the-mind-of-Jesus-for-yourself (for others), what then is the goal and purpose of Buddhism? In a nutshell, people go to Buddhism to seek *enlightenment*, a state of being that masters supposedly inhabit in their day-to-day lives. This state of being fuels the wisdom, it is said, of the greatest masters, leading them to be outstanding guides to liberate other men and women from a prison of their own suffering.

The state of Enlightenment has been called *satori*, which might be considered the spiritual "goal" of Buddhism. Satori is a state where there is a flash of sudden awareness, of infinite peace, of "getting the joke" of life — in this space there is no time, no ambition, no valuation — there is just the suchness of everything arising just as it should, an endless perfection. Masters are said to be permanently in this space, giving them phenomenal equanimity, calmness, and presence of mind.

"Getting" satori, or becoming enlightened, can be thought of in some ways like coming to understand mathematics. Mathematics is taught, but until you have the interior "flash" of illumination — until you "get" it — it is just an abstraction that has no real meaning. We can, for instance, talk about Godel's theories, but to really understand them we have to have had the interior, mental *illumination* of the theory in our own mind. Without this, we are just discussing concepts without any understanding of them, which would cause most mathematicians to roll their eyes if we were to share our uninformed opinion.

So too with Enlightenment. It is said the only way one can "attain" satori is through personal experience. You must experience the truth for yourself, not just the idea of the truth. The experience of satori is the experience of Enlightenment, a place where suffering at long last ceases to exist. The traditional way of achieving satori, and the most typical way taught to Zen students, is through the use of koans such as those found in the "riddles" students use to assist in realization. Examples include, "What was your original face before your mother was born?" or the now-clichéd, "What is the sound of one hand clapping?" Another method of reaching satori is meditation, in Zen called zazen. These two tools, zazen and koan training, are the equivalent of training your mind in something like a PhD course in mathematics. In a doctoral degree program you study with teachers, internalize the material, are tested, and then "have" the knowledge for yourself. Zen maintains it is the same with mindfulness training — students do koan and zazen training, gain the insights, are tested, and then have the *experience* (not just the knowledge) for themselves.

D.T. Suzuki:
... The discipline of Zen consists in upsetting this groundwork once for all and reconstructing the old frame on an entirely new basis ... Satori is the sudden

flashing into consciousness of a new truth hitherto undreamed of. It is a sort of mental catastrophe taking place all at once, after much piling up of matters intellectual and demonstrative. The piling has reached a limit of stability and the whole edifice has come tumbling to the ground, when, behold, a new heaven is open to full survey.

Satori comes upon a man unawares, when he feels that he has exhausted his whole being. Religiously, it is a new birth; intellectually, it is the acquiring of a new viewpoint. The world now appears as if dressed in a new garment, which seems to cover up all the unsightliness of dualism, which is called delusion in Buddhist phraseology ... Satori is not seeing God as He is, as might be contended by some Christian mystics. Zen sees into *the work* of creation; the *creator* may be found busy molding His universe, or He may be absent from His workshop, but Zen goes on with its own work. It is not dependent upon the support of a creator; when it grasps the reason for living a life, it is satisfied.

Satori is the "goal" of Zen Buddhism and yet Suzuki said, "It's not that satori is unimportant, but it's not the part of Zen that needs to be stressed." This paradox is at the core of Zen teachings, teachings designed to confound and confuse the thinking, logical mind to force it to stop and drop into a deeper insight.

Denis Kelly's life would become an expression of that very truth, that very statement, that very paradox. Kelly was barely past two years old when he had his satori experience on the floor of a rented house in northern Wisconsin. That place — satori — came to him from that moment on, easily and naturally. He had what most of us never dream of having: a safe place to retreat within our own minds. Becoming a Zen master some fifty years later wasn't as much of a choice as it was a response to that first, intense experience. It was Denis Kelly's inability to make sense of it and of his world that drove him first to the intensive use of psychedelics and eventually, a decade after that, to the monastery to train his mind in the vehicle of Buddhism.

When Denis Kelly discovered LSD in the mid-sixties he found a substance that mimicked this enlightened state. He could induce in himself and in others exactly what Suzuki had said: *sudden flashing into consciousness of a new truth hitherto undreamed of. It is a sort of mental catastrophe taking place all at once, after much piling up of matters intellectual and demonstrative. The piling has reached a limit of stability and the whole edifice has come tumbling to the ground, when, behold, a new heaven is open to full survey.*

FRANK, PRETTY BOY, AND JESSE HAD A GROWING BUSINESS that kept all of them very busy, which meant Kelly didn't have much time to check in on Cheryl. He let her use the classic Jaguar he'd bought, but she seemed to be bent on killing the poor car every time he went away. It was constantly ending up at a shop near his house where a buddy worked on it. He was getting regular repair bills of eight hundred dollars each month, and even though he would ask Cheryl to be gentler with the car, the bills kept coming.

For months he was too busy to pay it much attention, for eight hundred dollars to him was fast becoming pocket change. When he was delayed, though, on a flight to New York and had enough time to go back home, he found another bill from the shop in the mail.

"Goddamn it," he said. And the car wasn't in front of the house, which meant it was probably in the shop again.

He rode his motorcycle over to the shop to talk with the mechanic and see just what was going on. Three thousand dollars in bills was almost as much as the car itself was worth. Kelly figured it warranted a conversation. He pulled the bike up in front of the shop around lunchtime, but when he walked into the office the manager jumped to his feet.

"Kelly!" he exploded, "What are you doing here?" Kelly's eyes immediately narrowed. It was a strange greeting to give your best customer.

"What's gotten into you, Tommy?"

"Nothing. Nothing at all. What's up?" The man was clearly and obviously nervous and edgy.

"I'm just here to talk to Robert," Kelly said slowly. "About all these bills from the Jag." Kelly looked out and saw his 1959 Jaguar Mark 9 parked on the side of the building where the employees would park, out of sight from the road. He looked back at the empty bay, at Tommy, and back out at the car before it hit him in a flash.

"That *whore*," he exploded. Anger, long repressed, welled up from deep within him. "*Where is she*? Where are *they*?" Tommy, unsure what to do, stepped partially out from behind the counter. Kelly remembered Robert had a loft above the shop and he stormed into the bay. The manager stepped in front of Kelly, both hands held palms up.

"Don't go up there, Kelly," he pleaded. "You don't want to go up there. Trust me."

"Tommy," Kelly threatened, "Either get out of my way, or I will remove you from my path." Tommy nodded and, wisely, stepped out of the way. Kelly went up the back stairs to the loft and tiptoed into a darkened room, where he saw two bodies writhing under the sheets.

"Fuck!" he heard Robert yell, "Kelly! What ...." but that was as far as he got. Denis Kelly was a non-violent man and a pacifist. He hated conflict. Yet he had been forged from violence and abuse, and his pacifism was a reaction to that upbringing, a deeply held fear that he might ever end up like his own father. This required Kelly to stifle his anger all the time, to wall it away as "not him" whenever it arose. And now it exploded out of him in an uncontrollable flood of violence.

He leapt onto the bed and struck Robert with a hard right punch, knocking him unconscious. He turned to Cheryl and took her by the throat, lifting her out of the bed with a single arm. She was standing on the tips of her toes, gasping for air, eyes rolling back in her head.

Like with his daughter, Christine, seven years before, Kelly was suddenly outside of his own experience. He took in the filthy mechanic's apartment with dirty clothes strewn about, saw Robert unconscious and bleeding, saw himself standing and literally strangling his beloved to death. While violence had been programmed into his young brain, so had his visceral reaction to it, and in horror he dropped Cheryl and stepped off the bed.

"Jesus," he whispered, torn between shame, soul-wrenching pain, and fury. Cheryl was holding her throat.

"I'm sorry, baby," she coughed.

"The repairs — that's how you've been supporting your PMA habit." His voice sounded broken to his own ears, hollow. "I wondered how you were buying that stuff." He looked at Robert, who was now cradling his jaw, dazed, "You've been fucking my mechanic and then getting him to bill me for repairs he never did. Very clever of both of you. Very clever. And here I thought I was the clever one." He looked at the mess of the loft, shaking his head. Cheryl had access to a three-bedroom house, a yard, a car, and didn't need to work. "I'm such a fool," he said, barely above a whisper.

The walled-off part of his heart was busy creating a story of its own: *You're getting what you deserve, Denis. Trusting a woman. Trusting another. How many times do you need to learn the lesson?*

"I'm going to take the Jag, Cheryl," he told her, his tone eerily conversational, the affect flattened out of it. "I'll be back to pick up the Harley later, after hours. Robert can give you a ride home when you're ready."

He left the loft. His last view of Cheryl was her looking after him, crying and in shock, her neck red from the pressure of his hand. In a few days Cheryl would come back home to pack her things and, without a word, be off to live with a heroin addict and occasional lover of hers.

IN 1984 DENIS KELLY GOT A PHONE CALL.

"May I speak to …" there was a pause, "uh, Frank?" She laughed. "Or Denis? Kelly?"

"Ah," Kelly said, smiling into the receiver, "Someone from the old days. This is all three, speaking."

"Hi," the voice said, sounding nervous. "Hi. It's … it's Cheryl."

Kelly felt his stomach twist into a lazy loop. "*Cheryl*? My God — it's been — fifteen *years* since we spoke. How the hell did you find me?"

The voice laughed. "It wasn't too hard. You never were very good at being discreet."

He laughed. "No, I suppose not." He gave himself a moment to let the feeling sink in. "It's good to hear your voice," he said at last.

"Can I come in to see you? I know where your school is. Been by it a half dozen times before I decided to call."

"Of course."

"This afternoon?"

"Sure. I'll be here. Classes start at six. So come before, okay, so we can catch up?"

"Okay." A long pause. "Okay. I'll see you soon."

At 3 p.m. the door opened, and the shadow of a woman walked through. She was backlit by the street behind her and moved awkwardly inside, clutching her purse to her chest.

"Frank?" a voice said, quivering, "Denis?"

Cheryl removed her large sunglasses, and Kelly approached her.

"My God, Cheryl," he said. They stood looking at each other. The skin of her face was stretched thinly across the bone, and tears started pouring from her eyes. A thin hand was raised to cover her face as shoulders began moving up and down with sobs.

"Shhh," Kelly comforted, taking her immediately into his arms, feeling her thinness against him.

"Jesus," Cheryl said, wiping away tears. "You haven't aged a day." She laughed a little. "How is *that* possible?"

"I cleaned things up in my life," he said. "These days I live a life that's honestly a little boring."

She noted his shaved head. "You're not celibate, are you?"

He smiled at her. "Well, some things don't change."

He told her of his exploits in the last fifteen years. His stories made her smile. As he spoke, he was able to see her more clearly. Deep lines were etched into the skin around her mouth, running in wide arcs to her eyes, with worry lines thick across her forehead. Her hair was frayed and broken, cut not much longer than her upturned collar. An emaciated body was poorly concealed beneath too-large clothing, and Kelly guessed she was at least twenty pounds underweight.

"Your turn," he said at last, putting a hand on her bony knee, feeling his heart break. She told him she had traveled with some bands, gotten on and off drugs until she finally kicked them, and found herself currently battling alcohol and depression.

"I'm still with him, believe it or not," Cheryl said, meaning the heroin addict she'd run to after she'd left Kelly. "And he's still an addict." She lowered her eyes, her lower lip trembling. In a tiny voice, she breathed, "Can you help me, Denis, *please*?"

Kelly felt tears moving down his cheeks. "No one can help you but you," he said gently. "But I can give you a place to practice. I can help you get your diet straight, and start some practices to get your body and mind healthy again. I can put you in touch with healthy people who will inspire and encourage you. I can recommend some therapists that might help you to get your story straightened out. I can show you the seat, Cheryl, but you have to be the one to sit in it."

She nodded, weakly. "Thank you." She checked her watch. "I have to go."

She came back, three times in a month, and did some yoga and meditation. She spent time talking about how she might stop drinking and smoking and start getting healthy. And then a month passed without her coming in, and Kelly grew concerned. He waited another week, and then finally called the number she had given him.

A man answered after the ninth ring.

"Hi," Kelly said, "This is Denis Kelly. I'm an old friend of Cheryl's." He paused. "Her ex-husband, actually. I'm sorry to bother you, but I was hoping I might speak to her. Is she there?"

The voice was silent for a few long seconds. "I'm sorry to tell you this, but Cheryl's dead."

"What?" Kelly felt like he had been struck in the face. He sank heavily into the nearest chair.

"Dead, man."

"When?" he breathed.

"Few weeks back. Sorry."

"Oh," Kelly responded. "Oh," he repeated, unable to think or to feel anything but pain.

"Sorry." There was a noise like the man was going to hang up.

"Wait," Kelly said. "*How?*"

"Drank herself to death, man. Just a matter of time, I suppose." The phone went dead.

Kelly lowered his head into his hands. Cheryl was gone, dead before she had reached her fortieth birthday.

CHAPTER 8

CLEAR LIGHT WINDOWPANE LSD-25

IN LATE 1968, CHERYL LEFT TO LIVE WITH HER HEROIN addict lover. In the vacuum her absence created, Kelly threw himself into his life. It has been said that suffering is the first grace, perhaps because it propels some to seek a deeper truth and meaning. Although Kelly was eternally optimistic, seldom complained, and would have argued that his life was almost unreasonably good and happy, that was the mask that he presented to the world, and to himself. And certainly there was much truth there. But it was also true he was a survivor of serious childhood abuse, that he had caught not one but two wives cheating on him — including catching one actually in bed with another man — and that he had nearly been driven insane by the United States Army.

Kelly turned to Zen with a newfound passion. What he saw in the men and women he encountered in Zen centers was a transcendent wisdom, a way to rise above the petty smallness of the ego and its dramas, tragedies, and pain. More than ever he wanted to get away from the pain and vulnerability that relationships brought him, to find a place where he could simply be above it all, safe from the turmoil of the world. Because of this, he decided to take longer Zen retreats and to make his own meditation practice a more solid and steady part of his daily life.

In the spring of 1969 he was on a weeklong retreat in the Ventana Wilderness in California, which was owned by the San Francisco Zen Center. Spectacular cliffs and valleys bordered the property, and on the opposite side of the entrance were the exquisite Tassajara Hot Springs, which were free to visit. The easiest way to get to them was to cut across the Zen center grounds, which were not free to visit. Many people paid the admission and then walked or drove across the Zen grounds, the fastest and easiest way to get there.

A formal Zen retreat is an intense experience. Morning services start at 4:55 a.m., and students can expect to be either sitting or in walking meditation for most of the seventeen-hour day. Ending chants are usually sometime after 9 p.m. Some time is set aside each day for physical labor, usually to improve the grounds or the lodgings of the retreat center. It is contemplative work, and is done silently. Kelly was outside in the warm sunshine, weeding flowerbeds methodically and peacefully when he saw five hippies saunter up, laughing and giggling. The gate was staffed by a senior Zen priest, a middle-aged woman who had, Kelly knew, a disciplined practice, a very robust understanding of the Dharma, and genuine and deep spiritual insight.

Kelly was weeding a flowerbed only a dozen or so feet from the gate, and was within easy earshot of the conversation. Sweating, he wiped his brow with a gloved hand and smiled at the sight of the young hippies. Part of him wished he was with them, smoking grass, laughing, and having fun.

"Hey," a ponytailed young man, not long out of high school, said to the Zen priest. The woman nodded, her close-cropped haircut adding to her already intense look. She stepped from the booth, swathed in black robes, hands tucked neatly inside.

"We're looking to get to the hot springs," the kid said. "We hear they're like totally groovy and shit. Is it cool if we cut across?"

She smiled at them, coldly. Kelly stood and nodded to a fair-skinned young girl, her breasts clearly visible through her white, lacy shirt. She smiled back at him.

"I'm sorry," the Zen priest said, not sounding sorry at all. "But you have to pay. By the person."

The young man groaned. "Yeah, I get that's the *rules*, but we really don't have much money. We were hoping to just have a nice day in the springs. To go around your property will take hours. Could we just cut across your property? Please? We won't stop anywhere, and we're just going to sit in the springs for a bit, smoke some grass, and be on our way."

"I'm sorry," the woman insisted. "But the rules are the rules." She had placed herself partially in front of them. "You cannot pass unless you pay."

"I understand that," the young man said, "But we're asking you to, like, give us a break. We're just a couple of broke hippies who want to have a nice afternoon."

"You think the rules do not apply to you, but I assure you, they apply to everyone. If you don't pay, you don't pass." There was a glint of pleasure in her eyes. Kelly was suddenly certain that she was taking pleasure in being unreasonable, at having power over a half-dozen stoned kids. He felt his pulse rise and face flush, and approached the group.

"Hey," he said to the woman, "What's the big deal? Just let them pass."

The woman stared at Kelly with narrow eyes. "Mr. Kelly, is it? It is not your place. Go back to your work."

"Hey, fellas," he said, ignoring her. "You're looking to get to the hot springs?"

"Yeah," the ponytailed man said. "But it doesn't look like it's going to happen."

"I'll pay for you. Go ahead," Kelly stated. "Stop and enjoy the Zendo, if you want. The grounds are spectacular. And there's an open meditation at six in the small shrine room. You guys should check it out."

"You can't do that," the Zen priest replied angrily.

"You said," Kelly replied, glancing at her, "that all they need is money to pass. I have the money — it's in my room, in my wallet. I'll go and grab it, and you'll have your money and they'll have their pass. Everybody wins."

"No," she said, shaking her head. "No."

"Go," he said to the young man. "I'll take care of this."

"Hey man," the ponytailed young man said, "that's like super cool of you. Peace!" He looked nervously between Kelly and the priest, but when the woman said nothing they carefully and quietly walked around her, bursting into raucous laughter a dozen feet away.

The priest glared at Kelly, but all he felt was disappointment, not anger and certainly not any impulse to argue. He wanted to tell her that she would be better suited for the rigid rules and judgments of Catholicism instead of Zen, but checked his tongue. He went silently to his room, retrieved the proper amount of money, and delivered it to her. She took it without comment, he went back to work, and the incident was never spoken of.

As Kelly toiled in the garden, he realized that two things seemed to be true. One was that the Zen priest had a genuine and deep spiritual insight and knowledge. The other was that she seemed to be reacting in a conditioned way with pettiness, cruelty, and contempt for a group of kids that somehow upset her.

A bell was struck on the grounds, meaning he had ten minutes to get cleaned up and be in the retreat hall, or Zendo, ready to meditate. When Kelly took his seat with the twenty-five other retreat participants, his brow was creased and his thoughts heavy. If the Zen priest — who was highly trained and possessed deep insight — was not evolved enough to be past her pettiness, what hope was there for him? How would he insulate himself from the pain of the world, and from the pain held within his own heart?

THE YEAR 1969 SAW LSD USE SPREADING WELL BEYOND California to all areas of the country. Unlike the makers of other drugs, the major LSD manufacturers believed in it, and they were changing the world. It was idealism and not the desire for profit that drove their market. Because of this the major LSD families began to flood the market to create faster change in the world.

This flooding of the market meant the price for a hit of LSD dropped precipitously. In San Francisco, the drug was ubiquitous and could easily be gotten for free. Kelly, Russell, and Larry found themselves with thousands of unsold hits of acid, and they could not afford to sell what they had at the going rate without losing money.

Their business, barely running for a year, was suddenly on the verge of collapse. Kelly made an idealistic and poorly conceived trip to New York in the fall of 1969, believing he could meet with the editor of the *Village Voice* and somehow convince him of the cathartic and spiritual effects of LSD. The man, incredulous and enraged at Kelly's naïveté, threw him out of his office and out of the building.

Kelly was walking back to his hotel room along Third Avenue on his second day in the city, his hands in his pockets, watching as the city came to life in the deepening evening. He was planning on stopping for a brandy and then heading back to his hotel room for an early evening. Coming toward him was a petite girl with long black hair and a tiny face. She was wearing a very short leather skirt and dark overcoat tight at the waist. As she drew closer, Kelly saw she was staring at him with small but intense eyes.

"Hey there," the girl said as they passed, reaching out and touching his arm. "You looking for a good time tonight?"

Kelly stopped. Too much makeup was applied across her face, but underneath it was pale skin that was extraordinarily smooth. She had diminutive features — a small nose, thin lips, and narrow eyes. These features made her look very childish, but they also combined in a way that was remarkably beautiful. Her beauty momentarily muted him.

"Well, hi there," he said finally, smiling. He towered over her. "I'm sorry, but what did you ask me?"

"Cat got your tongue?" she cooed. "Would you like to come home with me?" Her lips, thin and red, parted as she licked them.

"You're a ...." Kelly said as her profession hit him, and he gave a small laugh. "Here I thought you were interested in *me*."

She took his arm in hers. "Who says I'm not interested in you?"

"Right," Kelly said, smiling down at her. "I kind of have a policy about that."

"Oh?" she said.

"I don't sleep with whores. No offense."

Her grip on his arm lessened, and as her smile faltered and her eyes fell, he saw the girl in her emerge briefly.

"I'm sorry," he said quickly, "I don't mean to be an asshole. Besides, given how beautiful you are, I have to admit I'm rethinking my policy."

"On whores?"

"On girls of the night, yes."

"Have you even been with one?

Kelly shook his head.

"There's a first time for everything," she said, suddenly confident and forward once more. "So, your place or mine?"

Kelly found himself excited and jittery at the thought of actually doing something that was clearly so against the norms of society. The girl pressed herself into his body, and he allowed his hands to come around her waist. He could feel her breasts against his chest and her hipbones under his large hands, and smell her slightly acrid breath that hinted of cigarettes. His pulse increased, and he found himself nearly aroused beyond his control. He was going to make love to a hooker. And he was going to enjoy every moment of it.

"My hotel is a short cab ride," he breathed.

"*My* place," she whispered, turning his ear to her lips, "has a custom-made bed and is only a few blocks from here." As she spoke her lips brushed his skin, causing a thousand goose bumps to ripple across his neck and arms.

"Then, my dear," he said, "your place it is."

They walked, arm-and-arm, down Third Avenue, cutting into the bottom of the East Village, which was in those days full of hipsters, junkies, musicians strumming guitars in the streets, prostitutes of all shapes and sizes, and an army of homeless people.

Kelly could hardly breathe. They arrived at her building, a run-down three-story walkup with a battered steel door. She unlocked it and they climbed two flights of stairs giddily, hanging onto each other like teenaged lovers. Her apartment was toward the end of the hall, and she unlocked three deadbolts to get inside. It was a typical New York two-bedroom, tiny but comfortable. They stepped into a cozy room done mostly in dark fabrics, with an old hardwood floor and exposed brickwork in the main room where an efficiency kitchen sat off to the right along one of the walls. The windows at one end were heavily barred. In her bedroom was the magnificent bed she had promised. It was a stately queen with a hand-carved frame draped in exotic fabrics.

"Take off your coat," she purred, "and stay awhile."

Kelly did as instructed, and she made her way to the bed and began to undress, facing him. He unlaced his shoes and kicked them loose.

He watched thirstily as she removed her knee-high boots and pulled off her socks, wiggling her toes at him. She then took off her coat, flinging it into a corner.

"Got your attention yet?" she cooed. Her arms crossed and grabbed the opposite bottoms of her shirt, ready to pull it off.

"Wait a second," Kelly managed, heavy with desire. "Hang on. Not yet."

"Oh," she said, smiling radiantly, "you want to do it?" Her hands came to her sides, and then she sat on the bed, crossing her bare legs.

Kelly sat down on a red recliner.

"Tell me about yourself," he said, surprising himself.

"What?" she asked.

"What's your name?"

"Summer," she murmured. "What else do you want to know?"

"Where you from?"

"Who cares," she laughed gently.

"I do," Kelly said. "Look, I've never done this. Maybe it's because of my upbringing or something, but I can't just sleep with someone I don't know. It seems somehow ..." he searched for the right word, "... un*civilized*."

She looked at him oddly. "What, are you religious or something?"

Kelly laughed. "Hardly. Look, I'll pay you for your time. Just talk to me, okay?"

She shrugged. "Whatever floats your boat, mister." She sat up on the bed. "I'm from upstate New York."

"You look *so* young sitting like that," Kelly observed, feeling a touch of sadness, followed by the thought, *because she is so young.*

"Does that turn you on?" Summer followed, smiling.

"New York," he stalled. "How'd you end up in the city?"

Summer sighed, crawling forward onto her belly and kicking her bare feet up behind her.

"You really wanna talk all night?" she teased.

Kelly shook his head. "Not all night."

"Then at least come and sit on the bed," she said, patting it.

"Okay," Kelly caved. He sat down, stiffly, next to her. "So you ended up working as a prostitute in New York City." He looked at her young face. "And you're not very old so you never finished high school. You fled your home and came to the only place where you could make money on your own terms. I get it, Summer. It takes one to know one."

"One of what?" she asked.

"A whore, of course," Kelly laughed. "As strange as it might seem, we're not so different."

She placed a hand on the inside of his thigh, and Kelly moved it off.

Summer let out a deep sigh. She rolled onto her back, looking up at the ceiling. "I'm the oldest girl ..." she began, her voice losing its seductive edge, "... the only girl, actually. My daddy died in a car crash when I was three, and my mom remarried a real asshole. He drank a lot. They had three boys together, and my mom started treating me like I was the competition." Her voice had grown metallic and guarded. "Is that enough?"

"My dad drank a lot too," Kelly said, leaning back into the headboard and putting his feet up on the bed. "He used to smack me and my brothers around a lot. Didn't break bones or anything, but I know what that kind of house is like. I left home at seventeen. Never finished high school."

She looked at him briefly. "Really?"

Kelly nodded.

"So starting when I was six, my stepfather used to come into my bedroom a few nights a week." She paused. "Hey, you want a drink?"

"No thanks," he said. "What happened?"

She smiled without humor. "At first he would just have me touch him, you know? But then he started touching me after awhile, and he would touch himself. And then when I was eight he started having sex with me. Told me he'd throw me out if I told my mom, and that I'd live in the streets." She glanced at Kelly, and offered a hollow laugh. "Nice, huh? When I was ten I bit him when he was giving it to me, bit him so hard I drew blood. That was the last time he ever tried that on me. But then he started to hit me, first with his hands and then with his belt. It got pretty bad."

"Shit," Kelly said. "I'm sorry, Summer. My dad damn near killed my little brother once," he added, "And I damn near killed him because of it."

She sat up and turned her back to him. She pulled her shirt off in one quick motion. "Normally I face a man when I take off my top. For a reason." Her bare back was exposed to the soft light of the room. Bright white scar tissue could be seen against her pale skin, running along her ribs, spine, and between her shoulders.

Kelly tentatively touched her back, running a finger along one of the scars. "Jesus," he whispered. He felt his heart blow open, and was suddenly and inarguably in love with the young prostitute. Instinctively, he touched his heart.

"Yeah," she said, laughing a little. "It was pretty bad." She left her top off and lay back onto her bed, her belly and breasts bare. "It was so bad I ran away at thirteen. I've been here ever since — three years now — working, trying to save up enough money to get into some kind of school. Trying to not get hooked on anything, or to catch any diseases."

Kelly took her hand and pulled her close to him. She brought her head onto his chest, and as his hands found her hair, smelling of the streets, she began to cry, softly, her face buried into his shirt. Kelly could think of no words to comfort her, so he did the only thing he could think of: He held her tightly and firmly against him. Summer began to sob, and for nearly ten minutes, her body convulsed against him.

"I think I snotted up your shirt," she sniffled at last.

"Shhhh," he breathed.

She fell deeply asleep, her small face in the crook of his shoulder, her arm thrown tightly around his chest and her legs wrapped around his. Kelly held her for an hour or more, until he heard the door of the apartment open and bang shut. Summer stirred.

She rubbed her eyes. "What are you doin'?"

"I should go," he said.

"That's just my roommate," she said sleepily. "Don't worry about it. She'll go to her room and she's real quiet."

"Oh," Kelly said, "but I should get going."

"We still need to do it," Summer said sleepily, her hand going to his belt. "I want to do you."

Kelly gently took her hand in his. "No, baby." He slid out from under her and, standing, ran his hands through his hair.

"I need to go, but I enjoyed your company," he said, setting two hundred dollars on her dresser.

"That's *way* too much," she said from the bed. "Oh my God! It would only be thirty *if we'd done it*. And we didn't do it!"

"Consider it a tip," he said, sitting back in a red chair to put his shoes on.

"For what? We didn't do it even. We didn't do *anything!*"

"The money's for you. Take a couple of days off, get some good food in you, and buy yourself something nice."

She climbed out of bed and threw her arms around him, kissing him on the cheek.

"Do you really have to go?" she asked, standing on the tips of her bare toes.

Kelly nodded. "I can't stay," he said. He didn't know why, but he knew he had to get back into the streets, where the cold city air could clear his head and stop his heart from racing in his chest.

"Jennifer," she whispered.

"What?"

"Jennifer. My name." She laughed self-consciously. "*Jenny Anderson*. How square is *that*?"

Kelly kissed her, deeply, and then she walked him to the door.

"Goodnight, and goodbye, Jenny," he said. She looked at him shyly, every bit the sixteen-year-old girl she was, nodded, and closed the door.

Kelly walked out into the crisp night air, breathing deeply. He had a few pints on the way back to his hotel, and he soon began thinking about the arrival of his old San Francisco pal Marty, who was flying in the next day. He could never have conceived then that Jenny Anderson and her story would be so intimately a part of him forty years after their only meeting.

As 1969 wore on, Frank, Jesse, and Pretty Boy refined the manufacturing of LSD-25. Business was slow due to the glut on the market, but things picked up enough that they were able to squeak by. They moved production into a bigger laboratory in the heart of North Beach, right under the nose of the authorities. Their new lab was in a building a block from a police station and directly above the center for the Chinese American Communist Party. They figured that no DEA agent or cop would look for a major LSD production ring a block from police headquarters, right off Columbus and Broadway and above the high-profile offices of Chinese American Communists. Only someone very clever and who disliked authority a great deal would even consider something so brazen.

They rented the upper two floors of the building, paying in cash, and set about upgrading their equipment. Kelly was convinced the price of LSD would turn around, but as they got closer to resuming production, it became obvious they had a problem that would not soon pass.

The three men had, between them, maybe an hour's formal education on economics. What Kelly saw was obvious enough:

few people were buying LSD, and those that were buying were used to paying next to nothing.

Kelly was walking through San Francisco one afternoon, thinking about how they might turn things around, when he paused to tie his shoe. There in front of him was a boutique clothing store and inside were dozens of people busily shopping and buying. He knew the store and knew a pair of jeans there were easily five times what a pair of Levi's cost. And yet the store was brimming with people. He smiled as an idea took hold.

The three men were out at dinner a few days later, talking business.

"Here's what we'll do," Kelly said. "My reputation is for delivering the finest stuff. Clear Light has done well, and its reputation is incredible. Shit, we've got all the people who supply all the bands as customers already. With our new lab we can refine it even more, right?"

Pretty Boy nodded. "Sure. We take a couple of days to purify each batch now, but we could repeat the process and get out more of the impurities."

"What if," Kelly said, "we became the makers of *the* most pure, designer LSD on the market? We'll charge *twice* what we are now, and three times what other people are charging."

Pretty Boy and Jesse exchanged a look.

"You've lost your mind, Frank," Jesse stated. "You're a fucking lunatic. The price for LSD is shit, and you want to charge more? Fuck, Frank. I'm no fucking economist, but that's the craziest shit I've ever heard. That's like offering premium milk at the corner store for ten times a regular jug. Who in their right mind would buy it?"

Kelly shook his head. "No." He thought. "It's not like milk — milk is a necessity. It's like offering Italian suits instead of seersuckers. Or Ferrari over Buick. We don't need to sell tons of volume to make money — we're a small operation that's going to stay small. But if we can increase our price and find the kinds of customers who can appreciate a finer product, it'll sell itself, and it'll be immune to dips in the market price. So what if we took two weeks to purify our product and produce one-hundred percent d-normal LSD?"

"You're crazy," Jesse repeated, taking a drag off his cigarette.

Pretty Boy pulled a pen out of his pocket and started to write calculations on a napkin. "Two weeks would cut our yield and would increase the purity to one-hundred percent, give or take." He looked up, somewhat sheepishly. "I can figure it more precisely with a calculator."

"Close enough," Kelly laughed. "So that would be two weeks to make, and then another two weeks to purify. A month for each batch, so we could make no more than twelve batches a year. I like it. I like it. We'll have people lined up dying to get their hands on it. I can sell that. I'm sure of it. Jesse?"

"I don't think it'll work," he said, pulling on his cigarette, "I think you're a goddamn idealist hippie fucking lunatic."

He looked at Kelly and Pretty Boy. "But then again, I've always thought that, so I ain't surprised. However," he smiled, "you're the one in charge of selling this shit, and if it doesn't work we can always go back to doin' what we were. Fuck it."

"Pretty Boy?" Kelly asked.

"I dunno," he said. "I just make the shit. Seems like it's worth doin' a run or two that way to see what happens."

Kelly nodded. "Okay. So it's done."

Kelly spread the word on the street that a new, ultra-pure acid was coming and that it was going to be priced accordingly. Before they had even finished their first yield or knew if it would work, he had tens of thousands of dollars in orders. The plan was working.

The month passed, and at the end of it the three of them were standing, looking at a huge sheet of pure LSD-25 as it came rolling off the last machine. It was almost entirely clear, with the lysergic acid encased in nearly clear, thin gelatin.

"The more pure it is," Pretty Boy commented, "the more clear. There will sometimes be a tint to it, but it should be mostly clear from now on." Another machine cut the large sheet of LSD into small, single hits. Each hit, exactly 250 micrograms, was one-tenth of an inch square and 6 mm thick.

In a few weeks, the name for it came back to them from the street: Clear Light *Windowpane* LSD. While it was three times more expensive than other LSD on the market, it was pure, which meant that many people would cut a single hit into four pieces, with a quarter more than enough to open the doors of their perception.

Frank, Jesse, and Pretty Boy refined their process, and Clear Light Windowpane went into the streets of San Francisco, spreading quickly to surrounding cities. Hundreds of thousands of dollars in cash came flowing in, and although much of that went back into the business, each man was making an average of ten K a month. Their lives began to reflect it.

Kelly bought sports cars in cash (but had them put in friends' names), wore custom-made Italian suits, had closets full of tailored clothing, owned several motorcycles (also in friends' names), lived in an opulent apartment (which he paid for in cash and had a friend hold the actual lease), and traveled the world on exotic outings, enjoying scuba diving and sunning on remote beaches and at incredibly expensive resorts. He bought the cape that had been worn by Marlon Brando in *Mutiny on the Bounty*, which he wore to social events, concerts, and parties. Of course, when Brando wore the cape in the movie, it draped gracefully to his ankles. On Kelly, who was a great deal taller, it came to his knees. He also bought a seventeenth century Roman Catholic French chalice, an exquisite work done in solid gold. He used the chalice to distribute free

LSD from when he went to concerts, mimicking the Roman Catholic ritual of Communion. He would enter concerts with a flourish, draped in his cape and distributing a hundred hits of Windowpane to anyone who wanted it.

He attended a Grateful Dead concert in San Francisco in late 1969, making his usual dramatic entrance. He found his way to the center of the arena and decided to sit down, in full lotus, and take a huge dose of Windowpane. An assistant took the chalice from him. With his eyes closed, he was transported out of his body and into another realm entirely. And what seemed like days later, he came back to himself, hearing in the distance a strange *swooshswooshswoosh* sound. The sound continued, and slowly captured his attention. It was coming from several places around him, *swooshswooshswoosh*, and he was unable to place what it might be. His eyes slowly came open, blinking in the open air of the stadium, and he was surprised to see that it was very early in the morning. The blue sky was overhead, and the stadium utterly empty except for him and four men sweeping up the trash, *swooshswooshswoosh*. They had swept most of the stadium clean, and were nearing the outer edges of the arena. But they had left a pocket of trash around Kelly, who was still sitting in Lotus position, so as not to disturb him. There was a fifteen-foot ring of beer cans, bottles, wrappers, bras, panties, and other debris circling him, a nineteen-sixties mandala of discarded and forgotten litter in which he was the centerpiece. He blinked a few times, carefully unfolded each leg, stretched, yawned, and stiffly stood. The custodians nodded at him, and he nodded back. He walked gingerly to the deserted parking lot, having no trouble whatsoever finding his car, the only automobile for a quarter mile in any direction.

KELLY LIVED LIKE A GOD, FELT LIKE A GOD, AND BEGAN to very nearly see himself as a god. As such, he took bigger and bigger risks, not just with the amounts of drugs he was taking, but also with every area of his life, feeling immortal and unstoppable. In just seven short years he had come from living on the streets, homeless and penniless, to having hundreds of thousands of dollars in cash at his disposal. He had money and power on a scale that seemed boundless and was nearly as famous as some of the musicians that were his customers.

There was, though, that walled-off part of himself that none of those things touched. It made a mockery of his attempts to hold onto happiness. It was unaffected by his speeches about how acid was going to change the world and that he was serving humanity. It scoffed at money and power, turned up its nose at sex and drugs and security, and cared not for his fame; it whispered of its darkness in the quiet hours of the night, of its unrelenting agony, and its unacknowledged pain. The more Kelly tried to surround himself with bright, beautiful things, the more he felt its power. He was only free of it when his consciousness was transformed by LSD, but the effects of the drug would inevitably fade, and there it would be again, where it always was.

He sat more and more at the San Francisco Zen Center, where Suzuki Roshi, a tiny, humble man, would give lectures in his broken English to ever-growing crowds. This simple man would pack an auditorium with eager listeners but seemed immune to their praise, to their attention, or even to their presence. Kelly marveled at the man for he knew the temptations that came from such prominence firsthand, and Suzuki seemed impeccable in every area of this life. After eight years watching him, listening to him speak, and sitting with him, Kelly — suspicious of any teacher or anyone who claimed to know more than he — suspected it was no act. The man seemed to possess something that few others had — a calmness, a confidence, a wisdom. Suzuki seemed to rest in the eye of the hurricane around which everything turned. Was that level of equanimity real, Kelly wondered? Could he obtain it without LSD?

CHAPTER 9

THE DOORS OF PERCEPTION: WHEN REALITY BENDS, AND BREAKS

ON AN INCREDIBLE SPRING EVENING IN NORTHERN California in 1970, a twenty-eight-year-old Denis Kelly sat in full lotus position in a beach house south of San Francisco. The house was of modern design and minimal in its decoration and taste. Kelly, alone, had spent the last hour preparing the space for his use. A small Buddhist shrine sat on a low altar in front of him, fine incense burned in a holder on his left, and some fruits and juices were on his right. He was sitting on a blue prayer rug and clad only in his Levi's. He was doing a kind of very deep, formal breathing known as Pranayama breath, his feet tucked up on top of his thighs. His mind was clear and grounded, and his body felt strong and supple. Outside of the house the sun was nearing the horizon. Long shadows ran through the windows around him.

The incense smoke curled upward toward the ceiling, and Kelly's breath slowed. His let his eyes close and heard the sound of waves crashing distantly on the shore. A breeze moved through the house, rustling the curtains as it passed. His eyes opened, and Kelly took a glass bottle off the altar. Inside were dozens of rose-hued crystalline needles, each one thinner than a sewing needle and about a quarter inch long. It was pure Clear Light Windowpane LSD-25, the first run off their latest batch of several million hits.

The sunlight filtering through the windows played across his palm where twenty-five-thousand micrograms of LSD — roughly a hundred hits — sat. This was one hundred times the amount Albert Hoffman had taken in April of 1943. Kelly had taken massive doses of LSD before, but this was the largest he had ever dared to take. He had no illusions about what he was doing. This was ritual suicide, but a suicide from which he would return. He knew his ego would fly into a thousand parts instantly, leaving nothing in its wake, but that he was in no physical danger. LSD has virtually no toxicity at all, so he was in no danger of hurting his physical body or brain. His mind, however, was a different story, and Kelly had never heard of anyone taking a dose as large as this.

There was a deep need for him to go to this place, to experience something outside of anything one could imagine or explain. He was ready to transcend his limited understanding of the world, to take a shortcut to the insights held by the greatest meditation masters, and to bring that realization back to the world.

His raised his open palm to his mouth and placed twenty-five-thousand micrograms of Lysergic Acid Diethylamide-25 under his tongue. He had only a split second to wonder what might happen next. He came undone in an instant — far too fast, actually. He was sitting there, in lotus, a man named Denis Kelly, and then there was a supernova — a violent, incredible flash of light followed by crushing darkness and, after that, nothingness. All in a microflash, a million times faster than the snapping of a finger. In another microsecond that nothingness too fell away so that any concept of time or of space came unglued. There was no longer a Denis Kelly, no longer a house, no longer a place called California; there was no time or space or form at all. There wasn't even *nothing*, for nothing can only exist in relation to *something*.

To say Kelly *went* somewhere or had *some kind of experience* would imply there was someone there to observe what was happening. He was entirely outside of time and was utterly disintegrated. Centuries and seconds passed, indistinguishable, and millions of lifetimes came and went. This was death; this was rebirth, this was heaven and hell and purgatory and the bard; this is what people walked around in life fearing, that everything they knew, everything they thought they were, that all the relationships that defined them, that the karma that brought them into being, that it all would simply vanish. In its place was a void that had no edge, no beginning, no time or being, no space, nothing whatsoever to define it, not even the concept of nothing and, most certainly, no individual ego. It wasn't even a void, which implies a duality, a boundary of some kind, a non-void to contrast itself with. It was as vast and as open as death, an extinction of being and a forced embrace of the vastness inside of a crushing black hole where even the laws of time and of physics break apart. Denis Kelly utterly and completely ceased to exist, even as a pure thought-form devoid of anything but its own existence. There was simply *nothing* except a singular consciousness, the end and beginning of all, beyond the reach of any thought, concept, form, idea, or organization.

After the passing of eons and traveling through light years, after the disintegration of the very fabric of time and space, a faint *sensuality* arose, a slim gossamer light threading through the darkness. The light was Consciousness itself; it led back to form and expression. There was a touch of fear that the thread would vanish, and there would be only darkness outside of time or place. But the thread grew stronger, and the consciousness split into experience and something that *could* experience. The darkness became active, like the sky just before dawn when the light must soon penetrate the night. There were still no concepts or thoughts, just disorganized fractals slowly congealing, combining and connecting to form ever more complex patterns. Eventually there was a kind of sensing, although what it meant or where it came from was impossible to determine. There was sense data, and it was being interpreted by something, a something that was somehow significant.

Scattered thought forms appeared like clouds moving across the wide, open sky. These thoughts were trying to organize themselves and the data coming in from the senses, but everything was running over the top of everything else. There was still no time, yet the information coming from the senses seemed to be following the pathways they were intended to follow. There was pure listening, pure feeling, pure emotion, without any pronoun, without an "I" to process them or create distance from those things. Eyes opened and became a brilliant field of blue, utterly out of focus. There was a particular expression of form that was unique, a body, and its owner began to rebuild its mind slowly, piece by piece, stacking the parts of itself into an organized whole that once again could know itself inside of time and place.

The tongue was strange, and the mouth very odd. Sound came in through the ears, and the repetition of noise was distantly familiar, almost recognizable. The eyes were open and seeing a blue kind of tapestry, out of focus and very intimate. The mouth was dry and somehow ... unpleasant. Yes, unpleasant. There was no valuation of the sense, just a knowledge of this being a sensation that could be harmful to the body, nothing more. And there was pain in the body, strong sensations that something was out of balance. There was no suffering or feeling of fear or withdrawal but rather a curiosity at the information crowding in. Pleasant and unpleasant sensations swam through the body, and very slowly a mind emerged to organize them.

Awareness spread. There was unpleasantness in the limbs, in the neck, in the pit of the belly where there was enormous pressure. The tongue was outside of the mouth, and was stuck to something that the eyes could not make out. All of these sensations at last came together, and an entire body was born into a singular awareness. The body attempted to move, but the tongue was stuck onto something, so it had to be pulled free, one taste bud at a time. Hands came down next to the chest and pushed, lifting the torso away from whatever it was so close to. The eyes took in a blue carpet that the tongue had been stuck to, evidenced by a large circle of drool. The legs were in lotus position, with the bare feet tucked up inside of the knees, and were entirely, completely numb. *Fallen over.* He had fallen over onto his face at some point, and had been lying there for some unknown amount of time.

From instinct, one of the hands reached to the right and grabbed a bottle of juice, feeling the sweetness wash over the mouth and slide down the throat. Stretching the legs out onto the mat, his blood began to give them sensation before the realization hit: the bladder was very, very, full. The legs were far too numb to support a body, and so, crawling and moaning, the man made his way to the porch, giggling on occasion, the legs exploding in intense sensation with every prickly movement. He gradually clawed himself to his feet, feeling those maddening prickly sensations intensify. The bladder was disgorged into the bushes beyond the deck.

"Ahhhh...."

It was night. There was a distant memory that this body belonged to a man known as Denis Kelly, but that information was largely irrelevant, as were the stories and emotions that defined him. The illusion of time still had not returned, and so the reality of an inevitable dawn had little meaning in the living darkness. As far as the man knew, it was eternally dark here, and he was just some curious expression of consciousness that didn't need to be understood. He had no expectation of time returning or of the sun ever rising again, nor any concern if this was to be the state of things for eternity. There was just the timeless present, sublime and perfect.

The man went down the stairs of the deck to the street where another flight of stairs took him to the beach. The sand was cool against his feet. There was a strange smell in the air, something that some part of his mind registered as "unpleasant," although there was still no valuation that "unpleasant" was "bad" or to be avoided. He was incapable of considering things morally, in terms of good or bad, or worse or better. There were simply sensations — some pressing, some opening, some constricting. All sensations were just information that came into his mind, free of the need to organize them into a system. Walking through the night down the beach, the man saw that the water was dark, but that it had an otherworldly red hue to it. He walked to the water's edge. As far as he could see in every direction dead fish bobbed up and down with the current. His bare feet stepped on their dead bodies, and he could feel the roughness of the scales against the arches of his feet. The smell of death was very strong and, still clad in only Levi's, he wandered into the coldness of the Pacific Ocean until the water reached the middle of his thighs. He walked along the shore that way, moving past the millions of fish in a red sea of death, a smile touching his face, arms outstretched. He looked up into the cloudless sky at the thousands of stars twinkling down at him. A red tide, the bacterial bloom that can kill millions of fish, had spread across the waters around San Francisco, and would be written about in the papers the next day. But to Denis Kelly it was just an expression of the perfection of God, perfection that was perfection no matter if it was a red tide, a holocaust, or a beautiful flower. The manifest is beautiful in the eyes of God no matter its purpose. God had no valuation — everything was part of Its perfection, part of the Absolute. Even though we humans struggle with our limited morality and terribly limited view, in the eyes of God there is nothing but perfection everywhere and at all times, there is only One Mind, there is only One Consciousness that pervades all.

Back in the house, he sat down to gaze outside into the darkness. His mind was still, and the thoughts that did arise simply came and then fell away again, without attaching to anything. There was a deep clarity and peacefulness, a being outside of time and of place as if he was floating through a pleasant dream and didn't need to bother with the rules of an ordinary world. An intuition came to him as strong and as clear as if someone had spoken it directly into his ear: *Go to India. You will find there what you are seeking.* Fire erupted in Kelly's belly and spread to his heart, and he knew there was no time to lose. He quickly gathered the shrine and his other belongings.

"India," he said out loud, somewhat surprised at the sound of his own voice. Still clad in only his jeans and wet to the waist, Kelly picked up the phone and called his older brother, Patrick, not having any idea what time it was or any ability to even know how to operate inside a concept of time. Like the Swiss scientist Hoffman remembering that milk might help him the night he tripped in 1943, he was amazed on a certain level that he knew he had a brother and that he knew his phone number — things he was not yet conscious of yet could somehow access. There were two parts of him now, not yet integrated; the part alive to the suchness of existence and only in the moment, and the part of him that remembered the stories and emotions that made Denis Kelly a unique manifestation of the universe.

"Hello," came the familiar voice through the receiver, startling him. He had forgotten he had a phone up to his ear.

"Patrick, it's me. Listen, man, I gotta come by. I've just had a revelation. I gotta go to India." The words were awkward in his mouth, slow to form and come, and they barely made sense even to him.

Patrick said coolly, "Sure, man. Just painting here. Come on by." Kelly realized as he hung up the phone that he had no idea where he was, where his brother lived, how he had gotten to the house, or how he would get out of it. Somehow that didn't matter. The other part of him — the Denis Kelly part — would figure that out on the way.

Dashing down the stairs, Kelly opened the door to the garage and stopped dead in his tracks when he saw what was sitting there. A Porsche. A Porsche 911. A convertible Porsche 911. *His* convertible Porsche 911. Kelly suddenly remembered that he had money. Lots and lots of money. He laughed, placing the Buddhist shrine carefully on the floor of the passenger side. The seat and the steering wheel felt deeply familiar to him, as did the pressure needed to depress the clutch, the smell of the leather, and the feel of the car around him. He turned the key. The sound of the churning cylinders and exhaust was simply divine, and he smiled from cheek to cheek as he revved the engine a few times.

Dawn was sending ripples of light into the night sky, puncturing the feeling of timelessness. The roads were empty, and Kelly pushed the automobile through the twists and turns of the back roads as if it were an extension of his own body. Kelly looked into the rearview mirror at himself; looking back was a man whose hair was standing nearly perpendicular to his head in a kind of alien afro, with hugely bloodshot eyes so dilated that the blue iris had been entirely eclipsed by the black of the pupil.

"Holy shit," he said out loud, terrified at the sight of himself. He adjusted the mirror. "Bad idea. No more mirrors." In the distance he saw a toll gate, and slowed the Porsche down, easing it up to the booth. An African American man, not much past thirty, sat placidly inside. He looked down at Kelly as he pulled up, taking in the make of the car, the time of the morning with a glance at his watch, and most certainly the bare-chested, wet-jeaned, bare-footed, wide-eyed, crazy-haired white guy sitting in the driver's seat, Buddhist relics scattered on the floor next to him. Kelly simply looked back at the man, unable to remember exactly what he was supposed to do at such a place. He knew he was supposed to do *something*, but *what* he couldn't remember, so he simply raised his eyebrows and waited for instructions.

The man waved a large hand at Kelly, raising the gate and shaking his head. "Just go, man. Just go." Kelly laughed, and dropped the car back into first. "Thanks, brother," he said, then flew off in the direction of Patrick's apartment, still not having any idea where he was going. In what seemed like a moment, he was knocking on Patrick's door. The two parts of himself were closer together now, communicating with each other more easily.

"Hey bro," Patrick said, opening the door. "Had an interesting night, did we?"

"Listen," Kelly blurted, "I've got to go to India. I heard a voice"

"A voice?"

"An intuition. Whatever. The point is, I need to go to India to find what I've been seeking. But first I need you to shave my head." Kelly barged into the house, pulled out a kitchen chair and sat down in it as if his brother might pull a pair of shears from his back pocket and start cutting immediately.

Patrick clearly was Kelly's brother. Both shared prominent noses, sculpted eyebrows, and high cheekbones. Each had the rugged handsomeness of some Midwestern men. Patrick was smaller than his brother and more slight of build, but shared the same mess of hippie hair, long in the back and on the sides. Patrick had full lips to his brother's thin ones and he was, in a word, a *prettier* man. He was also an outstanding fine artist who often painted well into the night. Kelly was his patron, so Patrick had been able to live comfortably, if not extravagantly, on the money that flowed his way. At thirty-one he looked healthy and strong, if hopelessly the artist, despite the hours he kept and the abuses to which he subjected his body. He smiled at Kelly.

"Here's the thing, little brother," Patrick said calmly, as if trips to India and head shavings were what one would expect of an early morning visit from family. "We all come down. And when you come down the rest of the way, the high will be gone, but your head will still be shaved, and I'll be the guy who shaved it." He smiled. "I'm not sure I want to be that guy." He tapped his collarbones, winking at his younger brother, who had once broken both of them in a vicious fight.

"Goddamn it, Patrick," Kelly said, "I'm serious. I want you to shave my fucking head, *now*."

Patrick leaned up against the kitchen counter. "I know you do. But can't we have a cup of coffee first? The sun's just coming up. We'll have some coffee, we'll chill out, and if you still want me to shave your head after we catch up, you got it."

Kelly agreed, and Patrick brewed a big pot of aromatic coffee. The brothers sat and drank coffee, talking and watching the sun rise.

"You know," Patrick said after a long but not awkward moment of silence between them, "your eyes are different. They're on fire. Must have been some batch of acid you made this time."

"It's not the acid," Kelly stated, "Or rather, it *is* the acid, but it just opened up something in me. I can't explain it yet — but I'm me, but not me at the same time. There's more room in my mind than there's ever been before. It's like I'm Denis Kelly, but I'm also something bigger and broader than that, something where he can come and go." He thought a moment. "There's room in my head now for ... for ... the voice of God."

"I thought you Zen guys didn't believe in God?"

"We neither believe nor disbelieve," Kelly managed. "But this is the experience of it. It's beyond something I can express ...." he thought, then snapped his fingers. "It's just like *that*," he said, smiling, but his brother only shook his head.

"Okay, little brother," Patrick said, not condescending, but also not pretending to understand.

Kelly looked him square in the eye, glancing at the empty pot of coffee on the counter. He watched Patrick's coffee cup come up to his mouth, nearly empty.

Kelly smiled. "Coffee's done, Patrick. Now shave my fucking head."

IN 1992, SOME TWENTY-TWO YEARS LATER, SOMEONE IN the monastery tracked him down, telling him there was an urgent phone call waiting.

"Hey little brother," a weak voice breathed through the line. "Remember the promise you made me a few years back?"

"Patrick. Yeah, I remember."

"It's time."

When Patrick found out he had AIDS four years earlier, he had called Kelly, sobbing and suicidal, and threatened to kill himself with their father's service revolver.

"Fuck, Patrick. Don't shoot yourself. For starters, it's violent. Secondly, you'll leave a big goddamn mess that somebody — probably me — is going to have to clean up. When it's time, we'll do it right. You don't need to worry. Some pills, a nice ceremony. We'll send you off in style. You call me, and I'll make it happen. You know that."

"But the gun — so fast, so easy. It's just a click, Denny, and the show's over."

"Look," Kelly said, growing more forceful, "Don't be a moron. You let me come and get dad's gun from you, and I'll give you my word: You call me when you're ready, and I'll drop everything and come to you. I'll make it happen. I will kill you, Patrick, if I have to."

There was a long silence. "Any other man and I'd think they were just placating me."

"I *am* placating you, you idiot," Kelly said with a laugh. "But I'm also serious. And you know it. You don't need to suffer. You've got years ahead of you still. Go and do all the shit you want to do, and do it with an open heart. When it's time, you call me. But you gotta give me that gun, or no deal."

"I could buy another one."

"But you won't. Those are my terms. Gimme the gun, and I'll take care of you when you need me. Otherwise, put that thing to your temple right fucking now and pull the trigger."

"Christ, little brother," Patrick said. "Take it easy. Come get the damn thing."

The call had come, so Kelly booked the next flight out of New York to San Francisco. As soon as he landed he went immediately to the hospital where his brother was. An attending physician told him that Patrick's lung had collapsed when they had revived him a month earlier. Because of this, his breath was ragged and forced and he needed steady oxygen. The doctor told Kelly they were going to fix the lung as soon as Patrick regained some strength.

"I'll deal with you in a bit," Kelly said, causing the man to raise his eyebrows in surprise. "Where is he?"

Entering Patrick's room, Kelly was immediately overcome with the smell of death and decay. Kelly remembered Patrick's beautiful body, that of an artist whose sinewy muscles wound from his hands through his shoulders, swirling down his chest, over his back, and down his legs. In his prime, Patrick's whole body had exuded a natural, calm athleticism.

Patrick was now about eighty-five pounds. His exposed arms were bones with a thin layer of desiccated muscle with loose skin stretched across them. The cheekbones provided a striking contrast to fallen cheeks and a protruding chin. The eyes had sunken partially into their sockets, giving Patrick's face a distinctly ghoulish appearance. The once thick and mane-like head of hair had fallen out, and the skin of his head seemed in danger of sloughing off like bark sliding from a dead tree.

Kelly had to step back into the hallway where he took many long breaths to steady himself. It was not yet the time for tears.

Patrick had, many months before, lost the ability to eat, move, or do much of anything for himself. He was being kept alive through a concoction of medicines and painkillers delivered intravenously. He was dying of AIDS in a San Francisco hospital. The disease was ravaging his mind and his body, creating suffering that was difficult to witness much less comprehend.

Patrick stirred. When he saw his younger brother, a weak smile spread across his face. The two men embraced.

"Denny," he croaked, "my little brother. And with tears in his eyes. I look that bad, do I?"

"You look like shit, Patrick," Kelly said earnestly, squeezing the hand.

"Still shaving your head," Patrick said. "Thought you'd outgrow that phase."

Kelly smiled. His brother was still able to be witty, even though he barely had the strength to speak. "I'm a late bloomer," he retorted. "You missed the Mohawk phase."

Patrick sighed deeply, letting his eyelids come back down over his eyes. The smile faded from his face, and deep lines of pain, etched into his skin, became active. "Don't leave me here, little brother. You promised."

"You're goddamn right I did. You'll be out of here in two days, and at home we'll set you free, Patrick."

Patrick lapsed into unconsciousness. Kelly noticed his brother's toenails had grown so long they were curling, so he tracked down a nurse and got a clipper. He clipped each nail and then trimmed his brother's long fingernails. He washed his emaciated face and bathed his body with warm water.

Patrick came to while Kelly was washing him, and watched his younger brother for a long time.

"What happened to you," Patrick asked, quietly. "How did you get to be this fucking strong? Your eyes look like they're made of fire."

"A lot of things happened to me, Patrick. Life on the run. Prison. LSD-25 happened to me, a pure psychedelic experience. And then Eido Roshi happened to me." He smiled, "*Also* a pure psychedelic experience."

Kelly kissed his brother on the forehead before tracking down the doctor in charge of Patrick's care. He was a young doctor with exhausted eyes.

"I need my brother released into my care. Patrick. Patrick Kelly."

The doctor, sitting behind a nurses' station, didn't even bother to glance up.

"Can't do it," he stated. "He's got a collapsed lung. Too dangerous to release him like that."

"His lung is collapsed because you fucking collapsed it," Kelly retorted. "I promised him five years ago I would take care of him. He's going home to die."

The doctor looked up, Kelly's words having awoken him slightly. "Nonsense. We can keep your brother alive another year, easily."

Kelly glared at the man. "Another year? Are you serious?" Tears came to his eyes. "He's *been* dead for *three fucking months*. You've got a corpse in there, a demented corpse, and you think that's fucking medicine? You think that's fucking cool? I *am* taking my brother home with me."

The doctor, sensing this was going to take a sterner talking-to, reluctantly abandoned his paperwork and tiredly leaned back in his chair.

"Mr. Kelly," he stated paternally. "This is your brother. I know this is an emotional time, but please be reasonable. Our insurance won't let people walk out of the hospital on their own two feet, much less discharge a man with a collapsed lung. Do you know the amount of liability that would expose us to?"

Kelly felt a deep, pervasive thread of rage rise through the core of his being, but that anger brought him tremendous clarity and presence of mind. He cared far too much to allow his anger to come out in any way other than as an immutable force. He was careful to not raise his voice, but his words were so tight and powerful that the doctor looked at Kelly's chin so he didn't have to hold eyes that seemed as though they might carve a hole right through the center of him.

"I don't give a fuck about your *insurance problems*," Kelly stated. "I am telling you, he's going home to die."

The doctor did his best to present the most authoritative face he could manage, one that had never failed to work. "Mr. Kelly," he said, staring at Kelly's chin, "I understand the depth of your feeling, but it *isn't* going to happen. You can't just come in and take a patient out of here. It's against the law, for starters. It's not going to happen. Now, your brother is in very good hands here. He's well cared for. He will die, yes, and he may die at home even, but you must let us get that lung treated and get him to a place where releasing him makes sense. You need to be *reasonable*."

"Reasonable? *Reasonable* is letting him die."

"We're through here, Mr. Kelly," the doctor said, leaning forward. "There's nothing I can do to help you. Remove him and you will be arrested and your brother returned to his room. I will personally guarantee you we will have him out of here as soon as is humanly possible."

"I see I'm not being clear," Kelly said.

He leaned onto the counter, moving his face close the doctor's. "I want you to have a full day to think about this. Look at me, so you know I'm not fucking around. I'm coming back Friday. I'm bringing five of my buddies. All of us will be armed. I'm gonna *take* my brother outta here, and if the cops show up or your security people try and stop us, there *will be* a shoot out, because I am not leaving here without Patrick. I am taking my brother, by force if you make me. It will be great press for how this hospital treats its AIDS patients. The six o'clock news, who will also be invited to join me, will eat it up." Kelly's eyes were like live wires. Nothing Kelly said was an exaggeration or an empty threat.

The doctor swallowed hard, seeming suddenly like he wanted to retreat inside of his white, authoritative coat. "Be reasonable, Mr. Kelly," he managed in a small voice, but he looked down, defeated. Kelly simply stared.

"I'll talk to my colleagues. We'll come and get you."

Kelly nodded and, after a long moment's silence, said, "Okay. Thanks, doc."

Kelly went back to Patrick's room, where his brother looked at him weakly.

"How'd it go?"

"Friday, Patrick. We'll have you home in forty-eight hours. On my word." Patrick, knowing his brother well, smiled and closed his eyes. He was going home to die.

Two hours later the young doctor appeared in the doorway, beckoning Kelly outside.

"Look," he said, "we can let him go on Friday. You'll need to sign a few things first. Actually, you'll need to sign a whole lot of things, and so will your brother. We need to be cleared of any liability."

"Done," Kelly said.

The doctor hunched closer to Kelly. "And here," he gave Kelly a prescription for morphine. "Get this filled."

"Pain meds?" Kelly was confused.

"A warning, Mr. Kelly: If someone were to administer this entire prescription at once, it would certainly be fatal."

Kelly took the prescription, and nodded. He put his hand on the doctor's shoulder. "Thanks, doc."

"Remember," the doctor added, "people on feeding tubes cannot digest solids, so his meds will need to be ground into water and administered that way."

"How fast?" Kelly asked.

The doctor nodded. "The pills, Mr. Kelly, work very, very quickly."

Kelly put the white slip of paper into his coat pocket. The doctor held out his hand, and Kelly batted it aside. He hugged the man instead.

"*Thank you.*"

"Thank *you*, Mr. Kelly. Sometimes we forget to see a larger picture."

Kelly arranged for a hospital bed to be delivered to his brother's small apartment, and on Friday he came and picked up Patrick, wheeling him out into the waiting car where some friends lifted the emaciated frame into the front seat.

Kelly took Patrick to the ocean, and carried him down the steps to the water's edge where he held his older brother upright. Patrick looked weakly out over the water, letting himself be completely supported. They went back to the apartment, and spent the rest of the day and evening talking and telling stories.

The next day, Kelly again carried him down to the sea. While he was holding him, Patrick looked over his shoulder at Kelly, smiling.

"Little brother," he croaked, "you know I'm almost totally blind? I can smell water, but I can't see shit?" He swallowed as his smile deepened. "Do you think we've done enough bonding yet?"

Kelly laughed through his tears.

"Do you think I can go home and die now?"

"Yeah, Patrick. Yeah, you can." Kelly struggled and then sat him down, overcome with emotion. His hand fluttered across his face for a moment. "I guess I'm not ready to let you go yet."

Patrick reached out and held his brother's hand.

"You've held me long enough, Denny. Even though I'm the older brother, you were the one who supported me. Come on. Let's get it over with."

They went back to Patrick's apartment, and Kelly ground the morphine tablets into a glass of water. As the afternoon wore on, he and two of Patrick's closest friends gathered around the bed. They said their goodbyes.

"Here you go, Patrick," Kelly said, handing him the glass of water with the morphine ground into it. He helped his brother choke down the foul-tasting liquid.

"God," he said, leaning back, "that's awful."

"Sorry," Kelly said, stroking his head. "It'll be over soon. I love you."

"I love you too, Denis," Patrick said, closing his eyes.

Ten somber minutes passed. Patrick opened his eyes and looked around. "Denis," he whispered, "am I still alive?"

"Yes, Patrick."

"I'm ready, Denny." He sat up. "Why am I still here?"

"Fuck," Kelly whispered. "I don't know, Patrick."

"You promised me, little brother."

"I know, Patrick. Please, lie back down and rest."

"You promised."

Kelly leaned in close to Patrick. "I want you to listen to me very closely: You will not live to see the morning. I promise you."

Patrick nodded and closed his eyes.

Kelly called the doctor at the hospital.

"His stomach is too far atrophied," the doctor told Kelly. "We can't prescribe anything to inject into his IV. That's what it's going to take. You might need to bring him back in."

"I can't," Kelly said, "I gave him my word."

"Mr. Kelly," the doctor said, "Sometimes we just can't keep our word."

Kelly shook his head. "No, doctor, I always keep mine. Thank you."

He hung up the phone and called everyone he knew. A few hours later, as word of his dilemma began to spread, he was told to contact a dental surgeon he had casually known.

"Frank," the man said over the phone, using Kelly's drug-czar name from his San Francisco days, "hey — I was told you'd call. Strangest thing, man. I have a couple of surgeries tomorrow morning. I never bring anesthetics home with me — ever. For some reason I did tonight." He paused. "Now I know why. You come by and I'll give you what you need."

Kelly drove to the man's house, where he was handed two vials of liquid painkiller in a paper bag. His instructions were simple: plunge a needle into one, and inject its contents into the catheter sticking out of Patrick's chest. Repeat with the other vial. There was enough to kill five men. The eighty-five-pound, desperately sick, and already drugged Patrick would die instantly and painlessly.

Kelly drove back to Patrick's apartment a few hours before dawn. He sat the two little vials on the bed and filled the syringe once.

"You need to do it, big brother," Kelly said, and Patrick pushed the plunger down. Kelly filled up a second one. "Let's be sure, Patrick." Kelly sat on the bed, and cradled Patrick to his chest while talking softly. "It's okay, big brother. You're safe to go. Let go and fly, let go and fly."

Kelly would feel the life flow out of him and his body grow still, and then there would be a spark of life, and Patrick would open his mouth and take in an enormous gulp of air. He was no longer conscious, but somehow his body was still stubbornly clinging to life. Twenty minutes passed, and Kelly reluctantly lay his brother back down in the bed.

"What the fuck is going on," the woman at the bedside whispered. "How is he still alive?"

Patrick's two friends were terrified, and Kelly had no idea what to do. He went to the phone and woke up the dental surgeon, explaining what was happening.

"He's still *alive*?" the man said incredulously. "*Impossible.*"

"I assure you," Kelly said, "he is still alive."

"Listen carefully, Kelly. There is *no way* he can be alive. There is *no way*. Do you understand me? You are in some eso-teric realm, so you need to go back in there and do what you need to do. Because he's dead, Kelly. He's already dead."

Kelly went back into the room, and looked down at the gaunt, beautiful face of Patrick. "Okay, Patrick," Kelly whispered, tears flowing from both cheeks, "you goddamn stubborn sonofabitch. I should have known you'd make me do it. Not without a fight. Not without a fight." Kelly sat on the edge of the bed.

He lifted his brother's diminutive frame into his arms, cradling Patrick's body firmly against his own. Patrick's jaw rested on Kelly's shoulder, and with his right hand Kelly reached around and pinched the nose shut, holding him as close and as tightly as he could, just for a moment.

"It's time to stop taking another breath," Kelly said. "Just like that pinch you felt. Stop breathing. Go, Patrick." He felt his brother's heart come to rest and his body settle solidly into his arms. The animating energy of life passed from Patrick's limbs. There was the tiniest contraction of the body, a flutter of energy, and then stillness. He was gone.

Kelly laid him back on the bed, tucking his emaciated arms across his chest. Death creates a spaciousness that is impossible to describe, but Patrick's essence, freed from the body, filled the room and the mind of his brother. Kelly slowly and lovingly stripped Patrick's body, washing it carefully with warm, scented water, the way he had been trained to do. It connected the living to the dead, and was a last, loving gesture to perform on a loved one. When the body was clean, Kelly dribbled oils onto the skin and face, and then carefully wrapped Patrick in a white sheet, from head to toe. His body, scented, clean, and oiled, was ready for cremation. Kelly bowed and left the room.

He walked out into the street, where the sun was rising. The full humanness of what had happened crashed through him, along with thousands of memories of the two of them. Kelly fell to his knees on the concrete, he cried out, he beat his chest, he sobbed and wept and screamed at the top of his lungs like a madman. And then that too passed, and he went back in the house to play out the last chapter.

TWO DECADES EARLIER, THE EAST BOASTED A SLEW OF internationally known gurus. Many Westerners, unable to find a deeper wisdom in their homelands, flocked halfway around the globe in search of a meaningful life. The East promised an unspoiled land of wisdom that surpassed anything in the West, for it seemed uncorrupted by the things that were tearing Western culture apart at the seams.

Alan Marlowe, a Zen student and professional gardener who Kelly had known for some time in San Francisco, had been badgering Kelly to go to India for years to "drop into the really deep shit" that was happening there. In addition to being a student of Suzuki Roshi, Alan was also a student of Swami Gauribala Giri, a German-born Jew who had first become interested in spirituality after the First World War. He had originally converted to Buddhism, but when visiting India was browsing through the spiritual section of the Lanka Book Depot on KKS Road in Jaffna town. An old man snatched the book from his hands and said, "You bloody fool, it's not found in books!" The man's eyes were like two pits of fire, and Gauribala was instantly in rapture. He had met his guru, Yogaswami of Nallur, and began studying with him immediately.

Alan was a practicing Buddhist but his heart was with Swami Gauribala.

"You have to meet Gauribala! He's fully enlightened, and he has something for you!" Marlowe would say, at least a few times a month.

"Yeah, yeah," would usually be Kelly's response, "then why don't you stay with him?"

"Got a family, buddy. Gotta play dad. Hard to do that from Sri Lanka. Besides, Roshi's got it going on, too. He's just not as crazy as Gauribala. You'll see."

"Yeah, yeah...."

Patrick Kelly, keeping his side of the bargain, took a straight razor and shaving cream to his brother's long hair. With a newly bald head, Kelly used Patrick's phone to call Alan Marlowe.

"Alan, it's Kelly," he said into the phone. "I'm going to India. Tonight."

"Well, hey there, Kelly," Alan responded, not at all put off by being called and told this out of the blue, first thing in the morning.

"Tonight," Kelly repeated.

"Yeah, I heard you the first time."

"You want to come?"

"Sure. When's the flight?"

Kelly paused, his own impulsiveness to go to India somehow trumped by Alan's utter willingness to fly halfway around the world on twelve hours' notice. "Well, I don't know," Kelly admitted. "I still have to call the airline."

"Well, call them and then call me back. You're ready to see the Swami, huh?"

"I'm ready." Kelly hung up the phone and smiled. He had some great friends, that much was certain.

He booked the flights. Patrick had at long last gone to bed leaving Kelly with the run of the apartment. The next step was to find Jesse and Pretty Boy, his two business partners, and tell them that he was through with the business. No more dealing, no more drugs. His business was to be Awakening people, and drugs were not the answer. He phoned Pretty Boy's house, but the call went unanswered. He tried Jesse's house in Bolinas, a hippie community north of Stinson Beach. After two dozen rings, a voice tiredly answered.

"Christ," it said, "somethin' on fire?"

"Jesse. Frank," Kelly said. "We need to talk."

"Christ, Frank. Can't it wait until a civil hour?"

"Is Pretty Boy there? It's important."

Jesse sighed. He knew that Frank didn't cry wolf or add unnecessary drama to anything, so if he needed to meet the two of them, it was important.

"Why would Pretty Boy be at my fucking house, Frank?" Jesse asked tiredly, his voice heavy with hangover and cigarettes. "I'll track him down for ya. Come over after three. I think I know where he is, but I gotta make a few calls."

The phone went dead.

Kelly, with his freshly-shaved head, slid behind the wheel of his Porsche and drove into the city. He stopped and bought an all-white outfit for India — cotton, loose-fitting pants and a loose, white, button-down shirt.

"Whoa — nice hair, Frank," Jesse said with a wry smile, seeing the shaved head. Although one would never have guessed, Jesse was a classically trained musician who had attended Cornell a few years before. He'd been intimately involved in the protests there. He was very smart, but his mouth got him into trouble, especially with anyone who seemed to be claiming authority over him or over any situation.

Pretty Boy, ever the good scientist, tolerated Kelly's increasing focus on spirituality for the simple reason that Kelly never once tried to convince him of anything. There was a kind of mutual respect between the two men that left the need to come to terms with their metaphysics largely unimportant to their friendship. Pretty Boy was cleaning his circular glasses. Even though everyone in their social circle had long hair, his was still short and well-kept.

Kelly sat down. "I'm leaving the business, boys," he announced without any preface. Pretty Boy and Jesse, if they felt anything, showed no surprise. "I'm going to India tonight and I won't be coming back. I'm giving my share in the business to you guys, and you can take it and do whatever you want. But I'm out of it, for good."

Jesse pulled his long hair into a ponytail. He and Pretty Boy exchanged a quick look.

"Well, here's the thing, Frank," Jesse said at last, as gently as he could. "We all get high, man, but we all come down."

Kelly leaned forward, placing both palms on the table. "Goddamn it. That's the second time today I heard that. Look at me, Jesse. I'm done. I'm out of the fucking business. For good."

Jesse nodded sympathetically. "I can see you're serious, Frank. That shaved head tells me all I need to know. I can see the fire in your eyes, brother; I don't doubt you believe that one-hundred percent right now. I'm sure you'd stake your life on it." Jesse lit a cigarette, shaking out the match. "We've been working real hard, all of us. Shit, Frank, you've been putting in eighty-hour weeks for months now. Me, too. I need a vacation. You sure as shit need one. Pretty Boy could use some time off, too, I'm sure, to do, well, to do whatever Pretty Boy does when he's not working."

Pretty Boy smiled. "Yeah, Frank," he said in his soft, thoughtful manner, "go to India, man. We'll hold it all together till you get back. I can shut the lab down tonight, lock her up real tight, and when you get back, you get back. A month, a year, whatever, man. We all got plenty of cash."

"I could use some R & R myself," Jesse continued. "So we'll see you in a couple of months, Frank. We'll just shut it all down, and take some time off."

THE DOORS OF PERCEPTION: WHEN REALITY BENDS, AND BREAKS

"I'm done, Jesse," Kelly said, growing angry both at being so well understood, but also at being, to a certain extent, humored. "I'm telling you guys — I'm not interested in it any more. Take my fucking shares and have a good time. The business can practically run itself at this point."

"What, you gonna take a factory job when you get back, Frank?" Jesse asked, leaning back in his chair and raising an eyebrow.

"If I have to."

Jesse smiled in a way that seemed to show some wisdom about the way things really were. "We'll see," he said after a pause. "Men like us ain't meant to work factory jobs, Frank. Ain't meant for the cubicle. We're meant to be free. So we'll shut her all down 'til we hear from you again. Ain't no company without you anyway, Frank. Not sure what we'd do without you. That's the goddamn truth."

Pretty Boy nodded.

"I'm not coming back, goddamn it," Kelly said again.

"I know," Jesse said. "You need any cash?"

"I got plenty of cash. On my way to the safety deposit box after this."

"Okay, man. So we'll see you in a few months."

"I'm not coming back," Kelly repeated, standing up and shaking his head. "You two take care of yourselves. It's been a real nice run — we did good stuff. Changed a lot of minds and opened a lot of hearts. But I saw something this last time — I need to find a better path, a deeper path than this one. I'll send you a telegram." Jesse and Pretty Boy nodded in sympathy.

"Hear ya, Frank," Jesse said, grinding the butt of his cigarette into an overfilled ashtray. "Think you're onto something, man, I really do. You're just not a factory man, that's all."

Kelly picked Marlowe up, and the two of them headed to the San Francisco airport. As the plane bounced down the runway and lifted off into the air, Kelly realized he was ready to step into a larger world.

CHAPTER 10

THE AGE OF THE GURU

ALAN MARLOWE AND DENIS KELLY FLEW TO BANGKOK in the spring of 1970. It was Kelly's first time to Asia, and as he and Marlowe saw the sights, he was nearly overwhelmed with the otherworldly beauty of Thailand. It was a kind of paradise. But after a week, it was time to go. The great teeming mass of India was their destination.

India was like nowhere in the world. It was a place full of the extremes of wealth and poverty, of asceticism and indulgence, of squalor and grandeur, of hell and heaven on earth pressed so tightly together they bled into each other in ways that were as confusing as they were intoxicating.

Marlowe and Kelly flew into Delhi and took a few days to settle into the culture, feeling utterly alien in a land so different from theirs. They moved through northern India as awkward tourists, watching the turmoil of the millions of people and the nearly unimaginable conditions in which they lived. They noticed everything and were noticed by everyone. Kelly, at six-two, and Marlowe, two inches taller, towered above the native Indians. Both men had blue eyes and pale skin, and both had the rugged good looks that Indians had been seeing on billboards and in poorly-dubbed Hollywood movies for over a decade. They attracted nearly as much attention as one might expect of a movie star, with people often pointing at them and staring without embarrassment.

Their plan was to travel eastward through northern India, stopping in the town of Almora for a long stay. From there they could walk to visit a famous Buddhist teacher with whom Alan had studied. Lama Govinda lived on Crank's Ridge, named so because a lot of spiritual cranks had made their homes there. Govinda was German by birth and had fought in the First World War before becoming interested in Buddhism in his early thirties. He became a student of a Tibetan meditation master, Tomo Geshe Rinpoche, and traveled through much of the East seeking to deepen his understanding and his wisdom. A gifted fine artist, he also wrote *The Way of the White Clouds*, an autobiography that had come out four years before Kelly and Marlowe touched down in India.

Almora was an ancient town with narrow streets, cobblestone walkways, and arched buildings built onto steep hillsides. Kelly and Marlowe arrived by bus and rented a government-built hut. It was surprisingly modern, with running water and an in-house "toilet," which was a hole in the floor with feet prints next to it, directly under a showerhead. They settled in and on their second day hiked out to see Lama Govinda.

Marlowe had been to visit the Lama many times, and knew the way to his small, modest hut on Crank's Ridge. It had a beautiful stone walkway leading one off the path and to the front door. The house itself was of modest Indian construction. The Lama lived peacefully and quietly with his photographer wife, Li Gotami. He was nearing his 60th year. He had already traveled much of the world, including Tibet, and was considered by many to be a master of meditation in the Tibetan tradition. He was renowned for his scholarship, intellect, humor, speaking style, and gentle being.

Kelly and Marlowe knocked on his door without any advance notice, and were greeted by a frail and ill-looking man who Kelly thought looked more Chinese medicine man than German. He was narrow of build with a white beard and long white hair. His eyes were large and kind and very blue, and he had a prominent nose, full lips, and large teeth. He looked, Kelly thought, like a wizard.

"Alan!" Govinda said kindly. "Goodness! Wonderful to see you. Please, come in." His English reflected multiple dialects, but the hardness of a German inflection was plain.

"Govinda," Marlowe said, bowing his head. "This is my friend Denis Kelly."

Govinda took Kelly's hand with both of his, and Kelly saw the man's eyes were as intense as they were open. "Very glad to meet you, Denis," he said. "Now, come in!"

The three of them sat in a small study overlooking a tiny courtyard. They talked through the late afternoon. As the sun began to set a dark-haired and beautiful woman entered.

"Gentlemen," she said, "Anagarkia is not well. Please — he needs his rest."

"We are almost finished, my love," Govinda said. "Alan and his friend Denis came all the way from San Francisco, after all. Denis was just telling me about his first meeting with Alan Watts. And his friendship with the Grateful Dead." He looked briefly at Kelly, a twinkle in his eyes. "A very interesting young man."

"Nevertheless," she said, "You need your rest."

Govinda chuckled, nodding his head. "Yes, my love, you are correct. But let me attend to the dharma with these young men first."

She nodded, but turned the lights off when she left the room, no doubt to hasten their departure. As they continued to talk, the sun crept toward the horizon, leaving them in a gathering darkness that came so gradually no one noticed it. The room transitioned from sun-filled to dark, but the three men were so engaged in conversation not one noticed they were sitting in a dark room, lit only by moonlight.

"The dharma is being radically changed," Marlowe was saying, hours later, to Govinda. "In America, people are ripe for it. I mean, there's an explosion in awareness. People everywhere are tuning in and dropping out, and working to make a whole different kind of life."

"Mmmm," Govinda said, stroking his beard. In the low light, all that could be seen of him was the white of his beard and the glimmer of his eyes. "Perhaps. I've been to America, many times. I'm not so sure."

"The evidence is clear," Marlowe pressed. "The old structures are breaking apart, and there's a new energy and a new embrace of spirituality blooming in that space."

"These people of whom you speak, they have a practice?" Govinda asked.

"Some; but it's more than that. It's like Jung said — the collective unconscious of the species is itself evolving; people are getting spiritual insights without having to follow the old forms."

Govinda nodded his head. "Perhaps. But I'm not so sure it is that easy," he said. "And you?" he asked of Kelly.

"I agree with Alan," Kelly said. "Some people are in it for the good times, sure. But a lot of people are serious about waking up to a deeper truth — about treating the sickness in America with love and with kindness."

"Love is an interesting idea," Govinda noted, "but it's one that can imprison some minds rather than free them. Like fire, it depends on the mind using it to see how it will ultimately be used."

"Sure," Kelly said, "but you need to see it with your own eyes. I mean, all the structures that used to tell people what to do and how to live are falling apart. There are communes now where dozens of people live together and share all their food and expenses. Free love has replaced possessive relationships. Marriage is seen as bondage to an idea, to a concept, that enslaves women. Blacks too are finding not only a strong voice but a place within our larger culture." Kelly, passionate about these things, now sat on the edge of his chair.

Govinda nodded sympathetically. "Those sound like good things," he agreed, "and time will tell if they are lasting change or a simple reaction to what has come before — a kind of pendulum swing, if you will."

Kelly shook his head, unwilling to concede the point.

"Let me ask you, Denis. You and Alan are both students of Buddhism, yes? Of Zen?"

Kelly nodded.

"And you believe this same revolution is touching Buddhism as well? Reshaping the insights of how to best realize Enlightened mind?"

Kelly nodded aggressively. "Yes," he said. "I mean, if you think about the number of people who reach Enlightenment, it's like what, one percent of practitioners, probably?"

"It depends," Govinda said, "on a great many things. In the Tibetan culture, for instance, there is much more room and acceptance of these kinds of experiences, so I think a great many people called to practice do indeed gain genuine insight."

"Well, have you read Aldous Huxley?" Kelly asked. Govinda nodded. "So you know what he says. Hallucinogenics give people fast and easy access to the deepest spiritual truths. They give the experience of no-mind, of suchness, of emptiness, not as some concept you have to sit on a cushion for thirty years to understand, but as a direct experience, right now."

Govinda smiled. "I have that experience, right now, young man." He chuckled to himself. "You know, Denis, I spent the better part of thirty years sitting on a cushion." His eyes blazed in the darkness. "My heart tells me there is no such thing as a shortcut to spiritual insight. Drugs ...."

"Medicine," Alan suggested.

"Well, then we shall simply call it something outside of *yourself* then," Govinda corrected, smiling, "they can indeed, as Huxley suggests, give you an insight, a window, through which you can see the truth of the spiritual masters. Yet it is hardly practical to stay on LSD all the time. At some point one must take their seat and train their mind in the ways we have been taught. There is no substitute for the disciplined wisdom that comes in the sober hours of one's practice."

Kelly shook his head. "Look at Ram Dass," he said. "Without acid, he would never have gone to India in the first place to seek wisdom. His mind would not have been in a place where he could have received the teachings. It primed him for them, and made it far easier for him to see their wisdom with only two years of training instead of the usual twenty."

Govinda nodded. "Perhaps you are right, Denis. I am an old man, after all, and you and Alan are young and passionate. The world will fall into your hands and out of the hands of my generation soon enough. What is your experience of LSD, I am curious?"

"LSD has personally allowed me to die to myself, to see things that I could never have seen at my age. It's put me on a path, you see. With LSD I know I can gain deeper and deeper insights."

"Hmmm," Govinda said, "Perhaps. Time will tell if LSD is going to indeed be part of a spiritual practice in the future or if it is just a temporary manifestation of Spirit for your generation to help you lay down the groundwork for the generations behind you."

Marlowe and Kelly exchanged a glance in the darkness.

"What?" Marlowe asked. "Could you run that by me again?"

Govinda smiled. "Maybe, Alan, LSD is an externalization of the interior insight needed at this time to move your culture forward. In other words, it appeared at a time when it was most needed — appeared to help create the change you needed to bring the insights of the East to the West — without corrupting them."

"Okay," Marlowe said slowly, "But if that is the case — " As he thought, his gaze fell to the window. "Holy shit! Is that the *sun* coming up?"

Govinda and Kelly both leaned toward the glass.

"Oh my goodness," Govinda said, laughing, "We seem to have done a glorious job of being present in the moment, but all those moments together have brought us back to the dawn. You'll excuse me, Alan and Denis, but I really must get some rest this ... well, day. I'm afraid that my wife is going to be quite upset with me." He chuckled, standing with difficulty before walking them to the front door. He hugged Alan.

"Continue your quest, my friend. Your insight grows deeper each time I see you, but remember to seek the deep water and to avoid the temptations of searching in the shallows, yes?"

Alan bowed and walked out into the early morning air, cool and laden with moisture. Kelly lingered. Govinda took him by the arm. "The Dharma," he said, barely above a whisper, "has existed for thousands of years, changing slowly for a reason. What has come before has worked well; be careful about throwing out the forms devised to open the heart and the mind to the light of God. LSD might indeed open you up, but true spiritual awakening is ever-present, my young friend; while awake, while asleep, while dying, even now, between an old man and a young one." He winked at Kelly, who smiled back. "Enlightened mind does not come and go when you take LSD. You see, your mind and the mind of God are not-two. Your mind and your mind on LSD are the *same* mind, do you see? Your mind and my mind are not-two. There is only *one* reality, there is only one view, even though most of us only see the brightly colored garments in which it covers itself. LSD shows you this, but it is not this, it does not *cause* this. Do you understand?"

Kelly nodded but did not agree. It still seemed to him, though, that LSD might be the ultimate shortcut, a technology more akin to the cotton gin making the gathering of cotton easier and more productive. It didn't mean that the cotton picked by the gin was worse than the cotton picked painstakingly by hand. The result was the same, only with a lot less work.

Govinda closed his eyes for a long moment. "Perhaps it is not yet your time to see this truth. You have insight, Denis. I can see that. May your time in India put you in touch with what it is you truly need to see." He nodded and retreated inside.

Marlowe and Kelly started down the narrow path toward town. The darkness was morphing and changing hues as the sun pressed closer to the horizon. Coming up the path in the retreating shadows was a Tibetan monk, his head shaved and his body wrapped in red and yellow robes. Behind him walked a beautiful woman. Both the monk and the woman had their heads down and eyes lowered. Kelly saw a magnificent halo surrounding the monk, a kind of aura of light as if the

man were subtly illuminated from within. He was glowing in
the way Kelly had read that saints and other realized beings
sometimes did. Kelly rubbed his eyes and looked up at the
morning stars. Those were just fables, mythologies not based
on anything real. He looked back toward the monk, but the
aura remained, subtle but undeniable.

As the monk and he passed, their eyes locked, and the most
curious thing happened. Kelly's mind and the mind of the
monk suddenly were one. It was as if Kelly had plugged not
only into the monk's insight, but also his emotional state,
his heart, his overall being, and it was completely and utterly
inarguable that the monk was getting the same information
from him. Two men, one mind. And then the monk and
the woman walked past and continued onwards toward Lama
Govinda's hut, Kelly staring after him.

Govinda had said there was only one mind, one reality, one
God. That the ideas of separateness were a confusion, an illusion shattered by deeper insight into the true nature of reality.
And by design or coincidence, Kelly had just experienced that
truth viscerally. Laughing, he caught up to Marlowe, clapping
him on the back.

"Alan, it's going to be an interesting trip, I think," he said.

"Let's get some sleep," Marlowe said wearily. "I can barely
keep my eyes open." He lit a cigarette, and his exhale was like
a sigh.

Marlowe and Kelly went back to their hut to sleep. They
were planning on trekking into the mountains the next day,
taking five or six days to backpack through the Indian countryside. They napped for a few hours, then went into the town
to eat. Kelly, who was hungrier than usual, ended up eating at
two different places during the afternoon.

Marlowe woke Kelly up the next morning. "Come on,
cowboy," he said. "What kind of a Zen guy sleeps in past eight?
We gotta get trekking." Marlowe took a closer look at his companion. "Man, you don't look so good."

Kelly put his feet on the floor. He was dizzy, and shivering.
Considering it was already well into the upper eighties outside, he knew the combination wasn't a good one. He used the
shower and the toilet before making his way back to his hammock. Marlowe, who had been outside smoking, came back in.

"What's the word?" he asked. His six-four frame looked
comical in the cramped confines of the low-ceilinged hut.

"Not gonna happen," Kelly croaked. "Sick."

Marlowe picked up his pack, added a few things, and
smacked Kelly's foot. "Okay. I'm gone for the next four or five
days. You're a Zen guy, so get into it." He left.

Getting sick in India is par for the course in the twenty-
first century, and it was even more common forty years ago.
Kelly assumed he'd have diarrhea for a day or two, and then be
back on his feet no worse for the wear. As the day progressed,
though, his health spiraled downwards. He made more and

more frequent trips to the hole in the floor, and began vomiting as well. By midnight he was in excruciating pain and could no longer move on his own. Shivering, he slept next to the waste hole on the earthen floor. By morning he was unable to raise himself to his feet. With violent shivers wracking his body, in tremendous pain and unable to move, he suspected he was going to die before Marlowe returned.

Light came to the outside window and faded again, and he rolled around delirious, naked, and burning with fever. Kelly came out of a particularly deep sleep, and looked to the window over the bathroom. Perched there was an angel, its cherubic face looking kindly down at him. The angel's pudgy little arms crossed over the windowsill. When Kelly looked at the vision, it briefly met his gaze and then vanished, only to reappear a few moments later as if they were playing a game of metaphysical hide-and-seek. Kelly smiled and waved at the vision and it waved back before vanishing again. He laughed, and then was lost in darkness.

An unknown time later he was shaken awake. "Me-ster Kelly," a voice said in clear English, with an Indian accent. "Me-ster Kelly? Sir, I need your permission to treat you. Me-ster Kelly? Sir?"

Kelly opened his eyes somehow, and a dark-skinned man with circular glasses was leaning over him. The man was very thin and his face was very concerned. "Me-ster Kelly? Sir, you need to let me treat you. You are very sick, sir. You are dying!" Kelly was so close to death and his hallucinations so strong that the word "dying" echoed repeatedly in his mind, "you are dying dying dying dying dying dying dying...." It seemed to him the funniest thing he had ever heard. He cackled with delirious laughter, then lost consciousness again.

Kelly awoke in his hammock, surrounded by pillows and comfortable blankets. He opened his eyes slowly, taking in the light in the room and the noises coming in from the street. He wasn't sure where he was, but he slowly put it together. India. Northern India. Lama Govinda. Almora. Government hut. He moved his right arm, wincing in pain. There was a needle sticking out of the vein, with a plastic tube that ran up to a plastic bag hanging from a coat hanger on the ceiling.

"What the ...." he managed to say out loud. His mouth was incredibly dry, and he wondered how he might get to the shower for water without ripping the needle out.

"Ah, Me-ster Kelly," a man's voice said from behind. "How are we feeling today?" The owner of the voice came to stand next to him.

"You were on death's door, sir," the man said. "Typhoid fever, and a rather nasty streak of it. We got antibiotics and fluids into your system as soon as we could."

Kelly stared at the man in disbelief. He was thin and had round glasses and graying hair that was swept away from his face. His eyes were kind and paternal, like a loving father or uncle.

"Who are you?"

"My name is Amara. I live in England, Me-ster Kelly, where I have worked as a physician for 17 years. I was home visiting my family when my nephew told me he had heard a man vomiting and had seen a white man dying on the floor."

"A nephew?" Kelly said.

"Amire!" Amara called. A boy came shyly around the corner, a chubby Indian boy no older than six. Kelly laughed.

"I thought he was an angel," he said. "I saw him peeking at me through the window."

"He is an angel, Me-ster Kelly," Doctor Amara answered seriously. "Without him, you would be dead."

"You'll have to let me pay you," Kelly said. "You saved my life."

"No, Me-ster Kelly. Saving lives is what I do. I will not accept payment. You should be dead, sir. I was supposed to arrive two days from now, but I did not. Had that been the case, you would be dead. Had my nephew not been playing in this part of town, which he seldom does, you would be dead. You, sir, were not meant to be dead. Not yet."

"I have money," Kelly protested. "Let me give you some, for your nephew, at least."

"This is a different culture than yours, Me-ster Kelly. I am honored to have been able to save your life. Please do not offer me money again, sir. Do you understand?"

Kelly nodded, reluctantly.

"Good. I will be back in a few hours to check on you, and to remove the IV. Here is some water. I am sure you must be very thirsty. Don't drink too much — your body is getting what it needs from the IV right now."

Dr. Amara placed a cup to Kelly's mouth, who greedily drank.

He could feel the strength returning to his body, and when Dr. Amara took his IV out at the end of the day, Kelly went outside to sit and watch the town go about its business. He had lost 20 pounds off of his already-lean 180-pound frame, and knew he would need to rebuild his strength before he and Marlowe's journey could continue. The sun began to set, and out of the throngs of people a man emerged. He was very tall — Marlowe's height — but also very, very thin and dressed in all black. His face was gaunt and pale, and it contrasted with dark hair combed away from his face. He was coming directly toward Kelly.

"Hello," the man said as he walked up. He had a vaguely European accent that Kelly could not identify. Even though he was lanky, his eyes and mouth had a predacious look to them.

Kelly, weak from his battle with typhoid, nodded.

"You're ill," he observed. Kelly nodded again. The man's neck was very long, making his head seem to float above his body.

"I saw you come into town with the large fellow," the man said. He stared into Kelly's eyes for a long moment. He seemed to smell at the air with his prominent nose, "who is not here any longer."

"He's trekking," Kelly confirmed.

"Good. Then you need to come with me tonight. *I have something you need to see.*"

Kelly was struck by the phrase, the very one he had heard in San Francisco. The man's eyes, a dark brown, were impossible to read and full of a guarded malevolence. As he looked up from his broken chair, he was suddenly afraid.

"Why?" Kelly asked, not much above a whisper. "I don't even know you."

"Because," the man said, "You are obviously a seeker, and I have the thing you seek."

"A seeker?" Kelly laughed, a bit hollowly. "You got the wrong guy. I know better than to seek."

"You came here looking for something, some kind of higher truth, did you not?"

"That's true of about ninety-eight percent of the Westerners you see here," Kelly countered.

"Yes," the man breathed, leaning down. His lips pulled back to reveal tightly packed teeth, the bottom row crooked. "But you're *serious* about it. And that *does* set you apart. You almost died. I can *smell* it on you." The large nose, which had flaring nostrils, took a few long drafts of air.

The man straightened and looked down at the seated Denis Kelly. He considered for a moment, then swiveled a leather shoulder bag from around his back. He pulled out a human skull. Kelly felt his mouth pop open for a moment.

"You've got to be kidding me," Kelly said, almost laughing. "Seriously? A skull? Isn't that a bit dramatic, even for India?" His confidence returned; this man was a parlor magician with a fake skull, someone who took advantage of the weak-minded.

The man held the skull upside down, with his long fingers cradling the top of the head. The jawbone was missing, and there was no yellowing of the bone to indicate it had been in the earth, which meant it was fresh, had been bleached, or was an amazingly realistic replica. The way the man held it made it look like a bowl one might dip into water for drinking.

"You've got a whole thing going on over there, don't you pal?" Kelly dismissed, leaning back in his chair.

The man laughed. "I can smell the fear on you. It is such a constricting, narrowing smell." He licked his lips as his nostrils flared. "I am part of the cult of Kali. Do you know her?"

Kelly stared at the skull, which was level with his eyes since he was still sitting. Some of the remaining upper teeth had modern fillings of silver and mercury. He felt a shiver run up his spine. The man's eyes, always probing, had not left his face a single time. Kelly's confidence began to ebb.

"Kali, sure," Kelly responded, now feigning indifference. "She represents death, destruction, fear, and the consuming aspects of our reality, as well as the dark nature of the feminine. But she's also a creator, and a giver of life and birth." He paused.

The thin lips pulled back from their teeth in a smile of sorts. "Spoken like someone who has read about her, but never tasted her terrible energy for himself. Kali is the triumph of death over life — who do you think wins in the game of life and death? Where do you think you are heading? To unite with Kali is to make peace with your own terrible nature, your own terrible destruction at her hands; it is how you find your way through destruction, death, and suffering to the eternal life on the other side. The eternal life in this world. She offers us a way out, you see, if we are willing to do the horrible and beautiful things she demands of us."

Kelly looked from the skull to the man. "That so?" he managed. "Didn't know there was a way out."

"Oh yes," the man breathed. "Oh yes, there is a way. You are yourself a destroyer of things, are you not? Destroying what was to create something new?"

Kelly said nothing.

"I see it in you. You should come with me this evening. I will show you the things you need to see." The man put the skull back into its bag and, without another word or so much as a glance, walked back into the crowd. Kelly watched him go, shivered, and retreated inside. When someone knocked on his door that evening, he did not answer it.

Marlowe was back the next morning, and found Kelly meditating in the main room.

"Hey there," Marlowe said, noting how thin Kelly was. "You look like you had a more interesting time than I did."

Kelly looked up. "I found the best way to lose twenty pounds in three days on the planet. Turns out if you shit and vomit at the same time for just three days straight, the pounds melt right off of you."

Marlowe, dirty and smelling very much of days spent exerting himself, put his pack down. "The place smells like a shithole."

"It is a shithole, Marlowe. Besides, you smell like an armpit."

"Great," he laughed. "Shit and armpits. A true bachelor pad." He told Kelly about his hikes and the sights he had seen.

An hour later there was a knock at their door. Marlowe came into the room where Kelly was resting, "It's for you," he said, cocking an eyebrow. "Weird, skinny dude."

Kelly walked out and there, standing just outside the threshold, was the thin, dark-clothed European looking exactly as he had the day before.

"We had a wonderful time last night," he said, his lips parting to reveal those crooked, white teeth. Kelly stepped to the door's threshold but not beyond. "You should join us tonight."

"Not tonight," Kelly said, "But say hi to Kali for me." He closed the door.

"New friend?" Marlowe asked.

"You have no idea."

He and Marlowe were prepared to leave northern India for the island of Sri Lanka to see Marlowe's guru, Swami Gauribala. Each morning, though, Kelly felt too weak and sick to spend the entire day traveling on India's bumpy roads in one of its overcrowded and reeking buses. Every evening and every morning not long after sunrise the thin European man knocked on his door to see if Kelly would join him in the jungle that night. Each time he was professional in his demeanor, cool, controlled, and almost excessively polite.

On the fifth morning of his convalescence, Kelly was feeling much better, and strong enough to travel. He and Marlowe rose early on the sixth day, near dawn, and packed their things. Kelly was sitting outside, earlier than usual, looking off into the jungle that bordered the street to the north. Coming out of the woods and into the street was the thin European, stripped to the waist, grinning in the low light. Behind him four women in red saris trailed. All of them were heading toward Kelly. The man was thin but more muscular than Kelly would have guessed. He was also completely covered in blood. It was splashed across his torso, splattered on his face, thick on his hands, and matted into his hair. The girls, too, were caked in red.

"I *told you* you should have come with us last night," the man called as he drew close, those black eyes calm in their bloodsplattered face. The women held back. "I *still* have something to show you." The women laughed and were, Kelly noticed, holding hands. The man smiled and nodded, and then walked past Kelly and toward town. "Perhaps tonight?" he called over his shoulder.

As Kelly watched, he was certain it would have been *his* blood had he gone with them. It was not uncommon for people to simply disappear in India in those days and to never be found again. In India in 1970 you were stepping off the grid, and not everyone found their way back. Some went mad, others were murdered, still others renounced their old lives and disappeared into caves or jungles. It was a strange, magical, mystical, and terrifying place where the rules of what could and could not be were not yet set.

He went back inside and told Marlowe what had he had just seen.

"*Fuck*," Marlowe cried, bursting out the door. "Where'd he go? I want to see what they're doing!" He looked left and right, but the man and four women were nowhere in sight.

"You would have gone with them?" Kelly asked, incredulous.

"Are you kidding me," Marlowe gushed, "*In a second*! Kali worshippers! I can't *believe* you didn't go with him! And I can't believe you didn't tell me until now that's what that guy wanted from you!"

"Alan, I think they were going to kill me. Jesus, didn't you get a look at that guy?"

"Oh, don't be so dramatic. He was skin and bones, that guy. They probably just slaughtered a pig or something. Man, can you imagine how cool it would be to see *that*? Christ, Kelly, *what's the matter with you*? I have half a mind to stay another day!"

Kelly shook his head. "I've had it with this hut," he said. "We have a long trip ahead of us."

Marlowe smiled. "You're gonna flip when you meet Gauribala."

Kelly nodded.

"And the Island Hermitage is on the way. Let's spend a few nights there." Marlowe lit a cigarette, shaking out the match. "Yeah, fuck it," he said after exhaling. "Let's hit the road. It's time."

Kelly, relieved, went in to get his things.

They took a long bus ride to the airport, and then waited for hours to finally board a terrifyingly old propeller plane to fly to Colombo.

Sri Lanka's capital was fully modern in many ways, and a wonderful contrast to the more wild and unruly India they had just experienced. Cars clogged the streets, pollution fouled the air, and people teemed about everywhere, on foot, in cars, and on bicycles. As they made their way through the capital to find the best means of heading south to the Buddhist center known as the Island Hermitage, they were amazed at how strongly the sense of British identity still clung to everything. British accents were heavy on the tongues of the English-speaking citizens, and a rigid Colonial stratification was obvious everywhere one looked. The nation had recently become fully independent and socialist, but the revolution had failed to penetrate very far into the cultural norms of daily life. It was, at its heart, a comforting reassurance to Kelly that the world still made sense — the European had deeply unnerved him and implied there was an unpredictable and unreasonable world lurking not far from the comforts of a well-lit town. Kelly wanted to break the well-lit world apart, but not into the madness of Kali. He was more interested in love and fairness and kindness, not destruction and death.

Marlowe's spiritual teacher was a man named Swami Gauribala. Born as Peter Schoenfeldt at the turn of the twentieth century, he was a member of an affluent upper middle-class family with influential connections in the German government. After the First World War, Schoenfeldt left his home to seek a deeper truth. He wandered the near and far East, meeting numerous swamis, holy men, and other teachers. Eventually he settled with one of his German brethren, a man born under the name of Siegmund Feniger but who was in the 1930s going by the name of Nyanaponika Thera. Nyanaponika was the resident monk at the Island Hermitage in Sri Lanka, a Theravada Buddhist temple. When the Second World War broke out, the British interred all German nationals at the Hermitage. Schoenfeldt took vows and became a Buddhist monk, but grew unhappy with the teachings and the culture there. After WWII he gave up his robes and went seeking another teacher and another means of satisfying his spiritual thirst.

He turned toward Hinduism and met many Indian masters, such as Sri Aurobindo at Pondicherry, Ramana Maharshi at Tiruvannamalai, and other notable teachers. But still he was unsatisfied. Schoenfeldt was in a bookstore reading books on spirituality when the great Hindu master Yogiswami came in. The two men instantly connected; Schoenfeldt had, after decades of searching, found his teacher. He devoted himself exclusively to Yogiswami until he was given the spiritual name Swami Gauribala.

Marlowe and Kelly decided they would first visit the Island Hermitage where Gauribala had been interred during World War II. After they saw the Hermitage, they agreed they would travel north to Gauribala's ashram, in essence following in the Swami's footsteps. Getting to the Hermitage was relatively easy. It was located in Bolgoda Lake, a brackish, shallow body of water connected to the sea on the west coast of Sri Lanka. Kelly and Marlowe rented a hut near the edge of the lake off of the Hermitage grounds, borrowing a canoe to get to and from the temples on the lake's central islands. The Hermitage consisted of two islands, Polgasduwa and Metiduwa. The shallow water was beautiful and alluring, yet incredibly popular with two creatures Kelly was not fond of: mosquitoes and snakes.

Marlowe and Kelly spent a few days traveling between their hut on the shores and the temple grounds, joining the monks in their meditation and in their meals each day. When they had experienced the Hermitage fully, Marlowe suggested they continue north to see Swami Gauribala.

They rented a car and drove along the western coast of Sri Lanka, winding their way through the cities, towns, and countryside, watching the dizzying display of extremes journey past the window. They would pass beautiful teenage girls showing their bellies and, five miles later, pass girls holding automatic weapons. In as little as 20 minutes, slums of rotting earth and corrugated steel gave way to mansions that ran the length of a city block. It was like someone had thrown two worlds onto the same island and mixed them so thoroughly that it was possible to witness a corpse in the streets in the morning, and an opulent palace pool, complete with white-gloved servers, in the afternoon.

Marlowe and Kelly showed up at the ashram not long after sunrise and took a stroll through its sprawling grounds and dusty open spaces, taking in the diverse population of Americans, Europeans, Sri Lankans, Indians, and just about every other possible nationality.

Marlowe let the staff know that he was there so to inform Swami Gauribala. The two men were invited to the main temple for lunch. It was large and open-aired with a concrete floor and close to a hundred men and women seated on the ground in neat columns. In front of every person was a large banana leaf acting as a plate. Onto this banana leaf servers had placed seven stainless steel containers full of pungent Indian spices and vegetables. As Marlowe and Kelly entered, they noted the servers were walking down the columns with huge bowls of rice, scooping out large spoonfuls that they dropped, from standing, onto the banana leafs on the floor with perfect precision.

Swami Gauribala was seated with a few close attendants perpendicular to the main group, and Kelly and Marlowe were directed to spots on the floor close to him. Gauribala waved to Marlowe. He was of medium height and pale-skinned, with a large belly sticking out from the middle of his plump frame. His face was jovial and covered in what looked like freckles, most likely from being exposed to the intensity of the sun for so many years. His gray head of hair was utterly wild and a full gray beard, white in places, dropped leisurely toward his chest. Gauribala wore a traditional sari, a kind of half robe that exposed much of his body. Kelly, amused, thought he looked like Santa Claus on vacation — jolly, chubby, and a twinkle in his eye.

Kelly and Marlowe were served rice and after a group prayer and dedication they eagerly dug into the food. Kelly saw everyone was sitting on their left hand and eating with their right.

He looked to Marlowe.

"Most people don't bring their own toilet paper, like us," Marlowe whispered with a wink. "Gotta wipe your ass with something, my friend. Sitting on your left hand is a sign for respect, so you don't accidentally touch anything with it."

It seemed the thing to do was to spread the rice on the banana leaf, dump the veggies out, and then dump the spices on top and mix it all together with your right hand. Being a good Roman Catholic boy, Kelly had been taught to eat everything he was offered, and to eat all the food that was placed on his plate when a guest. So he dumped everything out, including the spices, noting out of the corner of his eye that the Swami had stopped talking. Kelly, though, was too hungry to care much, so he scooped great mouthfuls of food into his mouth with his hand, swallowing greedily. By the fifth mouthful, he heard the Swami begin to laugh, filling the room with snorts and guffaws.

"Stop, stop," the Swami said through laughter, "No one is supposed to eat *all* of that food! And certainly not all of the *spice*! This is our feast day!"

Kelly, cheeks bulging, looked over to Marlowe, who had sprinkled the spices into his food, leaving all seven stainless steel cups mostly full. Kelly was contemplating what this meant when his mouth exploded in a fiery protest. Tears ran out of his eyes as he fought to keep from spitting his food all over himself. The entire ashram was now looking at the red-faced American who seemed like he might burst into flame, choke to death, or both. Swami Gauribala was doubled over in laughter.

"Bring ... that ... man ... some ... water," the Swami gasped, and someone appeared with a large pitcher that Kelly gulped down greedily. Murmurs of laughter rippled through the group.

After lunch, Marlowe, Kelly, and the Swami stayed behind while servants cleared the banana leaves off the floor. Swami G, as many people called him, was delighted to see Alan, and he pressed him for information on the States, on his travels, and on his practices. Gauribala at last turned to Kelly, who had been standing politely off to the side.

"Tell me, what brought you here," he asked. Swami G's accent was a blur of dialects, at once German and Indian in its inflection.

Kelly was familiar with the clever wordplay of spiritual masters. He was determined not to fall victim to the Swami's famously biting wit.

"I came here with Alan Marlowe," Kelly said, nodding his head toward his friend.

"Ah, so you are a follower of Marloff, then," the Swami replied instantly. He could not pronounce Alan's last name correctly.

"No, Swami," Kelly laughed. "I am a supportive friend."

"I see," he said. "An honorable thing. And why were you in India?"

"I was told to come here in a vision."

"Oh," he said, smiling broadly. "A vision! From God. Then you are a lucky man, Mr. Kelly." The Swami considered for a moment. "Except, of course, that this isn't India. But a vision from God is something very rare. You should be honored."

"I don't know if it was from God," Kelly replied. "I don't know where it was from. It was more of an intuition."

"Oh, I see." The Swami smiled. "The good news is that God doesn't care if you believe in Him or not. So what then really brought you to India?"

Kelly stared at him. Had he not just answered that question? "I'm not sure," he said at last. "To find something. Something that's waiting for me here."

"Tell me, how does a hummingbird know how to get from South America to Europe?"

"Instinct?"

"Hmmm." The Swami's eyes were alight with joy. He smiled broadly. "Maybe instinct is just being one with the mind of God? Why are you here again?"

Kelly laughed, nodded and, wisely, said nothing.

They broke for the day, and later that evening after dinner, the Swami pulled Kelly aside.

"Mr. Marloff tells me that you make your living off of a kind of drug that transforms the mind."

"Yes, Swami," Kelly replied. "It's called lysergic acid diethylamide, and it's a chemical ...."

"Yes, yes," the Swami interrupted, "Based off of the similar chemical process that produces common aspirin. Made from the ergoline family and first synthesized by Albert Hoffman in 1938."

Kelly looked at him, surprised. "That's correct."

The Swami was wearing a white sari, and he rested his hands on his ample belly. His eyes always had a light in them as if he had just gotten the punch line of a great joke, and might burst into laughter at any second.

"I know what it *is*, Mr. Kelly. What does it *do*?"

It was Kelly's turn to smile knowingly. LSD was his area of expertise, and he was like a modern shaman transforming the consciousness of thousands with his particular potion. "The best ways to describe it, Swami, is that it lets you see the face of God."

The Swami's dark eyes opened wide. "But you don't believe in God, Denis, so what do *you* see?"

Kelly shook his head. "I neither believe nor disbelieve in God, Swami. But on LSD-25, even I see God."

The Swami laughed. "I see God all the time, right now, here between us!"

Kelly nodded. "I don't doubt that."

"Tell me, do you have any of this LSD with you?"

"Yeah," Kelly said. "About seven doses or so — 1,050 micrograms."

The Swami stroked his beard, thinking.

"I think that LSD is going to transform the way the world works," Kelly started, getting into his preacher mode. "I think we can break people out of their habitual patterns and self-destructive stories and create a better, more open world. LSD opens people's inner doors to their own true nature. It gives them the experience of that firsthand. So instead of being just an abstraction, it lets people ...."

The Swami held up his hand. "Let me see the LSD."

"I have to go and get it."

"I'll wait."

Kelly was unable to keep from smiling at the lack of pretense. Gauribala was about as different from the reserved and contained Suzuki Roshi as one could imagine. Roshi was always impeccably shaved, his crisp robes folding perfectly along their seams, and his voice measured and thoughtful. His Zen center was the picture of order and discipline, and it was run with far greater efficiency than a military barracks. Gauribala, by contrast, looked like a spiritual madman — hair askew, food in his beard, stains on his sari, and what appeared to be little to no sense of self-importance. The ashram was nearly always in a state of near-chaos, and it was only through the efforts of a few enormously dedicated students that the whole thing didn't devolve into anarchy.

Kelly fetched the acid, returned and handed over the small glass vial containing three hits of LSD-25. Swami G inspected them thoughtfully through the glass before dumping them into his hand. He popped all into his mouth.

"Whoa!" Kelly said, "That's a lot!"

"Now, leave me," Gauribala said. "I will see you in the morning." Swami G stood up and, with his hands clasped behind his back, made his way back toward his quarters.

Gauribala spotted Kelly in the morning coming across the ashram grounds.

"Denis!" he cried, running with all the enthusiasm of a child.

Kelly, more self-consciously dignified, waited for the Gauribala to reach him. "How was your trip," Kelly asked. "Did you see the face of God?"

Gauribala smiled. "I keep telling you, Denis, I always see the face of God. But I write in four languages, and I was forgetting all of my grammar. The mind forgets." He tapped his temple. "But that stuff you gave me allowed me to remember all of my forgotten grammar, so I stayed up all night writing and translating — I got so much done!" He clapped Kelly on the shoulders. "It was the most productive night I've had in years. I feel great today! I had no idea that's what LSD does. No wonder you like it so much. Do you have any more?"

Kelly stared back, at a loss for words.

Gauribala looked puzzled. "It doesn't help you get work done?"

"No," Kelly said at last, "Not exactly."

Gauribala shrugged. "Do you have any more?"

Kelly shook his head.

"Oh well," Gauribala said, turning. "I got a great start on a lot of projects last night. Hopefully the grammar will stick with me this time."

Kelly watched him walk off. LSD had, without exception, created profound effects on every single person Kelly knew who had tried it. Some people struggled with the way the drug broke down concepts and pre-formed ideas about how the world worked, some people loved the way it broke these things down. Some, like Pretty Boy, would swim in the lap of the Divine and lose themselves, even if the experience would be dismissed as mere hallucination the next day. Kelly had seen thousands of people on LSD, and never once had someone reacted the way Gauribala had.

If LSD broke apart the ego and let you see the Divine always present behind it, the way Huxley suspected, what happened to someone who took the drug but had already freed themselves from their ego? Did that mean they could then remember lost languages? Since they weren't attached to their egos or operating exclusively from them to begin with, when LSD caused the ego to fall away could it be their view of the world remained largely unchanged? Was that possible? Could Gauribala really have taken seven hits of acid and worked on scholarly documents all evening? Kelly walked the grounds, deeply lost in thought, and the next time he saw Gauribala he looked at him with a newfound sense of curiosity.

A week later Kelly offered to take Alan and Swami Gauribala to lunch at the very prestigious Galle Face Hotel in Colombo. Swami G readily agreed to go, and he dressed in more formal robes that would not stand out in one of the finest restaurants in the country.

After a short drive they arrived at the hotel, and the three of them were seated on the veranda. Their waiters were men dressed in formal Colonial servants' outfits. This included white gloves and impeccable suit coats, hats, belt buckles of pure silver, and black boots over top of white pants. Food was served on silver and crystal, and they had no less than four servers for their table of three. The Swami had a love of white wine, and two very fine bottles were ordered for lunch. As they were finishing their meal, Gauribala took a swallow of wine and turned to face Kelly.

"So," he said, dropping his smile. The sense of playfulness was gone, and in its place was a deadly seriousness. Gauribala's brown eyes were illuminated from within, and their fire pressed almost violently into Kelly, who stopped in mid-chew.

"*What are you doing*?" he demanded.

"Well, Swami," Kelly replied, swallowing, "I suppose you could say I'm practicing Buddhism." He smiled. Kelly thought that was especially clever, to say he was practicing Buddhism while eating, drinking wine, and talking. Very Zen, since it implied he was being mindful in all he was doing, and that there was nothing one could do outside of mindful awareness.

"Tsss," the Swami hissed, obviously and transparently disappointed. He dropped his eyes and shook his head. "Tell me," he asked, looking back up, "how does one practice an '*ism*'?"

Kelly opened his mouth but nothing came out. He was stumped.

Swami G shook his head. "*You don't*," he thundered, smacking the table. "You practice what *IS*!" The words hit Kelly with all the force of a bullwhip.

Kelly's mind searched frantically for something to say, perhaps witty, perhaps profound, and the eyes of the crazy Swami were heavy on his face. Kelly looked into their intensity and his mind stopped in the truth of the statement. A few seconds passed with no thoughts arising. A few more seconds passed, and still no thought. A few seconds more, stretching into a full minute. His mind was completely silent, and from that place he looked at the plate of food in front of him, seeing the depth of the silver platter on which the food sat. The light refracting through the crystal wine glass was as complex and magnificent as a sunset, of love between a child and her mother, of the depth of a sexual union, of the creative energy that had created the universe.

Practice what is!

Kelly felt the undeniable truth of the perfection of being; he *was* the undeniable perfection of being. There was no separation between him and Gauribala, or him and Marlowe, who was looking at him with a crooked smile. Kelly was one with the breeze, with the sun above him, with the ocean breaking on the shore below. Like a man who suddenly gets a punch line to an old joke, he understood a story that had confused him for years: the great Zen master Fa-ch'an was lying on his deathbed, surrounded by attendants. Outside his window a squirrel screeched. "It's just *this*," the dying master said, "and nothing else." Zen called meditation practice and instruction "selling water by the river" for the simple reason there was nothing to sell, no "isms" worth anything at all, nothing to teach. There only is what is, in this moment, right now. That truth was overwhelming Kelly, removing his ability to speak, to think, or to do anything but surrender completely to the perfection of what was arising in *this* moment.

Kelly looked at the fork in his hand as if he'd never seen one before, marveling at the craftsmanship of the metal. Everything was incredibly, achingly beautiful, and tears came naturally and effortlessly to his eyes in seeing the beauty of what simply *is*. His heart broke open and, naked and blown apart, he finally met Gauribala's eyes. "Aww, I'm sorry, Denis," Gauribala said in a gentle, ironic voice, "I didn't mean to *confuse* you!" He picked up the bottle, pouring more into Kelly's glass. "Here, have some more wine."

Swami G turned to Marlowe and began to chat happily, leaving Kelly, who was beyond language anyway, to sit with his mouth hanging open. He did not speak again through lunch, paid the huge lunch bill without comment, and walked behind Marlowe and the Swami as they got back into the rented car.

On their drive back to the ashram, Kelly realized that Swami Gauribala was a fully enlightened being, and the fullness of his realization made it that much harder to see through his jokes, kindness, and general affability. The roshis, lamas, and rinpoches in Buddhism (those who teach), and the monks, priests, and ordained teachers in Christianity covered themselves in fine robes, surrounded themselves with attendants and devotees, had formal ceremonies to contain their lectures, and rigid practices their students were to follow. Swami Gauribala wandered around in a sari with his belly hanging out, food in his wild beard, and was happy to sit in the dirt and wait for a student. He would just as comfortably talk with a toothless beggar as a visiting head of state. For Gauribala, *everything* that arose was the perfection of God. He was not, like Kelly, out to change the world for he saw the world *was perfect as it was*. It was evolving, perhaps, closer to an understanding of its own Divine Face, but it was perfect. How did one change or alter perfection? How did one judge it as

THE AGE OF THE GURU

incomplete? How could one attempt to change it and mold it to fit their narrow ideas of what *should* be? For Gauribala there was no need for ceremony, for fancy titles or words, or anything out of the ordinary, unless it was part of a joke that helped people to wake up, even just a little

This realization came to Kelly in the car less as a series of thoughts and more as an overall feeling, an understanding that appeared in its entirety. He turned to face Gauribala, but the Swami merely offered Denis a wide, open smile.

"Maybe," Gauribala said upon seeing Kelly's face, "You understand now why there is no need to search for wisdom."

If Kelly knew what was about to happen next, he might have gotten on a plane and headed back to America right then, while the world still made sense. Kelly was trying to break apart the order of the world, to turn it upside down through the distribution of LSD. In this way he hoped to plant the seeds of change. But the Swami was about to push Kelly through a portal that led to a world where the laws that regulate what is and is not possible no longer applied, where there was no physics, no time or space, no linear logic, no rationality, and the only rule was one of endless creativity and play.

Madness could break apart the ego and allow some to see the Perfection of what is; LSD did the same. But the great gurus could also fracture students' egos, and be there to help them integrate the maddening truth: everything was perfect as it was, and there was nothing one would ever find outside of the perfection of *this* moment. Every search took you away from the one place where freedom and happiness were patiently waiting, right under your very nose.

And yet most of us continue to buy water right next to the river. Kelly, at 28 years of age, was no different.

"I need to move on, Marlowe," Kelly told Alan a few days after dinner with Swami Gauribala. Marlowe was still in bed.

"Time to go, eh?" Marlowe replied, unsurprised. "Where to next?"

"I don't know," Kelly said. "But Swami Gauribala isn't the one. I don't know what I'm looking for." Kelly sat down on the packed dirt floor, feeling its coolness. "I mean, he's extraordinary. He's Awake, there's no question. And he's a great teacher. I see why you are drawn to him."

Marlowe rolled over on his bed so he could look Kelly in the eye. "So the journey continues. Good for you, man. Swami said I'm to do the namakarana samskara this week, so I'll be staying. Said he's got a surprise for me."

Kelly smiled. Marlowe would be taking a formal name in Hinduism, and become a formal disciple. He was happy for his friend, but was ready to hit the road again and see what else might come his way. The answer was out there ... somewhere.

That afternoon, when he saw the Swami walking with a few attendants, Kelly approached him in the street. It was a

blazing hot afternoon, and even though the sun shone merci-
lessly on the street, the Swami was smiling and happy as always
and seemed as if he were walking on the coolest and most
pleasant spring day in recent memory. His attendants, even
native ones, were sweating and appeared rather miserable in
the intensity of the midday sun.

"Swami!" Kelly called out, shielding his eyes.

"Denis," Swami G replied, smiling broadly. "You've come
to join me for a walk!"

"I need to talk to you, Swami," Kelly said.

"Of course," Gauribala said. "Come and walk with me."

"It's time," Kelly said. "This has been great, and I've
enjoyed my time with you, but it's not my thing. This isn't why
I came to India."

"But you don't know why you came," the Swami observed.

"True, but I know this isn't it."

"You have insight, Mr. Kelly, insight far beyond most
people your age. Yet you lack the wisdom to hold onto it."

"I'm sure that's true," Kelly admitted, "But I still need to
go."

"But why do you want to leave? I can get you anything here
you want. Anything." The Swami took a step back and looked
Kelly over from head to toe. "Money? How about money? You
know I don't care for it, but I have lots and lots."

Kelly shook his head, "No, Swami. I've got money. Lots
and lots, too. I don't need yours."

"I see." Gauribala put his hands on his hips. "Power, then?
You could run this entire community, Denis. Lots of power.
Heads of state come here, powerful men, men of influence —
you could manage all of them. I will send you to palaces and
to government halls all over the world. I will make you my top
student. Power."

Kelly, unsure how to take that, shook his head. "No,
Swami. I don't want power. Not my thing."

Gauribala pulled thoughtfully on his grey beard, his eyes
probing. "*Girls*? I can get you girls. You needn't be celibate,
Denis."

"No," Kelly replied, laughing. "I'm okay there, too."

"Mmmm," Swami G's eyes narrowed. "*Young* girls?"

"No, Swami."

Taking a step back, the light in Gauribala's eyes came alive,
and his eyebrows arched high into his forehead. "*Boys*, then?
We can do that, too, Denis."

Kelly laughed louder, "No, Swami, no money, power, girls,
or boys. I just need to leave."

"Well, *what* then?"

"Nothing. I just need to go."

"No, no, Denis. You do need *something*." Gauribala looked
around. To Kelly's great astonishment, he began to cry, sobbing without trying to hide his face or his tears. A full-grown
man and a spiritual teacher and master stood there, shoulders
shaking up and down, nakedly crying in broad daylight.

THE AGE OF THE GURU

"They all leave me," Gauribala wept, "*All* of them. Sure, they stay for a time, but then they get tired of it here, and they go back to wherever they came."

"Swami," Kelly pleaded, placing a hand on his shoulder, "Swami, for God's sake, get a hold of yourself!"

"No one stays," the Swami sobbed. "No one finishes their training. They all come and they all leave. There is no one to transmit my teachings to. No heir, Denis. What do you want? Zen? We *have* Zen here. Vajrayana? We *have* that. Hinduism? We *have that* too. Esoteric Christianity? Yes. Hedonism? That too. Kabbalah, perhaps? Yes. Everything you need is *here*, Denis. Everything you seek is *right here*."

Gauribala composed himself, partially, and kept an eye on Kelly's face.

"I'm sorry, Swami," Kelly said at last. "I understand. I really do. But I still need to go." Kelly, in fact, did not understand. It would take him another twenty-five years to understand the wisdom he was being offered, to really get the fact that there were no *isms* worth studying, and that Awakened Mind did not depend on the practice, on the master, or on anything outside of one's immediate realization.

"They *all leave me*," Gauribala moaned, crying anew, "*All* of them! You're no different. Go, *go*, Denis. *Leave*." And he turned and started to walk away, shoulders slumped, chest heaving. Some of his attendants were beginning to circle, looking at Kelly accusingly.

"Okay, *okay*!" Kelly cried, "Swami, I'll stay a *little* longer, but I can't stay here forever. Another week is all I can do. That's it!"

Gauribala turned, sniffing. He walked back to Kelly.

"You promise?"

"Yes, yes I promise," Kelly said. "Please, just stop!"

"*Good*." The word dropped out definitely, without a trace of sadness. The tears too were gone, and the Swami smiled at him again, going so far as to clap Kelly on the shoulder.

"We'll have to make this week count then, won't we?"

He turned, whistling, and walked away. Kelly was left with the distinct impression that he'd just been had.

The Swami sent a messenger to Kelly's hut that night. "Hello," the man said, bowing his head slightly as Kelly opened the door. "Swami asked for you to come with me. He needs you to arrange for a car. He wants to take Mr. Marlowe to see Guru Ma. Come. I take you to place where you call for car."

Kelly stepped out into the early night air. "Who is Guru Ma?"

"She is Yogiswami's wife." Yogiswami was the man who had been Swami Gauribala's guru, who had died at the age of 93, a powerful yogi said to possess miraculous powers. Kelly was suddenly nervous.

Two days later, Marlowe, Swami Gauribala, and Kelly got into a beat-up Tata, an Indian-made car.

"Marloff," Swami Gauribala said, "sit back and enjoy the ride. Denis will drive."

Kelly climbed in the driver's seat, which was worn through nearly to the springs beneath. The car was a rusted tan with a faded tan interior, and only about half the gauges worked. Kelly took it out of the ashram grounds and onto a dirt road that headed south.

"Where to?" Kelly said, his arm resting on the door. It was a hot day, as usual, and humid, and all three men sweated in the car.

"Just drive that way," the Swami said, pointing vaguely southwest.

They drove for thirty minutes.

"Which way?" Kelly would ask occasionally, and the Swami would point. The road grew increasingly unused and rough, and the worn suspension of the old car rattled and shook the passengers. Stones, sent flying by the bald tires, smacked against the car's undercarriage.

"Okay, now you turn right," Swami G said. They were driving on a large, flat plain. There were some patches of green, but mostly the terrain was rock, dirt, and sand, and Kelly could see at least twenty miles in every direction without obstruction. There were no signs, barely a road, no homes of any kind, no telephone or power lines, no water. There was just them, the desert, and nothing else. A kind of donkey trail was ahead.

"Turn right?" Kelly asked, slowing down. "Onto *that*?"

"Yes," he said, smiling as always. "Turn."

"Okay." Kelly drove slowly along the tiny trail.

After ten minutes, Kelly had trouble not focusing on the fact that they were now forty miles or more from anything at all, in any direction. The late morning was giving way to the brutal afternoon heat, and the sun bore down savagely on the roof of the car. The windows were letting in the ever-increasing heat, making Kelly feel like he was being slowly broiled. His eyes flicked to the car's temperature gauge every minute or so, which was making slow but steady progress upwards. They had no water, no food, no provisions of any kind.

The terrain ahead was utterly flat, and Kelly squinted through the rising heat that came off the ground in undulating waves, twisting and distorting objects ahead. He rubbed his eyes. They drove for another ten minutes, about as far from anything as Kelly liked to get. If the car broke down, they could very easily lose their lives in this kind of heat.

Ahead he saw objects through the distorting heat waves, tall shapes that seemed like some kind of columns. He squinted and leaned forward in his seat. As the car moved closer, he picked up bright colors, too.

"What the heck is *that*?" he said. Marlowe leaned forward from the backseat.

THE AGE OF THE GURU

"Looks like people."

"Impossible," Kelly stated. "Out here? Where would they have come from?"

Yet as the Tata sped closer, it became obvious that there were indeed four people walking together. They were wearing the orange robes of monks. When they were thirty feet away, Kelly let the car roll to a slow stop. The dust kicked up by the tires blocked their vision for a few moments but, as it settled, four ancient swamis could be seen standing only twenty feet in front of them. Their wrinkled faces and shaved heads looked as old as the rocks at their sandaled feet.

Swami Gauribala laughed and excitedly exited the car, hurrying up to the men and embracing each one.

"You can turn the car off," he called back to Kelly. "Marlaff, come. It is time."

"How can this be it," Marlowe said, leaning forward. "Dude, look at those guys! They're older than the fucking dirt! How the hell did they get here?"

Kelly turned the ignition off. "I don't know," he said, turning to face his friend. "I'll remind you, again, this was your idea." Marlowe grinned.

Kelly and Marlowe got out, and stood behind Gauribala.

The five swamis spoke to each other in Veddah, or at least that's what Kelly thought it might be. At one point Gauribala pointed to Kelly and Marlowe and all five men laughed. Kelly and Marlowe exchanged a look.

"Glad you're the one doing this," Kelly said, smiling. "And I thought the San Francisco Zen Center was an intense place." Kelly wiped sweat off his face.

"Come," Gauribala said, and the four swamis stepped aside. Only thirty feet away was a low hut with a rounded roof, no more than five feet off the ground at its highest. "Fuck," Kelly whispered to Marlowe, "I might have driven into that thing if we hadn't stopped. Did you see it?"

Marlowe, his eyes wide, shook his head.

"Come," Gauribala called again, less patiently. "Come now. She is waiting."

There was an opening in the hut's mud-and-animal skin roof, and smoke trickled out of it. Swami Gauribala lifted a leather flap at the front of the hut, indicating that Marlowe and Kelly were to go in. They had to drop to their knees and crawl, and found themselves more or less blind when they entered, for their eyes were used to the searing light of the midday sun. For a long moment, Kelly could see nothing at all. The hut was very hot, and smelled of herbs and smoke and incense and age. The floor was slightly dug out, so that Kelly could stand if he bent over at the waist. He dropped first to his knees and then, as he saw more, sat down on the surprisingly cool earth.

The whole hut was no more than fifteen feet across, with a fire in the very center. Marlowe moved toward the light, and as Kelly watched him he saw Guru Ma take shape out of the shadows. She was sitting on a straw mat in front of the flames, the flickering light falling sharply across her face.

She was far older than any living thing Kelly had ever seen: her face was deeply lined in a way that suggested the passage of much more than a century. The deep pleats around her mouth gave way to smaller channels of wrinkles that gathered in great numbers about her eyes. The collapsed shape of her lips suggested she no longer had any teeth to push against them. Absolutely white hair was pulled back tightly against the skull, flowing down her back in a long ponytail. She said nothing to them and instead hummed to herself in a soft, rhythmic way, her gaze deep in the flames. Her two hands, bent with age and swollen at the knuckles, occasionally stirred a small pot suspended over the fire. She would add herbs and then hum, giving no indication that she was aware of the two young American men sitting close by.

As Kelly watched her, he had the strangest sensation of youthful energy circling about her, light and playful, trapped but not contained in an ancient, grizzled body.

Kelly looked to his left and his right, realizing that the hut reminded him of a Native American sweat lodge. When he glanced back to the fire, Guru Ma was looking at him. Her eyes, even from ten feet away, were like nothing he had ever seen. They burned like black diamonds in her face and held a wisdom that was not of this world — a Divine Madness that saw right into his soul. He felt part of his mind give way and break free. Her lips parted in a toothless smile, and she cackled as Swami G crawled inside. Her laughter shook the very universe, and Kelly pulled himself up against the very back of the hut, knees to his chest, as far from her as he could get. His heart thudded against his ribs and blood swirled through his temples.

Marlowe glanced back at Kelly, all eyes.

Guru Ma spoke in Veddah to the Swami, and the two of them talked in low tones. She sat in front of a small fire; Marlowe and the Swami sat on the other side of it. Gauribala pointed to Marlowe, and Kelly saw Marlowe's body jolt when she looked at him. She spoke at length to the Swami, who translated into English, but Kelly was forgetting what was said almost as soon as it was spoken. She closed her eyes, and began chanting rhythmically, rocking back and forth on her little straw mat. The air grew thicker. She opened her eyes and cackled again, speaking to Swami Gauribala, who showed no trace of his usual self. He reminded Kelly more of Suzuki Roshi — set, serious, focused, almost menacing.

"Open your mouth," he said to Marlowe. She took a handful of brown, foul-smelling goop from the kettle and put it in Alan's mouth, then handed him a bottle of palmetto liquor. Alan grimaced and swallowed, and she smiled a toothless grin at him.

Kelly let out a breath of air. It was almost over. Guru Ma and the hut were making his head spin, and he longed to feel the sunlight on his skin and to be back in the car, driving, in control of the vehicle and of his own destiny again. Since it was clear that they had accomplished what they came out to do, he shifted his bodyweight to stand and leave. Guru Ma's eyes found his, and Kelly froze. She spoke, and the Swami replied in Veddah to her while shaking his head. She responded, uttering a laugh as vast and as open as the universe. Kelly felt another part of himself come undone.

"Come," the Swami said, frowning. "She's going to have you take vows and give you a Hindu name. She says you came here to be initiated."

"No, no," Kelly protested. "Tell her I'm honored, but not interested."

Gauribala spoke to her again, and turning back said, "Yes — you're in the right place at the right time, she says. Come." He pointed at the earth in front of him.

"You've got to be kidding me. I can't do this — I don't know her, and I'm not a Hindu."

"She says *come*," Gauribala said, his voice terse.

"Swami, no," Kelly repeated. His heart was pounding in his chest. "I'm a Zen guy."

The Swami turned completely around to face him. All humor and all playfulness was gone from his eyes, and the pudgy old German was as threatening as a savage warrior. "*Now*," was all he said, but it was with such force that Kelly scrambled over to the fire, taking Marlowe's place. Guru Ma laughed again.

Her eyes met his, and she offered a grin that exposed pink, toothless gums. The wrinkled lids came down over the fire-pit eyes, and rocking and chanting she prayed. After some time one of those ancient hands, the skin stretched over the bone, reached out and, with a surprisingly cold touch, opened his mouth. Her eyes opened. The other hand placed a scoop of the foul-smelling stuff into his mouth, and when he grimaced at the taste of it, she handed him the bottle of palmetto liquor. As he brought the bottle away from his lips, she smacked him in the middle of his forehead, and Kelly felt the room grow dim.

She spoke to the Swami.

"Your name," Gauribala translated, "Is Simhacootie. That means *young lion*."

Looking directly at Kelly, she said something else, and he heard the Swami translating into his right ear. "She says she has instructions for you: *Don't bite anyone*."

Guru Ma laughed loudly, clapping her hands together. The last piece of Kelly's sanity floated free.

She and the Swami spoke again, and then Gauribala bowed his head.

"Come."

The three men crawled across the dirt and through the leather flap. Kelly looked back to see the ancient woman sitting at her fire, smiling that toothless smile at him. He pushed the flap aside and stood upright, blinking and blinded by the intensity of the sun and sand. After a few moments, Kelly got his bearings. The foul taste was still in his mouth, but there was something else. There was no Denis Kelly anymore. All that existed was radical clarity, and he, Marlowe, and Gauribala walked back to their car by the four ancient swamis. When they reached it Kelly turned around, and part of his mind stopped. From one part of himself, he knew what he was seeing was impossible. At the same time he wasn't surprised in the least, nor did he feel much need to understand what was happening. There was no way to explain, given the world and the culture in which he was raised, what now stood before him. He might try and explain *away* the information coming from his eyes into his brain, but explain it he could not.

Marlowe, too, had stopped walking and was staring back in the direction they had come, his mouth hanging gently ajar. They were still in the middle of the large, flat, utterly empty desert plain. The sun still beat overhead, and the old Tata, rusted and dented, sat just behind them, its engine still pinging as it cooled. Marlowe and Kelly stood shoulder to shoulder. All they saw was the desert, wide and flat and brown. There were no ancient swamis, no hut with smoke coming out of it, no Guru Ma. As far as either of them could see it was just the three of them and the old Tata.

Kelly heard Gauribala laughing behind him, and the sound of a car door closing.

"Come, Simhacootie, come Atmanand. It's too hot to stay in this sun!"

Kelly got into the car. No one spoke for the long drive back, and it would be months before Marlowe and Kelly would speak of the events of that day.

"The Swami has been so kind to me," Marlowe was saying to Kelly a few days later. His large frame looked slightly worn out by the heat and deep sweat stains were etched into the sides of his shirt. The heat, Kelly noted, seemed harder on Westerners, and harder still on guys like them who were used to cool San Francisco weather. "I sent a letter to Nyanaponika Thera asking if we could bring Swami G up to see him. Do you know it's been almost 20 years since they've seen each other?"

"You think he'll be interested?"

"Who?"

Kelly laughed. "The Swami will be interested. But Thera seems like a cool cucumber. And didn't Gauribala leave his order and switch to Hinduism?"

"Yeah," Marlowe replied, "But they're both German, were both interred by the British, and both found spirituality far from their homes. I just don't think anyone's offered to bring them together."

Kelly and Marlowe were sitting on the ground outside their hut, both leaning back into the wall of the building. They were watching the sun set above the tree line, and taking in the clearness of the air, so different than California's.

"It's not too far away," Kelly noted. "We can drive him there."

"Not that far," Marlowe laughed. "Not that far for California. But here — shit, you remember the drive here. It's a day's drive even if we shoot straight there. Plus, with the Communists in power who knows what kind of shit we'll run into on the way — road blocks, checkpoints. It'll be an interesting journey. Probably better if we get a local driver for this one rather than try and do it ourselves, don't you think?"

Kelly smiled. "A German Swami being driven by two Americans to visit a Buddhist monk in an Indian car might seem like a bit too much bullshit for any sensible Communist. What about the Swami? Have you run it by him?"

"Nah," Marlowe said, "I want to surprise him."

"Good luck with that," Kelly commented, leaning back and putting his arms behind his head.

Later that day Kelly arranged for a car and driver, and Alan decided it might be better to not surprise Gauribala, who was overjoyed at the idea. After morning prayers the next day, Kelly approached the Swami. "So we're all set to take a drive to the Island Hermitage tomorrow."

"Yes, Baba. I know."

"Okay, listen Swami."

Gauribala was all ears and eyes. "Yes?"

"It's a long drive, and it's dangerous. I don't want to be on the roads after nightfall, so we should really leave by 9 a.m. Is that going to work for you?"

"Sure, Denis," the Swami said. "I see you in the morning."

The next morning Kelly got up at his usual 5:45 a.m. and did a forty-minute sit in front of the hut, watching the ashram come awake as the sun first lightened the eastern sky and then rose above the treetops.

When the driver and car showed up at 7:30, Kelly could hardly believe his eyes. It was a decrepit Tata sedan with a faded black paint job. The rear quarter panels looked diseased, with rust having eaten gaping holes in the metal. The interior had frayed seats, missing seat belts, and cracked windows, and the car sat on four bald tires. The engine, when turned off, sputtered and spat violently for a long moment before wheezing to a standstill.

The driver was a tall, very thin Sri Lankan who spoke English with a heavy accent.

"This is the best car you have?" Kelly demanded of the man.

"Yes, Me-ster Kelly. It is the best car we had. Very short notice. You want nicer car, you need call sooner."

"Yes, yes," Kelly said, going around to the driver's side and pulling a latch to open the hood. He checked the car's fluids, not wanting to strand the Swami or himself due to a lack of oversight. It was, he had learned, best to trust yourself.

Marlowe came down to the front of the ashram at quarter to nine, and smoked quietly while they waited. At about five after nine, they saw him come out of the temple, dressed in only his customary sari.

"Well," Marlowe said, taking a final drag off his second cigarette and tossing the butt into the street, "that doesn't look good."

The Swami waved at them, clearly intending on continuing to walk.

"Yo, Swami," Kelly called. "We're all set here."

"Yes, yes, I know, Baba. Just need to see a few people before I go." He offered a smile, waddling down the street, talking and laughing the entire way.

"Christ," Kelly breathed, checking his watch. 9:15.

By 10:30, Kelly and Marlowe were both sitting under the shade of a tree near the car, with the driver stubbornly behind the wheel of the Tata, sweating profusely in the intensity of the sunlight.

"Where is that fucking Swami?" Kelly snarled, checking his watch. It was now closing in on eleven. He sat down next to Marlowe, folding his arms across his chest. About ten minutes later the Swami's head came bobbing down the street, surround by a few devotees. Kelly jumped up and went to the group. "*Swami*," Kelly said, struggling to control his temper, "we need to hit the road. You agreed on 9 a.m., remember? It's a long drive, and the roads are not in the best state."

"Yes, yes, Baba. I need to say goodbye to a few more people. Just a bit longer."

"Swami, we'll be back in a couple of days. It's not that big a deal."

"Yes, Baba. Not much longer. I know you are very anxious to get going." He was off again, and over the next two hours Kelly saw him going this way and that, always talking and laughing to those around him. By 12:45 he was furious, and Marlowe dead asleep. Kelly went and found Gauribala outside one of his attendant's huts, talking to the man's wife about, of all things, gardening conditions in Germany. He had dressed in his robes at least, and was no longer in just a sari.

"Swami!" Kelly nearly shouted, "Look, I paid for that car and for its driver. We are leaving in the next five minutes, or we're not going at all."

"Oh my," Gauribala said. He kissed the hand of the woman to whom he was speaking.

Kelly led him back to the Tata and its driver, woke up Marlowe, and the three of them piled into the backseat. Marlowe and Kelly took the windows, and the smaller Gauribala took the middle seat. The car sputtered to a start and, with a few fits and starts, headed out on the main road leading away from the ashram. Kelly leaned back in the seat, let out a long breath of air, and started to relax. They were less than a mile out of the compound when the Swami, sitting calmly,

suddenly shouted, "Stop! Stop the car!" The driver brought
it to a slow halt.

"What, what? What's the matter?" Marlowe asked, alarmed.

"There," the Swami said, pointing to the right. "A Ganesha
shrine!"

"So what?"

"A Ganesha shrine?" Kelly asked. Ganesha is the Hindu
deity who appears as a multi-armed elephant.

"Yes. Ganesha is my patron saint. He protects travelers.
I must walk around the shrine once while offering prayers
whenever I am traveling."

Kelly looked at him flatly. "You've got to be kidding me."

"No, Baba. I am serious." He didn't *look* serious, and Kelly
very reluctantly got out, leaving the door open for Gauribala,
who did a kind of running waddle toward the temple.

"So this is your guru," Kelly said to Marlowe. "Holy elephants
in a country full of elephants? Multi-armed ones at that?"

Marlowe lit a cigarette. "Who knows with him," he said
with a shrug. "Can never tell if he's serious or not."

"Hmmph," Kelly said. "I don't see roshi in a loin cloth
running around worshipping elephants."

"I don't see roshi making huts and four old men and one
old woman vanish in front of our eyes, either," Alan retorted.

Kelly nodded. Point made.

The Swami, now sweating, came back to the car. "Okay," he
said, breathing hard. "Now we go."

"Great." They piled back in, and the car started off again.
Two miles later, the Swami again shouted for the car to stop
at another Ganesha shrine. Kelly was even more reluctant
and even less polite in allowing him to get out of the car.
He checked his watch: 2:15. Once Gauribala was back in,
they started moving again, going this time maybe half a mile
before the Swami called for the car to stop. The driver let the
car coast slowly to a standstill. Kelly looked out the window
where all he could see was an ancient pile of rubble with a red
ring of earthy paint around it.

"There's no shrine, Swami," Kelly said, not budging, his
arms folded squarely across his chest.

"That once was a Ganesha shrine. We must stop at all the
shrines, or Ganesha will get very angry with us."

Kelly turned to him, "Swami, you're an educated man.
How can you believe in such nonsense?"

"Nonsense! How can you say that?"

"Come on, Swami. I mean, clearly you're plugged into
something powerful. What do you need with these cultural
trappings of religion? It's no different than praying to St.
Anthony or to the Virgin Mary — fictions."

"Ganesha is not a fiction, Denis."

"The East," Kelly lectured, ignoring him, "has much to
teach the West, that much is sure. But the West has a few things
to teach the East. One of them is critical reason. Driver, keep
going."

The driver, who was being paid by Kelly, stepped on the gas. "No, Denis! Ganesha will not like that."

Kelly, feeling a touch of malevolence, all but snarled at the Swami. "*I'll* deal with your fucking elephant karma."

The Swami shook his head. "Oh, Ganesha is *really* not going to like that."

The car headed south, and soon went into a narrow road that cut though the rain forest. The road was in poor condition and rutted, and the trees thick and dense on both sides. The temperature dropped as the sun was hidden under the canopy of leaves, but the humidity became intense. Kelly checked his watch. 3:15. He looked around the driver's shoulder at the speedometer: forty kilometers per hour. Kelly did the math in his head. About 25 miles an hour.

"Driver," Kelly said leaning forward.

"Yes, Me-ster Kelly," he said, not looking back.

"Can you go a little faster, please?"

"Yes, Me-ster Kelly. But it is not a good idea."

"Look, I know the road is narrow, but there's no traffic, and we're late as it is. Step it up to sixty kilometers an hour, will you?"

"Yes." He stepped on the gas, and the Tata moved faster down the road. Kelly leaned back, and sighed again. The Swami was chanting quietly to himself. Marlowe was smoking as usual, and gazing out the window. The road dipped down and then came sharply up before making a sharp right turn, the driver not slowing down to take it. Kelly had to hang onto the door to keep from sliding across the seat. As they came around the turn, Kelly looked up along the road. Not far ahead someone had cut a tree down and placed it on two handmade sawhorses. It stood about five feet above the ground, was blocking the road entirely, and closing quickly.

"Driver!" Kelly shouted. "You see that barricade?"

"Yes, Me-ster Kelly," he replied conversationally.

"*Are you going to stop*?"

"I warned you, Me-ster Kelly, that it was not a good idea to go faster. The brakes are not so good." The driver then simply fell to his left so that he was laying flat on the seat, out of harm's way.

"Oh shit!" Marlowe yelled. The tree was set high enough that it would be hard for a car or truck to ram it off the road, and so it hit the Tata square in the windshield. The glass, which was not the shatterproof glass of modern cars, exploded inward in a thousand tiny projectiles.

Marlowe and Kelly, already ducked down, noticed at the moment of impact the Swami was still sitting upright in the seat, eyes closed, chanting. They grabbed him at the same time, pulling him forward and probably saving his eyes. The top of his head was shredded by the flying glass, though, and almost immediately began to bleed profusely.

The car coasted to a stop before the tree rolled off the hood and onto the ground. Sitting up, the driver wiped glass off his body, inspecting the shattered front of the car. The windshield frame was bent, and nearly all the glass was missing.

Gauribala was bleeding from the scalp, but upon closer examination they saw the wounds were superficial. They wrapped his head in a white towel that was lying in the car, making the white-bearded Swami suddenly seem like some kind of Sufi teacher. "I told you Ganesha was not going to like it," the Swami said quietly.

"Don't even start," Kelly said curtly. The driver was outside on the road, inspecting the car and muttering to himself about the boss man.

"I'll pay for the damage," Kelly called. "And take responsibility. Just get in the fucking car and get us out of here. That's a roadblock by a Commie guard station we just rammed."

Marlowe looked back. "Where are the guards?" he asked, looking at the deserted hut next to where the roadblock had been standing.

"Who knows? Taking a piss, maybe. Doesn't matter if we don't stick around to find out."

Marlowe nodded.

The driver, with a long face, got back in and pulled off, this time going far slower. All four men, looking miserable, squinted into air rushing in through the open windshield. Kelly, in a furious contraction, realized he had to take a piss. "*Fucking mother of....*" he muttered. "Driver, pull off. I gotta piss."

"But Me-ster...."

"I said *pull off.*"

"Yes sir."

Kelly, bordering on rage, stormed fifty feet into the forest on a footpath, smelling the intensity of decay wrapped so intimately in the smell of life and growth. He unzipped his pants just as there was a tremendous crash in the underbrush. He froze. By the sheer amount of noise he expected a tank to come rolling into view, flattening the forest as it went. There was a rush of gray motion in the distance, and more branches crashing down as the earth shook. A few smaller trees were ripped from their roots and tossed aside, and suddenly a fully-grown bull elephant was standing fifteen feet from him.

Kelly took a fumbling step backwards.

The bull's ears stood erect from his body while he shook his head from side to side, enormous tusks tearing loose the low-hanging branches. The elephant's trunk rolled up as his ears flattened. Breathing savagely, the huge head lowered itself closer to the ground, and grew still. The breath slowed and steadied itself, and Kelly realized, in a moment of profound horror, the elephant was about to charge. He looked around frantically for something to defend himself, but against an elephant one needed an elephant gun, not a stick. There was nowhere to run or hide or take shelter, so he did the only thing he could think of: he held out his hands, palm up.

The elephant roared and shook itself once more. Kelly closed his eyes, surrendering to the crushing death that was

coming. There was the sound of wood being shorn apart,
trees crashing down, branches being ripped loose, and then
silence. Kelly opened one eye, then the other, his hands still
out in front him, shaking madly. The bull was gone. All that
was left was devastation. Overturned trees and deep fissures
ripped into the soft earth made it look like a bulldozer had
drunkenly attacked the forest.

Kelly, zipper still open, stumbled back to the road, heart
in his throat. Peering into the clearing was the squat image of
Swami Gauribala, prayer beads in his hands, head wrapped in
the white towel.

He was smiling. "I warned you," he said, "that Ganesha
would not like this."

"Let's just get going," was all Kelly could manage to say.

When they got into the car he looked over at the smiling
Gauribala.

"Should I thank you?" Kelly asked.

Gauribala smiled. "Thank Ganesha"

They stopped at four more Ganesha shrines, and Kelly
joined the Swami in his prayers and in walking around the
temples, with no disparaging comments about worshipping
elephants. To this day Denis Kelly considers himself a devotee
of Ganesha. That night, they made it to the Island Hermitage
long after dark, well after Kelly's carefully scheduled plan had
predicted.

THE TWO OLD GERMAN GURUS HAD A TEARFUL AND BEAUTIFUL
reunion. They utterly forgot about Marlowe and Kelly, who
spent a few days meditating and enjoying the scenery, while
avoiding snakes and swatting mosquitoes.

Kelly and Marlowe were walking one night after sunset.

"It's time for me to go, Marlowe," Kelly said quietly. "The
driver was paid to go both ways, so just call that number I gave
you to arrange to take the Swami back."

"I figured," Marlowe said, with his usual good nature.
"How long ago was it that you told Swami you were going to
leave?"

Kelly laughed. "At least three lifetimes ago."

Marlowe nodded. "You're telling me. You find what you're
looking for, Denis?"

Kelly sighed. "It's crazy, given all we've seen and experienced. But no, I don't feel like I found what I came here to
find. I think it's still out there."

Marlowe, seldom judgmental, nodded. "I can dig that,
man. You gonna say goodbye to the Swami?"

"No, I don't think so. He knows, anyway."

"Where you heading?" Marlowe asked.

"Back to India. Back to the road. I'll see what arises, and
see what there is to see."

The two good friends hugged, and Kelly went back to pack his things. In the morning he was on a plane, flying to Delhi. He took to the streets again, wandering through the various cities and towns, looking for nothing, content to simply go where his feet took him. He ended up in northern India in the ancient city of Varanasi, along the river Ganges. He walked as a shaved-headed man, wearing local clothes and tanned from months in the sun. No one noticed him as he made his way humbly among them, eyes downcast, as much a part of the city as its worn cobblestones. No longer a garish tourist and obvious spiritual seeker, Kelly blended into the scenery as naturally as the street vendor or local cobbler.

Varanasi was the city where bodies were brought to be cremated, a Hindu necessity. Kelly walked through the impossibly old streets, taking in the smells and sounds of a city whose entire business, whose entire reason for being, was to handle the thousands upon thousands of corpses brought to be cremated each and every day.

The city's cremation grounds stood on two ghats, or platforms, along the river. Harishchandra, the smaller of the two, was open for cremation to all castes and religions. The larger, Manikarnika, was reserved for Hindus. Day and night, hundreds of pyres were tended by a caste known as the Dome, who have run the ghats for centuries. The pyres were lit, it was said, with an eternal flame that emanated from Lord Shiva himself, the patron deity of Varanasi. Surrounding the cremation grounds were hospices where the old and sick awaited death. Kelly found himself drawn to the ghats, and to the river Ganges, and his footsteps brought him to a low wall near the river where he took his seat, pulling his legs into full lotus. All through the night the crematoriums worked, burning hundreds of corpses while throwing thick smoke and ash into the sky. The madness of India was all around, and he sat in that position, hardly moving, until the sun rose again. Kelly left to find food before going back down to the river, retaking his place on the wall. The smells were otherworldly — death, excrement, burning hair and flesh, the thick rot coming off the water, heavy body odor, perfumes, spices, open-air markets of frying food, auto soot.

The dead were carried to the pyres all day and all night by wailing relatives. Some corpses were refused — those with leprosy, pregnant women, babies — all for a myriad of complicated cultural reasons Kelly didn't even pretend to understand. The dead were burned for the amount of time the family could afford, and for most that meant the skull and pelvis remained intact. The oldest male of the family would then stand over the burned remains of their loved one, and bring a wooden mallet down onto the skull. That noise was one Kelly never forgot: skulls fractured apart by wooden mallets.

The refused corpses were carried by their relatives down to the water, and stones tied to their limbs. They were cast into the water where it was believed the holy river would purify their karma and lead to better rebirths. Yet stones slipped off rotting bodies, and so the shore of the river had over a dozen half-eaten and partially-decayed corpses lying out in the open. Only twenty feet from Kelly were the remains of a woman. She was face-down, and a fleshy breast could be seen poking out from her torso. Both her legs had been eaten off by animals, as well as her right arm, and only the clean bones stuck out, white and straight. Inexplicably, her left arm was entirely intact, with even the fingers whole and unmolested and so plump and life-like he half expected her to make a fist at any moment. Her skin was a patchwork of gray blotches and was largely intact, probably because she had only recently washed to shore. There was no hair on her head, but her body was large and once had been matronly, he guessed. Something was strung around her torso, most likely the remnants of her clothing. Kelly watched a dog come up and grab her femur, attempting to pull her away with him. Over the course of the next hour, another five dogs came by and fought over her, each taking a small piece of the woman's rotting body.

Kelly counted no less than 15 other human corpses or skulls strewn about. He sat all through the night, hardly moving, surrounded by death and life. As the sun came up on the second day, he saw the ritual of Puja, or prayers, as people walked out into the fetid water to make offerings. The Babas, or Indian holy men, slowly worked at gathering the human remains off the shores. They then took them to be crushed and incinerated at last, but the process was slow, and the corpses seemed to come far faster to the riverbanks than they were removed. Some part of Denis Kelly knew he should have been horrified by the scene, or darkly possessed by it, but he was strangely neutral to what he saw. He was touched by the suffering of the families weeping over their dead and moved by the dedication of the Babas, but otherwise he felt merely open, calm, and unreasonably happy, especially given the starkness, the madness, of what surrounded him.

Later that day Kelly went to eat, and as he came down the Harishchandra ghat toward the Ganges, he took his place on the wall and sat again though the night. When the sun came up on the third day he realized that he had not yet slept. He should have been exhausted, but there was no fatigue, no tiredness, only the deep awareness of life and death as part of a sacred drama. He saw, in the new light of the day, the skulls and half-eaten corpses around him, watched the endless smoke pouring from the ghats, and in a flash recognized something profound: For two days he had been watching the life and death in front of him not as an American, horrified at people bathing in putrid waters or at the feral dogs scavenging human remains. He wasn't looking at things as a Buddhist, seeing the suffering and the impermanence of life, nor as a Christian seeing a battle between good and evil, nor as a traveler or even as a spectator. Kelly realized he was beyond any ideas or concepts of good or evil, or any need to explain what was arising around him. Life simply was; his need to catego-rize or rationalize made no difference at all in the reality of what was happening. The ghats, the suffering, the wailing of women, the dying cow, and the sea of death and bones and diseases and decay simply *were*, independent of Denis Kelly and inexorably bound to him at the same time. Elsewhere in India there were weddings taking place, and births, and first loves, and intercourse for the first magical time. Kelly was, he realized, no longer bound to his cultural programming, no longer bound by the need to stand in judgment of life, of others, of himself. He was free, and his purpose for coming to India clear: he was practicing what *is*, not an *ism*.

Uncrossing numb legs, he stood. With the City of Death at his back he made his way out into the cleansing air of the countryside on his way to Delhi, and was soon on a plane back to San Francisco. It was time to go home.

CHAPTER 11

THE RISE AND FALL OF THE ORDER OF THE GOLDEN FROG

A FEW WEEKS AFTER GETTING BACK TO SAN FRANCISCO, he called up Pretty Boy and Jesse, requesting a meeting. His business partners acted as if the conversation in Jesse's kitchen four months before had never taken place, and they welcomed Kelly back like he'd been away for a long weekend. There were no knowing smiles, no rubbing-in the fact they had known Kelly better than he had known himself, no jokes at Kelly's expense. They were happy to see him and grateful that his wanderlust seemed to be quenched. All three men threw themselves back into the business.

Kelly was convinced more than ever before that it was his experiences with LSD-25 that had opened his heart to the lessons of India. He had remained sober while there, but he believed the reason he had been so receptive to what the gurus had been saying was because he had already opened through the use of LSD. He was convinced that the gurus of the "old" world — Swami G, Govinda, Aurobindo, Osho, and many others, were missing the essential truth of LSD. They didn't see what he saw: LSD was allowing his generation to wake up much faster and in far greater numbers than previous generations. True spirituality, once the most elitist and misunderstood of all areas of human knowledge, was expanding out of the hands of a few powerful masters. And more to the point: Why sit on a meditation cushion, hour after hour, seeking something that you could experience immediately and powerfully by taking a little acid? Then meditation would serve to aid in remembering what one had already experienced, instead of spending years and years chasing some kind of transcendent experience through meditation.

Kelly saw LSD changing people all around him, leading them into a spiritual practice, a greater understanding of themselves in their world, and a more open heart. His choice to go back into the LSD business seemed not only natural and obvious, but a moral imperative.

KELLY FLEW BACK TO GREEN BAY TO VISIT HIS PARENTS. He was once again a wealthy manufacturer of LSD-25, and wanted to give something back to the parents who had raised him.

His parents picked him up from the airport and took him home for a homemade dinner his mother had prepared. His parents were not old, but they were getting older, and both had a greatly subdued energy from that of his youth. His father especially, although still an alcoholic, seemed to have mellowed considerably over the years, the demons of the Second World War beginning to lose some of their power. After dinner, Kelly leaned back in his chair, took a deep breath, and looked at his parents for a long moment.

"So, mom and dad," he began, smiling a little, "there's something I have to tell you both." Kelly's hair, now nearly seven months after his trip to India, was getting longish on the top and sides, and a scruffy beard covered his face. He wore designer blue jeans and a fitted sport coat.

Kelly's mother looked suddenly nervous, like an admission might be coming that could leave her in a place she didn't particularly want to go. She took in a deep breath and sighed audibly, nodding her head. She was ready for whatever potentially awful truth he was going to share with them.

"I want to send you both around the world. All expenses paid — travel tours, hotels, the works. All on my dime."

"No kidding?" his father asked. His mother, though, knew there was an admission buried behind the offer, and she waited patiently for Kelly to continue.

"No kidding. It's my way of giving back and sharing some of my success with those I love. However, you need to know where the money is coming from."

His mother sighed again. Here it was.

"I'm deeply involved in the counterculture movement," Kelly admitted, and both his parents nodded, not surprised at that particular admission. "I make my living these days manufacturing lysergic acid."

"That hippie stuff that makes people lose their minds?" his father asked, not as a judgment but as a genuine question.

Kelly laughed. "Not quite. LSD-25 opens one's heart and the mind to larger realities. It's helping to fuel the counterculture movement, and is behind a lot of the energy of the civil rights movement, the anti-war movement, and the general turn away from the structures of the past that have bonded people into a kind of slavery. Now, it so happens that by doing this, I've made a lot of money. So much that I literally can't spend it all." Kelly smiled. "God knows, I've tried. So I would like to send both of you on this trip, but you need to know how it's being financed."

"Isn't that illegal?" his father asked, leaning forward onto the table.

"LSD? Yes, dad, it is." Kelly said.

"Jesus, son, be careful!"

They gladly accepted his generosity, and had a wonderful time journeying around the world.

Their LSD manufacturing lab in San Francisco, above the Chinese American Communist Party headquarters, was not able to keep up with demand. It was decided to purchase land in Oregon to set up a much bigger laboratory that could produce much, much more LSD. It would have the added benefit of being isolated on a patch of private property.

By the start of 1971, the federal government was stepping up its prosecution of LSD manufacturers. Kelly heard a rumor there was a $50,000 cash reward from the Drug Enforcement Agency for information that led to his arrest and conviction. They had already been more careful than most. Only the three of them were allowed in the lab, they never spoke about business on the phone, and Pretty Boy and Jesse were virtually unknown to the larger community. Kelly stood out front as the fall guy, but he was also clever enough to never leave any traces (like property or cars), or to sell LSD on the open market.

Their LSD family was ingenious in its design. Pretty Boy and Jesse handled the lab and the packaging of the product. Kelly made the connections, but he sold only to about two-dozen handpicked people around the country — the "family." Those men and women, in turn, had their set connections so that Clear Light Windowpane only went into high-level channels. It was nearly impossible to find it on the street. Those "authorized" to sell it were few and known personally by Kelly. This setup made it very hard for the Feds to break into the family. The DEA was not interested in bringing down minor players, for they wanted to get to the actual core — to Kelly, in fact. Since Kelly had no dealings with anyone except those he already knew well, the Feds had nowhere to slide an informant into the system. The best they could hope for was to bring down one of the other family members and hope that person might roll on the others, but without proof (like a lab), it would be nearly impossible to get a conviction.

Their family was more like a wholesaler of LSD, selling to set and trusted family members who then moved it out to their trusted contacts. This kept the family close-knit and protected from informants, greed, and power struggles — at least for a time.

John, a friend of Kelly's, owned a poster company in Sausalito and was a trusted member of the counterculture scene. Kelly ran into him at a party in the Haight. Bell-bottom pants and a white silk shirt opened to nearly the navel made Kelly hard to miss, and John spotted him in the kitchen.

"So," Kelly was saying to a group of adoring women, "Billy Kreutzman's been teaching me to play the drums."

"Wow," one young girl, with long blonde hair, oozed. "You *really* know him? You must be really good at the drums!"

"I'm terrible, actually," Kelly laughed. "But it's not Billy's fault."

"Frank!" John exclaimed. "Hey man — how's it going?" John had on skinny grey jeans and a black Nehru jacket. A bright red button said *Legalize Spiritual Discovery* in a way that made the acronym very obvious: LSD.

"Hey John," Kelly said. "Good to see you, man."

John stepped closer to Kelly. "I'm still looking to get 3-4 grams of Windowpane for my cousin in Texas. Poor kid's been hounding me for months now."

Kelly laughed. "I know. Because you've been hounding me for months on his behalf." He put his arm around John. "What is it with you and that cousin," Kelly said, grinning. "I mean, what's the big deal about getting acid to Texas?"

"Because," John said earnestly, "They *need* it in Texas. What, we need more LSD here in San Francisco? This city is swimming in the stuff. But in Texas — man, there's a place where it could really do some good."

Kelly considered. "Good point," he admitted. "Hey, let me introduce you. John, this is ... wait, don't tell me." Kelly gripped his chin with his right hand. "Autumn. And Sunshine. And Sky. Girls, this is John."

"Hi John!" Autumn said. "Did anyone ever say you look like James Darren?"

John turned bright red.

"She says I look like Steve McQueen," Kelly said in a mock whisper, "only because she's hoping you'll tell her she looks like Twiggy."

"She kinda *does* look like Twiggy," John said earnestly, making Autumn giggle.

Kelly pulled John aside. He went on, "Today's your cousin's lucky day. I was supposed to send four grams to one of my family members, but it fell through, so it's sitting in my car."

"Not a good place for that much acid to sit," John observed.

"Yeah, no shit. So look, I'll run out and get it for you, and you can send it to your cousin."

John clapped Kelly on the back. "That's awesome. But I can't pay you right now — don't have that much cash on me."

"Don't sweat it, brother. Just pay me when you get the chance. Be right back."

Kelly went out to his car and brought in the four boxes of LSD. Each handmade box was about the size of a pack of cigarettes, and the face opened to expose an inside where forty glass vials each contained one hundred hits of Windowpane LSD, each hit a tenth of an inch square and six millimeters thick.

"Here you go, buddy," Kelly said, handing over the boxes. "Pay me back when you can. Now, where did those girls go?"

Two months later, Kelly got a call.

"Hey, Frank, it's John," the voice said. "How you doing, man?"

"John — with the poster company?"

"Yeah, man. Remember that favor you did me?"

Kelly laughed. He had forgotten about it completely. "Sure do, man ... now."

"Got your money, man. Why don't you swing by the poster store? Meet me?"

"Gonna be out that way later on. How about after dinner and we'll take care it?"

"Groovy, Frank. I'll be there from six on. Let me give you directions."

Two hours later, Kelly went to the complex where the poster shop was located. Discretion was not a hallmark of the early 1970s, in fashion, in autos, in sexual encounters, or in much of anything else. As such, Kelly was driving a blue, customized 1965 Cadillac. His hair was long and in a ponytail, he sported a beard, and he had on bell-bottom pants and a leather vest. Kelly parked the Caddy and went into the poster store, and from there up a flight of stairs to a large loft space. John opened the door and threw his arms around Kelly.

"Frank! I'm so glad you made it, man. Come on in!" The space was mainly used for John to store the many supplies of ink and paper he needed to run his business, but he had also converted part of the space into a livable area, with couches, chairs, and throw rugs.

"Hey man," John said. "This is my cousin, Paul, that young Texan so hungry for LSD."

Paul was a skinny kid who had a mop of hair that hung down to his nose. He sat, collapsed, on one of the couches, staring between his corduroyed pants at the floor. At the mention of his name, he limply raised his hand in a kind of wave. Kelly was instantly suspicious.

John was talking about an upcoming show they were going to see when Kelly put his hand up.

"Hang on," Kelly said. "What the hell is this?"

"Huh," John said, his smile slowly fading. "What's what, Frank?"

"Him," Kelly said, pointing at Paul. "He won't look me in the eye. What's he up to?"

"Whoa, Frank," John said with an uneasy laugh. "Take it easy, man. Don't get paranoid on me."

"You!" he jabbed a finger in the air. "What are you up to?"

"Frank, man," John cut in, "Hey man, chill out! Paul's cool. You don't need to get all upset."

"The hell I don't," Kelly charged. "You didn't tell me anybody else would be here. You know I don't like surprises, John. I'm a careful guy. He shouldn't be here, and he's hiding something. I can smell it from ten feet away."

Without warning Paul burst into tears. "*I can't do this,*" he sobbed.

"What," Kelly nearly shouted, "You can't do *what?*"

"I can't do it," Paul repeated. He jumped to his feet, hands over his face, and ran out the door.

John and Kelly stood in a stunned silence for a moment.

"John," Kelly said slowly and clearly, "you come clean with me *right now*. We go back, you and me. You better not be nailing me to the wall."

"I swear to God, Frank," John said. "I don't know what the fuck is going on." He looked out after his cousin, going so far as to step partially into the hall. "What the fuck *is* going on?"

Kelly was pacing. "Shit. He runs out the door saying he can't do it? He's gotta be wearing a wire, and the moment you paid me cash I'd be busted for selling four grams of acid. It's the only answer."

"Paul?" John looked puzzled. "But Frank — listen, man — I still *have* most of your acid."

"What?"

"I've been holding it for him," John said quickly. "I only gave him a *sample*. Couple of hits. He was supposed to be here to pick it all up, and to pay you for it tonight. Shit, man, how the hell did my cousin become a goddamn narc?"

Kelly thought fast. "If he was put up to his — if he's got a wire on him — we didn't say anything yet to implicate ourselves. No money has changed hands. But that means the Feds are here, somewhere, right now. We need to get rid of the stash, now. There's enough there to put us away from a long time."

"The Coke machine," John whispered. "We'll put it in there."

"What?"

"I have a key to the machine in the hallway so I can get Cokes whenever I want. Come on!"

The two of them walked quickly into the hall, checking right and left, and then went to the snack room where a soda machine stood. John opened the Coke machine with his key. He carefully put the four cigarette-pack sized wooden boxes, full of LSD, inside, and grabbed two Cokes. He handed one to Kelly.

"In case the cops spot us coming out of here," John whispered. He locked the machine up. "I'm sorry, Frank — I really don't know what's going on."

"We'll talk about it later," Kelly said, curtly. "I'm outta here."

He went back down the stairs and into the parking lot, quickly getting into his car. He put the keys in the ignition, and as he went to start the car, heard a tap on glass. A long-haired man in jeans and a flannel shirt was standing there, and Kelly put his window down.

"Help you," said Kelly hurriedly, looking back to the ignition, hoping to be asked for a smoke or for directions back to the city. As his fingers touched the car keys, he heard the distinctive sound of a trigger being cocked, followed by the feeling of a cold gun barrel touching his temple. Kelly's hands involuntarily opened and came into view, fingers spread wide. John's cousin Paul was thrust into the car, someone holding him by his hair.

"Is that him?" the man with the gun demanded.

"Never seen him before in my life," Paul lied, face wet with tears, and was promptly jerked out of the car. The gun's trigger clicked, and the barrel was pulled off Kelly's temple. The man with long hair stepped into view. "Excuse me, sir," he apologized, "I'm an agent with the Drug Enforcement Agency." He flashed a badge. "We're looking for an armed and dangerous man, and mistook you for him. My apologies."

"Jesus," Kelly breathed, "Good luck finding him." Heart pounding, he started his car and pulled onto the main drag. He saw the agent speaking into a walkie-talkie in his rearview mirror. Kelly pulled down a service road, heading back toward the main street that would get him back to San Francisco. The service road intersected another road a quarter mile in front of him, and Kelly saw two unmarked cars come flying toward him along that road, in opposite directions. They were going to try and block the road with their cars, and prevent him from leaving. Or so it seemed.

Had Kelly thought it through, he would have simply gone casually on his way. After all, he had no drugs on him, and there were no drugs in John's apartment. All they had was one kid's word that he'd heard from his cousin that Kelly was a drug dealer. That wouldn't have gone very far in court, or even been enough for them to detain him. Kelly, though, just had a handgun placed against his temple, and his system was flooded with so much adrenaline that his only instinct was to fly, and fast.

So instead of driving casually or assuming those speeding, unmarked cars could do nothing but briefly question him, he mashed the gas pedal to the floor. The 1965 Cadillac Coupe de Ville had a customized engine, brakes, suspension, and exhaust ... essentially a race car. The Cadillac took a huge breath of air through its carburetor, and Kelly's head was suddenly snapped back as the engine roared to life. In a few seconds he was doing well over 100 miles-an-hour and flew across the intersection, passing easily in front of the two cars. Both turned to pursue.

"Shit," he muttered.

Kelly had a great head start, and he pushed his car to the edges of its performance. He sped through the hills of Sausalito, switching back from one road to another, trying to gain distance, knowing the whole time that the clock was ticking. The pursuing cars fell far behind and eventually disappeared. Kelly doubled back on himself and took side roads and secondary roads, his eyes always flickering between the glow of city in the distance and his rearview mirror.

When he knew he had lost them for good, he turned toward home and slowed down to a reasonable speed. The Golden Gate Bridge stood between him and the security of San Francisco, and while it would be hard to make a discreet drive across the bridge in a customized Cadillac, he had no choice.

The two pursuing agents had figured exactly that and had taken up position on the north side of the bridge, their cars parked in the loose gravel off to the side of the main highway. Kelly spotted them from a quarter mile away and punched the gas. As he speed up they tried to pull out and block the road, but both cars lost traction in the loose gravel, and spun out like something out of a cheap detective show. Kelly flashed past and slowed down when he hit the side streets of San Francisco on the other side of the bridge, grateful it was nearing midnight and traffic was non-existent.

None of Kelly's cars were registered in his name, which prevented him from having to prove where he got the money to buy them. The Cadillac was registered to Michael, the barroom philosopher who made his living as a locksmith, among other things. Kelly, beginning to feel safe, drove at a more leisurely pace to Michael's house, where his old friend answered the door. He agreed to take the car and sell it in the morning. Over the next day, it became obvious the Feds had not managed to get the car's license plate, a near-miracle.

The next day Kelly called a meeting with Frank and Pretty Boy, after he had upgraded to a 911 Porsche. They were sitting at a table in the lab.

"We need to change things up. The Feds know me, and I just got away from half a dozen of them. They can't prove it, of course, and if Paul and John keep their mouths shut, they've got nothing on me."

"They got nothing on you even if they do roll," Pretty Boy observed.

Kelly nodded. "True enough. But I ran from the Feds so they know I'm hiding something."

"More to the point," Jesse said, holding an unlit cigarette in his hand, "you can bet your ass you pissed' em off plenty, not just by running all over town, but by running and getting away with it. Cops don't like that shit."

"Yeah, I know." He looked at his friends. "But I gotta tell you — it was one hell of a chase." All three laughed. "I need to get off the street for awhile, though, so I don't bring us any extra heat. Jesse, no one knows you. You'll need to take over sales and distribution, and I'll stick to the lab and manage it. It'll be a piece of cake — I know everyone already, so I can tell you where to go, who to meet with, all that shit. It's time to tighten the family. We're up to 28 people on the inside now, including the three of us. That's it. No one else but those 28. It's time to close the gates, boys. The family stays the same from this point forward."

Kelly had his 17th-century French chalice out of which he distributed Windowpane at concerts and parties. The week after that meeting, he had it melted down and cast into 28 small solid-gold frogs, with astrological symbols on their underbellies. Frank, Jesse, and Pretty Boy became the official leaders of the Order of the Golden Frog, an LSD family that had a lock on the procurement, manufacture, and sale of Clear Light Windowpane LSD throughout the United States and parts of Europe.

○

THE SAN FRANCISCO LAB HAD BEEN SHUTTERED AND THE Oregon lab was up and running at full capacity. Frank, Jesse, and Pretty Boy took lower profiles. They didn't feel any additional heat from the Feds after Kelly's car chase, and since the family was impossible to penetrate with informants, all three began to relax.

In late 1970 Kelly decided to make another quest, this time to visit a shaman whose fame was legend in counterculture circles. María Sabina was a Mazatec curandera, or folk healer, who lived in a modest house in the Sierra *Mazateca* of southern Mexico. She was known through the American banker and ethnomycologist Dr. Gordon Wasson, who had a life-altering experience with her. Dr. Wasson wrote about that experience in *Life* magazine, and brought spores of the fungus back to Paris with him. Its active ingredient, psilocybin, was duplicated by Albert Hoffman, the now famous chemist who first synthesized LSD-25.

Kelly traveled with his good friend Johnny, who was always up for seeing what lay over the next hill. Johnny looked a little like Kelly's old friend Alan Marlowe — he wasn't as tall, but he had a large build and a strongly masculine face. His hair was dark and wavy. His deep-set eyes were intelligent and intense.

Kelly and Johnny rented a Volkswagen "Thing," an ugly, square car that was basically shaped like a steel brick. It was slow but reliable, and it managed to get the two men through most of Mexico without incident. They met the Mexican Mazatec curandera, ate mushrooms with her, and explored the countryside before driving back toward the United States.

Kelly reflected on something that came as a surprise. Although his experience had been interesting and entertaining and poignant, it lacked the force of his trip to India. In some sense, his trip to see María Sabina felt like a spiritual dead end, with no real lessons or penetrating insights. No huts had vanished to make him question what reality was, no enigmatic koans had been issued and received, no glowing monks had been seen walking at dawn. As Mexico faded behind and he and Johnny entered southern California, Kelly realized that he was still seeking *something*. Despite his money, power, and amazing life, there was still an emptiness inside of him — a deep desire to connect to something that was outside of time and place and longing and death. As Johnny talked about girls and cars and their next vacation, Kelly wondered what it was he really sought. Why couldn't he just accept things as they were, like Johnny managed to do. Why couldn't he just be content with his wonderful and magical life? Why was it that even the masters — Govinda and Gauribala and Suzuki — that he *knew* spoke a truth he longed to possess for himself, why were these men also not enough for him?

San Francisco appeared in the distance, the beauty of the city shrouded in the swirling mists of the Pacific Ocean. As Kelly tasted the ocean on his tongue and smelled the fine salt being carried through the air, he realized he wanted to *know*. He wanted to take his seat in wisdom and to stay there. And for the first time, he wondered if hallucinogenics could get him any further, or if they had served their purpose.

DESPITE THAT INSIGHT, HE HAD A BUSINESS TO RUN AND responsibilities, and it didn't take long for Kelly to settle back into the ease of his daily routine. He lived as an underground shadow celebrity, known by many but virtually no one knew what he did to make his money. There were rumors, sure, but Kelly was very careful to never talk about where his money came from. Kelly too, while social, was far more reclusive then other counterculture fixtures. Not much of a partier, he would sometimes slip into gatherings to socialize with friends, and then just as quietly slip back out again. He was a study in contradictions: he tried many drugs but never became addicted to any; he was a counterculture icon, but also highly disciplined, often rising with the sunrise to practice yoga, run, and meditate. The counterculture was beginning to split along the seams. Those like Kelly, a small minority, were using drugs to expand their consciousness and heading more deeply into spirituality and deep inquiry. The rest were using drugs to deaden consciousness or to bolster their egos, and they were heading in a different direction altogether. While this split was not yet obvious, it was beginning to be seen in the lifestyles of those around him.

One of Kelly's routines after completing a new batch of LSD was to drive back and forth between San Francisco and the property he and the boys had purchased in Oregon for the new lab. There was a small restaurant along the way that specialized in organic vegetarian food. Kelly always stopped there to eat, and he came to know the owner well. One Friday he was on his way north, and pulled into the restaurant's parking lot after closing time, hoping to get a bite before everyone went home. There was only one car in the lot, and Kelly parked and walked up to the front door, peering in through the glass. He knocked.

"Hey Frank," the proprietor answered dispiritedly, unlocking the door. He was a true hippie, with hair that came down nearly to his waist, and a thin blond beard.

"Hey David," Kelly said. "I know you're closed, brother, but could you just give me some greens or something, man? Been a long drive, and I'd rather not put crap in my body if I can help it."

"Yeah, sure," David said, "Come on in. I'll fix you some-thing up."

Kelly took a seat near the kitchen, and heard a few refrig-erator doors open and plates being moved about. Five minutes later he had an exquisite pear salad sitting in front of him, with a side of toasted whole grain bread. Kelly dug in, and David sat across from him, moving his great mass of hair out from under him before sitting down.

Kelly ate in silence for a few moments before he actually saw the man sitting across from him. David's blue eyes were heavy, and there were deep circles under each one.

"So," Kelly said, "you look like you've got something on your mind."

David let out a long sigh. "Man," he said, "it's just this place. You know how much I love this place. Good, whole food that's sustainable."

Kelly nodded.

"But fuck, Frank," he said, "There's only eight fucking hip-pies a day that come in here. I throw out most of my food. Rent is killing me. I can't keep this place open, man. I'm almost eight grand in debt and there's no end in sight. I would keep this place open, but I can't get a loan from the bank carry-ing this kind of debt. So I might have to just close the doors, declare bankruptcy, and walk away. It's fucked up — I can't even afford to order food anymore." He looked suddenly self-con-scious. "Shit, man. I didn't mean to dump all that on you."

Kelly finished the last of his meal and pushed the plate away, dotting his face with a napkin. He took a sip of the ale David had sat before him. "You know how much I love this place. I would really hate to see you go. But I understand. You're just twenty or thirty years ahead of your time." Kelly thought a moment. "Let me ask you this: if you had that eight grand right now, would you pay off all your debt and be free and clear to keep running the business? Or you would you declare bankruptcy, walk away from your debt, and take that eight grand and travel Asia for two years?"

David looked back, clearly not in the mood to play with abstractions.

"I mean, the way I travel, you could only afford to travel a year," Kelly corrected with a smile. "But you — you could easily stretch it out for two years. See the world, sit with some gurus, travel and eat and fuck and let the wind drive you, man. What do you think?"

David brought his elbows onto the table, placing his fingers on his temples. "I dunno, Frank."

"Humor me," Kelly persisted.

David sighed. "I don't know what I would do, man. All I can see is debt right now, and the fact that my suppliers aren't going to let me order food much longer if I don't pay them."

"Gotcha," Kelly nodded, standing. He conspicuously checked his watch. "Well," he said, "I gotta get outta here. It's getting late, and I've got another hour ahead of me." Kelly took off his vest, which had numerous hidden pockets sewn into it, and began pulling out $100 bills. David's blue eyes were so wide that the entire iris was visible.

"There's your eight grand," Kelly said with a smile, "minus my dinner tonight, of course, and the ale. So I'm gonna go, brother, and I'll be back in two weeks. If you're still open, I'd love a free meal and a free beer. If not, then I know you're on your way to Asia. Good luck with your decision." He turned and headed out the door. As he pulled his car out of the parking lot he saw David peering after him from inside the restaurant. Kelly laughed and waved.

Two weeks later he swung into the darkened parking lot, as promised, and was delighted to see that a large "For Rent" sign hung in one of the windows. David had made his choice.

Kelly flew to South America a few weeks later to secure more base for the manufacture of LSD. Jesse picked Kelly up from the San Francisco airport in his Jaguar. His dog Blackberry was, as always, in the backseat, along with a pile of debris.

"Hey ya, Frank," Jesse called when he spotted his friend. "Hop on in."

Kelly got in, pulling the door shut.

"Jesus, Jesse," he said, looking around. "This car's a real mess, man."

"Fuck off," Jesse said dismissively and without a trace of anger.

"And it smells like shit in here, too," Kelly observed. "When's the last time you washed that fucking dog?"

Blackberry groaned at Kelly, and Jesse shook his head. "You can take the stinking bus next time, you prissy bitch."

The two men talked business as Jesse pulled the car into a McDonald's.

"You want something, Frank?" Jesse asked.

"Don't touch that stuff," Kelly said.

Jesse ordered three Big Macs. He pulled the first burger out of its wrapper, took a bite, tossed the bun out the window, and threw the meat patty into the backseat where Blackberry caught it in midair, chewing noisily and drooling all over the fine leather upholstery. The same routine was repeated for the next two Big Macs. Jesse then tossed the bag and wrappers out the car window, wiping his hands on his blue jeans.

"I don't suppose there's any point in telling you that you're littering," Kelly commented.

"Fuck off, Frank," came the response.

Kelly was unable to keep himself from laughing, and knew better than to lecture Jesse on why feeding his dog or himself a steady diet of Big Macs was not a great idea, or why throwing one's trash on the highway wasn't exactly enlightened behavior. Sometimes you have to accept people where they were, without qualifications, simply because you love them.

A few weeks later, Jesse and Kelly were standing outside of a Grateful Dead concert, very high on LSD. Jesse, as always, had a cup of coffee in one hand and a cigarette in the other. His Jaguar was a few feet away with Blackberry's head resting on the passenger side window. Kelly knew Jesse was getting really into heroin, a drug Kelly steered clear of. Even in the anything goes heyday of the early 1970s, heroin was taking down bigger men than he.

"Man," Kelly said, "you need to get into better shape, man. We're not kids anymore, and we can't keep doing the things we used to. You should start doing yoga. I'd be happy to teach you — it increases flexibility, strength, balance — you'll be amazed at how much better and in-tune your body will feel. It'll help you get off that shit."

"Christ, Frank, don't lecture me," Jesse complained, "I'm doing just fine."

"Jesse, I love you — come on ...." Jesse sat the coffee cup down as Kelly was talking, and without letting go of his cigarette did a complete back flip, landing squarely on his feet again.

"Holy crap," Kelly exclaimed, mouth opened. He had forgotten that Jesse had been a gymnast in college.

"*That's* my yoga," Jesse said, grinning and putting the cigarette back between his lips.

PART OF KELLY'S LIFE WAS SEMI-FREQUENT MEETINGS WITH family members, distribution connections, suppliers of raw materials, and others involved in running a multi-million dollar LSD manufacturing business. Like many businessmen, Kelly conducted these meetings in some of the finest restaurants in Marin County, dining over finely prepared foods while sipping exquisite wines. He had a table permanently rented at a restaurant called the Trident in Sausalito, so he could sit and get dinner or lunch anytime he wanted.

One evening he entered the Trident for a meeting, and saw immediately it was packed with people standing three deep at the bar. Overhead was beautiful modern art in an Aztec style, and one mural went from the lobby down a flight of stairs to the restaurant, which overlooked San Francisco Bay. Kelly made his way through the crowd, down the stairs, and toward his table, where a half dozen men were waiting to do business. He was wearing a fine silk shirt and tailored slacks, with his hair pulled back into a ponytail.

A young woman, wearing a shirt that was see-through, stepped in his way, and he stepped to the right to move around her. She stepped to her left. He stepped to his left, and she followed by stepping to her right. He stopped and, reluctantly, took his eyes off of his back booth and looked down at her, raising his eyebrows and giving her his most indignant of looks. Pretty young things that were interested in him were nothing new, and Kelly's impatience was obvious on his face.

"Excuse me, darling," he condescended, moving to step definitively around her. She stepped in his path again, and reaching up ripped his shirt open to the navel, sending five buttons flying into the restaurant. She reached her hands inside his shirt, digging her fingernails into his ribs painfully and, leaning forward, bit him incredibly hard on his exposed pectoral.

"Ow!" Kelly exclaimed.

The young woman stepped back, and cocked her head at him.

"Do I have your attention yet?"

Kelly grinned. "I'd say you do," he said at last. "But I have a meeting. Would you be so kind as to wait for me at the bar?"

She nodded, and Kelly made his way back to his table. Pretty Boy shook his head as Kelly sat down.

"That girl," he said, incredulous, "just ripped your shirt open *in public*." Pretty Boy was dressed in khakis and a button-up white shirt.

"Sure did," Kelly noted with a smile.

"How do you *do* that?" he asked. "Jesus." Pretty Boy sighed, looking down at his drink.

"I," Kelly said, "didn't do anything. But I'm going to," he checked his watch, "In about forty-five minutes." He winked at Pretty Boy.

KELLY WAS A CLOSE FRIEND OF A STREET HOOKER, DANI, and often gave her a couple of hundred dollars to get herself off the streets for a few days and take care of herself. She was intensely sexual, smart, witty, and also completely neurotic and utterly hooked on heroin. Dani always happily took Kelly's money, but was forever trying to pay him back by having sex with him.

"Come on, baby," she cooed one afternoon at the Trident after Kelly bought her lunch. She put her hand between his legs. "I just wanna say thanks the best way I know how."

"Sweetie," Kelly replied with a smile, "I don't fuck whores. Except when I inadvertently fuck myself. But you know, Pretty Boy hasn't been laid in ages. He's wound so tight I'm afraid his head might blow off."

"I'll fuck him, Frank!" Dani nearly exploded.

Kelly laughed. "That was easy. It's a huge favor, so thank you, darling. But there are rules. I want you to listen carefully. Pretty Boy and I are going to have a meeting here in just a little bit. You could hit on him when he goes to the bar. Nice and natural. Hit on him, seduce him, take him across the street to the hotel, and blow his mind."

"You got it, Frank!"

Kelly sighed. He loved Dani, but knew she was trouble for someone like Pretty Boy. "One more thing: Pretty Boy's going to fall in love."

"You're crazy!" she said, shaking her head. "Get out of here. He's like a wealthy chemist."

"Exactly my point," Kelly said. "He'll fall in love with you the moment he lays eyes on you. Listen to me, Dani: he doesn't need your kind of energy in his life. You're fun, and I love you dearly, but you're still a junkie, baby."

"I know, Frank," she said, dropping her eyes. "A girl can't be perfect."

Kelly laughed, despite himself. "No, I suppose not. Pretty Boy can't handle you, and I don't want you to do anything but fuck him this one, single time. That's it. He's going to ask you for your number, and you are not to give it to him. He's going to want to see you again, and you're going to say no." Dani was half-listening, and Kelly was suddenly afraid the whole thing could blow up in his face. He then thought of Lou, the Chicago mafioso who had stolen all of his belongings, and of the army company commander he had almost killed.

"Dani: give me your eyes," he said, echoing the company commander. Her large, beautiful blue eyes looked into his, and he had her complete attention. "You give him your number, and I'll fucking kill you." Chicago Lou's line.

Dani's eyes went wide, and she stopped chewing gum for a moment. He didn't mean it, of course, and she knew that, but she also knew he was very serious about it.

"We clear?"

She nodded slowly and solemnly. He smiled inwardly — those two catch phrases got people's attention, a fact he was never to forget.

An hour later Pretty Boy strolled in and had his meeting with Kelly. Afterwards, he went to the bar, where Dani slinked up to the shy chemist while he was waiting for a cocktail. Pretty Boy was hit on, seduced, and had his brains fucked out that afternoon, and never once knew or suspected anything was out of the ordinary. His spirits were greatly lifted for weeks afterward, and his confidence with women remarkably improved. A month or so later, he found a steady girlfriend who would become his wife. She was a sweet girl — a fall-down alcoholic, it was true — but as Dani said, a girl can't be perfect.

JESSE BECAME THE DISTRIBUTOR OF THE ORDER OF THE Golden Frog. Kelly, as the head of the family, continued his lifestyle, attending concerts, eating at the finest restaurants, wearing tailored suits, taking diving trips to remote corners of the world, driving exquisite cars, and having the means to do what he wanted whenever he wanted. He had an open

and honest relationship with a woman he had met in a lin-
gerie store, before going to India in 1970. Brenda was an
athletic blonde whose blue eyes were quick and steady. She was
the perfect complement to Kelly — grounded and calm, she
had little interest in metaphysics, meditation, or in changing the world. After she and Kelly became lovers in 1971, they
quickly became best friends. Her pragmatic and unemotional
nature was a powerful obverse to Kelly's fiery and wild one,
and they entered into a decade-long open relationship that
would define both their lives.

The austere and rigid discipline of Zen grounded Kelly
amid what appeared, from the outside, to be a wild and carefree
existence, although the truth was far more complicated for a
man who rose at 5:45 to meditate daily. The Zen retreats Kelly
attended meant not seclusion and quietness, but an utter lack
of privacy through communal housing, along with a 4:30 a.m.
rise and lights out at 9 p.m. Food was simple, and beverages
limited to coffee, water, and tea. Every minute was accounted
for, and the roshis made no distinction between the rich or
poor, the personable or awkward, or men or women. It spoke
to his meticulous nature and his deep curiosity about what truly
drove the insanity of life. In a world where he could have and
do just about whatever he wanted, the humility, simplicity, and
clarity of the Buddhist temple was deeply nourishing.

By 1974, Kelly had personally turned thousands of people
onto the insight and power of LSD, and had watched as the
experience of the drug transformed their lives. Part of this was
the fact that when people did LSD in his presence they were
drawn in by Kelly's insight, confidence, and expansive mind.
As a kind of urban shaman, he was able to draw out the type
of experience he wanted people to have. The horror stories of
people having "bad" or destructive trips were not something he
experienced. When Kelly came across someone who had experienced a dark LSD trip, he would explain how the drug showed
a truth of their own mind, and would offer to guide them on
their next trip to brighter and more insightful places.

His belief that a spiritual practice, combined with the regular use of LSD, was the most effective way to open the mind
to the truth of the universe was as strong as ever, and so in
1974 he, Jesse, and Pretty Boy decided to purchase a second
property outside Portland, Oregon, through a myriad of
dummy companies, and built a new and larger lab.

The Brotherhood of Eternal Love, the biggest producer of
LSD in the world, also believed LSD was changing the world
for the better. They knew of Kelly, and donated a new formula
for processing LSD that would increase productivity from
twenty to nearly one hundred percent. Kelly rented an industrial storage unit outside of Portland, and planned to move
his lab's equipment there to be refitted.

With the new formula, they now had the ability to make five
times the amount of LSD they had before, without changing anything else. Kelly, Jesse, and Pretty Boy hatched a

preposterous and ambitious plan: They would build out a lab large enough to make two billion hits of LSD in two years. That was one hundred times the twenty million hits they had made to that point, over nearly six years.

When exposed to air, sunlight, and heat, LSD slowly breaks down and becomes inert. If Kelly was going to make two billion hits in two years, it meant he also had to find a way to safely store the drug, out of the air and the heat. It wouldn't take up much room, for one gram of pure LSD-25 contained four thousand hits. Pretty Boy devised a way to pack the LSD in nitrogen gas cyro-packs, and Kelly decided they would purchase land in the Canadian northwest and bury the drug in barrels, underground. Cold, dark, and inert, the LSD would stay good forever. With the two billion hits in storage, the lab would be permanently shut down, and the Order of the Golden Frog would be able to continue to provide the same amount of LSD to the world for 100 years without any interruptions in its distribution. Clearlight Windowpane would continue to be a cultural force for shaking up consciousness long after Frank, Pretty Boy, Jesse, and the other 25 family members had died and new ones had been anointed to take their places. It was a beautiful and ridiculous plan, but given all they already accomplished, it seemed well within their reach. In the summer of 1974, the three men began to turn the dream into a reality.

The first order of business was closing down the operating lab in Oregon and moving the equipment into storage. They quickly sold out of their remaining stores of LSD. When the business had been running, people had paid one hundred percent of the money up-front, and usually had to wait two months to get their order filled. Kelly put the word out that no new orders would be taken for a few months. Kelly and Pretty Boy did the hard work of setting up the new lab on a remote stretch of property in Oregon, and all of their old equipment was cleaned and waiting for them in the industrial warehouse space.

Kelly had state-of-the-art locks put on all the doors to the warehouse, but was concerned that the roof of an adjacent house, which they used on occasion, might leak. A group of contractors was hired to replace it, and one of the roofers was a volunteer deputy and fireman who grew suspicious of the three young men who never went to work, drove expensive, brand-new 4x4 trucks, and seemed to be having way too much fun. He reported his suspicions to the local police, who came to investigate. They found only a maze of paperwork that pointed to a very complicated array of companies and individuals, all of them impossible to reach. But the DEA had longer arms than the local police, and word spread up the chain of command that there was a lot of equipment in storage that was the same kind of equipment one needed to convert ergot tartrate into lysergic acid diethylamide-25. The word on the street was that Kelly still had a $50,000 bounty on his head, and the DEA was eager to make an example of such a flamboyant but impenetrable target.

Kelly showed up at the warehouse one day and was sitting in his car looking over some notes about when production could start back up. He saw a ponytailed man, a little older than he, walking along the outside of the warehouse, hands buried in his pockets. He had on a flannel shirt and torn jeans, but his eyes were far too alert for a hippie wandering through the property. The man noticed Kelly looking at him. Their eyes locked for a split second before the man dropped his gaze. But it was too late — a transmission had occurred, and Kelly knew instantly he was being watched. The man continued to walk, hands in pockets. He rounded a corner and was gone.

"Fuck," Kelly breathed. How far, he wondered, had the Feds gotten? Had they found the second lab? Were they watching all three men, tracking their movements?

Kelly got in his truck and drove to the nearest payphone, where he called Pretty Boy and Jesse and scheduled a meeting at a downtown Portland restaurant that was always very crowded and loud.

"So what's up," Pretty Boy asked as he sat down. He was wearing khaki pants and a blue, button-down shirt. Oval glasses were pushed up high on his boyish face, and his beard was, as always, neatly trimmed.

"Let's wait for Jesse," Kelly said. "I don't want to go through this twice."

They ordered drinks, and by the time they arrived Jesse was sitting down at the table as well, wearing faded jeans and a jean jacket.

Kelly explained about the agent.

"I think the gig's up," he finished. "The Feds are watching us, so we can't move that equipment or we'll give away the location of the new lab, too. Right now we're not breaking any law, so we have nothing to worry about."

Jesse, whose hair was matted and greasy, ground out his cigarette. "Hey man, fuck the fucking Feds. They've never managed to get us yet, so fuck' em. You saw a guy make eye contact and you're jumping to conclusions, man. You don't know if that dude was a Fed. Come on."

"I know it, Jesse," Kelly stated. He was absolutely certain, and six years later his suspicion would be confirmed when he met the very same DEA agent face-to-face.

"You don't know shit. Why would they change our locks out? Don't make no sense. Look, let's get the production started again, so we can get some fucking money coming in."

"Jesse," Pretty Boy said, "You okay, man? You don't look so good."

"Fuck off," Jesse spat at him. "Look, I can't afford to take a fucking vacation. It's gonna be hard enough making ends meet just taking a few months off. You're talking about an indefinite closing? Based on some fucking eye contact? Fuck you. Fuck that."

Kelly and Pretty Boy exchanged a look. "Jesse," Kelly said, "We can't just pretend like nothing's happening. We need to keep laying low — it ain't worth prison."

"They got nothing on us, man," Jesse nearly shouted. "Don't go and get all fucking paranoid on me, Frank. I haven't noticed shit out of the ordinary. They been chasing your ass for four years, and haven't gotten nothing yet."

Kelly nodded. "Hear that. But I'm not going to fucking prison, Jesse, just because you didn't save up some money. Christ, Pretty Boy and I have nearly three-quarters of a million saved between us. How the fuck did you even manage to blow all that money?"

"Fuck you. So money ain't my thing. Look, let's just agree that we'll be back in business in two months if we don't see anything else that's weird."

Pretty Boy shook his head. "Maybe," he said. "I'm with Frank. Not willing to serve hard time because we're impatient."

"Fuck," Jesse said, disgusted. "Fine." He stood up, glaring down at them. "Feds got nothing, just like always. Cocksucking motherfucking parasites buzzing around us. Can't touch us." He threw a five-dollar bill on the table and left, leaving Pretty Boy and Kelly to look after him.

"He's addicted," Pretty Boy said at last. "Heroin. You see how red his nose is?"

"He had long sleeves on, too," Kelly noted. "Might be hiding his tracks. Fuck, Larry," Kelly said, using Pretty Boy's real name. "I'm worried about him. Russell's always been a loose cannon, but this is different. Keep your ears open, okay, and let's make sure he doesn't sink the ship on us."

Pretty Boy nodded. "Always knew this trip had to end sometime, Frank."

Kelly nodded. "Maybe. But the fat lady ain't sung yet."

JESSE WAS THE PUBLIC FACE OF THE ORDER OF THE GOLDEN Frog. He began to promise Windowpane LSD, pocketing their cash with no intention of using the money for anything but heroin. He ran this scam for a few weeks until Kelly caught word of it.

The next day he drove to Bolinas unannounced. As Kelly neared the house, he saw trash strewn everywhere about the yard. He pulled his truck past the 18-wheeler that sat idle next to Jesse's ramshackle home. Jesse had bought the rig along with a huge tree saw setup and had cut a deal with some shady characters in Costa Rica to cut down exotic lumber and then haul it back to the States. As with so many of Jesse's ideas, it never got beyond the concept phase, and now the huge rig sat on his property and collected dust. On occasion, Jesse would start the truck up with the intention of doing something, then snort some heroin and let it idle through all 250 gallons of gas.

Kelly shut his truck off and sat a moment, looking over the long grass, the empty beer cans and bottles, and the debris stacked on the porch. With a sigh he opened the truck door and got out, walking up the path to the front door.

The smell of rot and decay was everywhere. The door opened, and Jesse offered a tepid smile. A few days of stubble clung to the pasty skin of his face, and his normally compact body looked thin and weak. His eyes were watering, and they were weak and unfocused.

"Hey Frank," he said, barely above a whisper. "Come on in."

Kelly stepped inside and stopped. The foyer was packed so densely with boxes that there was a literal path one had to walk to make it from the door into the rest of the house. The boxes were chest high and full of tools, magazines, knick-knacks, and other useless things. Kelly wound through the maze and into the living room, where the same sight greeted him. In this room there were several pathways of boxes so one could go to the dining room, the kitchen, or up the stairs.

"Jesus, Jesse," Kelly said, "You ever think about throwing a few things out?"

Jesse, walking in front of him, shrugged. There was dog shit every few feet that Kelly had to step over, and the house smelled like a combination of a kennel and a garbage dump.

They came into the kitchen, which was filthy but at least reasonably clear of clutter. Blackberry, Jesse's lab, was curled in the corner with a litter of puppies around her.

"When's the last time you cleaned? Or let the dogs outside to shit?"

Jesse shrugged his shoulders again. "Fuck it, Frank. I'll burn the fucking place down when I get tired of it. You want a beer?"

Kelly shook his head, pulled out a chair, and sat.

Jesse was about 36, but looked far older. Deep circles ran under his eyes and his cheeks were sunken and pale. Like so many heroin addicts, he had lost interest in food. Much of the mass that formed his stocky body had fallen away. He was still dressed in his trademark jeans with a dirty white muscle shirt covering his torso.

"You keep smoking with all these boxes in here, that might just happen with you inside," Kelly noted. He paused a minute. "Sit down, Jesse."

"Fuck you, Frank," Jesse exploded, his pale cheeks instantly crimson, "You don't tell me what to do in my *fucking* house."

"Jesse," Kelly said, looking at his friend lovingly but firmly, "sit the fuck down before I knock you the fuck down."

Jesse bristled and puffed out his chest, but Kelly held his gaze. Even through the fog of heroin Jesse could see that Kelly had become more muscular and more willful than ever. He knew that Kelly was deeply physical and would do exactly what he threatened. He sat.

"*Fucking asshole,*" he muttered.

"Word came back to me," Kelly said. "You've been making bum promises to people. Promises I had to make good on."

"Oh, come on," Jesse said incredulously. "Fuck, Frank, that new lab will produce so much shit we'll be kings again, man. People can fucking wait."

"No," Kelly corrected, leaning forward on his elbows, "People will *not* wait, Jesse. It's *my* business. I'm the patriarch of this, not you, and it's been my word and my reputation that brought us all that business in the first place." He took a deep breath. "We've been different from the very beginning, Jesse. We've run this thing with integrity which is why no one's ever been hurt, no one's gone to jail, no one's ever been screwed over, and we've always had each other's backs no matter how much money was coming through."

Jesse nodded, exhaling through his nose.

"You broke that bond, Jesse. Made bad promises, and stole money from our family."

"Oh come on, Frank," Jesse laughed. "Don't get all fucking moral on me, man."

Kelly's gaze was unrelenting, and Jesse withered under it.

"You're out, Jesse," Kelly said at last, "You're out of the family. The Order has been informed, and no one is to have anything to do with you without my permission. I love you, but you're a fucking mess and you need to get yourself cleaned up."

"*Fuck you*, Frank," Jesse cried, slamming his fist into the table and standing halfway up. "You fucking cocksucker, you can't just take it fucking away from me like *that!*" Veins stood out on his neck and forearms, and his lips began to tremble. He looked like an old, sick dog backed into a corner.

"I can, and I already have," Kelly said, not wincing or looking away even as spit from Jesse's outburst clung to his face. "Christ, Jesse, you're in no shape to put up a fight, not now, and not on the streets trying to rescue your reputation. You're a fucking addict, and addicts can't be trusted. It's not you, Jesse, it's the drugs. You get yourself clean, you get yourself back together, and you're back in. You're back in the family." Tears were running down Kelly's face.

"Fuck, Frank," Jesse whispered, covering his eyes with a trembling hand and sitting back down. "What the fuck am I supposed to do for money, man? For fuck's sake, man. I burned through all my cash. I ain't gonna take no factory job."

"Jesus, Jesse," Kelly said, "Man, you can do whatever you want. Get clean, and come back to the family. Come back to us. I'd loan you money but you'd just buy drugs with it." Kelly shook his head. "I love you too much to do that. I'll take you to any clinic you want. I'll pay for any rehab center in the country. But I can't give you any money, or let you have any access to the family. I can't. I won't."

Jesse's hand stayed over his eyes, trembling violently, while the other hand held the burning cigarette.

THE RISE AND FALL OF THE ORDER OF THE GOLDEN FROG

"I love you, Jesse," Kelly said, his voice unsteady. "I didn't want to do this. Get clean. Lean on me to get clean. And you're back in the family."

Jesse didn't move or say a word.

"Fuck," Kelly exhaled. He stood up, and made his way through the mazes of boxes and back out the front door, through the yard full of trash. As Kelly opened his truck door he heard the screen door yank violently open.

"Hey Frank," Jesse bellowed from the doorway, "*Fuck you*, man!" He lumbered onto his front porch, his face bright red, contorted with rage. "You fucking turncoat motherfucking narc fuck!" The tirade of curse words continued to fall as Kelly got into his truck.

"Jesus, Jesse," Kelly said quietly. He turned the key and slipped the gearshift into reverse.

It was, he knew, absurd. His life was turning into an absurd caricature of itself. One of his best friends was standing in a heroin-induced fog twenty feet away, screaming obscenities. An 18-wheeler was sinking into the cement of his driveway under its own weight, with a portable sawmill inside that had never been used. It was crazy, and it was burning them alive.

Jesse picked up a rock and threw it wide as Kelly turned the truck around and drove down the driveway, his face nearly as tight as his grip on the steering wheel.

Kelly and Pretty Boy continued to lay low over the summer of 1976, waiting to see what the Feds next move might be. On a warm August morning, Kelly left his house in the suburbs of Portland for a run. As he ran down the block, he passed the trash truck. The men dumping the cans conspicuously avoided making eye contact as he ran by. There were two white men loading trash and one driving the truck, and all three seemed a little too square-jawed and clear-eyed to be working on one of the lower rungs of the employment ladder. Kelly turned his head for a second look, noticing their clothes were clean, and faces clean-shaven.

"That's not good," he muttered.

Later that week he went out in the afternoon for a jog, and this time noticed a man walking a German Shepherd, a man he had never seen before. Like the garbage men, this man failed to make eye contact or to say hello in the normally very friendly suburbs of Portland, and the man seemed a bit too intense in his casual indifference. Kelly's pit of anxiety grew deeper.

Two weeks later he went out to fetch his newspaper, and as he bent down a glint of sunlight came across his eyes from the tree across the street. The sun was at his back and as Kelly stood and scanned the tree he spotted something that made his heart hiccup in his chest: a camera, aimed directly at his house.

"Oh shit," he said, snatching the newspaper and rushing back indoors.

"Brenda," he called, "can you come here?"

"Hey baby," she said, drying her hair with a towel, fresh out of the shower. Kelly leaned in close to her, and whispered in her ear. "Go sit in the bedroom window, and just look casually out, like you're enjoying the day. Tell me if you see a camera in the tree across the street, aimed at our house. The big maple tree in the Laurel's yard on the left side about half-way up. With any luck," he added, "I'm just losing my fucking mind."

Brenda, eyes wide, disappeared upstairs, and came back down a minute later, her face telling Kelly everything he needed to know.

"There's a goddamn camera pointed at our house!"

"Fuck," Kelly breathed. "I've gotta go and give Pretty Boy a heads up."

"I don't want to stay here, either, Denis! That's creepy — a bunch of Federal agents staring in through our bedroom window! I'm going to close the blinds."

"No!" Kelly said, "We can't do that. Can't let them know we're onto them. Not until I figure out what we're going to do."

"I'm not staying here without you," Brenda stated.

"Okay. Go to Rachael's house. I'll call you later."

Kelly met Pretty Boy at the empty building where they were going to install the lab.

"Hey Frank," Pretty Boy said as Kelly walked up. "Already went through the lab. Clean."

Kelly nodded. "You see anything weird around you?"

Pretty Boy shook his head. "Checked out the trees around my house," he said. "Didn't see anything. But Frank," he smiled, "I'm not the one with the bounty on my head. I'm just the chemist, man."

"Don't I know it," Kelly said.

"You think they might have cameras on the building?"

"Maybe. One way to find out."

Kelly broke left and Pretty Boy right. Ten minutes later Pretty Boy called out, and Kelly walked over to him.

"Check it out," he said, pointing.

In one of the trees 100 yards away, across a ravine, a camera bracket was mounted, and under the tree the grass was matted as if men had been lying in that spot. Wires were coiled under some brush.

"To power the camera," Pretty Boy noted, "they must have used a portable battery or a car battery."

Kelly knelt down and inspected the grass. "This can't be more than a few days abandoned. Shit." He put his hands on his hips. "Once they realize that they have all the evidence they're going to get, they might arrest me with what they have and see what sticks."

Pretty Boy's eyes narrowed in thought. "Yeah, I could see that."

"Turn us against one another, get testimony and convict on that. Wouldn't be that hard to roll some of the younger family members though intimidation, or if they have small counts against them. Would be a circumstantial case, but a strong enough one to put us all away for conspiracy to manufacture LSD, I would guess."

"You think you're more at risk than me or Jesse?"

Kelly nodded. He smiled at his old friend. "I don't know if you realize this, Larry, but I haven't exactly been living a modest life."

Pretty Boy smiled back.

"And I think that pisses 'em off more than anything else." Kelly pulled his keys out. "Alright. Let's get outta here. I'll talk to you tomorrow."

"Hey," Pretty Boy said, "How's Jesse?"

"Don't know," Kelly said. "He won't return my calls. He's Jesse, so I'm sure he's finding a way."

"Probably by going through the nearest wall."

Kelly nodded. "Yeah, most likely. I might have to hit the road, Larry. You think you could loan me a hundred-grand?"

"Sure, Frank. Follow me back to my house, and I'll give you a briefcase."

"Thanks, Larry. I'll come straight there. Think it's best."

It turned out that was the last day he would ever see Pretty Boy.

CHAPTER 12

ON THE RUN

KELLY PULLED HIS CAR INTO HIS DRIVEWAY, RESISTING the temptation to see if the camera was still in the tree across the street. He let himself in through the front door and walked through the living room, then came to a dead stop. A book was sitting in the middle of the floor, doing a split around its binding.

His house had been searched, and the agents hadn't been very careful to return things to their original place. Kelly didn't know if he had surprised them and forced them to rush out of his house, or if they were so confident of his arrest that they were not bothering to hide their tracks at all. Either way, it was bad. Very bad.

Getting arrested was to not be in a position of power. The only way Kelly planned on dealing with the Feds was to turn himself into them after his lawyer negotiated terms. Kelly moved swiftly through the house, packing bags for himself and for Brenda. He had 250K in cash, another 40K in gold Krugerrands, and an extensive wardrobe. He cherry-picked what he could so that when Brenda walked in she was greeted by four large bags and a very intense-looking Kelly.

"We have to go," Kelly said without pretense. "Right now. They were in the house, and they're going to arrest me at any moment."

Brenda, ever flexible, wiped a few tears from her eyes, got a favorite jacket, and was ready to go. Kelly risked a phone call, asking a friend to pick them up to "go to dinner" immediately, and said that he and Brenda would be waiting "where you picked me up that one time."

They slipped out of the back door with the four heavy bags, and scrambled down a back path through their backyard, jumped a hedge, and had to slide down a fifty-foot embankment to emerge on a quiet street. Their friend pulled up a few minutes later, and Kelly and Brenda piled in.

"Where to?" their friend asked.

"Take me to that dealership by the flea market."

"What's up, Frank?" the man asked.

"The less you know the better off you are," Kelly said, and the man nodded gravely. He dropped Kelly and Brenda at the dealership. Kelly bought an International Harvester 4x4 in cash off the lot. He spent the afternoon loading it with water and groceries. Kelly pulled into a parking lot, turning to the woman that had been his lover for over two years.

"So this is it," he said. "We're going to be on the run now. You don't have to come with me if you don't want, Brenda. You've broken no laws, and you can stay here and live out your life and wait for me to get this mess cleaned up."

Brenda shook her head a few times.

"I love you," she stated. "And I'm going with you no matter where we end up. We'll beat this thing, together."

"I love you," Kelly managed, leaning across the seat and kissing her. "We'll need to get you a fake ID. But it'll take the Feds a few days at least to realize we're gone, maybe more. I'll have Johnny come by and take care of the house until it's obvious they know we're gone, then he can just put all our stuff into storage."

Brenda smiled. "He loves to play gangster. He'll love it." She turned her head and looked out over the road. "So that's it, then. No more San Francisco."

Kelly shook his head. "You know," he said, "I always wanted to visit a national park."

Brenda looked back. "Which one?"

Kelly grinned. "All of them."

With $300,000 in cash, gold, and jewels, he and Brenda headed north, beginning their five years on the run.

A few months into their trip, he traded the 4x4 for a VW pop-top minivan with tags and title that were good for a few years. He and Brenda journeyed to nearly every state, visiting the national and state parks, staying in their van, keeping themselves warm with campfires and love making.

The first year went by quickly and wonderfully, but Kelly wasn't a wanderer at heart, and his strongest desire was to root somewhere. He stayed mobile long enough, he hoped, for his trail to grow cold. Without credit cards or checks or bank withdrawals, it was impossible for the federal government to track him. In 1977 he and Brenda passed through Northampton, Massachusetts, and fell in love with the town. They rented a three-room, cathedral-ceiling apartment with fireplaces in the countryside in Ashfield. It was attached to a country estate home. Kelly converted a walk-in ten-by-twelve closet into a kitchen.

GETTING A FAKE ID IN THE 1970S WAS DIFFICULT, TIME-consuming, and risky. The first thing to do was to visit a local library where one would go through the obituaries in old newspapers. Infant deaths were listed, and Kelly would find a boy's obituary from the 1940s. He would write down the name and address and then write to the city or county registrar where the child was born and had died, pretending to be one of the parents, and sending a cashier's check for payment. He would claim he needed a copy of the birth certificate for his records. The first five times he did this, the hospital sent him the original birth certificate. Once he had a real birth certificate, he would write to the social security office and inform them that he had left high school and joined the seminary. As a Brother of the Holy Cross, he had never needed a social security card. In the letter, he would explain he was leaving a life of the cloth and moving back into the secular world, where he would need a social security number to get a job and pay his taxes. Once he had a legal birth certificate and a legal social security card, he could get a driver's license, insurance, and even sign a legal lease. He had legally resurrected a dead child from the grave.

The only problem was that Kelly had been on the Fed's watch list for nearly half a decade. The sixth time Kelly tried to change his name this way, the process took a very long time, and Kelly decided it was likely the ID had been diverted through the DEA, so he left that birth certificate and social security card in his lawyer's hands with a warning that they might have been flagged and were on a federal watch list.

It was in 1976 that the DEA finally realized that Kelly had given them the slip, and that there would be no more labs producing LSD where they might catch him red-handed. They arrested all of the other family members on conspiracy to manufacture LSD charges, who then all rolled on Kelly in exchange for leniency.

Once a month Kelly would call a pre-selected payphone in San Francisco at a specific time and date. Johnny was there to answer, and to provide him with information on what was happening with the family and the DEA.

Four months into his trip, there was an especially sobering exchange. "You've got a warrant out for your arrest," Johnny informed Kelly, who was standing in a gas station outside of Spokane, Washington. Johnny was an attorney and had plenty of friends in and around the courthouse willing to funnel him what would eventually be public information. "Eight federal counts, each one carrying a maximum penalty of five years. Looking at forty years if you get pinched, Frank."

"Shit," Kelly said into the plastic receiver, looking out at the expanse of the countryside.

"All the family members have been arrested, and all of them rolled on you."

"That's okay," Kelly said, "I was the head of things. Most of them were just idealistic kids looking to change the world."

"Looks like they'll all get just probation in exchange for testifying," Johnny noted. "But I've got some bad news, Frank."

"More?" Kelly laughed uneasily.

"Russell wouldn't roll. And he cursed out the judge or some crazy shit. He's been sentenced to five years."

"Fuck," Kelly said.

"That's not the worst news. Pretty Boy rolled. They managed to get the chemist for the Order of the Golden Frog to say under oath that you were the brains and the head of the operation. He got probation in exchange for his testimony. He's off, scot-free."

Kelly felt anger rise in his gut at the betrayal. "I've got his hundred-grand loan," Kelly said at last. "Think that just might make us even." An 18-wheeler drove past, temporarily drowning out Johnny.

"Ok. Gotta run here. I'll call you in exactly thirty days. You remember that little organic restaurant where we sometimes ate with that gorgeous Asian hostess?"

Johnny was quiet for a long moment as he thought. "Where Dani showed up that one time in tears and needing money?"

"That's the one. There's a phone booth on that corner. Talk to you in thirty days, at 9 a.m. your time."

"Be safe, Frank."

BECAUSE JOHNNY WAS AIDING AND ABETTING A FEDERAL fugitive, he too was at risk. Forgetting about Kelly's warning about the birth certificate and social security card, he went ahead and applied for a passport arranging to pick it up when he was going to be visiting Kelly and Brenda in Boston later in the year.

Kelly and Brenda, Johnny and his girlfriend, and one other couple reserved adjoining suites in downtown Boston and spent a fun week sightseeing, partying, and relaxing. Johnny informed Kelly that he needed to go to the courthouse to pick up his passport in case he too had to flee the country in a hurry.

Kelly considered the risk. He had been incredibly careful on the run. Maybe his concerns about the original birth certificate and social security card being tagged by the Feds were overblown. He considered staying at the hotel while Johnny went to get the ID, but then decided to tag along.

A blizzard hit Boston on Saturday and covered the city in over a foot of heavy snow, shutting the city down. By Monday the streets had been cleared and public transportation was up and running, but the city was much sleepier than normal, a refreshing change. There was little commuter traffic, and many people stayed home and out of the cold, leaving the streets beautiful and deserted.

All federal and state offices, however, were open for business. Kelly and Johnny got up early, dressed in suits and bundled up against the cold. The courthouse was only a few blocks from their hotel, and they stepped out into a frigid morning. Plumes of moisture condensed around every exhale, and the two men laughed and joked all the way to the steps of the building. The sky was forlorn and low, still heavy with moisture. An occasional snowflake floated by. The city seemed abandoned, and the fallen snow had been pushed into huge piles, making the concrete sidewalks feel like a low-lying canyon.

They climbed up the long stairs to the courthouse and entered a large foyer made mostly of stone and marble, and as silent as a mausoleum. Kelly had bought a *New York Times* and he sat on a bench near the stairs as Johnny went off to find the passport office.

He checked his watch again. Five minutes had passed. Kelly's eyes moved over the words of the newspaper, retaining nothing. Eight minutes. He flipped through the entire *Times*, having read a total of maybe a dozen words. Ten minutes.

The sound of running caught his attention, and three men came running down the stairs, their sidearms visible in shoulder holsters as they tore by the bench. Kelly carefully folded his newspaper, checked his watch one more time, and stood. The doors were twenty-five feet away. He started walking toward them, sweating heavily. Fifteen feet to the doors, and he let his pace increase.

"Whoa there, buddy," a voice said from behind. "Hang on there just a moment."

Kelly stopped and turned. A young agent, wearing a cheap gray suit, approached. Two other agents, a little older, flanked the younger one.

"You came in with Kelly," the young man asserted. "Hands up!"

The young man patted him roughly down, and then pulled his wallet from inside the suit jacket.

"What is this about, gentlemen," Kelly said at last, having found his voice. "Please be careful with the suit," he condescended. "It's tailored."

The young agent pulled out Kelly's license, which said Paul Killdare, and his insurance card.

"What's your business here, Mr. Killdare?" the older agent asked.

"*Doctor* Killdare," Kelly corrected, absurdly and spontaneously. "Obstetrics." He literally looked down his nose at the agents. "I just came in to buy a *New York Times* and warm up a bit," he said, sounding annoyed. His tone made it clear that he would only tolerate a small delay.

"*Gotcha*," the young agent said, "Fucking liar! I knew this guy was with Kelly." He pulled his handcuffs off his belt. "Turn around, asshole!"

"What have you got?" the older agent asked.

"Two addresses; his insurance is registered in Ashfield. His home, in Boston."

Kelly turned to the older agent. "Would you please explain to your vulgar young colleague that for those of us who make more than ten grand a year, it is beneficial to not insure your automobile in the city of Boston, for obvious financial advantages. The home in Ashfield is my vacation home, where my car is registered, and where it is registered quite legally, I assure you." Kelly glanced disdainfully at the younger agent.

"Now, is there anything else I can help you gentlemen with today?"

"Bullshit," the younger agent said, uncertainty coloring the edges of his words. "He's lying."

"Shut up, Kent," the older agent said. "Give him his wallet back. We're sorry to have stopped you, Dr. Killdare. Please enjoy the rest of your day." The agent wrote down Kelly's information in a small notebook.

"Thank you," Kelly said, taking back his license and tucking it into his pocket. "And good luck." A nervous impulse to begin chatting nearly overwhelmed him, and he immediately turned and walked briskly toward the door, away from three armed federal agents who were looking for him. He pushed the doors open and stepped into the cold air, moving down the steps and back toward the hotel, barely resisting the urge to look back or to break into a run. When he raised his hand to the hotel's doors, it was shaking. It wouldn't take the agents long to realize that they were holding the wrong man, and Kelly walked quickly back to his room.

Despite the cold, he entered with sweat standing out across his forehead. Brenda was curved into the bed, her blonde hair spread across a pillow. A bare foot protruded from the sheets.

"Baby," Kelly said gently, sitting on the bed. "We need to go. Now."

She sat up, immediately awake. "Why? What happened?"

"They got Johnny, thinking he was me. I told him about that fucking birth certificate. They stopped me on the way out, but bought my alias. But they're gonna figure out Johnny's not me sooner or later, and put two and two together. They saw my license with our Ashfield address on it. We need to get back home and pack everything up."

"But we just finished it," Brenda said, a tear welling at the corner of her eye and then slowly running down her cheek, leaving a glistening trail on her skin. Kelly reached up and wiped it away. "It's such a beautiful place."

"I know, darling. I know. But we can't stay. I don't know if they'll remember my address, but they'll remember the town, and I'll get picked up for sure. Johnny's probably telling them the truth right about now, which means we have to get out of this state before the afternoon."

Brenda threw the covers off the bed, exposing her thin and naked body. She pressed her lips against his neck. "Okay," she whispered. She planted her feet on the ground, stood and stretched, and got dressed.

Kelly was amazed at how quickly and resolutely she packed and was prepared to start all over again. Before they left the hotel room, he took her into his arms.

"I forget just how strong you are sometimes, only because you're also so amazingly soft and beautiful and graceful," he whispered. "I'd be lost without you."

"I told you," Brenda said, "I love *you*, Denis, and that's all that I need."

He nodded, and together they drove back to their apartment, packed their car, and in two hours were gone.

While Brenda and Kelly were nervously driving back to Ashfield, Johnny was refusing to say anything whatsoever. Johnny didn't have his real license on him, so the Feds had no way of determining his true identity with what they had confiscated, and he didn't say a word for two entire days.

After they had arrested him in the courthouse, he was transferred into DEA custody and spent a night in an otherwise empty federal holding cell. On Tuesday he was taken into an interrogation room early in the morning, where he was given the good cop-bad cop routine, threatened with a long jail sentence, and told that they would arrest Brenda and send her to jail, too. Johnny sat and smirked at the agents, which caused them to get more and more angry.

Halfway through his second day in custody, one of the agents was going over what had become an old threat.

"Eight federal counts, Kelly, eight. You're looking at forty years easy. But you work with us, you give us something, and we'll see about maybe letting you serve at least some of those sentences consecutively. You keep just sitting there with that blank look on your goddamn face and you're going to be collecting social security in prison before you see the light of day. We're going to arrest your girl too, and charge her with harboring a fugitive. That the kind of guy you want to be known as? We got over two dozen written testimonials ...."

The other agent in the room stood up. "Holy shit," the man interrupted. He smacked the file that was opened on the table. "This says that Kelly's eyes are *blue*. This guy's are *brown*! We've got the wrong fucking guy!"

"True enough, gentlemen," Johnny said, breaking his silence. "My name is Jonathan Miles, *Esquire*. And I'd like to speak to my lawyer."

The two agents' mouths hung open.

Kelly and Brenda took a long, leisurely drive toward the middle of the country, staying in select bed-and-breakfasts, four-star hotels, and fine resorts. They ate dinner in the most expensive restaurants in town, wearing tailored clothes. When people noticed Kelly and Brenda at all, it was only to admire how well the charismatic couple suited each other. A master at hiding in plain sight in the more elite sectors of society, Kelly would be nearly impossible to find once he had a head start.

AFTER A FEW WEEKS ON THE ROAD, KELLY AND Brenda decided that the bucolic town of Woodstock, New York, would be their new home. With new fake IDs and new cover stories, they quickly settled into the rhythm of life, living in the open, eating out at restaurants and attending yoga classes and lectures in town. They lived as if they had nothing to hide and were quickly welcomed by their neighbors. Kelly began to be drawn, with increasing intensity, to the dharma — Buddhist teachings and Buddhist communities. Kelly had legally become Charles Stephens, a new alias and the name of an unfortunate child who had died 35 years before.

By 1977, Kelly had heard of a very unusual Tibetan Buddhist teacher named Chögyam Trungpa Rinpoche. Trungpa was born in 1939 in Tibet and was only three years older than Kelly, and he too had lived a remarkable life. In 1959 (when only 20 years old) he was the head of the Surmang monasteries in eastern Tibet, but was forced to flee from the invading Chinese to India, going over the Himalayas on foot. He moved to Scotland in 1963 to study comparative religion at Oxford and gave up his monastic vows. He saw that Western students were too distracted by the exotic dress and culture of Tibet, and that he was too distracted by Western women to remain celibate. In 1970 he moved to the United States and became known for his ability to present highly esoteric Buddhist teachings and concepts in easily understandable Western terms.

In 1973 Trungpa had established more than 100 meditation centers throughout the world. Originally known as Dharmadhatus, these centers are now known as Shambhala Meditation Centers. He followed in 1974 by founding Naropa Institute, which later became Naropa University in Boulder, Colorado — the first accredited Buddhist university in North America. Trungpa believed that an enlightened society could be actualized and he taught and wrote relentlessly about spiritual matters. The practice of his Shambhala vision was to use mindfulness/awareness meditation as a way to connect with one's basic goodness and confidence. He believed that secular meditation would bring dignity, confidence, and wisdom into the lives of those who practiced, and would change the world. Kelly, who was still quite attached to changing the world via the distribution of LSD, was naturally drawn to the ambition and philosophy of this teacher.

As Trungpa became more famous and had more and more Western students flocking to him, his teaching style began to shift. Like the enigmatic koans in the Zen tradition, Trungpa started to intentionally confuse and misdirect his students in an attempt to dismiss their expectations. A truth that every spiritual teacher eventually comes to realize is that as long as the students think the teacher possesses something special and extraordinary, they will never have the insight for themselves. Eventually Trungpa's style of teaching came to be known as *crazy wisdom*, meaning he said and did outrageous things to help jar his students out of their self-inflicted ignorance. These startling pranks were supposed to help free people from their habitual stories and emotions and thoughts by shocking them into a larger and deeper spiritual reality. His reputation was that of a fully enlightened being who nevertheless liked to drink, have sex, and cause trouble — lots of trouble. Kelly, needless to say, was intrigued. Some of Trungpa's students let Kelly know about an upcoming lecture, but warned him that Trungpa would show up late to toy with people's expectations of timeliness and what a spiritual teacher was "supposed" to do.

Kelly and the others showed up for the 9 p.m. lecture at 11 p.m., where they found a crowd restless with a combination of anger, resentment, and anticipation. Kelly took a seat, and about a half hour later Trungpa doddered out from behind a screen on the stage, an enormous glass of wine in his hand. He was a handsome man with a full head of thick, black hair and a broad, dark face. Heavy glasses gave him an air of scholarship, and his tailored suit hinted at a lean body. He sat on the stage and looked out blurrily at the audience, all of whom were intently staring at him. The glass of wine came up to his lips, and he let out a sigh. He moved a little strangely, due to an auto accident in his youth that had left him partially paralyzed on one side.

"Go home," he said, smiling. "There is still time." He smiled, lowered his head, and stood on his uncertain legs before disappearing behind the stage. The audience sat in stunned silence, and no one moved for at least two minutes. Kelly looked at their shocked faces and open eyes, and finally threw his head back, roaring with laughter. The lecture was over.

Kelly immediately signed up to do a thirty-day retreat at the Karmê Chöling in Vermont with Trungpa. The retreat initially was very challenging for Kelly, not because of its length but for its lack of rigidity. Deeply comfortable with the military precision of Zen, he found the lax attitudes and lax enforcement of rules distracting, and very nearly left early. Trungpa, though, had a method to his madness, and by the third week the group had self-organized and created a very tight and powerful bond.

Over those thirty days he was amazed by Trungpa's phenomenal insight and the true depths of his insanity and depravity. Yet there was no question the man was absolutely galvanizing those around him, from those who angrily left in disgust to the senior students who bent over backwards to excuse and justify the inexcusable and unjustifiable. Both views seemed, to Kelly, to be missing the point. He saw through Trungpa's madness to the lesson behind it, and thought he was sharp and smart enough to manage this kind of teacher. Trungpa was like Kelly — confident enough to believe that he could single-handedly change the world. Kelly deepened his relationship with Trungpa and decided that it was time to deepen his own training.

Woodstock was a very hippie-friendly town and the long-haired Kelly and Brenda walked through downtown on their way to get breakfast. It was a beautiful morning with a sky

that was as deep and blue as it had been in months. Long ten-
drils of white clouds floated languidly overhead. Huge trees
shaded the streets, their roots distorting the bricks attempting to bind them into neat squares. Brenda and Kelly walked
down an uneven sidewalk stained a deep red. The windows of
the downtown homes afforded views of antiqued parlor rooms
and pressed tin ceilings, yet the staples of a hippie community could be seen everywhere. Posters like ERA NOW and
PARDON DRAFT DODGERS were taped against windows.
Many houses had the tools of woodworking, metallurgy, and
other artisanship spilling into their front yards.

"I need to deepen my monastic training," Kelly said, and
immediately felt Brenda's grip loosen from his arm. "I feel
so much clearer in my mind, and so much more focused in
my life. It's like there is just so much more space, you know, a
quietness that never goes. I want to take a long retreat — one
hundred days."

They walked half a block in silence, Brenda's long, blonde
hair obscuring her face.

"That's four months," she said at last, quietly.

"I know."

"That's a long time to be away, Denis."

"I know it is. I figured you'd probably take a deeper cut
with Alan." Alan was a tennis instructor Brenda had met and
become romantically involved with. She and Kelly were still
in a very much open relationship, although they seldom and
only very consciously added on it.

"Yeah, he's okay," she said. "But he's not you." They came
to the diner where they were going to get breakfast. Brenda
turned to face him. Her eyes mirrored the blueness of the sky
over their heads.

"It's tough sometimes," she said, lines appearing around
her eyes and forehead. "You're part wild man, extrovert,
party host, runner, and yogi, and part monk and philosopher.
I never know who I really fell in love with."

Kelly smiled. "And you like some of them more than
others."

The lines deepened. "I was raised an agnostic."

Kelly smiled sympathetically.

"I have little interest in monks, philosophers, or theo-
logians, Denis. I don't need God, or no God, or anything
like that in my life. What's wrong with just living? Why do
you need to rage against things *all the time*? Why can't you just
be?" Brenda, excluded from a growing part of Kelly's life,
felt the heat of this separation, and her words were like steam
escaping.

"Meditation *is* just being."

She shook her head. "Not the way you practice it. Most
normal people practice it that way, yeah, but with you it's all
intensity and fire and life-or-death. Why can't you just *be*?"

Kelly's smile faded. "Because, Brenda, I have to know. I
have to know the truth."

"What truth?" she nearly cried, exasperated. "Maybe there *is no truth*, Denis. Maybe this is all we get. Can't you be okay with that?"

He offered her a smile whose edges were tinged with sadness. "No."

"*Why?*"

"Because that's not my experience. I've died, Brenda. I've died and been reborn. Through LSD, through meditation, through insight, through Swami Gauribala. Hundreds of times now. I know a truth deeper than this." He opened his arms to indicate everything around them. "I know a truth that doesn't come and go, that always was and always will be, that doesn't fade with the passage of time or any changing circumstance. I need to deepen my understanding of it, deepen my insight." His blue eyes spilled over with the fire of his passion.

"Where is this leading?" she asked.

"Leading? I don't know. Waking up is not a casual affair, Brenda. Christ prayed so hard in the garden he sweated blood. While the other's slept from exhaustion, he prayed so hard he sweated blood. The Buddha took his seat and resolved to either die from thirst and starvation, or to Wake Up. No more living in ignorance, no more living in delusion. I know now what it takes."

She shook her head, very subtly. "Do you really think it's that hard?"

Kelly laughed. "For a stubborn asshole like me, I do."

"Do you think you'll be some kind of teacher? Some kind of religious guru?"

"I don't know, Brenda. Maybe." He considered the question. "Maybe," he repeated.

Her eyes at last dropped. "What is this thing that whips and drives you? I don't understand it. In my worst nightmare, I never dreamt of being a minister's wife."

"A *minister?* Christianity and Buddhism are as different as folklore and science," Kelly lectured. "They have nothing in common. Buddhism is all experience and open curiosity, and Christianity all faith and repression. They share nothing."

But Brenda had turned her back and was pushing through the doors into the restaurant.

LATER THAT YEAR KELLY RETURNED TO BOSTON TO SERVE as the Tenzo, or cook, for Trungpa and the sixteenth Karmapa, Rangjung Rigpei Dorjé. The position was an honorable one, and Kelly spent a month preparing, learning the finest Japanese preparation for the red snapper he was going to cook. The day he was to serve food to Trungpa and the Karmapa, the two men were sequestered with a number of attendants and senior students in a closed room not far from the kitchen. Dinner was scheduled for 9, and Kelly made all the necessary preparations. Having remembered Trungpa's penchant for lateness, Kelly planned the dinner to be served at 11 p.m., a safe delay, he figured. At 10:30 he approached the wooden doors where Trungpa and the Karmapa were sequestered. An attendant stood in front of the doors, his arms folded neatly in front of him and his gaze off in the distance.

"Dinner's ready," Kelly said to the man, who nodded politely.

"One moment." The attendant slipped as quickly as he could through the door, but drunken laughter and a slew of moving bodies were divulged. A few seconds passed and the attendant again quickly opened and closed the door. He resumed his position, back to the door and hands folded neatly in front.

"Rinpoche is not ready for dinner yet."

"It's fish," Kelly reminded him, a little sharply. "Prepared to be served hot. If it cools, the whole thing will cave in on itself." The attendant nodded and politely smiled, but did not move.

Kelly went back to the kitchen and cleaned the dishes. He put away his spices and the dishes, cleaned the counters, and folded all the towels. At midnight he took his apron off and hung it up. On the kitchen's main table his snapper sat in its pan, the red skin caved into the sides, cold and ruined. The side dishes, garlic mashed potatoes with horseradish and handmade gravy, a green bean dish infused with honey and tarragon, and handpicked mushrooms sautéed in red wine and fresh spices, were cold, their sauces opaque.

Kelly walked into the hallway and toward the attendant, and halfway there could hear the raucous laughter and giggling coming from behind the doors. Kelly was deeply resentful of having his time and his talents taken for granted.

Fuming, Kelly moved toward the doors like a projectile.

"You ...!" Kelly shot at the man. "I've got a message for that Tibetan cocksucker: he can go fuck himself." The attendant, who was one of Trungpa's inner circle, had seen many strange things in his day, but had never heard his teacher referred to quite like that. Kelly spun on his heel to leave as the doors to the room opened with a flourish. Trungpa emerged with a huge smile on his face.

"Charrless," he slurred, using Kelly's alias, "where's our food?" He clapped Kelly on the back. "Come! I am sure you have prepared something incredibly delish...delicious for us, no?"

Kelly went to the kitchen and brought the food in, serving it onto dishes for the nine people in the room. It was devoured amid heaps of lavishing praise about Kelly's cooking prowess. He stood silently with folded hands, listening to their compliments and watching them eat. As he cleared their plates afterward and brought the last of the dishes to the kitchen, the stoic attendant pulled him aside.

"Did you hear how much they enjoyed your food? You must be quite a chef!"

"I could have served them dog shit, and they wouldn't have known the difference," observed Kelly. "I fixed you up a plate if you're hungry. It's in the fridge, third shelf down."

"Are you okay?" the man asked, genuinely concerned.

"Yeah," Kelly said, "I'm fine." He smiled. "I'm better than fine, actually. I'm great."

"He teaches through 'crazy wisdom,' you know," the attendant, whose job was often to manage the shock Trungpa created, noted apologetically.

Kelly paused for a moment. "In my experience, there's nothing crazy about wisdom."

Back in his room, Kelly slept soundly with the knowledge he would leave in the morning and never return to study under Trungpa. He had finally gotten the man, finally understood his teaching methods and how effective they were at breaking people apart. Kelly even saw how well he had been played, with Trungpa taking the joke as far as he could, pushing Kelly's buttons for maximum effect. It was, he had to admit, clever from start to finish.

"See the perfection" was one of Trungpa's favorite expressions, by which he meant that from the non-dual, Enlightened mind, from satori, everything was perfect. Your master was drunk? So what? He tried to sleep with your wife? So what? See the perfection! From the Absolute, there was no valuation, there was no ego, there was nothing that wasn't utterly perfect as it was. Despite what religion taught, the truth was that God didn't take sides or share our morality or our valuations. Everything that arose was Perfection, just as it was. Kelly had no doubt that Trungpa was, like Swami Gauribala, a fully Enlightened character. He suspected Trungpa's crazy wisdom was a smokescreen for self-indulgent behavior and an excuse to not do psychological work on his small, relative ego. The man was unquestionably an alcoholic and a sex addict, but Kelly also knew nothing Trungpa did mattered if one truly "saw the perfection."

As he zipped his bag shut and headed out the door into the coolness of the Boston morning, a critical truth had taken shape for him: He saw how Trungpa's brand of crazy wisdom worked in retreats and weekend workshops and lectures, worked for the suburban middle-class Americans drawn to him who needed to learn to break the stubborn drudgery of their lives. Kelly, though, was trying to get back to sane. He was done with crazy.

His upbringing was crazy. A fourteen-year-old boy bringing a loaded shotgun into his parent's bedroom was crazy. His fleeing from his wife and daughter, working for the mob, and living on the streets for weeks on end was crazy. He had somehow along the way become one of the biggest LSD manufacturers of the 1970s and there were half a dozen DEA agents combing the country for him at that very moment. Crazy. Jesse had been lost to heroin and was doing hard time, Cheryl was lost to PMA and alcohol (as were a good many of their friends). Crazy was killing him, and killing those he loved. Crazy was Kandinsky whispering to him on the army base about necklaces of ears, crazy was the Kali worshipper covered in blood with topless women behind him, crazy was Swami Gauribala making a hut and an old woman and four ancient swamis vanish into thin air in defiance of everything that was possible. Crazy was Kelly's *life*. He had enough of crazy to last a lifetime.

Although Brenda loved and supported Kelly, she was relieved to hear he had left his teacher. Perhaps, she thought, he might make meditation and Buddhism more of a hobby and a side interest, like going to the gym or taking up a new sport. And for a while, Kelly did just that. His home practice was set and disciplined, and he rose before sunrise to sit, usually practicing the form of concentration meditation taught in Zen. He was still not looking for a teacher, but rather someone who might embody the perfect teaching, and through whom Kelly could deepen his own insight. He was still in charge, still the boss of his own life, and utterly unwilling to give away much power in any relationship, be it with his partner or with his so-called guru.

In 1978 he came across an article by the Rinzai Zen master, Eido Shimano Roshi, who pleaded that no more PhDs be sent his way. "They already know everything," he had written. Kelly, who was a two-fisted intellectual, loved the description. He was drawn to Zen already and Eido Roshi had just opened a monastery through the Zen Studies Society in the Catskill Mountains, not that far from Woodstock. He decided to drive down and investigate further.

The drive was magnificent. Located on 1,600 of acres at the end of a climbing, two-mile private drive and bordering a state park, the land around the monastery was heavy with old sugar maple trees and thick grasses, the roads were seldom used. The first thing to come into view was Beecher Lake, black-green in color, and surrounded by deep forest on three sides. The 19th-century Beecher House, the name of the family who once owned the land and where Harriet Beecher Stowe wrote *Uncle Tom's Cabin,* passed by on Kelly's right. And then the Zendo came into view, in all its perfection, and Kelly's breath caught in his throat. It was like love at first sight. The main building was huge and perfect, a Rinzai Zen temple in the American forest built to the absolute standards of perfection insisted upon by Eido Roshi. A team of monks, nuns, and laypeople labored over the building, lavishing attention on every detail so that it appeared as if it had been built only hours before.

Like something out of Imperial Japan, the buildings on the temple grounds were white structures with brown framing, their roofs sloping downwards on gentle, upturning angles in classic Japanese style. Kelly got out of his car and went inside, where he came across rooms with tatami flooring, meticulous meditation halls with rice paper walls, a wooden kitchen that was about the cleanest thing he had set eyes upon. For decoration, there were immaculate porcelain vases, detailed pottery, wooden carvings, and fresh flowers. Kelly felt like he had been transported halfway around the world and two centuries back in time, and he loved the timeless feel of the spaces and the orderliness that defined every inch of every room. This was a world where everything made sense, where every item had its proper place, where a clear and unquestioned hierarchy ruled over everyone, and that had but a single purpose: to Awaken.

He stayed for a public meditation, and immediately signed up for their next long retreat, a 100-day Kessei.

"A four-month retreat?" Brenda questioned when informed. Her lips tightened. She and Kelly were sitting in their beautiful kitchen, the afternoon sun filtering in through the large window. Dinner simmered on the stove a few feet away.

"Three months and ten days, really," Kelly corrected.

"Do you remember what you told me when I took too much LSD?"

Kelly smiled. "You can never take too much LSD, Brenda. You always take the right amount."

She shook her head, ignoring the comment. "I saw myself as completely, utterly alone in the universe, unable to connect to anyone or anything," she said, tears coming to her eyes. "It was the most frightening thing I ever experienced, and when I told you later on, do you remember what you said?"

"Not really," Kelly admitted.

"You told me it was *fantastic*. That most people never had that thought of aloneness, much less the experience, and that it was a gift."

"In that case, I agree with myself."

She sighed. "You're not getting what I meant, or what I mean. What I mean is that we — that all of us — live not just in separate worlds, but in separate universes. Every single person. We are all alone, Denis, all completely and utterly alone. That was what I experienced, and I don't want to experience it ever again. How do you think it feels to have you vanish from me for months on end? Do you think it's pleasant?"

"Come with me," he offered. "You can live on the grounds too, do some of the sits."

"No," she stated, hard and certain. "Meditation is like LSD. It brings up those same feelings for me, Denis. Of being alone."

"I know," he said gently, "I know that feeling, Brenda. I know it better than most. You stumbled onto the truth, though. You did. It seems scary, because you're viewing it from the perspective of our small, battered egos. We come into this world naked and alone, and we leave the very same way. Everyone dies alone, Brenda, regardless of their power, gender, family size, or any other external fact. You can't take any of it with you — the money, the friendships, the memories, the experience, the wisdom, the laughter, the dreams, the fears — it *all* gets stripped away in death. It's all an illusion, and in that sense you are indeed completely alone. You saw that you are an individual drop of water, one of billions, all in their separate little sphere."

Brenda shook her head.

"There's a question in Zen," he said. "How do you keep a drop of water from evaporating off a rock?"

Brenda sighed, and shrugged.

"'You throw it into the sea.'" He blew. "What you saw was that you are a drop, and the ocean doesn't much notice the drops. It's just too big. But you're missing the central point — which is *you're the ocean*, Brenda, not the drop. You can't actually be separate from anything or anyone. It's as impossible as saying your arms and your legs aren't part of your body. You can say it, you can even believe it, but that doesn't mean it's true. We think we're these billions of separate drops of water, you see, but really we're the ocean they come from, and return to. We're the end, and the source. You felt alone because there is only One Mind, One God, One Truth, although we forget when we get lost in our egos, and it feels scary when seen from the tiny us. Don't you see that? Don't you see there is only one mind in this room *right now*?" Kelly's own realization, deeper than ever before, was flowing through him.

She looked away. "I don't know what you're talking about. Meditation is just boring, Denis."

Brenda stood and went to the stove, stirring the contents of a pot, her shoulders hunching forward. Kelly rose and moved behind her, reaching around her waist and lifting her shirt so that he could press his hands against her belly.

"I love you," he whispered in her ear. "It's okay that meditation and Buddhism aren't for you — I've never asked you to make them yours. But I need to do this, the same as I've always needed it. I would like to know I have your support, that you believe enough in me to let me go, and know that it will make me a stronger, better person."

Brenda turned around, her eyes large and wet and open. "You *are* a strong, good man. I don't need you to be any different than you are right now."

Kelly pulled her close, burying his face in the sweet smell of her hair. "But I need it," he whispered, tears surprising his cheeks, "I need it, Brenda. I need it."

"Why, Denis?"

Kelly's eloquent speech abandoned him, and he merely took Brenda's hand, and placed it on his heart.

During Kelly's 100-day retreat, he was able to get to know the monastery's abbot, Eido Shimano Roshi, much more intimately. Eido Roshi was an unparalleled meditation master who ran his Zendo with all the order and precision of a drill sergeant. His teaching style was very Zen — intense, brief, and unadorned with unnecessary lectures, concepts, flourishes, or emotion. In many ways he seemed the opposite of the wild and unpredictable Trungpa, although Kelly did notice that Roshi's attention seemed to flicker when attractive women crossed his line of sight.

Kelly knew that Eido Roshi viewed him as a typical American male, an ignorant barbarian, but through the hundred-day sit Kelly called on his inner warrior to maintain an impeccable presence. Rinzai Zen required that the practitioner not move at all once the meditation bell was rung — no scratching, no adjusting, no moving a numb leg out from under the body. One took their seat in silence, as a warrior, and resolved to face whatever arose without turning away, without letting one's attention wander. Physical pain, emotional discomfort, and intellectual boredom were all faced in stillness and without reaction. The training was simple: if you could stay present on the cushion to whatever arose, even as you passed 16 hours of meditation a day, you were training yourself to stabilize your insight and be able to bring it into your turbulent, changing life. You could face whatever arose in your life without giving into the impulse to turn away, to minimize your suffering. You could, as Swami G might say, finally be able to practice *what is*.

The hundred-day Rinzai training was about having the courage to stay present to whatever your mind and body threw at you, to resist the urge to turn from pain and turn it into a mental and emotional concept — suffering. It asked the practitioners to face their discomfort as merely data coming from the senses, and to face their emotional and intellectual discomfort the same way. The practice was designed to teach equanimity, or self-control and awareness, no matter what arose in life — pleasure, pain, boredom, jealousy, anger, lust, longing, sadness. It was designed to interrupt the habitual impulse that we all have as humans — to turn from pain and toward pleasure as fast as we can, a practice that in the long run leads to greater ignorance and suffering.

The practitioners were asked to sit with the koan, or question: "Does a dog have Buddha nature?" and to concentrate on the response: "Mu!" This koan is designed to give the meditator the experience of One Mind or No Mind.

Kelly felt like he had been born for this kind of training. Thirty days into the retreat he developed a terrible head cold that caused his nose to run constantly. Many of the other men and women, when sick, would excuse themselves for a few days until they recovered their health more fully, but Kelly showed up with two tissues. He took his seat and twisted the tissues into a kind of a tampon, jamming one into each nostril. With white tissue paper jutting out of his nose he took his seat, breathing through his mouth. Nothing would cause him to give up his seat, especially not a head full of snot and a pounding sinus headache. He did this for several days, until the cold began to subside, as immobile on his cushion as if he had been cast in bronze.

Eido Roshi made no comment about this demonstration of resolve, determination, and innovation, but Kelly was beginning to realize that little escaped the old master's attention. Kelly was a barbarian, it was true, but he was also a warrior who had little in his life or in his mind that he feared. At the end of the retreat, Eido Roshi gave Kelly the informal nickname of *Charus*, thinking that Kelly's name was Charles Stephens and knowing virtually nothing of Kelly's true life. *Charus* came from Eido Roshi's inability to pronounce "Charles," so he converted Kelly's name into something he could pronounce.

"IT'S YOUR BIRTHDAY," BRENDA SAID ONE DAY. "THIRTY-SIX years on this planet. I've got a surprise for you." She blindfolded Kelly, led him outside, and put him into a limousine. They drove for a half hour. Then the car stopped and the door opened, letting in a terrific sound. Brenda slid the blindfold down. They were standing on a tarmac and a small, chartered jet was in front of him, the pilot smiling and standing next to the plane.

"What the hell?" Kelly asked, turning to Brenda.

"Happy birthday, baby," she said. "Come on."

The two of them were flown to St. Bart's. When they arrived they were taken by another limousine to a resort. Eight of their closest friends had also flown in to celebrate Kelly's birthday in style.

As the party hit its stride, Kelly was leaning over an old friend, Anna, whose large brown eyes seldom were off him. As she and Kelly talked, they kept touching each other's arms, stomachs, and necks. The party went until the sun came up, and at last everyone had gone back to their own apartments, except for Anna. Brenda and Kelly sat on their couch looking out into the dawn, and Brenda leaned into him. "How was your birthday?" she asked.

"My God," he responded, putting his arm around her. "It was the best one I've ever had." They heard the bathroom door open, and Kelly's head turned to see Anna emerging.

"You like her?"

"Well, yeah," Kelly grinned. "I mean, what's not to like?"

Brenda snuggled further into him. "Well, she's been celibate for about a year now. She dated a whole bunch of assholes in a row, and just doesn't really trust men. But she likes you, and she trusts you. I spoke to her — she wants to be with you."

"She does?" Kelly felt his heart beat faster.

"She does," Brenda repeated, nestling further into him.

"What do you think about that?"

"I think it's your birthday," she said, and looking down he caught her smile. "You should have whatever you want."

"Okay," Kelly blurted, almost before Brenda had finished speaking. "You want to join us?"

"No, baby. This is a gift for you. Not a gift for us to share." She sat up and looked him in the eye. "Happy birthday." Brenda, who was topless and wearing only a pair of tight shorts, stood and met Anna by the bathroom door. Trying not to stare, Kelly saw them conspiring and giggling as Anna blushed deeply. Brenda brought Anna over and directed her onto the couch next to Kelly. She then kissed him deeply.

"Have fun," she whispered, padding off on bare feet to the spare bedroom.

Kelly took Anna to the master bedroom. As he began to make love to her, Brenda put on soothing music for the two of them. He and Anna made love passionately and beautifully, and their moans filled the house. When Kelly arose late in the morning, he walked naked from the bedroom to the kitchen, and found that Brenda had cut fruit for both him and Anna and left it on a tray. Kelly went into their spare bedroom and found Brenda curled up in the bed, sleeping soundly, and he kissed her check before returning with the fruit to the master bedroom. Kelly fed Anna fruit and served her juice before making love to her again. She left in the early afternoon.

"You weren't jealous," Kelly asked Brenda later in the day, "knowing we were having sex only twenty feet from you?"

Brenda shrugged. "Sure I was. But I love you. Jealousy is all about me — love is all about you. If you truly love it, you can truly give it away, right? Because it's not about you anymore. If you want her, I want you to be happy, and you're not my possession, Denis. I can't keep you. Besides, it was a birthday you'll never forget."

"Right," he managed, astounded at the profundity of her teaching. Brenda, who knew nothing of Zen or Buddhism or Eastern philosophy, had just uttered a more profound truth than he'd ever heard fall from the mouths of the roshis or lamas he knew.

"Do you know how much you mean to me?" he asked, and when Brenda smiled he took her into his arms.

Two months later Brenda approached Kelly when he returned from a morning jog. His morning ritual was to rise at 5:30, sit for 45 minutes, take an hour run, and have breakfast at 7:15. He was just sitting down, a large bowl of fruit and yogurt in front of him, a towel around the back of his neck.

"Hey honey," Brenda said, kissing him. She sat down, her expression telling him she wanted to talk, but wasn't sure how to begin. He smiled to himself, taking a few large spoonfuls of fruit mixed with yogurt, and watched Brenda's mind work itself around.

"What's on your mind, sweetie?" he offered.

She laughed. "That obvious?" she said, surrendering. "I met an art dealer last night. He wants to meet up with me again tonight ...."

Kelly cocked an eyebrow at her. "And you want to fuck him?"

"Maybe, maybe not," she laughed, "But maybe, yeah. You know him, actually. Mark."

"Yeah, I know that guy," he agreed. He felt a contraction of jealousy arise deep inside his stomach, sliding up his esophagus and into the back of his throat. "He's good-looking all right. And rich, sophisticated, educated." Kelly forced a smile. In other words, Mark had some of the things that Kelly didn't, namely a deep knowledge of fine arts, music, and culture. Kelly was more the self-taught philosopher with rough-hewn good looks. Mark, by contrast, was much more of a groomed man — formally educated at good schools, he reflected the most avant-garde opinions on art and art theory. His perfect eyebrows sat above clear, sharp eyes and clear skin, and he wore only the most fashionable clothing.

Brenda was intensely focused on him, watching as he ruminated.

"If it's not okay ...." she began.

"No, no," Kelly said, surprising himself, "I want you to. I want you to enjoy it — to enjoy him." Brenda came around the counter and threw her arms around him. "I love you," she whispered.

It was edgy, he had to admit. With most of the other men she'd been involved, Kelly had never felt very threatened. He had, after all, money, power, influence, a natural athleticism, and a fearless personality. This guy, though, had some of the things that he self-consciously lacked.

That night Brenda went out on her date with Mark, and Kelly considered what he should do. Certainly he didn't want to dwell on what was happening, but he didn't want to run from it, either. He ended up on their couch watching a ball game, something that partially held his interest. He was very surprised to hear the door open at 11 p.m. and, looking over the couch, saw Brenda stroll in.

"Hey hon," he said, feigning disinterest. "You forget something? Date going okay?"

"No," she said, plopping her purse on the counter and taking off a shawl.

Kelly turned fully around. "You're not back for the *night*, are you?"

She shook her head, coming around and sitting down next to him, kicking off her shoes. "Yes, I'm back for the night."

"Oh, this is too delicious," Kelly said, smiling. "What happened?"

"We had a nice dinner — his knowledge of wine is as exhaustive as his knowledge of art. And I admit, I began to think that any man that learns so easily must have learned how to be one hell of a lover. So I let him know I wanted to go back to his house."

"And?" Kelly was sitting forward.

"And I fucked him," Brenda said, bluntly. "And he was *terrible*. Dull, predictable, and no staying power." She lowered her eyes coyly. "Nothing like the treatment I get at home."

Kelly laughed and stood up. "Okay, darling. Come on," he said, taking her hand. "Let's see if we can't put things right." He took her to their bedroom and made love to her. Afterward Brenda, satisfied and smiling, breathed, "*That's* what I'm talking about."

CHAPTER 13

AN INSTITUTIONAL MAN, PART II

KELLY LIVED AS A FIRST-CLASS FUGITIVE, BUT HE AND Brenda were obviously unable to work since the last thing they wanted was a paper trail tied to their IDs. Four years into life on the run, their money, which had seemed infinite, was dwindling. Kelly knew he would need a substantial amount of that to pay legal fees and fines if he was arrested or turned himself in. It was time to find a legal way out.

Kelly had a prominent San Francisco criminal defense attorney, Mark Topel, representing him. Topel was a brilliant young lawyer who was as incredibly gifted at law as he was opinionated and sure of himself. He was more than a match for Kelly's outsized personality, and the two men worked well together. In late 1979, the San Francisco DA approached Topel and let him know he was ready to strike a deal. The DA was about to leave for private practice and he wanted Topel on his friend's list, as well as a conviction on Kelly so he could close out the case. Topel and the DA worked out the details together. For Kelly, who called Topel from pay phones, the news came as a huge surprise.

"Listen, Denis," Topel told Kelly on the phone, "The Feds are ready to deal."

Kelly took a deep breath. He was standing outside a small market outside of Woodstock. The moment of truth. "What do they want? Some kind of ...."

"You," Topel interrupted. "Plead guilty to conspiracy to manufacture LSD. Serve an eighteen-month sentence with good behavior, get out in sixteen and a fifty-K fine."

Kelly's eyes widened. "Sixteen months and fifty grand?"

"That's the deal."

"Are you kidding me?" Kelly looked around. He loved Woodstock, but his heart was in California, where it had always been. "Fifty grand and just over a year in the joint. That's what they offered?"

"That's what they offered," Topel replied, matter-of-factly.

"That's incredible!" He had been getting used to the idea that he might serve out the remainder of his life behind bars if caught. "Christ, Mark, how did you mange to pull this one off? I thought that the case hinged on...."

"Prosecutors," Topel interjected, "are much more practical fellas when they're about to step into their own private practice. He wants a conviction, wants it off the books. DEA wants a conviction — had an agent on your case die already. Case is getting cold. Everybody wins. So you're telling me yes?"

"Well," Kelly said, smiling, "if you'd stop interrupting me every two seconds, I would have been able to tell you that *yes*, I'm in."

Topel laughed. "I interrupt because I know what I'm doing, and because I'm charging your ass by the minute, so shut up and listen. I'll draw up the paperwork and let them know you're ready to play ball."

"Christ," Kelly breathed. "Does that mean I can come back into the open? That I can move back to San Francisco, open a school, and lead an open life again?"

"Yeah, you've really suffered these last few years, haven't you?"

Kelly laughed. "Well, you told me that running time is doing time, right?"

"Yup. So you've knocked five years off your sentence already. They'll deal. But don't do *anything* until we get a response *in writing*. When we have the paperwork locked away, I'll let you know. Clear?"

"Sure, sure," Kelly said, "But I can start to shut things down here? Prepare to move?"

"No," Topel said, "don't do anything yet. This is just the first step. We gotta get a lot of other steps into motion. Go take your lady out to celebrate, sure, but know that tomorrow I might call you and say the whole deal's off."

"Okay."

Topel hung up, and Kelly threw his arms into the air.

He jumped into his car and raced home.

"Brenda!" he nearly screamed, running into the house.

She was in the upstairs bedroom.

"Baby," he said, bursting into the room. "I just spoke to Mark Topel. We're close to getting a deal with the government. We might be able to *go home* soon."

Tears came to Brenda's eyes, and she threw her arms around Kelly. "Oh my God — you mean we might get to lead something more like a normal life?"

Kelly held her close, and grinned. "Well, as normal as you and I can get."

KELLY PROPOSED TO BRENDA NOT LONG AFTER THE GOOD news from Topel. She accepted, and they agreed that the marriage should happen after Kelly served his time, not before. It would give them both something to look forward to, and be an important symbol of their lives entering a new phase. They made plans to cut their connections in Woodstock and to start over in San Francisco.

Kelly spoke to Topel once again, who said the DEA was serious about settling, and it was now only a matter of weeks before they had a finished deal in writing. Kelly knew there was another important person who had to be told. He made the drive from Woodstock to the monastery Dai Bosatsu, and requested a meeting with Eido Roshi.

"Roshi," Kelly said, meeting him in his small office. He bowed.

"Charus," Eido replied. "Sit." He gestured toward a chair.

Kelly sat. "Roshi. I have something to tell you."

Eido Roshi nodded, sitting back and folding his hands across his lap. If he was eager to hear what came next, nothing in his face gave that away. The overhead lights gleamed off Roshi's shaved head, and his eyes were calm and steady.

"I've been living under an assumed name, Roshi — a fake name. I'm not Charles Stephens. I've been on the run this whole time from the federal government. I was a major manufacturer of LSD in California and in Oregon, and I've been living underground for the last five years. My real name is Denis Kelly. I've just made a deal that will allow me to return to San Francisco, serve a short sentence, and then I'll be a free man."

Eido Roshi, never one to be taken aback, simply nodded, his expression and body language not changing in the least. "How long you serve?" he asked.

"I'll likely serve sixteen months in prison, but I'm moving back to San Francisco for good. I'll fly out for sesshins and to continue my training under you."

Eido Roshi nodded. "Prison good place to practice," he noted.

KELLY FLEW BACK TO SAN FRANCISCO TO MEET WITH Mark Topel at his office. Topel was a striking man whose thick black hair and piercing eyes, combined with his sharp features and muscular body, gave him a slightly predacious look. He was dressed impeccably, and he smiled when he saw Kelly walk through the door.

"Good news," he said, right to business as always. He had a folder in front of him. "Got the deal I promised you. Eighteen months, sixteen with good behavior. Fifty-K fine."

"It's a great deal," Kelly said. "I broke the law. Actions have consequences, and I always knew I'd have to face the music some day. I can live with eighteen months."

Topel leaned back. "So the prosecutor and the DEA are happy. They tell the judge they recommend eighteen months and that you've agreed to the terms with no trial. The judge agrees, stomps his gavel, and then they set a sentencing date where the judge gives you the time the DA recommended. Everybody's happy, everybody wins. You serve your time and are out in sixteen months for good behavior. You will be a convicted felon," he cautioned. "Forever."

Kelly shrugged his shoulders. "Don't need to own a gun," he quipped, "I can live without voting, and I doubt I'll be going into the banking industry, so I don't think that's going to matter so much. So I'm free to move back into Marin, and to live out in the open under my real name?"

"Almost," the attorney said. "There's one more thing. You've been successfully on the run for over five years. To say you're a flight risk, in their minds, is a mild understatement. They want to secure a half-million dollar bond to ensure you don't run again."

"I'm nearly broke," Kelly said. "There's not much left — certainly not that much. I can pay the fine, and barely pay you, but after that I have nothing."

"You must have something? Come on, Kelly — all that drug money and you didn't buy anything nice for yourself?"

Kelly shook his head. "Unless you count fine Italian clothing, I don't own anything. Never did."

"Then you'll have to turn yourself in, and spend the pre-trial period in jail."

"How long is that?"

The attorney thought. "Could be a bit of a wait. Couple of months, at least. Maybe more, depending on about a million things."

Kelly shook his head again. "No. Sixteen months is enough. What are my other options?"

"Friends and family can put up bail for you. Houses can be leveraged, cars, loans taken out, IRAs, all kinds of stuff. As long as the government has all its money, it'll let you be a free man. But," Topel smiled, "they'll have you by the balls then. If the deal changes, and you run, the people who put up their houses and money will lose everything."

Kelly's eyes narrowed. "So don't let the deal change."

Topel nodded. "Never do, Kelly," he said dismissively. "Never do."

Over the next few months, a formal deal was secured. Kelly's parents put their home up for bond, and many of his more respectable friends put their homes on the line as well. In the end, Kelly cobbled together the half million dollars in assets to let him live in the open, as Denis Kelly, for the first time in over a decade. He and Brenda packed their modest belongings in Woodstock into a moving van, and made the trip back to San Francisco.

To celebrate both their return to the Golden State and their engagement, Brenda and Kelly decided to have a party. Many of Kelly's old friends, including Marty, Johnny, and Michael, were invited, along with some of the old Order of the Golden Frog family members.

As a new decade came into view, Kelly and Brenda were leading a life much different than the heyday of the 1970s. The fine suits, sports cars, motorcycles, wild parties, and exotic trips all over the world had given way to a more modest way of being in the world. The money that hadn't been spent was set aside for lawyer's fees and federal fines likely to be in excess of $50,000, so his and Brenda's lives reflected a new-found concern with budgeting, eating in, and economical getaways. Starting his new life and a new way of being, Kelly began teaching yoga and meditation while he awaited trial and sentencing. While he had always taught friends and associates, he was becoming a formal public teacher for the first time in his life.

Not long after they settled into their new home in Marin County, Kelly met Kim, a half-Japanese, half-Native American woman of boundless energy and shy sexuality, fluent in English and Japanese, and employed by a major Japanese state-run television company. She was also an expert potter and a chef, and was young and bright. With Brenda's blessing, she and Kelly became lovers.

Kim became Kelly's mistress, moving from an occasional lover to a steady one, and although Brenda was aware of the growing strength and the intensity of their relationship, she said nothing. She and Kelly had, after all, been in an open relationship since the very beginning, which on the whole had brought them closer together.

For much of human history, marriage had been more about politics and power than about love; affairs were for passion while marriage was more functional, designed to sire children and improve social status. There were unwritten rules around mistresses that had long been in place: The married man would provide financially for his mistress, would never bring the mistress to the same social circle or events where his wife would normally be expected, and would never allow the mistress to be in the same room as his wife. In other words, there was a hierarchy of status, and the wife sat at the top of it. These were simple rules that preserved the complicated social dance of marriage, mistress, and status. Open relationships were a little different, but the rules weren't much changed. Kelly managed to step all over them with a single move.

Brenda's back was turned as she cleaned some dishes, and Kelly sat down at the kitchen table, having just returned from a run. Their engagement party was only ten days away.

"So," Brenda said, not turning around, "I hear that Kim is invited to our party on Friday." Her tone, matter-of-fact, gave away nothing.

Kelly took a few swallows from a glass of water. "Yup. It's a big party, and we're pretty much inviting everyone we've ever known, so I thought that inviting her wouldn't be a problem." Kelly could feel a heaviness between them, a thickening of the emotional air.

"I see," Brenda said, cleaning the last of the glasses. She turned and leaned back against the counter, her t-shirt an inch above the waist of her jeans, exposing a sliver of muscular stomach. She pushed her hair off her shoulders. "And you don't see a problem with that?"

Kelly bristled. "Well, no," he flashed, a red flare shooting off in his mind and warning him to slow down and pay attention. He pushed on, however. "No," he stated, more strongly. "I mean, you know about her. She's been a part of my life for a while now, and this is a big night for us. I just wanted to share it with everyone who is close to us, that's all."

Brenda's arms folded themselves across her chest. "I see," she said. "The fact that she is your mistress and would be at *our* engagement party doesn't create a problem?"

"Well," Kelly stalled, feeling his face flush.

"It might be called a conflict of interest," Brenda noted, "in some circles. Or just unwise in other ones."

"Oh come on," Kelly dismissed. He got up and walked over to Brenda, sliding his hands around the small of her back. She had gone rigid and cold as a statue. "You're the one I love, Brenda. You're the one I'm going to marry. Kim knows that. She cares about both of us, and just wants to be here to celebrate our big day. It's not a conflict of interest." His arms pulled Brenda in, hoping to crack the armor. She allowed herself to be held, but remained aloof and distant and withdrawn.

Kelly let her go. "Okay, then? Come on. It's our *engagement* party. I'm pretty sure Kim has the idea!" He smiled, and Brenda looked away.

The next morning Kelly found her sitting, with dark circles under her blue eyes, at the kitchen table, staring at an engagement ring that sat in the middle of the table. Kelly picked it up.

"What's this?"

Brenda sighed. "I called off the engagement party, Denis," she said, not raising her eyes.

"You did what?"

"Called it off," she repeated, unnecessarily. As always the case with Brenda, there was no storm, drama, or emotional outburst, just a steady and solid statement of what she felt.

"Did you even think to talk to me about it?" Kelly said angrily. "Are you fucking serious?"

"I did try and talk to you about it, yesterday. But you weren't listening." There was no bitterness in her voice. "It's okay," she said. "I think the engagement was a bit rushed. We have a lot of moving pieces in our lives, including keeping you out of prison. The engagement and marriage should probably wait until we settle those things, until we can make it more of a priority. A choice and not a reaction."

"Brenda," Kelly began, feeling his equanimity waning beneath the flush of his face. He could not bear the thought of her suffering all night, as the circles under her eyes implied, or the thought that he might have been the cause of it. Shame welled up deep within him, and he raged against it. "Come on. Don't be like that. You don't want Kim to come, don't worry about it. Forget it. She's off the list. I told you that."

"That's hardly the point, Denis," she said, looking at him in her stubborn, German way. It wasn't enough, nothing he could now say could change her mind, and he knew it.

"I want something permanent," she whispered, "something that I know will last. I need that, Denis."

"Permanent?" Kelly flared, "*permanent*? There is nothing permanent in the world, Brenda — not you, not me, not *this*," he indicated the apartment with a sweep of his arms. "Not one thing in the whole goddamn world is permanent." The fire and passion of his eyes sought hers, muted and reserved. But Brenda refused to raise them to his challenge. She merely shook her head once more.

Feeling impotent and enraged, Kelly stormed out of the kitchen. He changed into his jogging clothes and headed out the door for a long run, flying through the streets with clenched teeth, moving as if death itself was stalking him. A very old story was chasing him, threatening to break into his conscious mind — that he was selfish, worthless, unwise, hurtful, and worthy only of his own shame and self-loathing. He pushed himself furiously through the streets, feet pounding into the pavement.

Under more normal circumstances, he might have been able to slow things down, to take some air, and in that expansiveness gain perspective. He might have been able to climb inside of Breda's mind to see how she was obviously and understandably hurt by his choice to invite Kim, and how that had triggered an old story starting with his mother, and Grace. But the situation was far from normal, and Kelly had to focus on his legal strategy for a rapidly approaching court date.

A few weeks later Kelly, Brenda, and Topel went to the courthouse again, this time to be arraigned. U.S. District Court Judge Stanley Weigel, a 73-year-old judge known for his fair-mindedness and general soft touch in the courtroom, presided. The prosecutor, DA, and the judge were supposed to be in total agreement on the sentencing, and Kelly's attorney had signed off on the deal. The arraignment was really little more than a formality, where the judge would rubber-stamp what had already been resolved to everyone's satisfaction, saving the court money and time and aggravation.

Everyone in the courtroom was then startled when Judge Weigel, for some unknown reason, rejected the deal, a very rare occurrence. He told the stunned DA and defense that there would be no deals in his court, and that Kelly would have to go to trial. Enraged, Topel nearly took the DA's head off after the hearing, but the DA was just as shocked.

"Word of this gets out," he told Topel and Kelly, "my reputation is shit. How the hell am I supposed to offer people deals if the goddamn judge won't go along with *my* recommendation?"

He helped Kelly arrange for the case to be moved to the Oregon Federal court, since Kelly had manufactured LSD in both California and Oregon. Kelly drew the Honorable James M. Burns, who told the Oregon DA that there would be no deal in his court either — they would need to plead their case to him, and he and he alone would decide sentencing. This wasn't good, but there was nothing that could be done now except to run, and Kelly wasn't willing to do that.

Judge Burns' reputation was as a tough but fair judge, and Topel told Kelly he was facing five years in prison if the judge rejected the original offer presented in San Francisco: All other charges would be dropped in exchange for Kelly's guilty plea to one federal charge of conspiracy to manufacture LSD, for which Kelly would serve 18 months. It was anybody's guess what might happen.

Kelly and Brenda drove to the sentencing in Portland, and Topel met them at court. The DA presented the evidence against Kelly, which included not only the testimony of all his former "family" members, but also Kelly's own confession. He noted that Kelly had an unusual background, including many long years spent studying Buddhism, his dedication to the practice of yoga and the Kanzeon Zen yoga school he was running.

"Denis Kelly," Judge Burns said.

"Yes sir," Kelly responded, standing, his heart pounding.

"You are hereby charged with one federal count of conspiracy to manufacture a Schedule 1 narcotic, lysergic acid diethylamide. How do you plead?"

"Guilty, your honor."

"So be it. This court finds you guilty of one count of conspiring to manufacture LSD. You are hereby sentenced to 24 months in a federal penitentiary."

Kelly turned back to look at Brenda, who looked relieved it wasn't five years.

"For the record," Judge Burns continued, "I want to note that I don't think it will do you or society one bit of good to put you behind bars. But due to your notoriety, and to not discourage the agents who pursued you and the substantial investment of time and resources dedicated to your capture, I feel obligated to give you this sentence." The judge looked down at Kelly, who stood with his hands folded in front of him. "Do you have anything you would like to say, Mr. Kelly?"

"Yes, your honor," Kelly responded, "I would like to note that LSD-25 was able to change the hearts of thousands of people for the better, including me, and that getting it out into the world was something that I considered a service to humanity. The exposure to lysergic acid is itself a spiritual...."

Mark Topel stomped on Kelly's foot. "Aaand ..." Kelly said, glancing over at the glowering Topel, "*and* that's it, your honor."

A two-year sentence meant Kelly would serve 20 months with good behavior. An additional half-year over what he had hoped he might receive.

Brenda and Kelly had, after the cancellation of their engagement party, not brought the subject up again.

Not long after the verdict he was sitting at home, on the couch, and watched as Brenda came in from the grocery store. Carrying a single bag, she set it down on the counter, sighing, and the curve of her long and graceful neck in the light of the fading afternoon was almost unbearable. Her breasts pressed against her shirt as she moved back and forth from the pantry, and Kelly got off the couch and approached her, wrapping his arms tightly around her waist. They made love next to the apples and bananas and cans of tuna fish spilled onto the counter, and Brenda's reserve came unhinged as an orgasm caused her to shudder against Kelly's chest.

Afterwards, she was dark and glum. "What am I going to do without you for 20 months?"

"It's a long time," Kelly admitted. He smiled, taking her hand in his. "It'll be the longest retreat I'll take in a long time, I can promise you that."

Brenda pulled away from him and, pulling her clothes back on, resumed putting away the groceries.

They had a huge costume party the night before Kelly was to report to prison, and he attended wearing the black-and-white stripes of a prisoner, pulling a plastic ball-and-chain behind him. As the party got into full gear, Kelly made sure he went from person to person, requesting that they not visit him in prison.

"Why not?" his old friend Johnny, dressed as a pirate, wanted to know. "Come on, Frank. It'll lift your spirits to see some of your old buddies in there."

"Bullshit it will," Kelly said. "The last thing I want is to see my old friends surrounded by cheap furniture that's bolted to the floors, with a bunch of toothless degenerates for company. I'll see you when I get out."

"Prison's making you grumpy," Johnny said, "and you haven't even set foot in it yet. So you want me to give you my word I'll stay away from you?"

"I do," Kelly said.

"No can do," Johnny said. "I hate to go against your wishes, Frank, but how am I supposed to gloat if I can't see you?"

The party went into the late hours, and Kelly, tired but happy, climbed into bed with Brenda as the sun rose. A few hours later, after a sumptuous breakfast, Brenda drove him to the minimum-security Pleasanton Federal Correctional Facility.

Brenda was clearly scared for him, but didn't want to say so. "You be careful in there," she said as they drove. "Don't let your mouth get away from you. Watch your back. Make a lot of friends as fast as you can."

"I'll be fine," Kelly consoled, not at all sure that he would be.

"I can't believe I'm driving you to prison," Brenda said.

Kelly sighed. "I always knew I'd have to pay the price for the life we lived, somehow. All and all, it's not so bad. Military service members get shipped overseas all the time, and sometimes their families don't see them for six months. At least you can come and see me at prison, as awful as that thought is." He considered. "And as much as I don't really want to see you there ... I mean, I want to see you, of course ... but Jesus, what an awful place to have to visit someone."

She followed the signs for the prison, located in a wide expanse of bright desert.

They drove into a parking lot and moved toward the front gates. The romantic in Kelly saw Brenda getting out and throwing her arms around him, and they would exchange powerful words of love and devotion. As the car came to a stop, he sat blinking in the bright morning sun. He looked over the many gates and fences, and imagined himself standing before them, looking back at Brenda. He imagined as she, slender and perfect, blonde hair illumined by the fierce sunlight, raised a hand in a wave, her perfection framed by the expanse of the white sand and blue sky.

He opened his door and put his feet onto the warm asphalt.

"Okay," Brenda said, still firmly seated behind the wheel. "I'll see you soon." She leaned across the seat and kissed Kelly's cheek. "Take care of yourself."

"I love you, baby," Kelly said, his voice wobbly.

"Me too," she said. Brenda was not one for excess emotionality or displays of overt sentimentality, which was, of course, part of what he loved the most about her.

Kelly got out and closed the door, and Brenda waved goodbye. The car moved slowly away, and in a few moments Kelly stood, alone, in the parking lot. He turned to face the prison.

Kelly was about to become an institutional man for the second time in his life.

FORTUNATELY FOR KELLY, PLEASANTON WAS AN EXPERImental federal prison that housed 200 men and 100 women. The prison was founded with the idea that the men and women in it should maintain their skills of non-criminal socialization while they were incarcerated — they should be ready to step back into society as soon as they were released. Because of this, its inmates were mostly non-violent first offenders like Kelly.

Every prisoner had his or her own room, was able to wear street clothes, had windows that looked out into the bright California sunshine and that opened a few inches for fresh air. There were tennis courts, a football field, and access to the outdoors. The idea was that by keeping new prisoners like Kelly active and feeling part of society, and helping long-serving prisoners to begin the process of adjusting back to the real world, the prison would help inmates better adjust to their lives when they were released. Kelly could hardly believe his luck.

Of course, as anyone with a brain could tell you, putting men and women in the same prison was a horrible idea, and the running joke was that the guards spent all their time "guarding the beaver," trying to prevent the prisoners from having sex in the closets, on the walkways, under the tables, or anywhere else they might get more than thirty seconds of uninterrupted time. In the bizarre model of prisons at that time, one inmate was given no extra time for stabbing a fellow male inmate, while another male inmate had his good time taken away and was sent back to a maximum security prison for having consensual sex with a female inmate.

And there were strange conspiracies, like the time Kelly was playing football with a co-ed team, and a couple wanted to have sex. The group ran the ball as far from the 300-pound guard as they could, and then formed a wall of people. The couple dropped to the ground and began to have sex.

"Hey!" the guard called, and began to run, very slowly, toward them. After stopping twice to catch his breath, he finally arrived only to find nothing out of the ordinary.

Kelly spent his days playing tennis and soccer and football, jogging, reading, and meditating. He got permission to set up a Body-Mind program, where he taught marathon running, Zen, and Astanga yoga. It helped Kelly refine his teaching skills with a unique blend of "students," for in prison everyone was trying to hustle someone somehow. Most of the people went through his program for the singular purpose of hoping it might reduce their sentence — they hung around just long enough to determine if it was having an effect on their time served and, if not, they left.

Brenda came to visit once a week, and his friends utterly ignored his request to never visit, so Kelly sometimes had more visitors than he knew what to do with. It was, he had to admit, very nice to socialize with his friends, and it didn't make him depressed or homesick, like he had feared. The only trouble was every single time he had a visitor, he would meet them in a common room and not behind glass. It was just the kind of nightmarish room he had imagined, where the plastic tables and chairs were bolted to the floor, the walls concrete, and the lighting harsh fluorescent. Because he was not separated from his guests, he had to be thoroughly strip-searched every time he went back into the population.

Big Tony was nearly always the man responsible for checking Kelly's body for drugs, knives, cigarettes, pills, or a thousand other contraband items. Tony was a thick-necked 28-year-old who wore his hair in a military cut, and whose barrel chest strained against his uniform at the shoulder, the chest, and most noticeably, the gut. His eyes were the dull blue of faded denim, strained and tired, and nearly lost in the folds of his large and fleshy face.

The drill was always the same: Kelly came back into the guardroom and stripped naked. With a penlight, Tony would check under Kelly's tongue, armpits, between his toes, and under his penis. Then Kelly would turn around, bend over, and spread his cheeks for a penlight inspection of his nether regions.

Big Tony and Kelly had gone through this drill about fifty times, and had an easy and friendly chemistry about it.

"Take off your clothes," Tony said through a fog of disinterest.

Kelly did as he was told, still immersed in his own thoughts.

"Tongue out," Tony managed, peering into Kelly's mouth and under his tongue with a flashlight. "Lift your dick up," came the next command. Tony looked like he was about to collapse into himself, and as Kelly lifted his penis up he saw Tony's jaw clenched so tightly the muscles were bulging from his temple all the way down to his neck. His nostrils flared as his breath came and went in shallow gasps. Tony stood an inch taller than Kelly, but his arms were the size of Kelly's legs, and the meaty fingers of his right hand kept fluttering over the handle of his nightstick.

"Bend over and spread your cheeks."

"Hey Tony," Kelly said, gently, bending completely over at the waist, his hands spreading himself wide. "Listen man, how many times have you looked at my asshole? Christ, man, I might be the prisoner, but you're the one serving time."

"Shut the fuck up, Kelly," Tony snapped, his voice quivering. "None of your fucking Zen bullshit today. Stand back up. Put your fucking clothes back on."

Kelly dressed slowly. "Isn't there anything else you can do, man?" offered Kelly. "Some other profession? What do you want with prison life, man? It's obviously toxic for you, but you're still a young guy."

Tony's fluttering hand settled firmly on the top of his nightstick.

"Hey man," Kelly said quickly, "I just see a brother in pain is all. Don't mean any disrespect. I'll shut up," he added.

"Fuck," the guard said and, to Kelly's astonishment, sat down, head in hands, and began to sob. "Man, I ain't got no choice. Got two kids and a wife. Only got a high school education. Nothing else. I ain't qualified to do nothin', failed to get into the police academy cause I'm too fucking stupid, and can't get out from under the hole I'm in to make somethin' of myself. Fuck — I don't wanna look under dicks and between ass cheeks for the rest of my life..." He let out a few wracking sobs.

Kelly, now dressed, sat down next to him, and put his hand on Tony's hulking shoulder.

"Hey man — sometimes it's darkest just before the dawn, right?"

"How do you do it?" the guard asked.

"Do what?"

"Keep a sense of humor. You're in fucking *prison*, but you always bust my balls, always make jokes, usually make me and all the other guards laugh. You seem *happy*. How the fuck is that possible? You're on the fucking *inside*. Ain't *nobody* happy on the inside unless they're crazy. And you ain't crazy, neither. But you're right — I'm the one serving time. I'd fuckin' beat you to death for sayin' that if you weren't so right."

"We're all serving time," Kelly said. "All of us. Don't kid yourself. But some of us have learned to relate to it differently. My life sucks, Tony. I'm in prison. My girl is fucking another guy."

Tony gave him a look. "That pretty thing that visits you?"

"That's right. My fiancée. It hurts bad sometimes. She leaves, and goes and gets to fuck him, and I get to go to an eight by ten cell and hold my dick in my hand." Kelly took in a deep breath of air. "I'm losing her," he admitted. "Right in front of my face. Ain't nothing I can do about it. Nothing 'cept tell her how I feel about her."

Tony's eyes welled up again.

"Prison sucks. I can't change that, Tony, but I can change what I do with it. I think any day spent alive is a blessing, be it in prison or diving off the coast of Hawaii. Look at this — you and me sittin' here talking 'bout life — this is the tits, man."

A smile came to Tony's thick face for a moment. For the second time inside of five minutes Tony astounded him.

"Will you help me?"

Kelly's eyebrows shot up involuntarily. After a moment's pause, Kelly grinned. "Well, here's what we can do. First, we'll start with the way you think, and then we'll get to the way you feel. You like to read?"

"Fuck no," Tony said.

"Me either. Hate books almost as much as I hate writers. But I got a few books for us book-haters. You might like' em. And listen — I'll be outta here before too long. You should come and train with me on the outside. I can't help you, Tony, but I can give you everything you need to help yourself."

Tony checked his watch. "Come on, Kelly," he said, "I gotta get you back."

"I'll bring the books by the guard station," Kelly offered.

"Sure," Tony said, then thought better of it. "Actually, just bring 'em with you the next time your old lady comes to visit. I'll take 'em from there."

"You got it." Kelly knew it wouldn't look good for a guard to be getting chummy with a prisoner. Tony became a kind of informal student of Zen for Kelly's remaining time in prison.

Mark Topel suspected that Judge Burns had been intrigued by Kelly's file, which showed time spent in a Zen monastery, a serious yoga practice, a long history of teaching, and a strong desire to help people who were suffering. So seven months into Kelly's sentence, he requested what is known as a "review of sentence." This was very unusual given the relative short length of the sentence.

Normally a judge would laugh off such a request, but Topel was the top defense attorney in San Francisco for a reason. He knew that Judge Burns would likely shake his head at the boldness of the request, but also suspected the judge would have to peek at Kelly's record out of curiosity.

And that's exactly what happened. What Judge Burns saw was that Kelly had become a model prisoner. He had started a yoga/Zen/physical embodiment school in prison, was counseling other prisoners, and had several positive notes from guards.

And Judge Burns did something virtually unheard of: He ordered Denis Kelly's immediate release, surprising even Topel.

"Immediate" is, of course, a relative term in prison bureaucracies, and when the paperwork came through, the prison staff assumed that Kelly had snitched on a fellow prisoner behind all of their backs. That was the only way they could figure he could get a short sentence reduced even further. Since they figured he had gone around their backs, they decided he should be punished. The warden let Kelly know his paperwork was almost through, and that he would be a free man anytime. Weeks dragged by, and the warden and his staff took great pleasure in watching Kelly's growing anger at the repeated delays, at making the Zen guy lose his cool. Kelly unwittingly played into their hands, letting himself grow furious and spiteful. Every few days he was called into the warden's office to be told his release would be delayed "just a couple more days," putting him into a purgatory of hope. He stopped sleeping, stopped practicing, and grew increasingly miserable. Time slowed to a crawl, and every night Kelly went to bed dreaming of being released, only to watch the next day drag itself along one agonizing minute at a time.

One month after the order of his "immediate" release, Kelly found himself sitting on the concrete floor of his cell, looking at the light reflecting off the metal of the bed frame and the seatless toilet. Though the window he could see the moon in the distance, and she seem so free, so otherworldly, and he allow himself to sink into the blackness of his longing. Over a long and sleepless night, he realized how much he resented the warden, the government, the U.S. Army — these systems that seemed to abuse and repress him.

An hour or so before dawn, Kelly had an illumination: He could not think or feel his way out of prison. He was trapped, literally, and no amount of will could change that. He thought of Eido Roshi, and how he had said prison would be a good place to practice. Kelly was in the strange land of insomnia, unable to be fully awake or asleep, and so he unfurled his blue prayer rug and sat, pulling his feet into full lotus position. He faced the moon framed by the window, and brought his attention to the moment the way he had been trained to do.

He struggled amid the turmoil of his emotions and thoughts and desires, their fire burning upwards in his chest. Through the thick glass he could see the stars boiling and twisting in the night air, their passion stretching tens of thousands of light years in every direction, right through the darkness of the night sky and into his prison cell. The moon, her face one-quarter hidden, took her cool light closer to the horizon, and as the dawn shimmered across the night sky, Kelly broke free.

He was suddenly inside of one of the Buddha's teachings: *attachment* was part of what imprisoned people. Attachment kept you from experiencing *this* moment — it kept the mind caught in an idea and disconnected from what was actually occurring. Attachment was as much at the root of human suffering as anything, and it was just that — attachment — that had been making Kelly miserable. The truth was he had no power in prison. It was up to the warden to release him whenever he saw fit, and there was nothing Kelly could do. Topel had filed complaints, spoken to the judge, and done everything he could, but it was the warden's prison, and the warden claimed the paperwork had been lost.

Kelly experienced his hope of being released as an attachment, and in that sense similar to the hope that one might find happiness through marriage, or wealth, or having a certain kind of house, or through a family, or by accomplishment — hope, seen through the lens of attachment, was a purgatory that placed happiness in an imagined future. But all Kelly had was the moment, and in that moment he was sitting barefooted in full lotus position inside of a federal prison. That was what arose, and the only power he had was whether he would accept the unfolding of the moment, or would fight it with the prison of hope.

Kelly's body was imprisoned by the federal government and by a petty and cruel warden. His spirit, though, was imprisoned by *his* choice alone. He was free, unbounded and unlimited, and nothing and no one could disturb the equanimity of his deeper, truer self. He might be in pain, but he was choosing to suffer.

After that morning, Kelly took the only course that made any sense: complete surrender. He saw the pain of the men who were taking delight in his torture, and he opened his heart to their suffering. He kept teaching those, like Big Tony, who wanted to learn from him, and he practiced nearly every moment of every day.

It took a long time for the game to grow old with the warden and his staff. Kelly no longer seemed to care that he was being held in prison for no reason, but they were convinced they could break the Zen guy, could make him lose his temper like he had in the beginning. But they could not, and nothing and no one could get to Kelly anymore. He took joy in the regularity of prison life, in being fed and clothed without any effort, in not having to think about how he spent his days, and he felt tremendous compassion and love for all those he came across, especially the warden.

Three full months after his order for an "immediate" release, two months after his breakthrough and surrender to the moment, and eleven months after he was incarcerated, Denis Kelly was released from Pleasanton Federal Correctional Facility, his debt to society paid in full.

○

BRENDA PICKED UP KELLY AT PRISON, AND IT SEEMED TO him that everything was right where it had been before his incarceration. Brenda was loving in her own intense way, and they spent a few weeks reconnecting with each other

Kelly was a free man but a broke one, and he made plans to reopen his Zen Yoga school to start making money as fast as possible. A new life began to come into view that didn't involve LSD or running from the law. A few months out of prison, Brenda found Kelly reading in the back room. She came in and sat across from him.

Over a decade after they had met, Brenda was as beautiful as the first day he had seen her. As she sat down she sighed, and her blue eyes held sadness, and resolve. The symmetrical arch of her eyebrows seemed exaggerated into long ovals. He lay his magazine in his lap and looked at her, feeling his pulse quicken and his breath grow shallower.

"You're going to keep pursuing Zen, is that correct?"

Kelly nodded.

"How far?" She sat with her legs spread, hands clasped together between them.

Kelly shrugged. "To the end, I suppose," he said.

"What does that mean?"

Kelly exhaled. "Until I wake up, Brenda, for good. Until I'm free of *this* prison." He tapped his head.

"Why?"

"It's something I've sought ever since I was a toddler. And each year I get a little closer to being able to stay in *this* moment. But I keep falling back asleep."

Brenda's lips tightened for a moment. "I told you before that never in my wildest dreams did I expect to be the minister's wife. And that's what I'd be — the roshi's wife."

Kelly shook his head. "Not the same thing, dear. Not by a long, long way."

Brenda, though, didn't respond. "I'm leaving, Denis. I need to make my own way in the world. You've supported me all these long years, and I'm grateful for it. You've been so strong, in so many ways. I've never been as close to any human being as I have been to you."

"What?" Kelly managed, sitting upright and letting the magazine he was reading topple to the floor. "What?" he repeated, unable to believe his ears.

"It's time for me to go," she stated. "To live a life on my own. To be my own woman."

"Come on, Brenda," he said, his voice breaking. "It doesn't have to be like this. Christ, I'm out of prison only a few months."

"I can't stay, Denis," she said.

"So live somewhere else," Kelly said, surprising himself. "Just stay with me," he choked. "Just don't leave, Brenda. Not now. Not after a decade together. Not when it's all about to get so interesting ...."

She cut into his sentence. "I need to not be surprised anymore by life. By the craziness, by the impulsiveness, by the passion, by this endless thing that drives and whips you into a fury. I can't understand it. I understand you, but I can't understand this *thing*, this madness, that pushes you."

Brenda raised her eyes to her lover.

"*You do understand it*," he said, barely above a whisper but with all the intensity of a scream. "You understand it all too well. You just turn from it, and I turn into it. But you know it, Brenda, you know it better than most."

She shook her head. The heat of his words was thrown onto her face in a slight flush of the skin, but his Brenda, when she made up her mind like this, was more solid than iron. She was gone, and there was nothing Kelly could do or say that would stop her. While he had been able to endure the indignity of prison with poise and insight, it was thoughts of Brenda that had helped him to remain so strong.

"It's not about *you*, Denis. This is about *me*. About what I need to do, where I need to grow, how I need to find my strength and my own view. The truth is we're heading in two different directions. I didn't want to see it before, but I see it now, clearly."

Kelly felt the tears and the muted rage of his being — always present, always repressed — boil from the pit of his groin up through his stomach and into his heart. The last thing he ever wanted to be was like his father — full of anger, violent and reactive — so he stuffed the anger that arose and in its place felt a deep and pervasive anxiety. Kelly didn't know if he believed in soulmates, but Brenda was as close to what that must be as he could imagine. They had lived in the lap of luxury, traveled the world together, dined at the finest restaurants, run from the Feds, made love in a thousand different places, partied with Alan Watts and the Grateful Dead and a dozen other cultural icons, bared their souls, loved and lived and lost. Each of them had once dared to be utterly naked and vulnerable, and always found the other willing to provide cover and protection. And now that Kelly was at long last clear on what he was here to really do, she was rejecting his path ... she had followed him everywhere, but would not follow him on the path to Awakening.

His lip trembled and, with a lowered head, he reached out and took her cold hand in his warm one, letting the sobs take him away with them. When he finally looked up, she was gone. She was physically present, but her strong will and stronger determination meant she had already left the relationship, had already left him even though she sat only a foot away. Kelly felt his powerlessness, and his rage spilled forth. The pain was too great, and his heart felt like it might burst in his chest.

His face contorted in a spasm of contraction and anger and, reaching out, he slapped Brenda across the face. His eyes were fierce and his body tense, and he leaned in, daring Brenda to show him something, to let loose her fury, to attack him, to scream and yell and abuse him. He wanted to feel her own anger at being slapped, wanted to know that she was still in the room, still bound to him. Brenda's blue eyes blazed for only a moment before sadness consumed them. She lowered her reddening cheek. After a moment, she rose and quietly left the room to pack her things.

Brenda was gone. The days afterward were far more difficult than prison, and Kelly wandered their apartment, lost. In the quietness there, a truth began to take shape in his mind.

He realized that he had struck her out of anger, out of passion, but the anger masked something deeper and more perverse: He was afraid. Afraid of being alone, of being abandoned, of not being good enough, of losing the best thing that had happened to him. He felt guilt for his arrogance of bringing Kim to his own engagement party and over not being more responsive to Brenda. He cared so deeply for her, loved her so completely, that he would have gladly given her his life. He would have given her anything except the one thing she was wise enough not to ask: that he give up Buddhism, for that would mean giving up more than his life. She loved him too much to ask such a thing, and so she left him with all the dignity and grace she had demonstrated through their years together.

Somehow out of his deep caring and his fear, violence had emerged. Rather than sit across from Brenda and tell her he was terrified she was leaving him, that he cared for her more than any other living human being, rather than share that truth and invite her to meet him in that place of vulnerability, he had slapped her. He had become violent rather than expose his heart, and his fear. What sort of insanity could have driven him so far away from the depth of his true feelings?

Kelly brooded over what had happened with Brenda for weeks, but time provided little in the way of answers. When he at last picked up the phone to call her, it was to offer a simple message.

She picked up the receiver and they exchanged greetings.

Kelly listened to the sound of her breath for a long moment before speaking. He closed his eyes, and his grip grew tight on the receiver.

"I understand," he said, simply.

"I knew you would," came the response. "You know me too well not to." She then added, "I too understand. I love you."

"I love you too."

"Goodbye, Denis."

"Goodbye, Brenda."

Patrick and Denis Kelly, with their mother, mid-1940's

Denis Kelly, AKA Frank, mid-1970's

Denis with friends, the night before going to prison, 1980.

Rock climbing in the mid-1980's.

Kelly's daughter Vanessa, 1982.

Ashtanga Yogi, backbend, 1983.

Yoga, 1983.

Denis Kelly, now "Jun Po" Denis Kelly after becoming a Zen priest. 1984.

Jun Po Denis Kelly after being ordained, on the streets of NYC. 1984.

Jun Po Denis Kelly, Zen priest, 1984.

Kelly with his mother, mid-1990's.

Jun Po Denis Kelly receives "inka", becoming the 83rd Patriarch of Rinzai Zen. With his teacher, Eido Shimano Roshi. 1992.

Jun Po Roshi with the men of the ManKind Project, late 1990's.

George Burch, Dai En Hi Fu, receives "inka" from Jun Po and is elevated to "roshi", mid-2000's.

Jun Po Kando Denis Kelly Roshi, 2011
Photo Credit: DarrinHarrisFrisby.com

Jun Po Kando Denis Kelly Roshi, 2011
Photo Credit: DarrinHarrisFrisby.com

PART THREE

"*If some are still dominated by their former bad habits, and yet can teach by mere words, let them teach …. For perhaps, by being put to shame by their own words, they will eventually begin to practice what they teach.*"
— *St. John Climacus (John of the Ladder), seventh century, from* The Ladder of Divine Ascent

"*If you are going through hell, keep going.*"
— *Winston Churchill*

CHAPTER 14

OF SAINTS AND SINNERS

KELLY THREW HIMSELF INTO THE BUSINESS OF RUNNING his small Kanzeon Zen Yoga Center. He worked from 6 a.m. till 11 a.m., rode his bicycle home, and then ran classes again from 6 p.m. till 9 p.m., six days a week. The pain of Brenda's leaving was fresh in his mind, as was his confusion at his violent reaction to her.

Traveling to India had once changed his life, so Kelly thought it was time for him to make another trip. Perhaps this would provide the clarity he sought. His plan was to spend several months studying under Pattabhi Jois, the master yogi in Ashtanga who had few equals. Life in India was cheap by American standards. He would be able to stretch his modest savings a long way there. He rented a spacious apartment near Pattabhi's house where the master lived and trained. Pattabhi was a real character in his own right, a yogi of almost unparalleled realization and skill, and not above the occasional demonstration of his humanness.

Kelly flew to India and then journeyed to Mysore, located in the southwest of the country. Pattabhi Jois taught out of his modest home, not out of some huge ashram like Kelly had envisioned. The orientation talk was held in the small basement studio of Jois' home, where a dozen or so Western students, including Kelly, had gathered. Pattabhi explained a little about how they would train and what they could expect, and afterward pulled Kelly aside. "One of my nieces will be cleaning your apartment for you, and cooking your meals. You will pay her one dollar a week."

Kelly scoffed at this. "I can afford to pay her more than one dollar a week."

Pattabhi shook his head sternly, wagging his finger in Kelly's face. "This is a radiant, beautiful Hindu goddess who is doing this service for you, and for me. Do not take this happy creature and convert her, with your morality, into a capitalist pig by giving her a single extra dollar." Kelly's mouth popped open. He was, after all, a man who had given a near stranger $8,000 on a whim — a kingly sum in the early 1970s. "Our culture," Pattabhi continued, wagging his finger more aggressively, "is not your culture. Our culture has been in place for thousands of years, and it has worked for a reason. We do not need or want your values here. We will come to *your* country when we want to learn *your* ways. But you are *here*, to learn from us. *So learn*." He waited until Kelly's eyes registered the profound truth of what he had just said, then turned and left.

Kelly's days were beautifully simple. Rise at five a.m., meditate for an hour, then have a very light breakfast, three hours of yoga training under Pattabhi, a break for lunch, then more yoga training in the afternoons. It was a glorious program designed to deepen one's exposure to and training in yoga. Kelly fully expected that he was going to walk away from his time at Mysore with many stories about Pattabhi Jois, and how this master teacher pushed, prodded, and opened him — another kind of Swami Gauribala.

There was a beautiful gray-haired man who came into their morning meditations every day, but who would excuse himself ten minutes into the hour practice. Kelly would see him afterward, sitting quietly in the sun, sipping coffee, his eyes incredibly alert and aware. His hair and his energy were that of an older man — certainly someone in his sixties — but his face was free of worry or of any wrinkles, and had he dyed his hair he could have easily passed for someone in his thirties. After the fourth day of seeing him sitting and drinking his coffee, large and alert eyes taking in everything, Kelly approached the man.

"Hi," he said, sitting down, holding his own cup of coffee in his hands.

"Hello," the man said. "I don't know how you do it."

"What's that?" Kelly asked.

"Sit for so long. You are much better at it than I am." The man smiled. There was something lyrical in the man's tone, something calming about his presence. Kelly looked at him a little harder. His eyes were still and tranquil, yet vigilant. They possessed a kind of fierce softness that reached right into Kelly, and while it was strange to realize, Kelly fell in love with him almost immediately. It was as effortless as looking at a great painting and feeling something in yourself soar. Kelly's focus had wandered for a moment as all of this information moved through his mind, and when he looked back the man was watching him closely.

Hundreds of colorful parrots passed overhead, calling to each other and landing in nearby trees.

"There's a sight," Kelly said, breaking free of the trance. He looked back at the Indian man. "I'm Denis. Denis Kelly."

"You are training?" Kelly asked.

"No, not really. I am writing a book on Pattabhi Jois, and so am here as a kind of journalist, I guess." He laughed.

"Are you a journalist?"

"No sir. I am a retired professor. I used to be the Dean of Students at the University of Mysore." He extended his hand. "My name is Su Bara Char."

Another week passed, and the professor followed a similar routine. He would join the students in the morning meditation, and then depart early, finding a comfortable spot in the sun where he would drink his coffee and take notes in a notebook, looking as rooted and tranquil as the ancient trees under which he sat. He never attended the yoga classes, but waited in the garden outside, writing and sipping his coffee or tea.

Su Bara Char and Kelly spent most of their early morning breakfasts together, getting to know one another.

One morning, Kelly asked him about his family.

"No, Mr. Kelly, I do not have a family," he replied, but something in his eyes made Kelly press for more information.

"No one?" Kelly asked. "You don't have a wife or a consort of some kind?"

Bara Char laughed. "You are very perceptive, Mr. Kelly. I have a great love, yes, it is true." Bara Char's eyes twinkled.

Kelly smiled. "So you do have a partner?"

"Yes, Mr. Kelly. She is a goddess." Bara Char's face looked illuminated from within. "She is my great love and I am blessed and humbled by her company."

"So you two are married?"

"Married? No, sir. We fell in love many many years ago, but she was married to a close friend of mine, and so we never consummated our love. It is not necessary, anyway." He smiled.

"She is still married to your friend?"

"She is a Brahman, Mr. Kelly. As such, marriage is always for life. Her husband — my friend — died many years ago, but she must remain faithful to him."

"But," Kelly asked, confused, "you're celibate, in other words?"

"Yes, Mr. Kelly. It is their way, you see. "

"How long have the two of you been in love?"

"Almost thirty years."

"But you — you've had other lovers, other loves?"

"No, Mr. Kelly. She is all that I need, all that I ever wanted."

Kelly could only stare back. "So what do you do with her," he asked at last.

"Many, many things, Mr. Kelly. My love for her, and for God, is all that I need in this life. I am a very, *very* lucky man." Bara Char sat back and smiled radiantly.

"No kidding," Kelly managed. In time, he shared his own story of heartbreak and LSD and prison and spiritual discipline.

At the beginning of the third week, Professor Bara Char pulled Kelly aside. "Mr. Kelly," he said, being more forceful than Kelly had yet seen, "you need to leave this place and come with me. Together we will explore the temples here in southern India. There is something you need to see."

"Temples?" Kelly's tone dismissed the notion. "Professor, I've seen plenty of India, and plenty of temples. I'm here to study under one of the greatest living yoga masters — the same man you're writing a book about!"

"That is not why you are here, Mr. Kelly."

Kelly just raised his eyebrows, laughed, and walked away.

As the days passed, the professor became increasingly adamant that Kelly go with him and visit Hindu temples.

"Listen, professor," Kelly said, irritated, after a week of saying he was not interested. "I am *not* going to go to look at the temples. I've already seen enough of India, as I told you. I'm here to train with Pattabhi, and nothing else. This is all I need and want right now."

Bara Char smiled, revealing his white, evenly spaced teeth. "There is something you need to see, Mr. Kelly. You need to visit the Hindu temples in the south, where they are still uncorrupted and have treasures not yet plundered to behold."

Kelly shook his head, putting his hand on the man's shoulder. "Thank you, professor. But I'm here for Pattabhi Jois. To train with him is an honor, and I'm not going to leave his side to sightsee."

Another two weeks passed, and while Kelly and the professor talked about a great many things, Bara Char never stopped insisting that Kelly leave his training to travel.

"Okay," Kelly said one morning after their meditation. "I'll go. But only on one condition: You come with me, as my guide, as you first offered."

Bara Char clapped his hands together, his eyes shining. "Oh Mr. Kelly! I would be honored! And my cousin is a driver. He will take us wherever we wish to go. Now, a few things." Bara Char rattled off directions without a pause. "The first thing is that many of the temples that take government money must be open to tourists. We will avoid those, and only go to temples for Hindus — much more sacred and special. They do not allow heathens in, Mr. Kelly, like you." He smiled. "So, you will shave your head and put on robes and paint your face and body, and I will tell people that you are a prominent and famous American Hare Krishna, who is spreading Hinduism to the West. In this way, they may allow a Westerner to enter the sacred grounds."

"I'm a Zen guy," Kelly noted, "but I can pass for a Hindu I suppose. How long do you want to travel? I really don't want to be away from Pattabhi for too long."

"We will travel, Mr. Kelly, until you get what you need." Bara Char smiled broadly. "But if it eases your mind, I don't think we will need more than two weeks."

Kelly sighed, and with a nod surrendered.

Two days later the men were in the backseat of a large sedan and were being whisked across southern India by a very quiet driver. The professor knew a great many people, and the three of them stayed as guests in the homes of half a dozen people. For those who have never experienced what it is like to be the guest of a Hindu Brahman family, it is an opulent, beautiful thing. Fresh flowers, perfumed sheets, the finest foods and drinks the family can afford, and a level of respect and kindness worthy of a head of state. Over the first four days together, they visited no less than twenty temples, and got into about a third of them.

Professor Bara Char would explain who Kelly was to the priests guarding the temple entrances, and nod toward Kelly, who stood regally with his freshly shaved head, naked except for a loincloth around his genitals. The professor would cajole, bribe, and otherwise insist as forcefully as he could that Kelly had to be granted access. Sometimes the priests relented, and sometimes they would simply laugh at Kelly, shaking their heads and shooing them away. Because some of the temples possessed ancient statues made entirely of gold and encrusted with jewels, many had armed guards from the Indian army standing watch in the corners, machine guns at the ready.

In the temples where they did get access, Bara Char would never enter with Kelly, but would instead wait in the car. Kelly would go into the rectangular-shaped temple grounds and make his way to the temple located at the rear of the compound. There he would stand with another fifty people, and eventually be granted access to the temple itself. The inside of the temples were large, full of hand-carved stone and wood, and at the far end stood the closed doors of a shrine.

With incense heavy in the air, the temple priests, chanting intoxicatingly, would eventually open up the doors of the shrine to reveal gold or bronze statues of Indian gods and goddesses, always bejeweled and dazzling. The doors would stay open for five or so minutes before the priests would shut them. Kelly would see many of the Hindus around him go into an ecstatic state, sometimes collapsing, sobbing, or being so disoriented that they would have to be led outside. The group of fifty people would then be ushered out of the temple and back to the temple grounds. Kelly would go back to the car and to Bara Char, who would study Kelly intently for a moment or two before telling him the location of the next temple they were to visit.

Days passed, and Kelly grew weary of seeing the same thing again and again.

"I get it," he said to Bara Char one day, "I understand how the mythical-poetic structure of the Hindus is not that different from Roman Catholics praying to Mary and the Saints. I feel the Hindu's energy shift, I see the ecstatic states they enter. My appreciation of the depth and the beauty of Hinduism is greatly deepened. What is it you want me to see beyond that?"

But Bara Char only shook his head and smiled kindly.

Kelly entered a temple on his fifth day, so much like the others, after walking across the meticulously maintained temple grounds. He was ushered in with about fifty other people, the only Caucasian on the entire temple grounds, as had been the case at every temple. They stepped into the darkened temple, and as Kelly had seen before, there were temple priests, burning thick camphor incense and chanting. Twenty feet away stood the closed shrine, and the chanting and the music intensified. Kelly was a head taller than the next tallest man, and so had a clear and easy view of the shrine doors. He knew the drill well by now: The chanting would go on for two or three minutes, then the doors would open to reveal the statues of the deities, people would swoon, then the doors would close and priests would escort all of them back outside. Kelly watched with a wandering attention as the shrine doors slowly opened, revealing two solid gold statues encrusted with jewels, Shiva and Shakti. They stood maybe three-and-a-half feet high and were dazzling to behold, cast forever in a frozen dance, each deeply engaged with the other. The gold was clearly pure, and the statues very obviously ancient. Rubies were embedded as eyes with painted and sculpted features that were remarkable in their artistry.

The chanting intensified, causing Kelly's heart to open to the beauty of the voices. The smoke was heavy in his nostrils with the crowd adding to the intensity of the southern Indian heat. Shiva's golden head turned and his ruby eyes looked out over the crowd, causing many people to gasp or begin chanting, and a few to faint. Kelly stared, wide-eyed, and blinked. He had just shared a group hallucination. How interesting! But then Shiva's golden leg came down to the ground, and Shakti too turned and faced outward. Both deities smiled, going through some kind of mudras together, moving gracefully from one position to the next, their faces full of joyous love. They moved fluidly for many long minutes, until their bodies began to once again grow rigid. Shiva first came to his original position, the animation slowly leaving his body. There was only a beautiful gold statue standing, lifeless, as it had been when Kelly entered. Shakti too slowed and took up her original position. Before her head turned she looked out across the crowd and met Kelly's eyes with her own ruby ones. Kelly felt an opening in him beyond anything he had ever experienced before, a movement of energy through his body that blew his consciousness into the corners of the universe. He was suddenly not sure if he still had a physical body, for he was all energy, all movement, and felt the most pure and divine feminine love erupt in his heart. The shrine doors came to a close, and the priests harshly pushed the worshippers out, many of whom, like Kelly, were barely able to walk.

Kelly stepped out into the midday sun, feeling its warmth across his skin, a more sensual touch and more intimate connection than he had ever experienced in the embrace of a woman. Tears ran down his cheeks without effort or awareness, and the earth felt as if he were walking across a pregnant belly, and so it was with reverential feet he trod the grounds. He got lost twice in the simple rectangle, and smiling soldiers gently guided him toward the front gates. Kelly wandered out into the street where he saw the car with the professor inside. He got in and sat down. Bara Char clapped his hands together, touching Kelly's heart. "*That* is what you needed to see, Mr. Kelly," he said gently. Kelly stared at him, struggling to understand the words, yet unable to forget them. "You have received the divine feminine into your own heart. You will never again be the same. That was what you needed to see. Thank you for the deep honor to have shared this experience with you."

Kelly was incapable of speech, and would not be able to utter a single sound for three days. His saintly companion guided him into the homes where they slept, helped to feed him at times, and simply let Kelly swim in the sea of acceptance and healing that had overcome him. Kelly was no longer like an anthropologist looking at Hindu culture from the outside, but rather was living it from the inside. He was Hindu; his mind and Krishna's were one; he was loved and beloved, eros and agape, evolution and involution, the source and the end, utterly and completely wrapped in perfection.

Kelly went on to continue his training with one of the greatest yoga masters of the twentieth century, and yet his teacher had been a retired dean of students, a humble and modest man who loved a woman with the whole of his being, yet who was forbidden to consummate that love. So he served her, and Kelly, and everyone else he came across, the fire of his sacred heart burning into anyone who was able to feel it. Kelly realized this man was a true saint, a man who lived on devotion to God and to his fellow human beings alone, expecting nothing in return. His kindness, insight, and fiercely open heart showed Kelly what it meant to truly be the change one wanted to see in the world.

As Denis Kelly prepared to return to the United States, he realized that sometimes God does indeed walk among us.

○

BACK IN CORTE MADERA IN CALIFORNIA, KELLY SETTLED into his life as a Zen and yoga teacher at his Kanzeon Zen Yoga Center. His small studio had classes six days a week, from 6 a.m. to 11 a.m., and from 6 p.m. till 9 p.m. He made enough money from the business to live modestly, and flew to New York for sesshins (seven-day meditation intensives) under Eido Roshi. In 1984, he took formal vows and became an ordained Zen priest.

The phone rang in his studio one day in late 1984, and Kelly picked it up.

"Frank!" said a gravelly voice. "Holy shit! This number actually fucking works."

"*Russell*?" Kelly said, shocked, feeling a certain sinking in his stomach. "Jesse?" They had not spoken since the day, a decade before, when Kelly had gone to his ramshackle home and kicked him out of the family. Since then Jesse had served four years in a prison for conspiracy to manufacture LSD (after threatening the judge, who gave him the maximum sentence allowable). He was released from prison and out a few weeks when he was pulled over, and firearms were found in his trunk. He was arrested for a parole violation, and given another five-year sentence. A decade of life had already been spent in prison.

"Yeah," Jesse responded, "It's me." Kelly could almost hear the grinning on the other end of the phone.

"Jesus Christ, Jesse — it's good to hear your voice." It *was* good to hear his voice, but other than that Kelly wasn't sure what he was feeling.

"You too, Frank. So can we meet, like face-to-face? I don't much like phones."

Kelly considered. "I don't know, Jesse. I don't know. I've got to sit with this one. I've moved on, you understand."

Jesse said nothing.

"Give me your number, and let me call you back, okay?"

"Sure thing, Frank. Sure thing." Jesse knew, of course, that "Frank" would call him back even if Denis didn't think it was such a good idea.

Denis Kelly indeed thought about it, and decided that there was no way he could not see Jesse. He wouldn't deny his old friend and confidant that connection, and he had a strange feeling that it might be his last chance to do so.

Kelly called the next day, and Jesse picked up on the first ring.

"Frank?"

"Okay, Jesse," Kelly said slowly, "let's meet. There's a restaurant called *Greens* at Fort Mason in San Francisco. It's the San Francisco Zen Center's organic vegetarian restaurant. I'll meet you in the parking lot at noon, and I'll buy you lunch. Okay?"

"Awesome, Frank. Thanks so much!"

Kelly had $3,000 saved, and he decided on a hunch to bring it with him — he suspected that Jesse had called because he was in trouble, and the kind of trouble that only cash could get him out of. He put the money, in $100 bills, into a white envelope and slipped it into his coat.

Kelly was waiting when Jesse pulled up in a 1972 Dodge pickup truck that was several different colors and in the middle of losing its exhaust. Jesse got out of the driver's seat, and Kelly at first thought his eyes were playing tricks on him. It seemed that the decade hadn't passed. In Jesse's right hand was a cup of coffee, in the left a burning cigarette, and his black hair was pulled back into a ponytail. He wore the denim jacket, the blue jeans, and the scuffed and dented cowboy boots he had always worn, and even had the cocky saunter of a 25-year-old. But as he got closer, Kelly saw a different man coming into view. Jesse's face had grown hard — there were deep lines across his forehead and mouth. His skin was slightly jaundiced, and deep circles had taken up permanent residence under his eyes.

"Frank," he said, his lips parting in a smile that revealed half a dozen missing teeth.

"Jesse," Kelly replied, putting his arms around his friend, and feeling his heart swell. They hugged for a long moment. "Good to see you." Kelly blinked back tears.

"Come on," Jesse said, "I'm starving!" They walked up to the restaurant, and Jesse looked over the menu. Mostly vegetarian food greeted him. He looked at Kelly. "Can we go over to that bar across the street? I need to get a little grounded before I put this healthy hippie shit into my body."

Kelly laughed. "Sure thing, Jesse."

In the bar, Kelly ordered a seltzer, and Jesse ordered one vodka after another. After the third one, he said, "Okay, Frank. Now I'm ready for that hippie shit. Come on."

Over lunch, Jesse told Kelly that while in prison, he had learned to speak fluent Spanish and had made connections with the Columbian mafia. He also told Kelly he was working as a longshoreman in San Francisco. Kelly was impressed — the longshoremen had a powerful union, high wages, fantastic benefits, and were generous all around with their people. Some men spent half their lives just trying to get into that union, and Jesse had landed it without any effort. Halfway through the meal, after they had caught up, Jesse came to the reason for his phone call.

"So Frank — they've made me an offer. The Columbians. I can get back into the business and have suppliers and sellers all lined up. It's a piece of cake. All I need is a loan to get started, man. Just a small loan."

"Jesse," Kelly said, "Shit, man. You know you're no good at it. You're not cut out for the business. Plus I don't have any money anymore. I haven't for a long time — I live like a monk now. I've left our old life behind. I'm a fucking Zen and yoga teacher."

"Well, good for you, Frank. Good for you. You always were a natural leader and teacher and into all that healthy shit." Jesse smiled. "I've always been a little rougher around the edges." His eyes narrowed. "Come on, Frank. You always have a stash set aside."

Kelly stared across the table at him. "Jesse, I'll say it again: You were terrible at the business. You don't have the right personality — you're too hot-blooded. You know that's true...."

"*Fuck you*, Frank!" Jesse nearly shouted. "What the fuck else am I supposed to do?"

"Jesse, *you're a longshoreman*. Shit, man, you make great fucking money. It's stable, it's local, and you're set for life. Retirement, benefits... what the fuck else do you want?"

"Fuck you, Frank! You work a fucking factory job, man. Not me."

Kelly sighed. "Well, what about something else? I found a weird niche that suits me."

Jesse shook his head. "What, I'm going to teach mother-fucking Zen? Are you kidding me? I learned my lessons, Frank. I learned them the hard way. Ten years of hard time. You think I'm going to fuck up again? I need money to go back to work. I need a loan."

Kelly pushed his finished plate away. "Well, how much do you need, Jesse?"

"Three grand should get me started."

"Ain't that something," said Kelly, quietly. He felt the envelope pressing on his ribs inside of his coat, and couldn't suppress a smile. They stopped the conversation as the check came and Kelly paid, then went back out and sat in Jesse's truck.

"Listen, Jesse," Kelly said. "Don't do it, man. If you get that kind of money, do something else. You're just no good at the drug thing — you don't have the right temperament. You feel too much, and everything gets to you. You're too arrogant, too angry, too prone to being impulsive." Kelly laughed, and Jesse grinned back at him. "You've got authority issues to boot, just like me. You've already spent most of your adult life in prison. Isn't that enough?"

"Christ, Frank," Jesse said, looking out his window. "I'm forty-fucking-seven years old with two major felonies on my jacket. I hate the longshoremen. What am I going to start over at? What? Accounting? Or do you really expect me to be *happy* loading freight on and off boats when I'm an old man just trying to hump it out to a miserable, broken retirement? Is that really what you see for me? Doing that kind of work?"

Kelly said nothing.

"So let's say I fuck up again, Frank. So what? I get to go out the way I've always lived. At least I won't die broke." He lit a cigarette. "I'll pay you back, with interest."

"It's not about the money, Jesse, you know that," Kelly said. He took out the envelope and let it slip from his fingers to the floorboards.

After a pause, Kelly said, "You dropped something, Jesse."

Jesse looked at it for a long time, then picked it up and slid it into his coat. "Thanks, Frank," he said at last. "Thanks for the advice, too. You always were the wise one." He started the truck, which rattled noisily to life.

Kelly got out and tapped on the hood once. He watched Jesse pull out, his arm out the window and a cigarette dangling out of his mouth.

A few years later he received the $3,000, plus compounded interest and a few thousand dollars on top of that, a princely sum for a man making his living teaching yoga and Zen. There was no return address, and the money was encased in a large plastic frog . A note said simply, "Hope you're enjoying busing your Zen dishes." Kelly laughed so hard he doubled over.

Kelly never saw his old friend ever again, and ten years after their meeting in the parking lot he heard Jesse had died from a massive heart attack. The news hit Kelly oddly, for he was sad to hear his friend was gone. But Jesse — Russell — had died as he had lived, defiant to the end.

◯

DENIS KELLY HAD UNFINISHED BUSINESS WITH HIS FATHER. Kelly and his dad had a cordial but distant relationship, and after prison Kelly decided he needed to come to terms with who his father had been, and was.

William Kelly had gone into middle age and then into his retirement years a largely unchanged man. The psychological wounds of the Second World War had faded over the decades, leaving tough scar tissue in their place. Bill, as friends called him, was a disciplined soldier and staunch Midwesterner, and he watched as that discipline gradually eroded as a slow and steady alcoholism took its toll on his mind and body. Although only in his mid-sixties, he was overweight and out of shape, and so unpredictable in nature that his own grandchildren were afraid of him and wouldn't sit in his lap.

Kelly flew back to Green Bay and surprised his semi-retired father with a ten-day fishing trip to Canada, something he'd wanted to do his whole life. They chartered a plane in Green Bay that flew them to Canada. They had enough gear to eat and fish for a week, and didn't have to worry about additional supplies because the pilot was paid to fly in every day.

Father and son flew over hundreds of miles of unspoiled countryside, until an expansive lake came into view. The seaplane touched down on the water, and motored a quarter-mile to a dock. A modest cabin sat overlooking the lake, just up from the shore. Kelly and his father jumped onto one of the pontoons, and from there unloaded their gear onto the dock, including the remains of a twelve-pack of 16-ounce beers his father had brought. Although his father liked hard liquor, he never drank it when he was around his adult son.

"When you come back, bring more beer," his father told the pilot, who nodded. The plane was unloaded, and his father wandered off to relieve himself. Kelly put his arm around the pilot.

"Listen to me. I'm paying the bills, right?"

"Sure are," the pilot answered. He was a young, thin man whose blonde hair and facial stubble were about the same length. He looked back at Kelly through a pair of mirrored aviator glasses.

"Okay," Kelly said. "You bring a drop of alcohol to this island, you don't get paid. Do I make myself clear?"

The pilot looked past Kelly at the point where his father had disappeared.

"The old man's not going to like that," the pilot observed.

Kelly smiled. "Nope, he's not."

"You're the boss," the pilot said amicably, and climbed back into his plane. He fired up the engine and turned back toward the open water.

Bill Kelly came back out on the dock, and he and Denis stood shoulder to shoulder to watch the plane take off. Once it was gone, they took in the beauty of the huge lake, bordered on all sides by a heavy tree line. It was still early in the morning, and the sky was a pristine blue.

"Look at how clear that water is," Kelly noted. "You can see down, what, eight or nine feet?"

"Gorgeous," Bill Kelly agreed, cracking open a beer.

The cabin came with a fishing boat, and after they unpacked they motored out on the lake to fish. The lake was so well-stocked with northern pike that they had to throw back the first dozen fish they caught because they were too big to clean and eat, and finally Kelly caught one small enough to provide a normal-size meal. They each drank a few beers, and by the time they went back to the cabin to cook and clean the fish, they were both feeling quite relaxed. After dinner they built a fire outside, and watched as thousands of stars came out to dance and twinkle over their heads.

In the morning, they heard the pilot returning. Kelly and his father helped unload fresh supplies, and after the plane was empty Kelly's father scratched his head.

"Hey, where's the beer?" he demanded of the pilot.

"Oh, shit," the pilot said, feigning forgetfulness. "I forgot!"

"Well," Kelly's father said, "okay, but don't forget again."

The pilot was off, and Kelly prepared breakfast from the ingredients the pilot had brought: organic eggs, whole grain breads, yogurt, and vegetables.

"Christ, son," his father said, examining the plate of food. "No bacon? No butter? No biscuits? You call this stuff food?"

Kelly just smiled. "It's good for you, dad. And it's all there is."

His father sighed and ate.

That day father and son fished and chatted and enjoyed the secluded beauty of the lake without a drop of alcohol.

On the third morning they again heard the plane sputtering toward the dock. It had no sooner come to a halt than Bill Kelly's rear end was hanging out of the plane's door. Kelly walked up to the plane, hands in pockets, where his red-faced father was now standing.

"You forgot the beer!" he accused the pilot.

"Damn," the blonde pilot said, not very convincingly. "You're right. Must'a slipped my mind again."

Kelly's father looked at the young pilot, then at his son, then back to the pilot.

"Fuck you both," he said, the words harsher than his tone. He lumbered back into the cabin, knowing that his son had gotten the better of him.

On their fifth night, the two men ate a great dinner inside the cabin. Afterwards they went out to a clearing by the water, built a small fire, and sat with outstretched legs. The sun, heavy in the sky and close to the horizon, set fire to the water and the tops of the trees before the lake slid into gloom.

"Okay, Papa," Kelly said. "Can we get real?"

Bill Kelly was not a fool. After the alcohol had been shut off, he had quickly figured what his son's likely motivation was. So he nodded his head, putting his large hands behind his head and stretching back into a comfortable recline. "Figured somethin' was on your mind," he said, his voice a low rumble.

"Prison taught me some things." Kelly began, "Like how I wanted to live my life when I got out, and the kinds of relationships I want to have in it. I've been looking at myself, dad, and at the kind of man I am. You know I'm a pacifist."

His father nodded.

"Well, the reason I hate violence is because of how we were raised. I was afraid of my own anger because I didn't want..." the words caught for a moment, "...because I don't want to be like you." The senior Kelly nodded, not showing the least sign of offense.

"I came here to say goodbye, Papa," Kelly continued, softly. "I just want you to know this will be the last time I'll see you, and I wanted to say it to your face." His father sat for a long moment, eyes lost in the fire. Kelly had to search to find the hard, defiant man who raised him, for sitting across from him was a man fast becoming old, whose body was falling into disrepair and who could no longer badger and bully the way he once did. The sharp lines of his masculine face had given way; his face was now soft, the angles rounded. When his father at last looked up, Kelly saw the comments had hit their mark, but there was also a defiant twinkle in his father's eyes.

His father leaned forward. "Why, son?"

"Why? dad, you're an abusive alcoholic whose grandkids are afraid to sit on his lap. You used to beat the shit out of me, and Michael, and Patrick. I know you have your share of demons you had to face, but it only excuses so much. I'm here to tell you that you and I are through if you don't change, and I wanted to tell you that to your face. I love you, and you're my father, but I cannot and I will not stand by you any longer if you keep drinking. Enough is enough."

"Okay, son," his father said, sitting back. "But if we're going to have *this* conversation, we need to get our terms straight. For starters, I'm not an alcoholic."

Kelly stared back at his father, who just a few days before had all but sprinted to the plane to search for beer at 8 a.m.

"You're kidding me," said Kelly at last, incredulous. "You've been drunk for forty years!"

"Yes," his father admitted, his mouth pursing thoughtfully. "That's true. But I'm a Kelly. *We're* Kelly's, and Irish."

"What the fuck does that have to do with anything?"

"Kelly's aren't alcoholics, we're drunks."

"Oh right, dad," Kelly said, temper flaring. "And what's the difference?"

"An alcoholic can't stop drinking. I'm a drunk — I can stop whenever I want."

"Bullshit," Kelly shot back, "I mean, come on, dad. Stop whenever you want? When was the last time you went more than two days without a fucking drink?"

His father shrugged. "I've just never had a reason to quit."

"Never had a... never had a reason? *Never had a reason*?" Kelly's eyes flashed. "Your *life has been shit* for forty years. You and your fucking *drinking problem* have alienated most of your family. And you're telling me you don't have a reason to quit?"

His father sighed. "There you go again, son," he said. "I don't *have* a drinking problem. You have a problem with my drinking. Let's get the order right. I drink because it works for me."

Kelly shook his head, speech abandoning him. His father, smiling slightly, poked at the fire with a stick, and a great rush of embers lifted into the sky.

Kelly could feel rage trying to break free of him, and he remembered slapping Brenda. Rage. Anger. Caring. He cared about this relationship, and he wasn't going to shit all over it by being violent. Not yet, at least.

"Whatever you want to call it, dad, the bottom line is that you and I are through unless you quit drinking."

"Yeah, I get that, son," he responded, good-naturedly. "I heard you the first time. Now look, I don't want to lose you." His eyes glinted in the firelight. "But I need a *good* reason to quit drinking."

"You...." Kelly managed.

"For instance," his father continued, "If I had me a nice, brand new RV that I could take your mother south in during the winter months, cruise the country in style; well, then I might have a good enough reason to quit drinking for good."

Kelly stared back in amazement, his heart pounding. "You want me to *bribe* you?"

"Bribe?" his father said. "Jeez, son. Not a bribe. I told you. A *reason*."

"I would think," Kelly said defensively, "that losing your son might be reason enough."

"It's a fine reason," his father noted. "But keeping a son *and* gaining an RV make it a no-brainer."

"I see," Kelly said, folding his arms across his chest, "And what do these RVs cost?"

"Forty grand."

"You're kidding. Tell me you're kidding."

"Well, it so happens my neighbor has one with a couple of thousand miles on it. Will give it to me for twenty grand."

"Dad, I just told you if you don't stop drinking, I'm never going to speak to you again. I'm not bluffing."

"I know you're not, son. You never did."

"Well, I'm *not* bribing you to stop drinking," Kelly said. "I can't believe you. I really can't believe you."

"I'm just being honest."

"Well," Kelly said, standing. "Fuck you and your honesty, then."

Kelly walked angrily away from the fire and into the woods, stomping his feet violently into the ground. "Stubborn, stupid sonofabitch," Kelly muttered, kicking at the underbrush. Here he had opened his heart and given his father a stark choice, and somehow his dad had managed to make a joke out of it. *What an asshole*, Kelly fumed as he came to the lake's shore. *He needs to control everything*, Kelly thought, kneeling down by the water and dipping his hand into it. *Abusive, arrogant control freak. Who the fuck does he think he is?*

Kelly stood and walked the shoreline, and looking back could see the light of the fire dancing in the trees a few hundred yards behind him. An RV. He smirked. It was ridiculous. So ridiculous that he began to see it a little differently. William Kelly was a mean drunk and unrepentant about his mistakes, but at the same time he loved his family very much. He would never let Denis walk away after accusing him of being a drunk. Pride alone meant that he would have to rise to Denis' challenge, and more importantly he loved his son. He could have agreed to stop drinking, but it was important that Denis understand who was still the boss, who was the father and who was the son.

"I'm not an alcoholic. I'm a drunk," his dad had said, and Denis was suddenly laughing. By the time he circled back toward the fire, a smile had come to his face. His father hadn't moved, and was once again sitting with outstretched feet, hands behind his head.

"Okay, Papa," Kelly said, sitting back down. "Only because you played especially dirty and brought mom into it, I'll agree to pay for *half* that RV. That's it. And you quit drinking, for good and forever, on your word."

"Okay, then, son," his father said, nodding his head to the deal. "On my word, the word of a Kelly." They shook hands.

The rest of their fishing trip passed lightly.

True to his word, Bill Kelly never again touched a drop of alcohol. Perhaps it was just to prove a point in his stubborn, Irish way, perhaps because no one had ever sat him down the way Denis had and shown him the pain he had been creating, or perhaps he had finally grown tired of numbing a pain that had, in his old age, at long last begun to fade. Whatever the reason, William Kelly gave up his beloved cognac and beer. He remained a drunk, it was true, but a sober one.

About a year later, Kelly was once again visiting his parents. After dinner, he and his father were doing the dishes.

"Papa," Kelly said, "so listen. I've been doing all this work on myself. Men's work, therapy, and I've found out there's a reason why we drink and do drugs. We're running from something. It was true for me — I was running from my own anger, at you, at mom, and the whole fucking world. Once I got in touch with it, it lost its power over me. It freed me to focus on things that are more important, and it helped to open my heart to true intimacy. It's part of why you and I have an actual relationship now."

His father nodded. "Sure, I get that, son. But I stopped drinking, didn't I?"

"Yeah, dad, you did. But what I'm saying is that even though you've stopped drinking, you've never confronted the reasons that led to it in the first place."

His father nodded. "Sure. Get that too. But you got your mother feeding me mush in the mornings for the last year instead of my bacon and eggs, and I don't ever complain, do I?"

"No."

"And I've never complained about not drinking anymore, have I?"

"No, dad."

"Or fallen off the wagon."

"Not that I've heard."

"And I have relationships with the grandkids, right? They crawl on my lap again? Love their pa-pa?"

Kelly nodded.

"Well," his father smiled, "so you think we can leave my mind alone?"

Kelly laughed, putting away the last glass. "Yeah, okay."

"Don't worry. I hear what you're saying. I really do. If I change my mind," his father put his arm on Kelly's shoulder, "you'll be the second one to know, I swear."

A few years later his father took a fishing trip with his buddies, and he was the only one to catch a fish. He had come home laughing and proud, and died that night in his sleep.

CHAPTER 15

AN INSTITUTIONAL MAN, PART III

BY 1987, THE ZEN YOGA SCHOOL IN SAN FRANCISCO HAD good attendance, and Kelly was making enough money from it to live comfortably, if not luxuriously. He had a housemate to keep his rent down, drove a used car when he wasn't bicycling, and dressed in second-hand clothes from the many hip San Francisco clothing resellers. On occasion he would pass acquaintances from the old days who had known the flamboyant "Frank." They seldom recognized him.

There was a 17-year-old girl who lived near his school and came in from time to time to visit Kelly and talk about her life. She was delightful, tall and thin, with deep brown eyes and thick brown hair. Like so many 17-year-olds, her life was, she believed, complex and fraught with all manner of drama, love, redemption, delicious love affairs, and wrenching heartbreak. Kelly took her under his wing in a paternal way, for he was old enough to be her father. She loved his unconventional advice and approach to life, and the fact that he didn't seem judgmental about anything she told him. She unfolded like a flower, sharing things that she wouldn't dare reveal even to her closest girlfriends. In return, Kelly got to be a force of good in her life, a light that she could rely on in a world that seemed dark and tragic and aligned to satisfy its own needs.

She came in one Friday afternoon after class, and, kicking off her shoes, sat down in lotus position on the practice floor, watching as Kelly read a newspaper.

"Hi, Claire," he said, watching her watch him.

"Hi," she dropped casually, clearly distracted. Claire sat for a few moments, then uncurled one long leg, extending it out on the floor in front of her. She wiggled her toes, leaned forward, and brought the other leg out in front of her, wiggling all ten toes at him.

"So my mom threw me out of the house," she said in a defiant tone.

Kelly shut the paper, and laid it on the desk.

"What happened?" he asked simply, giving her his full attention.

Claire's composure broke. "She's such a *bitch*. She went through my *room*, and found some pot and because of that she accused me of being a pothead and a fucking whore and all kinds of *bullshit...*" She broke off and buried her head in her hands. "So I told her to fuck off," she continued through sobs, "And she told me to get out. So what the fuck am I supposed to do? Where am I supposed to stay?"

"Claire," Kelly consoled, "it's okay. Your mom was probably just blowing off steam. But you're coming of an age when you'll need to decide if living in that environment will ultimately serve you." Kelly knew the girl's mother was an alcoholic and had a nasty temper. "Believe me, I know. It's not easy when you have parents who are so steeped in their own shit, their own ignorance, that they can't help but hurt you."

"She's just a cunt," Claire spat.

"Yes, but she's also in pain, Claire," Kelly offered. "She's afraid of losing you, and knows on some level you're becoming a woman and will soon leave her — just like everyone else has. So she's trying to protect herself the only way she knows how."

"By being a cunt?" Claire asked defiantly.

Kelly leveled a gaze at her. "Yes, by being a cunt," he stated.

"Well, it's working."

"I know, but the sad thing is it's not really what she wants. What she wants is to be close to you."

"So why doesn't she just tell me that?"

Kelly sighed. "Probably because no one taught her how."

"What do I do?" Claire implored. "I don't want to go back there."

"I'm not saying you should. Just because that's what your mom really wants doesn't mean you *should* go back to her. Not if she's shitting on you with her own ignorance." He thought a moment. "You got somewhere to stay?"

Claire shook her head, two more tears dropping onto the carpet.

Kelly sighed. "You can stay with me for a bit. I've got a spare room and you're welcome to it until we can figure out a solution for you. There's no need to run away, *or* to run back. Make your decision from a place of spaciousness. Take some time and some space to let the emotion out, and then see what arises from there."

"Oh, thank you!" she cried, and getting up threw her arms around Kelly, making him laugh.

"You're welcome, kid."

That night, Kelly made up Claire's room, and went to bed around 10 p.m. Sunday morning she came in at 8 a.m., after being out all night. Kelly awoke to her kicking off her shoes, and fully dressed she slid into bed with him. They snuggled more closely together, and then they were kissing. She tasted of cigarettes and stale alcohol. The sensation was odd, and both of them looked at each other as if they found out at that moment they were cousins. Yet her body was warm against his, and she was young and soft and very pretty. Lust overrode intelligence and wisdom, and despite everything Kelly knew his hand made its way under her shirt and closed around a firm breast.

She exploded out of bed. "Jesus, Denis!" she said, grabbing her shoes. "I don't think of you like that! I just wanted to be held. What's the matter with you?" She left upset and, Kelly sensed, hugely disappointed.

"Christ," Kelly muttered, sitting up and rubbing his face with his hands. He got up and went to the bathroom, clicking on the light. Kelly saw his reflection in the mirror. He was still fully erect, and the lights glinted off his freshly shaven head. His gaze fell on his eyes. A 45-year-old man looked back, a man who had trained his mind and his body well beyond what most people considered possible, and yet was as undisciplined in the face of temptation as a 12-year-old schoolboy. His intention had been to continue to serve Claire, as he had all along, but somehow he had lost control of himself. He thought of the Indian saint Su Bara Char, and of his platonic embrace of the woman he loved, an embrace that demanded nothing in return. Kelly saw a man-child staring back at him, a man-child pretending he was an Enlightened being, and for the first time felt the full weight of his pretentiousness and arrogance. He was Denis Kelly, the rebel, and he would never take vows to a master, never surrender to a man. He sought teachings, not teachers, because he believed teachers were too flawed. What a bunch of horseshit. He was the flawed one, projecting his weakness onto those much stronger and wiser than he. For 45 years he had refused to surrender, and for 45 years he had allowed his narcissism to run roughshod over his life. The result was him fumbling for boobs in bed like a horny child.

"Fuck," he said, shaking his head.

It was not his view of himself that it was okay to use his training and insight to bed a child. Kelly's own playful, adolescent frivolity had betrayed him, and while he knew that philosophically there was, as Trungpa had taught, "nothing but perfection," practically speaking this was bullshit. Even though he could relax his mind and touch in with his own Perfection in that moment, it didn't matter — Claire knew nothing of this insight, wasn't a student, and only knew the very real pain she was in. Whether or not it was real in an Absolute sense was a bullshit bypassing of his own responsibility. When his actions hurt real people through his own ignorance, the Absolute offered no solace. Kelly, naked, slid to the floor, choking on his shame and his anger and his self-judgment.

He spent a long, sleepless night coming to terms with an ugly truth: his spiritual insight was not stable and his transformation far from complete. Kelly was still utterly bound by his conditioning. He was, in essence, no more free than a well-trained dog, reacting to what life dealt him in a highly conditioned way, rather than making conscious choices.

He did not bother to show up at his own school for the next two days, and on the third day drove to the shadow of the Golden Gate Bridge. No one noticed as a lone man, barefoot, walked to the apex, climbed over the guardrail, and stood poised over the dark waters below.

His reaction to Claire had exposed the ugly truth of his life. Still a narcissist, he was no closer to a stable spiritual insight than he had been twenty years before. He leaned out over the water again and again, wanting to let go, to snuff out his consciousness, to get away from his pain, his judgment, his self-loathing. Under the stars, with an occasional car going languidly by, he came face to face with what had brought him there. He wanted to kill himself, but didn't really want to die. What he wanted was to be free from the prison of his own mind, his conditioned behavior that caused him to react to life with so little consciousness and compassion. The easy way out, he began to see, was to jump. The hard way would be to return to Eido Roshi and surrender himself utterly, without qualification, and be trained until he was awake or dead. To surrender to a man. To a flawed man.

Kelly had told Brenda that *waking up was not a casual affair.* But he hadn't really understood his own words. He knew, standing on the Golden Gate Bridge, that what he sought couldn't be found as a hobby or something he did a few days a week. It wasn't an hour-a-day practice. It could never be found on a retreat, or kept after a seminar, or gotten from a book, and no amount of LSD would ever allow him to keep his insight. Disciplined and sober silence was the only way to hold the wisdom he craved. It was the greatest crossroads he had yet faced. Would he turn into his fear and resistance and make a choice to Awaken, or would he continue to do it his own way, the way that had succeeded in changing little about him? He knew he had to live the truth of his practice in every moment of every day.

Kelly stepped back from the railing. He would yet find a way to penetrate to the root of his contraction and self-absorption, he would kill the part of himself that thought he was a teacher, an Enlightened being, a wise man. He would kill the part of himself that insisted on doing things his own way, in his own time — the cowboy, the loner, the rebel, the wild man.

He would yet be reborn, he swore to himself as he returned to his car. He would yet serve.

Kelly called Eido Roshi and told him there was a crisis, and the roshi told Kelly to come to New York City. They then met at the New York Zendo, on East 67th Street, where Kelly presented what had happened.

"Mmm," Eido Roshi responded, his voice deep and penetrating.

"So I want to go back to school," Kelly said. "Go to NYU and get my degree. I'll be your *inji*, your assistant, and simply arrange my school schedule to work around the monastery's."

Eido Roshi shook his head. "No, Jun Po. Come to the monastery."

Kelly shook his head. "I told you. I've been institutionalized. I'm not interested in doing it again."

Eido Roshi considered. "The head monk is leaving, Jun Po," he countered. "There is no one to take his place."

Kelly thought of his vow to surrender. But a monastery? Surrendering was one thing. Living a monk's life was another.

Eido Roshi had been watching Kelly's face. "What would it take to get you there?" he asked.

Kelly laughed. "It would need to come out of the sixteenth century and into the twentieth."

"How?"

"Well," Kelly began, "if I was to run the monastery, I would bring in body practices like yoga, mind practices like psychotherapy, environmental practices to raise awareness of what we're doing to the world, and create outreach programs so non-Buddhists could rent space for other kinds of retreats to broaden our exposure to other modalities, to other kinds of mind and spirit training."

Eido Roshi considered. "You would want Zen students to go through these things?"

"Some of them, yes." Kelly said. "Give them training in mind, body, environmental awareness, *and* spirit."

"Jun Po," Eido Roshi asked, "would I have to do any of these things?"

Kelly smiled. "You mean set them up and run them?"

Eido Roshi nodded.

"No, roshi. I'd take care of it all."

He smiled. "Would you expect me to practice them, to set an example?"

"No, roshi."

"Okay, then." Eido Roshi's eyes twinkled. "We have a deal."

"Roshi," Kelly said, bowing. He went to speak but, overwhelmed with emotion, struggled to make the words come out. "Eido Roshi," he started again, evoking his master's name to fully get his attention. "Do you think I can be trained?"

Eido Roshi considered deeply.

"Jun *Po*," he said at last, slowly, drawing out the words. Kelly held his master's eyes. Eido Roshi's lips moved in the smallest hint of a smile.

"I think," he paused, "you...are...worth...*civilizing*."

Kelly drove back to the Catskill Mountains and to Dai Bosatsu, the Zen monastery. He had first entered the monastery in 1978, and had taken formal vows in 1984 to become a Zen priest, but he had always maintained a strong attachment and interest in his life outside of his practice. No more. Kelly walked through the doors of the monastery, resolving to stay there as long as it took.

Perhaps this was what Brenda had sensed, this level of intensity, of insanity, that drove and whipped him. He was no sage who went to bed one night and woke up the next morning in harmony with the mind of God. He wasn't Saul, struck down by God in the desert with his heart set aflame. There was no instant conversion from dark to light, no turning of a switch that would transform him into an Enlightened sage.

For Kelly, it would take years of discipline, practice, failure, and frustration. It was only his word to himself — wake up or die — that would keep him in the monastery for the next six years.

○

TO UNDERSTAND KELLY'S EXPERIENCE FROM 1987 THROUGH 1993, it is important to understand what a Zen monastery does, what the point of training in one ultimately is, and what it means to surrender yourself there.

Kelly entered Dai Bosatsu with the experiences of LSD-25 firmly rooted inside of him. LSD-25 allowed tremendous insight into the true nature of reality, but that insight was not grounded in a disciplined practice that gradually allowed someone to internalize and adapt to the radical truths it allowed the mind to see. Eido Roshi would help Kelly to ground his insight, make it stable, whole and complete, through practice and repetition.

Life in a Zen monastery is a very beautiful, very controlled thing. It is, in essence, a benevolent dictatorship where the roshi teaches the "dharma" — the sacred teachings of Buddhism passed down for thousands of years, refined and augmented by each generation of masters. The goal is to help students "wake up," or realize their own true nature, and to pass on the dharma to the next generation.

What does that mean, to "wake up?" Beyond the ego or the higher self, there is another place, a place from which those two kinds of ego arise. This is the "ground" or "suchness" of being, where we can see not only our ego, but also the higher self that contains it. This "ground" rests in a place of paradox when seen from the ego, or even from the higher self. When one is "in" this place, there is no time, no need, no grasping after things to make us "full" or "happy" or "free of pain." The ground of being is a place where everything arises, the ego, the world, the very fabric of the universe. When one is in touch with this place, one is imperturbable, unmovable, beyond even the conception of fear or contraction. And this place does not come and go, it does not arise and disappear — the *realization* of this place might arise and disappear, the ability to sit in this place might come and go, but the ground of being is the ground of being — it is always already present. It is the only true thing one will experience in life, for the simple reason it does not come and go. This is what is meant by "waking up" or "Enlightenment" or "Enlightened Mind." The word "Buddha" simply means "awake" — the historical Buddha awoke from the dream of his own mind to see a deeper reality. It was this state that Eido Roshi had mastered, and it was this state that Denis Kelly was seeking.

A Buddhist monastery is designed to help the men and women there to not only have this realization of the "ground of their being," but also to stabilize that realization so that it is no longer fleeting. To "take their seat" there, preparing them to go into life and marriage and conflict and love-making and bankruptcy and death with a realization that is permanent and unshakable, that is no different from the very mind of God.

When a student has demonstrated a thorough understanding of the teachings and attained a high level of "realization," he will usually become a lineage holder, and be given the designation "roshi." (In Tibetan Buddhism, this same process takes place except realized teachers are given the title "lama.")

Life in a Zen monastery is not easy. Morning meditations start before 5 a.m., life is highly structured and regimented, and there is virtually no privacy or free time. For those like Kelly that came to study the dharma seriously, they begin an intensive meditation practice and an intensive study of Zen koans, 1,400 "riddles" that are designed to help break the ego free of its habitual conditioning and understanding, allowing a man or woman to have the realization of the ground of being — to "wake up." A "koan" (pronounced ko-on) is a question designed to have an answer that creates a paradox in the small mind or ego. The paradox can only be resolved when one has a deeper realization — from that realization the paradox ceases to exist. It is through koan training and practice that Rinzai Zen masters will test and train their students.

A less confusing way to think of this might be mathematics. There are very complicated "proofs" to mathematical problems that can only be solved by very deep insight into the nature of mathematics. A student must train his mind in the arcane language of math, and then have a mental insight into the problem before he can solve it. He must not only give the correct answer, but also demonstrate how he got to the correct answer — the "proof."

So the now-classic koan, "What is the sound of one hand clapping?" has no answer in the conventional, logical mind. One hand cannot make a clapping noise by itself. In a Rinzai Zen monastery, a student will be asked to answer this koan, or one like it, in the presence of the roshi. If the answer is incorrect, the student will be sent back to the meditation hall to contemplate more, sometimes for months before they are asked back to try the answer again. What happens is that most of us try and answer the koan with our ego, with our small mind.

It's not so much that there is a correct answer as there is a correct "place" *from which* one answers. There is a famous story about Suzuki Roshi, who founded the San Francisco Zen Center, lecturing to his students about a question concerning the teachings. The next day, he asked the same students a question, and one of his students answered him by repeating exactly what Suzuki said the day before.

"No," the roshi said, shaking his head. "That is incorrect."

The student, flabbergasted, protested. "But roshi! That's exactly what you said yesterday!"

Suzuki Roshi smiled. "Yes, but when you say it, it is wrong. When I say it, it is right."

The other students laughed, but the point was a serious one: the student's answer was incorrect because it lacked the insight behind the words. It was the equivalent of the virgin telling you that sex was "something that's amazing." The answer is correct, but it lacks the insight of experience.

Zen "koan" training is the same thing. There are about 1,400 Zen koans, those enigmatic riddles designed to help a practitioner "wake up." They are broken into five divisions. The first division is designed to help the student gain insight into the true nature of mind, insight into the true nature of Buddha Mind, to get out of their dualistic, evaluative mind. The second division of koans is about physically embodying that realization, to be able to answer with more than just your mouth. The third division is about language koans, embodied awareness, usually expressed through poetry. The fourth division is the difficult-to-pass koans, ensuring that the student has truly mastered their insight and cannot be tricked into giving an answer from their dualistic, limited egos. The final division involves the Ten Precepts in Buddhism, or in how to live one's life now that one is Awake, which should flow naturally and spontaneously. Compassion for all beings, for instance, arises naturally and effortlessly when one has given up attachment, a paradox from the ego's perspective, which thinks that non-attachment could mean non-compassion.

EIDO ROSHI GAVE DENIS KELLY THE CLASSIC FIRST KOAN of the 1,400 koans to master. It was what is known as the "mu" koan. The koan is simple: A monk asked Joshu (a Chinese Zen master), "Does a dog have Buddha-nature or not?" What he was asking was Buddha-nature, or that ground of being, "true" for a dog — was it true for *all* sentient beings? Or was it only humans that had this "ground of being." Joshu answered "*Wu.*" In Japanese, this translates to "Mu," which when translated to English is often translated as "no," "none," or "no meaning." Kelly's task was to sit with this koan, for months and months on end and train his mind around it. He and Eido Roshi met regularly, in the sacred ceremony of dokusan (a meeting with an Enlightened master and a student) and discussed the koan.

"So," the roshi would say in his deep, slow voice, "Does a dog have Buddha-nature?" And Kelly would answer. Sometimes he would say "no," sometimes he would say, "Not-knowing," sometimes he would say, "mu," but his answers were always met with Eido Roshi shaking his head. Kelly knew the answer was *mu*, but Eido Roshi never accepted his answer.

"Back to the zendo, Jun Po," he would command, and Kelly would return to sitting, hour after hour, day after day, week after week.

One afternoon a few months after Kelly had come to the temple, Eido Roshi and Kelly were relaxing outside on a small deck overlooking some gardens.

"Roshi," Kelly said, "you told me that *Jun Po* means 'dharma cruiser.'"

"Mmm," Eido Roshi said, cocking an eyebrow.

Kelly came from a military family and knew that the classic military formation for navies included a slow aircraft carrier, fast but minimally armored destroyers, supply ships, personnel carriers, and, of course, cruisers. Cruisers circled the fleet and kept it safe — they ensured that the convoy got from point A to point B unharmed, and had an idealized combination of firepower, armament, and speed.

"So when you say dharma cruiser," Kelly asked, "You mean like in the navy, the lightly armored ship that protects the fleet?"

Eido Roshi looked at Kelly for a moment. His eyebrow cocked high into his forehead. "Noooo," he said at last, and put his hands up on an imaginary steering wheel. "More like...*Toyota!*" Eido Roshi gave the steering wheel a few imaginary turns left and right.

Being demoted from a huge naval vessel to an imported car was simply too much, and Kelly Jun Po let out a laugh so loud it was heard all across the grounds of the monastery.

The monastery was its own kind of voluntary prison, in many ways much harsher than Pleasanton Correctional Facility had been. There was communal sleeping, communal eating, rigidly enforced wake up and lights out times, and a restricted vegetarian diet. Privacy and free time were non-existent. Kelly had committed to staying in the monastery until he "woke up" — until he shattered his old habitual patterns and took his seat in freedom. Eido Roshi's initial training for all students centered around the "Mu" koan (does a dog have Buddha-nature?), and Kelly had failed this test again and again.

Towards the middle of this first year at the temple, he resolved to sit until he got it. Kelly, like the historical Buddha, decided he would not move, eat, or do anything until he broke through and got the Mu koan correct. For 72 hours he sat in the meditation hall, taking no food or water or rest. He just sat. He sat until his legs were numb to the waist, his back felt as though it might fail him, his eyes looked like someone had ground glass into them. At the end of his third day, utterly manic, he had his breakthrough. He crawled off the cushion, dragging himself to his feet and, lurching through the halls of the monastery, sought the roshi. He found Eido Roshi in his study, and with bloodshot eyes, bad breath, and an exhaustion so deep he could hardly tell the waking state from the dreaming one, he gave his answer. "Mu," he said.

Eido Roshi gave a short shake of his head. Wrong again. Kelly felt all the energy flow out of his body, almost as if the life was taken from him. He collapsed. He would never get it. He would never wake up. He was unteachable, a true barbarian. Eido Roshi looked at his student closely. When Kelly met and held his eyes, Eido Roshi began to tighten his face, screwing his features into a ball of contraction. His face turned violently red, his jaw muscles distended the skin below his ears, and his nostrils flared as breath came and went violently. He had Kelly's attention.

Roshi then brought his right hand up next to his face and drew it into a fist, the knuckles white and the arm shaking from the force of the contraction. The whole of Eido Roshi's being was under tension, bound in on itself. His eyes shot out an unrelenting rage and frustration; they bristled with contempt, with ambition, with self-hatred. Kelly saw a parody of himself in them, and he sat forward. Eido Roshi then let it all go in a flash: The tension vanished from his face, the color drained from his skin, and his eyes grew calm and open. He was as still and as calm as a lake in the midsummer sun. Only his fist was still tightly clenched. Eido Roshi then broke eye contact, turned his face and blew on his fist, *phewww*. As the breath crossed his hand, he opened it, then turned and smiled at Kelly with a body that was utterly, completely relaxed.

Kelly popped. In a flash, he got the koan, he got the joke, *he woke up*.

"Jun *Po*," Eido Roshi said very gently and very slowly, "*Does...a...dog...have...Buddha...nature?*"

Jun Po, eyes alight, smiled and shook his head. "*Muuuuu*," he said in a rumble, speaking from the pit of his belly. Eido Roshi nodded his head. "*Muuuuu*," he said again, laughing. Jun Po Denis Kelly had passed the koan test. Like the story with Suzuki Roshi and the student who had repeated, verbatim, what Suzuki had said, Kelly had finally answered the koan from the right *place*. It wasn't just the correct answer, but rather the correct answer *from* the correct understanding. It was an insight spoken not from his conceptual mind, but rather from the depth of his actual realization and understanding. He was revealing his insight, not talking *about* what that insight might look like. Kelly had experienced the truth of "Mu" in a profound, experiential way, and that was what Eido Roshi had been pushing him to do all those long months.

The shift required in Kelly's mind to make this leap, to have this understanding, was enormous. No longer seeking the manic disintegration of LSD-25, he had deconstructed his own ego without any external chemicals to aid the journey.

What Jun Po told Eido Roshi was "Nooooo" as in "know the truth of your own mind, know the truth beyond duality, beyond the very question. Know!" It was "know/no" — what he revealed to Eido Roshi was saying *no* to dualistic mind and to any conceivable dualistic content. It was Joshu's *mu* manifesting through Kelly. It was an Absolute "no!" speaking to the very dualistic nature of the question, and from that place, one should "know" a deeper truth. *No! Know!*

In the weeks and the months afterward, Eido Roshi and Kelly began to go through the 1,400 classic Zen koans, selecting 108 of them to be used for training other students at the monastery. The second part of Kelly's training was ready to begin. The koan insight was important, but so were the ethics that came from the realization. How does one live one's life in the context of the realization of the ground of being?

"SO," EIDO ROSHI SAID A YEAR INTO KELLY'S MOVE TO the monastery, "Next month I leave to return to Japan. It has been many years since I go home, and I plan on staying one year." Eido Roshi's round face was as always, a mask of restraint and calm. He exuded an air of deep authority and awareness, and there was little doubt that he was in charge. "So," Eido Roshi continued, looking Kelly hard in the eye. "Will you take the monastery?"

Kelly stared back. He had been a priest for only a few years, and was far from the most qualified or tested student in the monastery. Much more importantly, he wasn't a dharma heir or lineage holder, and putting him in charge would be bound to create a real headache of bruised egos, internal politics, board of trustee arguments, and backroom deals to undercut Kelly's authority. Kelly immediately suspected, of course, that Eido Roshi was all-too-aware of this.

"Roshi," Kelly said at last, "You want me to run the monastery even though I'm not your dharma heir? Even though you haven't empowered me?"

"Yes, Jun Po."

"I've heard some bad ideas in my life, but this is the worst one I've ever heard."

Eido Roshi smiled.

Kelly considered. He was already running the monastery. And it would be an interesting challenge.

"Okay," Kelly said, slowly. "But if I'm to be responsible for all *your* children, then you have to promise me something."

Eido Roshi ever so slightly raised a thin eyebrow.

"You have to leave me alone *completely*. It's *my* monastery. I run it as I see fit. No phone calls, no checking in, no interfering. Do that, and I promise that when you return it'll be in better shape than when you left."

Roshi's eyes narrowed. "Okay, Jun Po," he said deeply. "We have a deal."

True to his word, Eido Roshi departed for Japan a month later and left Denis Kelly as the acting abbot. He was to not only run the sesshins — the seven-day long intensives that including rising at 4 a.m. and spending seventeen hours in either sitting or walking meditation — but also in conducting *daisan*. Daisan is the sacred ceremony in which those on sesshin meet with a senior student to discuss their practice, and what has arisen during their sit (it's called *dokusan* if one does this with a master). Due to the fragile state such intense sitting can trigger in people, it is a position that is not to be taken lightly.

Kelly ran sesshins, deepened the psychological work for those living in the monastery, brought in one hundred percent organic food, taught daily Ashtanga yoga classes, and established an "open space" program to use the facilities for other purposes to help expose Zen students to other forms of learning. Within a few months, the feel of the temple was remarkably different. It felt like a modern integrated spiritual center and not just a medieval Japanese one. Eido Roshi would joke months later, referring to the concentration meditation taught there, that the monastery was "no longer just a concentration camp."

Kelly knew more than one person was rooting for his failure. In the strange paradox of spiritual centers, the backroom politics and positioning can be very nasty and intense, probably because it is in the shadow of the organization. Spiritual people are not "supposed" to be nasty, petty, jealous, and ambitious for power, but they are still people, and they still have the same impulses, neurosis, and weaknesses as everyone else. In fact, they may even have more of these things, which is part of what drove them to a monastery to begin with. Kelly was relatively young, not a senior student of Eido Roshi or a lineage holder, brash, arrogant, and sure of himself — just the kind of man who could succeed brilliantly or fail spectacularly.

There was a soft knock on his door. "Come in," Kelly said, and Hozan entered.

"Hozan," Kelly said, bowing slightly. "Welcome. How can I help you?" Hozan was about Kelly's age, but his stooped figure and compressed gait gave him the aura of a much older man. He was an American, and his Caucasian features were often creased with worry. He held his hands together at his heart, and his fingers tapped nervously against one another.

"I think there is a problem," he ventured cautiously. Kelly knew Hozan had the ear of the board that controlled Dai Bosatsu, and could sway them with his inside knowledge and ostensive concern for the well-being of the monastery, and Eido Roshi's reputation.

Kelly, who was folding laundry, continued without saying anything.

"I understand your problem," Hozan began, "Roshi put you in charge, but you're not a roshi. You are not a recognized dharma heir. And only a dharma heir can use the dokusan room to do daisan. There are rumors and talk about the fact that you are breaking sacred protocol, and that this offense could get back to roshi."

"Hmm," Kelly grunted, "I see." He knew that Eido Roshi had people reporting back to him in Japan — despite having promised that he would not interfere and would leave Kelly to run the temple as he saw fit, Eido was no fool. Likewise, Kelly suspected that Hozan was the very person spreading the idea that using the dokusan room was violating sacred protocol.

He folded a few shirts in silence, considering. Everyone knew Kelly to be a strong personality and self-confident teacher who never backed away from confrontation, and Hozan probably suspected that Kelly would dismiss any concerns about his authority to teach. That he might even welcome the challenge to his authority. Eido Roshi had, after all, left him in charge. But while Kelly hated politics and internal maneuvering in a place like a Zen temple, he also understood that these things were intrinsic to human beings.

"Okay," Kelly said, folding the last shirt and placing it in a drawer, still not turning around. "I will from now on conduct daisan in *another* room. Put me in the conference room, and we'll just have the participants come there for it. Doesn't matter to me — put me in the boiler room if that makes people more comfortable. The pipes will keep everyone plenty warm."

Hozan stared back and blinked a few times, his fingers fretting around one another. He nodded and silently withdrew, and in the emptiness of the room, Kelly smiled. It was a clever solution: if only a roshi could use the sacred dokusan room, then Kelly would do daisan in a conference room. He sidestepped completely the issue, which was that some of the senior students were upset that Kelly was conducting daisan at all. They had hoped to entrap him, but Kelly *had* been empowered by Eido Roshi, and so he played the situation to the letter of the law.

Ten-and-a-half months after he left, Eido Roshi called the temple and asked for Kelly.

"Roshi!" Kelly exclaimed, picking up the phone. "Good to hear you."

"You too, Jun Po," came the deep voice in response.

"But," Kelly said, smiling into the phone, "It's only been ten-and-half months. You promised me one year, roshi. Are you all right? Did something go wrong?"

Eido Roshi chuckled. "Oh, Jun Po. How are things?"

"Here?" Kelly said, knowing full well that roshi knew every single thing that was happening, "Things are great, roshi. Just like I said. Temple is in better shape than it's ever been, just like I promised."

"Good, Jun Po. Good. So, you did a good job for me. I would like you to fly to Japan, and to travel with me. It's my way of saying *thank you*. See you in Tokyo, Jun Po."

IN JAPAN, THERE WERE SCORES OF RINZAI ZEN TEMPLES without priests to run them. While formal Zen was slowly dying, Zen roshis were nevertheless treated almost like royalty. Rinzai Zen traced its lineage directly to the Samurai line, and it was by far the fiercest of the Zen traditions. Soen Nakagawa Roshi, Eido Roshi's teacher, had taught the Crown Prince of Japan.

The centuries-old Rinzai temples sit on some of the most sacred of land in Japan, and they are among the greatest architectural treasures on the planet. Kelly had, before he left, contacted Kim, the half-Japanese and half-Native American woman he'd unwisely invited to crash his engagement party. She was living in Japan and agreed to meet Kelly to act as his interpreter.

Not long after he arrived, a group of Rinzai Zen masters were invited to dinner at the Imperial Palace and taken there in a stretch limousine. A "barbarian" and "round-eye" given access to the Imperial Palace itself is an honor and a rarity that is difficult to describe. The palace is located right in the center of downtown Tokyo, a square kilometer of land surrounded by a moat, exquisite imperial gardens, ancient trees, and meticulously arranged medieval structures. Tourists are allowed in only twice a year, and even then are never allowed access to the innermost areas of the sacred grounds.

Kelly's limousine passed through a formal gate and over the huge moat that isolates the palace from the rest of the city. They pulled up in front of the palace, a surprisingly modest structure with iron gates and a wall of stone closing it off to the small road. Curving pine trees framed it on either side, so the car had to cross another small bridge.

As their limousine pulled up, a dozen geisha spilled forth from the palace in formal dresses, their feet in eight-inch heels and their faces entirely masked in white makeup. Each woman carried an umbrella against the light rain and opened the doors to the limousine. With tiny steps clacking on the cobblestones, the women led the group through the iron gates and into the almost unimaginable beauty of the Imperial Palace itself.

To *eat* in the Imperial Palace is an indescribable honor for a Japanese, much less for a six-foot-two native Midwesterner who didn't speak a single word of the native language. The fact Kelly was allowed was proof of a few things. One was how much pull Eido Roshi actually had. The second was how much Eido Roshi truly respected and honored Kelly.

The level of detail in the palace was stunning — everything in sight had been impeccably crafted by the best artists in the country, from the handmade tables to the exquisite plateware. The geisha exchanged their eight-inch high heels for socks, and stood silently behind each man, attentive to the slightest needs. Every sip of water from a glass meant it was immediately filled to the top, any stray speck of food was immediately wiped clean, each cup of sake was kept brimming.

From the reception they went upstairs to the dining area, where they were seated and served food on ancient Imperial plateware — and served the same foods the emperor himself had eaten 300 years before. Although dinner was entirely vegetarian, a Kaiseki meal, Kelly could have sworn he was being served steak, fish, and pork, along with a dizzying array of seaweeds and vegetables.

Halfway through the meal a bishop in the Rinzai Zen order looked over at Kelly, and began to speak to him in Japanese, his deep voice carrying through the room. Kim quickly interpreted.

"So," the large-faced Bishop spoke slowly, "You look like a reasonably intelligent barbarian." He smiled, letting Kelly know he was joking — a little. "I understand there are a number of teachers of Zen in America. Why did you choose that man?" He glanced to Eido Roshi.

Kelly sat with the question a moment. This was no light exchange, for this bishop was a highly realized teacher with an unshakeable reputation. Kelly wanted his answer to be thorough, but succinct.

"Every time I saw Eido Roshi, he was sitting," Kelly said, and Kim translated. "The other teachers in America, they teach, but you hardly ever see them practice. Eido Roshi is the most disciplined meditator I had ever seen." Kelly watched the bishop's round face as the words were translated.

The man first smiled, then turned red, then threw his head back and very nearly spit his sake onto the table, a rare sight in such a formal setting. He spoke again in Japanese, this time much more quickly, laughing.

The translation came: "Because *he was sitting!* That is your answer! Don't you know that the reason he sits *is because he has to*? What do you think, that Zen mind comes and goes? That Enlightenment comes and goes? That one is more present on the cushion than out in the world! *Students practice. Masters live!*" He laughed again, resuming eating after a pause. Kelly sat with this a long moment, and realized he had just been handed another koan. He looked over at his teacher, his master, one of the greatest meditation masters of the twentieth century. Eido Roshi caught his eye and smiled just a little, causing Kelly to laugh so hard tears came to his eyes.

Kelly went to the Ryūtaku-ji Temple, the main Rinzai Zen temple founded by Hakuin Ekaku, who had reinvigorated Rinzai Zen in the sixteenth century, saving it from ruin. Soen Nakagawa, Eido Roshi's teacher, was the current abbot. Soen was born in 1907 and had spent most of the twentieth century in a state of deep *satori* and awareness. He was a controversial figure in his day, for he was playful by nature and modest in a way that didn't sit well with the rigid formality and even more rigid hierarchy of Zen. Soen never wore the formal robes of a roshi, preferring instead the simple robes of a monk. He only took advantage of the roshi's private residence when he was on retreat; the rest of the time he ate, bathed, and slept in the same space as his students, obliterating the distinction between them, and could often be found cleaning the toilets after his students, an impossible modesty in Imperial Japan.

Kelly was more than a little nervous to meet him. Eido Roshi had trained him well in the art of the Japanese Koan, the enigmatic phrases used to gauge a student's grasp of Enlightenment, and Kelly knew he would be tested. He was, after all, one of Eido Roshi's top students and had been made acting abbot for one year, no small honor. Of all the students under his charge, Eido Roshi had brought him to Japan. Given Soen's reputation for unpredictable playfulness and fierce, penetrating insight, Kelly had no idea what to expect and he was extremely anxious.

Kelly was shown the beautiful temple and grounds, then led up a hill to Soen Roshi's private residence, used when the old master was on silent retreats. Soen was waiting for him there. The house was modest and meticulous, and Eido Roshi and Kelly entered a small greeting room. Soen Roshi was busy preparing ceremonial tea, and bid the men to sit down. Eido Roshi sat silently by the door, and he indicated Kelly should approach the old master.

Soen was a tiny man with bronze skin and shaved head, stooped at the shoulder and humble in bearing. Kelly towered over him and self-consciously hunched at the shoulders. Soen looked Kelly deep in the eye and was unable to keep from smiling.

"How do *you* do?" he asked in a thick Japanese accent, breaking the silence and raising an eyebrow. The fire of awareness burned in his eyes, as did a mischievous twinkle. Kelly was overcome with a powerful realization and clarity, as deep as he had experienced in his life. His training allowed him to stay present to the experience and respond instantly from his own Buddha-mind.

"How do *you* do?" he responded, taking the teacup in his hand and emphasizing the word "you."

Soen picked up his cup and leaned forward. "*Who* wants to know?" he asked, holding Kelly's eyes. A smile touched his lips again.

Kelly answered quickly: "*Who* is asking?"

Soen chuckled and leaned away. "Who *indeed*." He broke eye contact, pouring the tea into the cups and whisking it around to create a light foam across the top. He handed a cup to Kelly. "*Have a little more tea.*"

That was the entirety of their first conversation. Eido Roshi and Soen Roshi spoke to one another in Japanese for a few minutes and then Kelly and Eido departed.

It took Kelly ten years to realize that this had been a koan test of its own, and that his insight had been validated in front of two great Japanese meditation masters, sealing in his succession. He was a barbarian, it was true, but he was also an *Awake* one.

In his second year at Dai Bosatsu, Kelly was formally made vice-abbot to Eido Roshi. Soen came to the monastery to visit, and afterward the three men flew from New York to Tokyo. He and Eido Roshi would occasionally speak a few words in Japanese, but otherwise all three men flew in silence. About halfway through the flight Soen got up and walked to the emergency exit of the plane. He came back, chuckling, and gestured for Kelly to follow him up to the small porthole that looked out at the endless expanse of the afternoon sky. Soen pointed.

"You see?" he said, smiling, and Kelly leaned over and looked out into the emptiness. He stood back up. "There's nothing there, roshi," he observed, and Soen chuckled. His tiny, round face was alive with humor. He gently shook his head in disappointment.

They walked back to their seats. Half an hour later Soen elbowed Kelly in the ribs, and, chuckling, again made his way to the front of the plane. Kelly followed. Once there Soen pointed out the window, laughing and prodding Kelly. "You see?" he asked again.

Kelly peered out the window. Sky and clouds and sun. "Roshi," Kelly said, "There's nothing there." Soen chuckled and shook his head, and, seemingly satisfied, went back and sat down. Twenty minutes later, Kelly again felt the elbow touch his side, and Soen was walking toward the exit row, bidding Kelly to follow. Again, he did.

"You see?" Soen asked once more.

Kelly saw nothing. With a start he burst into laughter, and Soen Roshi joined him.

"Yes, yes, Jun Po," Soen said, "you see! There is *nothing*. Just *emptiness*." Smiling, he made his way back to his seat, leaving Kelly to look after him in amazement. The koan dialogue came in many forms, and Kelly's insight was always being tested.

Japanese temples are benign dictatorships. It had worked this way, and worked well, for a dozen centuries and Eido Roshi saw no reason to change that. As such, he ran his monastery tightly. He was always aware of exactly what was happening, from back-alley politics, to personality conflicts, to problems with the building, to things the board of directors might be considering. He knew exactly what was happening at all times, a testimony to his detail-oriented personality and his belief that it was, in the end, *his* monastery.

Dai Bosatsu, founded by Eido Roshi, saw him in residence most of the year and leading trainings all year round. One of those trainings always fell during the week of the 4th of July. Roshi absolutely loved fireworks, and it gave him tremendous pleasure to be able to watch the spectacular fireworks in New York City once a decade or so. But his service to the monastery came first, and so he settled for his students placing candles inside of floating paper bags on the lake that sat on Dai Bosatsu's property. He would come down to the dock on the night of the 4th, in his robes, hands held neatly behind the back, and watch as the hundreds of candles inside of paper bags floated across the water peacefully. After twenty or thirty minutes, he would walk back to the Zendo and go to bed. It lacked the dramatic punch of a fireworks display, but it was very Zen.

Kelly knew that his roshi loved fireworks and knew even more certainly that it would be almost impossible to surprise him. In the middle of the winter of 1989 he pulled aside a handful of trusted conspirators, secured a lot of extra cash — almost $20,000, most of that his own — and set about preparations. Six months later, he was ready.

Roshi was leading a very large seven-day sesshin with a few dozen people who had signed up to do the intensive seventeen-hour days of sitting and walking. Bedtime was normally 10 p.m., but on the 4th of July they stayed up a little later than usual so Roshi could make the walk from the temple to the lake, and watch the hundreds of candles floating on the stillness of the water in the recently settled darkness. He had failed to notice how Kelly had been vanishing that week whenever he had the chance, and getting up nearly two hours before the 4:30 a.m. wake-up call. He failed to notice too that Kelly and a few other senior disciples were not part of the group walking down to the lake.

Roshi, hands clasped behind his back, walked out onto the dock, watching as the candles floated serenely. It was a warm and still night and a gentle breeze pushed the candles in beautiful, peaceful eddies along the water's surface. The trees were heavy with leaves and they murmured quietly in the evening air as crickets chirped by the thousands. The night was clear, with the stars standing out starkly in a dark sky.

Several hundred yards away, on the far side of the lake, Kelly was dressed in all black. In front of him was a foxhole he had dug out by hand, and there were two other foxholes on either side of him, twenty yards apart. Inside each was about $6,500 worth of professional fireworks, and two of his co-conspirators were hunkered down in their holes. Kelly had not only secured the permits to have the show legally, he then used those permits to contact professional fireworks manufacturers. He had made more than a dozen trips to pick up scores of high-powered explosives, planning exactly how they would be lit to ensure the most spectacular show. It took him hundreds of hours of work, all done in the most intensive secrecy.

Eido Roshi stood on the dock, his senior attendants behind him, his face a mask of contentment, restraint, and discipline. The forty or so sesshin attendants lined the shores and, forbidden to speak or make eye contact on retreat, took in the candles silently, likely thinking of their friends and family enjoying barbeques and laughter.

On the far side of the lake, masked in darkness and conspiracy, Kelly lit the fuse of the first skyrocket, with a battery of explosives arranged in the order in which they would be lit. The fuse hissed into the rocket's casing. A second later an eruption of flame drove it into the sky, leaving a thin trail of smoke and sparks behind. Kelly then barked orders to the other two men, and they began lighting fuses carefully. His countless hours of secretive work were about to pay off: all Kelly and the other men had to do was light the fireworks in a set formation, using six foot sticks with flares on their tips.

On the dock, roshi's attention went to the single streaking firework moving up into the dark sky, and he allowed himself a smile, thinking someone had lit off a large bottle rocket from the woods. One-quarter mile into the air, it disintegrated in a perfectly spherical ball of red and orange, the explosion echoing off the trees.

A few seconds later, a half dozen fireworks went up, creating falling mandalas in the sky. After twenty minutes of steady fireworks, all three men had reached the end of their supplies. Kelly let the sky grow dark again, and the silence of the night reluctantly returned, with a few brave crickets offering a cautious chirp. As a murmur went up from the sesshin attendees, the sky lit up again.

Kelly had carefully planned the finale, and fireworks went off without interruption for five steady minutes, two and three at a time, filling the night air with light and smoke as the artificial thunder clapped and roared. Finally the sky went dark, with only the candles on the lake swirling in muted color. The students attending retreat exploded into cheers and chatter, whooping and hollering excitedly. Eido Roshi's arms had fallen to his sides. His normally composed face was a mix of awe, gratitude, and shock, but he quickly tucked his arms behind his back and set his face. Without a word or gesture he quickly left the dock and made his way back to the monastery, indicating that his attendants should not follow.

Kelly, blackened, burned, and covered in mud, ran laughing from his foxhole toward the temple. As he came up to the rear entrance, he spotted Eido Roshi's diminutive figure coming intensely toward him, and stopped. Tears streaked Eido Roshi's face, and his lips trembled with uncontrollable emotion. He threw himself onto Kelly's chest, beating him with his fists, sobbing. The two men hugged, cried, and laughed. After a few moments Eido Roshi released Kelly, composed his face and body into that of the master once more, and entered the building silently.

The door to the temple clicked shut, and Kelly stood overlooking the gentle curve of a valley, whose shadows rose, uninterrupted, to meet the sky. Behind him a single bulb burned, while just beyond the reach of its light darkness pressed in. Over his head two thousand stars twisted and boiled, set afire in the stillness of the country night. Kelly, not as good at composing himself as his master, sat outside in the sweetness of the summer night air, and let tears flow freely down his smiling face.

CHAPTER 16

THE CHAINS OF THE PAST

AFTER NEARLY SIX YEARS OF LIVING AND TRAINING full-time at the monastery, Eido Roshi determined that Denis Kelly was to become the eighty-third Patriarch in the Rinzai Zen tradition. (In time, Eido Roshi would elevate a woman, Roko Sherry Chayat, to the roshi position as well.) Kelly was the first student of Eido's to become a roshi in his own right. He now had to take his seat not as the ex-hippie free-love LSD manufacturer who had a spiritual practice, but as a fully-realized and fully-trained Zen master. Kelly took *inka* in October 1992, the transmission of mind, lineage and energy that has been a part of the Zen tradition for thousands of years. Part of the ceremony involved passing what is called the five Gates, where five monks stood between Eido Roshi and Kelly. Each monk asked a koan to Kelly, and they alone determined if it was answered correctly. This was done at the end of a seven-day retreat, with the forty retreat participants forming a circle, inside of which Eido Roshi, Kelly, and the five monks would perform the ceremony. Eido Roshi sat at one end of the circle, and between him and Kelly stood the five monks.

"Does a dog have Buddha-nature," the first monk asked, and Kelly's eyes narrowed. "*Mu*," he said deeply and slowly, drawing the word into a long growl. The monk stepped aside.

The second koan was asked, Kelly answered correctly, and the monk stepped aside. The third monk folded his arms, barring the path forward. He asked his koan and Kelly answered, but the monk shook his head. Wrong. Kelly dropped into his immediate experience. The answer to the koan had been correct. He had answered from the deeply awakened part of his being, with an open heart and an embodied gesture. The man asked again, and Kelly answered. The man shook his head once more. Wrong. Kelly considered, and the two men held one another's eyes as the monk asked for the third time. Without warning, Kelly head-butted him, sending him stumbling backwards. "Ug," he cried, hands flying up to cradle his face as he dropped to his knees. Kelly stepped over him to the next monk, who was staring with wide eyes. He and the next monk let Kelly easily pass. With a smile, Kelly took his seat at the feet of Eido Roshi, who nodded and smiled back. The ancient ceremony of *inka* began.

Afterwards, Jun Po Denis Kelly Roshi was handed his own *keisaku*, the flat wooden stick that is used to whack sleepy students in the back during long retreats. The fear of being struck kept many students focused, for a monk at any time might smack someone they thought were not focusing properly. Kelly hated the *keisaku*, because in his experience too many of the monks hit from a place of closed judgment or psychological shadow, and not with an open heart. As his first act as a roshi, he broke the *keisaku* across his knee, tossing it to the ground. There would be no corporal punishment under his leadership, a strong break from tradition.

Eido Roshi was classically Japanese — deeply ethnocentric, and convinced that the Japanese were the only truly civilized people on the planet. Eido Roshi thought there was no such thing as Zen outside of Japan, which meant that he expected his American students to become, in essence, fully Japanese in their interpretation and embodiment of Enlightenment. For Kelly to succeed, Eido Roshi implied, Kelly had to become Japanese. But there lay the trap: Denis Kelly was an American raised in a post-war Roman Catholic working class neighborhood in the Midwest. He was almost quintessentially American, and even though he had turned from the dominant culture decades before, the counterculture itself was also uniquely Western. There was nothing even remotely like it in homogenous Japanese culture, which valued conformity and order above all else.

The truth was that Japanese culture did not work in America — it was amazing that Eido Roshi had as many students as he did, but those he attracted were those who tended, like Kelly, to be looking for a rigid form to turn away from some painful part of themselves. Kelly didn't believe the Japanese were "better" at meditation or achieving spiritual insight than Westerners. The Japanese had indeed created an amazing culture that was solid and uniform and stable, but in other ways they had stifled individuality, creativity, and honest emotional expression. Sexism, racism, and imperialism were not, in Kelly's eyes, high Buddhist ideals, and yet they were without question part of the shadow being cast by the Rinzai school, and part of the larger Japanese culture.

Kelly came back to the question again and again after receiving *inka*: what did it mean to be an American Zen Roshi nearing the twenty-first century? He knew that for Eido Roshi it meant honoring and keeping completely intact the old ways of doing things. To Eido Roshi, evolution was something that occurred in other parts of the world, but Zen was just Zen, perfect as it was, and Enlightened mind was just Enlightened mind.

While Eido Roshi had allowed Kelly to bring yoga and therapy and other modern forms of self-exploration to Dai Bosatsu, he had never done those things himself, with the exception of him learning the first series of Ashtanga yoga. It was not properly Japanese, and so he stopped as quickly as he had started — Eido Roshi's wife, in fact, once ran through the Zendo as students were practicing yoga, nearly shouting *this is not a yoga school!* What Eido Roshi taught was Imperial Zen — Zen the way it had always been taught. "Go back to the Zendo," the line used to admonish students to train harder to break through their blockage, was not always the right thing to say, Kelly was realizing. Sometimes, "go to a therapist, then come back to the Zendo," was a more appropriate command. Or, "go to the gym and train your body, and get your diet straight, and get your relationships in order, and *then* come back to the Zendo." Or, "transform your understanding of your impact on your environment, and then come back to the Zendo." Zen, for all its strengths, had huge blind spots. It was focused on the Absolute — on what is known as the Awakened Mind, but tended to ignore the *relative*, and too often that meant that the ego that was transcended stayed fractured and broken and neurotic, and when the practitioners finally realized their own ground of being, that realization was forced to flow through a twisted and neurotic ego.

Kelly had seen plenty of this in his day, saw it in himself and in Eido Roshi who, despite his mastery of Zen, was still a fully flawed human whose eye could wander into unwise places.

Kelly suspected that Zen alone wasn't enough — that unless you were one of the incredibly rare people who woke up so completely that it transformed all of your mind (which out of seven billion people might include no more than a few dozen individuals), the small mind mattered. What that meant, exactly, he would have to discover for himself. Eido Roshi and Kelly parted ways not long after he received *inka* in 1993. His time at the monastery was over, and his life as a Zen roshi was about to begin. The student had become the master, and Jun Po Denis Kelly Roshi's real time of learning was about to begin.

KELLY MOVED FROM NEW YORK TO BOULDER, COLORADO, that same year. There he found himself immersed in a town that offered some of the most cutting-edge psychological work in the country. He was drawn to something called the Hoffman Process, an intensive eight-day workshop that had the participants go deeply into their family of origin's roots. Even though Kelly was fifty years old, an age when many men decide to put a stake in the ground and declare, "This is who I am!" he knew that the chains of his past were still binding him in the present. Even though he was a full-blown roshi and Zen master, he knew that his ego was still deeply conditioned, and he wanted to gain an understanding of how his upbringing had shaped who he was, binding him in so many places where he came into contact with the freedom of his Enlightened mind.

A few days into the work, he was asked to make a list, one hundred items long, of what he didn't like about his parents. After ten minutes, he had over eighty things listed for his father, and not a single entry for his mother. The person leading the group looked at Kelly's sheet.

"That's interesting. Your father was a real sonofabitch," the man nodded, looking at words like *alcoholic, short-tempered, abusive, unfair, cruel, uneven...*

Kelly nodded.

"Mom was an angel, huh?" There wasn't a single negative word under the column for his mother.

"My mom was as much a victim of my father's insanity as the rest of us," Kelly defended. "She *was* an angel."

"Uh huh," the man said. "You told me your story yesterday. I don't seem to recall your mother ever stepping between you and your dad."

Kelly opened his mouth with a ready defense, but it died there. In his mind, it had always been the boys and mom against dad, but suddenly it seemed a little less clear. He felt his face flush. "Well..."

"Did she ever demand your father not hit you?"

"No, but look, it wasn't that simple."

"Did she ever put herself between your dad and your brothers?"

"No, but that would have been crazy!"

"Or remove you boys from the house so you couldn't be abused anymore?"

"No, but look, it's not like that. She was as afraid of him as we were."

"Uh huh. She was an adult, no?"

Kelly said nothing.

"Just saying that might be one thing you could put down," the man offered, tapping at the column before walking off to another participant.

Kelly looked at the sheet in front of him, with dozens of negatives listed for his father and not a single one for his mother. Was it possible? Should she have defended them, at least tried to make a stand to keep her sons from being abused?

Over the next few days of painful emotional exploration, Kelly was forced to see a pattern in his life to which he had been blind: He didn't trust women, and he had not his whole life. He viewed them as perfect angels in his conscious mind, capable of redeeming and saving him from himself, but the truth was he always expected betrayal and abandonment, and when it came he wasn't surprised in the least. Grace had likely cheated on him, and had frozen him out of her life; Cheryl was caught in bed with his auto mechanic; Brenda had left him after deciding that she couldn't support Kelly's decision to devote himself to Zen, and also needed to find her own voice and her own strength. He, of course, had played his part in sabotaging all three of those relationships. Since Brenda left him in 1982, more than a decade before, he had kept himself guarded and detached through every additional relationship. He was beginning to see why.

Kelly left the eight-day intensive with a profoundly altered view of himself, and a deep thirst to do more "shadow" work, or bringing what was unconscious to his consciousness. Soon afterward, he met Sandra, a beautiful and embodied woman who was shy, quiet, and reserved. She had a soft power in her eyes that touched him deeply, and they became lovers not long after they met.

○

IN ADDITION TO BEING A MARATHON RUNNER AND ACCOM-plished yogi, Kelly was also an avid technical mountain climber. He set out to solo climb the Flatiron Mountains just outside of Boulder for a casual, one-day climb. He free-climbed the middle Flatiron, no small feat for even a young climber, hiking over to where he could rappel down the back-side with climbing ropes that had been attached and left on the mountain for other climbers.

It was a magnificent summer day, and he loved to push his body, feeling the strength flow through his limbs and torso. But Kelly felt a nasty surprise when the end of the rope he had climbed down dangled a hundred or so feet above the ground. He had few choices: climb back up to the top and choose another, longer rope and start down again, or free-climb down the remaining distance. His reaction was to prepare to free-climb down, an utterly illogical choice for any experi-enced climber. There was a paradox at play here. Kelly's mind was highly trained: He could remain in stillness as impulses, emotions, and thoughts came into his consciousness. He felt none of those things. And yet, he had not yet learned to con-sider why those particular impulses arose in the first place, or why he reacted to them in such a predictable, conditioned way.

So although it was with great equanimity he chose to free-climb down, the truth was that he would eventually come to see that he had a choice in that moment, and while his impulse was to climb down, that impulse was a highly conditioned response to fear and anxiety. Take control immediately and get yourself out of this situation, his reactive mind insisted, compelling him into action.

And so, standing on a tiny ledge, he let go of the rope, then shook off his climber's belt and backpack, watching them fall to the ground. He surveyed the territory below, and found a secure place to hold onto the rock face, detached his harness, and began free-climbing down.

About forty feet from the bottom was an outcropping that was bigger than he had gauged from above. He could not get his body around it by holding onto the mountain with his hands and stretching his body around it to find foot holds on the other side. He was trapped: There were no paths open to the left or the right for him to move parallel to the ground to find a better route down. He would have to somehow go over the outcropping, and the only way to do it was to hang from one arm while stretching the rest of his body over until his feet found something. Then he could use his free hand to find another hold, and release the first hand so that he could slowly move over the outcropping.

He found a hole in which to jam his left fist, which allowed him to work his body over the outcropping. The pocket of rock in which his hand was stuck seemed dry, but it turned out there was a pocket of moisture and moss inside of it. It was a fissure in the rock, and without warning Kelly's hand popped out of its secure place and slid down three feet of fissure, dislodging his feet and other hand. Now his entire body was hanging from one hand, and as he scrambled to find his footing or secure his other hand, he felt the tendons begin to let go from the strain on them. After an excruciating thirty seconds, the inevitable occurred: his fist opened involuntarily, and came free from the rock face forty feet above the ground. He pushed himself off as far as he could so he wouldn't smash into the mountain side on his way down, and landed in a kind of crouch on a tiny patch of bare earth between massive rocks.

He heard more than felt bones shattering on impact. Kelly lay on his side, his consciousness scattered but intact. He was alive, and he looked around slowly and carefully. He was lying on his side, and next to his left elbow was his left leg, positioned at an impossible angle. The left leg was bent back towards him as if his knee bent both ways, and his knee had clearly been obliterated. Throwing his left foot back down where it belonged, he could feel the catastrophic damage. He took a few deep breaths, looking to his left hand, which he saw was at a ninety-degree angle halfway to the wrist, cleanly broken in half. That's not good, he thought. Okay, you're running out of time. You're going to go into shock no matter what you do, so you better do something and do it pretty fast.

He impulsively snapped his left wrist back into its proper position so he wouldn't have to keep looking at it, then pressed his right hand into the soft ground, pushing himself up on his right knee, hopping to standing on his right foot. He wobbled for a moment, until the right foot snapped under him, the tendons and ligaments ripped free, unable to support any weight. He collapsed again, momentarily blinded by pain. He knew his body was deeply in shock, insulating him from feeling the full effects of the damage. He experienced the pain as a tremendous amount of neurological noise, like a radio station broadcasting static at high volume.

Kelly considered: He had a demolished left knee and possibly broken ankle on that side. His left wrist was broken cleanly, as was his right ankle. His head and spine seemed more-or-less okay, at least compared to his limbs. He pulled himself up against a rock with his unbroken right arm, and lay back breathing slowly and steadily, focusing his mind. He had very limited time before he would become confused and delirious, and needed help, immediately. But there was nowhere to go, and nothing to do but wait, so he let his breath deepen and tried to stay focused there, not allowing the growing static of shock to take control of his mind. He felt himself slowly begin to shut down, the brain directing energy away from his head and limbs into his torso to keep him alive as long as possible. He began to shake and tremble uncontrollably.

He heard a man and a woman talking somewhere, on a trail that ran below his position. He waited until they were clearly within earshot, then called out to them. "Hey down there! I need help!"

The voices stopped. "Hello?"

"Yeah, I need help. Gonna need a helicopter. I fell off the mountain, and broke just about everything. It's real bad."

"Holy shit! What should I do?" came a man's voice.

"Like I said, I'm very seriously injured. Go and get help immediately!"

"Yeah, yeah of course!" the words were excited and jumbled. "Holy fuck! Hang tight, fella. We'll be right back!" Kelly heard scrambling and sliding somewhere below, and a few moments later, feet on the trail again. "Hey," the man called, "Where are you?"

Kelly explained which mountain he had fallen off, and off of which ropes. Kelly knew he would have to wait until the couple went all the way down the mountain, a solid forty-five minutes, then to a pay phone to call 9-1-1 to scramble a mountain rescue crew. He did the math in his head, and figured it would be well over an hour before anyone would come and get him, perhaps more. He saw, lying broken and bleeding on the cliff, that he was being offered an exquisite gift. He was able to experience his body and mind dying, perhaps long before his actual death, perhaps not.

After a very long hour, Kelly heard the sounds of a helicopter above and the crackle of hand-held walkie-talkies below. Paramedics were soon surrounding him, but they were unable to airlift him out due to the angle of the mountain and the position of Kelly's body under it. He was instead wheeled out in a kind of human wheelbarrow.

Thirty-six hours later, he awoke to find Sandra sitting at his bedside. "Shhh," she said as he opened his eyes, confused. "I'll take care of you. Don't worry about a thing."

Kelly looked down his body, seeing three casts. "How bad," he managed.

"They had to rebuild your knee," Sandra whispered, bringing a spoonful of yogurt to his lips. "Had to rebuild your ACL and meniscus, and a bunch of stuff I don't remember. And your ankle was in pretty bad shape. Ligaments were all torn, but no break. And a double compound fracture of the wrist."

"Frankenroshi," Kelly groaned, managing a smile.

"But they said you may walk without a ... a limp..." Sandra said hopefully.

Kelly laughed. "Doctors." He shook his head. "I'll do a hell of a lot more than... than that." He spent the next few weeks in the hospital mending and doing therapy, and Sandra almost never left his side. She fed him, brought water to his lips, bathed his body, read to him, massaged his temples and his feet, and served him with the whole of her being. She arranged to have food brought to him, organic and vegetarian, so that he never had to touch hospital food.

His injuries would be with him for the rest of his days. Kelly would never again be able to jog, and he would only attempt to climb once more in his life: on the one-year anniversary of the fall. His recovery was relatively fast and the pain was manageable, in part because of his yoga practice and dedication to exercise. Yet a year would pass before he was free of a cane, and he would never quite walk the same way again.

By the time Kelly was released from the hospital, he had fallen completely in love with Sandra. With so much time to reflect, he was able to see where his heart had been blocked. He and Sandra moved slowly but consciously closer together, and Kelly was able to share how vulnerable he felt by exposing all of himself. Sandra responded with kindness, love, support, and complete acceptance, and within a year they were living together.

IN THE MID 1990S, KELLY AND ANOTHER DOZEN AMERICAN Buddhist teachers were invited to visit the Dalai Lama in India.

"You're going to India?" Sandra asked him, amazed. "To meet the Dalai Lama, personally?"

Kelly looked at the invitation in his hands. "Well, guess it's time to go and see dad," he said with a grin. "Find out if we've been bad boys and girls, or good ones."

The fourteenth Dalai Lama was acknowledged by just about every serious practitioner of Buddhism as having penetrating insight into the true nature of mind. His insight was not in question, but some Americans thought his cultural programming from Tibet did, in fact, strongly color and influence his beliefs, and not always in the most insightful ways, especially around topics like homosexuality, oral sex, the role of women, and masturbation, where the Dalai Lama could sound strikingly like a Roman Catholic bishop.

The Dalai Lama was hosting the conference to answer questions that were arising with the first generation of American teachers of Buddhism, and to see if he could impart any wisdom or clarity where Western cultural confusion might be creating problems in their understanding of the dharma, of teachings.

A dozen Western Buddhist masters, from many different backgrounds, were brought to India to participate in the conference. They sat in an audience, with His Holiness on stage taking their questions. Kelly was near the front, and he listened as one of the American teachers brought up a troubling question: A high ranking Tibetan teacher had gotten into trouble for sleeping with some of his female students, and had been sued and forced into a kind of hiding from the uproar he had caused.

This problem, it should be noted, has been a long-standing one in spiritual communities. For some, like Osho (also known as Rajneesh) and Papa Free John (also known as Adi Da), they dealt with this by having "free love" communities, where sex was encouraged as part of a spiritual practice, to take away the taboo surrounding it. Many other spiritual teachers had been accused of sexual misconduct, from Kelly's own teacher Eido Shimano Roshi to Chögyam Trungpa Rinpoche to the Indian yogi Pattabhi Jois. And it wasn't just non-Christians, either — in another decade, the dam would break on the Catholic Church, exposing an epidemic of sexual misconduct within its ranks. Clearly, sex was problematic for all of us, including our spiritual teachers.

"How do you explain his behavior, your Holiness," the questioner asked, perhaps hoping for a psychological explanation. The Dalai Lama, smiling, leaned forward.

"The problem," he said, gently, "is that their insight is not deep enough. When the insight of your true nature is deep enough, it transforms *all* parts of us, so that Basic Goodness and compassion naturally and effortlessly arise. This prevents the kind of deluded behavior we see with him." He sat back.

Kelly, incredulous, waited for someone to challenge the statement. He raised his own hand and the Dalai Lama pointed to him.

"Your Holiness," Kelly offered, "may I use a word here?"

"Please," came the answer.

"*Bullshit*," Kelly dropped, and a collective gasp went up from the audience. Father Geiger would have been proud to know Kelly was still making his philosophical arguments much the same way he had forty years before.

The Dalai Lama chuckled.

"I know this man we're speaking of," Kelly continued. "He took three three-year cave retreats where he saw *only* his master and lived in the wilderness with no power, no heat, no bed. That's nine years of the most intensive monastic training. He trained with *you*, your Holiness, for a *decade*. And he spent another decade training in the States. This man trained for *thirty years*, and you're telling me his insight isn't deep enough? I've met him, I've talked to him, I've practiced with him, and I'm telling you, that explanation is, with all due respect, *bullshit*, your Holiness."

Kelly sat back, smiling. The Dalai Lama nodded his head and chuckled again, his eyes shimmering behind the thick lenses of his glasses.

"That is because *your* insight isn't deep enough," he said with a kind-hearted smile.

Kelly's mouth popped open. As the Dalai Lama waited patiently for Kelly to respond, he couldn't think of a single thing to say.

KELLY WENT BACK TO THE UNITED STATES TO FACE THIS
dilemma fully. Was the Dalai Lama correct, or was there a
better and more accurate explanation that took into account
the insights of Western psychology? Was it possible to be completely and fully Enlightened, and still make the kinds of
profound mistakes that some teachers made? Was that a problem with their small, conditioned mind, was it as simple as the
Dalai Lama believed, or was it a combination of those two? In
Kelly's mind this was not a problem for the philosophers to
figure out, but rather something one had to experience for
himself. The only way to get to the answer was to throw one-
self into the messy territory, and see what happened.

Kelly knew the angels and demons that had given birth to
him had created a man rife with contractions and conflicting
energy, and he knew he needed to come to a far better understanding of his own origin. Kelly was beginning to realize
that Brenda had been onto a powerful insight: He had indeed
been whipped and driven by *something* for most of his life. He
had been reacting to events and situations as much as he had
been choosing his actions. Six years in the monastery had
interrupted his habitual conditioning; he was able to notice
the conflicting emotions and drives that would arise inside
of him, but still was more driven into action than making
choices freely.

The years of meditation had created a stillness in his mind
that made seeing what arose there easier. In the quiet he could
sit with his arising impulses, emotions, and thoughts. For
most of us, we react to life — someone cuts us off in traffic,
and we get angry right away. If we're late for something, we
rush and get angry at people who get in our way. Our reactions are conditioned, meaning that for most of us we don't
notice that the energy of the emotion must first arise, and
then we have to react to it. That we could, in fact, choose a
different reaction if we could slow the whole process down.

Kelly, because of his insight and quietness of mind, had
greater freedom to choose his reactions, but he had little
understanding *why those particular impulses arose within him in the first
place.* Perhaps the difference was cultural or perhaps it was
indeed because his insight wasn't deep enough, but Kelly did
not agree with the Dalai Lama. His Holiness, after all, had
lived in the rigid container of a monastery for his entire life,
and was a man who had taken a monk's vows of celibacy. In
Kelly's experience, it was intimate relationships that were the
most likely to activate one's old conditioned patterns and allow
for the emergence of emotional energy that one would never
encounter in a monastery. Kelly believed that the teacher he
and the Dalai Lama had been discussing that day had suffered
a powerful breach of integrity, not because his insight wasn't
deep enough, but because he had been sheltered emotionally

and practically for most of his life. Sexuality was one of the most potent and least developed parts of the human animal, Kelly knew, and if you never engaged that part of yourself in messy, real-world situations, you never saw just how broken you could actually be. He wasn't certain of his position, but he was certain he would find a deeper answer to the question.

○

KELLY AND SANDRA ENTERED A TWO-YEAR PROGRAM OF Buddhist-oriented psychotherapy called the Ayala Process, with Thomas Huffman and Reta Lawler acting as his teachers. Reta and Thomas were both Gestalt therapists and had studied with the great Indian mystic and teacher Osho Rajneesh for many years. Kelly, true to form, threw himself into the emotionally expressive work — catharsis, gestalt, bio-energetics, shadow revealing, and looking into the foundations of one's psychological structure. It was a small, Boulder-based community that allowed him to study intensely the patterns and shadows of his own psyche, and to expose the messy parts of himself for all to see.

One of the tools of the Alaya Process was to have people hold a deep crouch until they literally fell over from exhaustion. Most people would weep, scream, or otherwise express the extreme emotions that would arise from so much exertion. Kelly, though, would hold his crouch until he was covered in sweat and shaking, and when he at last collapsed he did so without any noise whatsoever.

"Seems like you're pretty good at stuffing what you're feeling, Denis," Reta noted one day. "Afraid to make a little noise, are we?'"

She walked off and Kelly, on the floor, looked after her, panting. Losing control, expressing emotion — these were not considered very "Zen," and of course Kelly loved Zen because of how much discipline and control one learned, no matter what arose within the mind. You simply sat in stillness, in non-reactivity. Kelly sat up, thinking. He *had* wanted to scream, to shout, but he had stuffed that desire. Why?

Over the next two years, he would come to use the Alaya Process to express himself publicly in ways that he could never have imagined before — showing anger, shame, and fear as they arose. By 1995 he was becoming adept at seeing his small, conditioned self — the little boy, for instance, who had learned to abhor violence so that he would not become like his father, or the sexually promiscuous twenty-something looking to define himself in opposition to his own upbringing. Or the grown man deeply distrustful of women because his own mother had not "protected" him against the abuses of his father.

Through the Alaya Process he came to know that his narcissism had been formed because he had to fend for himself from a very young age, and he was fearful of giving away any of his "power" to another. That was the story of his life, and he had defined himself for over fifty years against the backdrop of that story. The Alaya Process taught him he was free to author another story entirely. That was one hell of an insight — he and he alone was the author of his life.

He and Sandra were driving one Monday morning, with heavy snow falling against the windshield. They rode in a comfortable silence for awhile, until Sandra asked him a question.

"So how are you going to integrate what you've learned with Zen?"

"Well," he said, "this shadow work has been so consuming, I haven't quite settled that yet."

She nodded.

"Let me ask you something. Do I seem more humble since I started all of this therapy?"

Sandra laughed. "Denis," she said, taking his hand in hers. "Honey, modesty is not your strength."

He sighed, and laughed. "I know. But the whole reason I started this damn therapy was to get to the bottom of my narcissism. But I think it's actually strengthening it. I mean, the neurotic stories of being human are endless! So I'm broken, okay, so are we all. I get it. But so what!"

There was a long silence. "What are you getting at?" Sandra asked softly.

"The Alaya Process taught me that therapy's important when you have strong conditioning to unpack and make conscious — which God knows, I do. So I climbed inside the fact that all of us, from the Dalai Lama to the homeless guy on the street — are *entirely* conditioned, right? Our genetics, our upbringing, our innate traits all conspire to make us predictable, conditioned creatures who have an illusion of free will that is largely that — an illusion. For most of us, when someone says or does a certain thing, we react in an entirely predictable, conditioned way. Most of us are slaves to ourselves, to that conditioning. We're not free in any sense of the word."

"I see that," Sandra said.

Kelly gripped the wheel harder and shook his head.

"Learning how our upbringing creates reactive patterns is important, but there's a trap there. The ego loves nothing more than to talk about itself, about how neurotic it is, about how it has been hurt and abandoned and made to suffer in childhood, middle school, high school, the first marriage, the first job, by being forced into the role of a woman in a patriarchal system or as a minority in a racist society or the role of a white male in an anti-white male society or the role of a homosexual in a heterosexual culture — the stories and the victimizations go on and on and on. I was abused by daddy. Okay. And mommy didn't protect me. Okay, too. But so fucking what?"

Sandra laughed. "What are you getting at?"

"I'm not sure." He took the exit for the hot springs they were going to visit, and slowed down at the first traffic light. "So I was a victim of my parents, as we all are, and was living that unconsciously. Now I've made it conscious, so it's no longer driving me. I'm more free there."

"Sure," Sandra said. "I've seen the change in you, Denis."

"But the trap," Kelly said slowly, thinking, "is that there is no real 'me' to fix. That's the problem. That's why shadow work can become its own form of addiction. Something that is unreal and impermanent — me — getting more and more into the dirt of that, without ever seeing the truth: I'm not real, and I will die and when I die, everything I am, think, feel; every relationship I've ever had, every mistake and love I've ever known, will be gone. That's it, Sandra, that's what the problem has been. Look at Boulder! Therapists and psychologists assume that the egos sitting across from them are real, that they themselves are real."

Sandra's eyes narrowed, and she let his hand slip from hers. "How can my ego not be real?"

Kelly shook his head vehemently. "Egos come and go — they're real sort of, but not permanent. They are shifting and changing and impermanent, just as the stories of us are shifting and changing and impermanent. I lost my sanity entirely once, remember? Our egos vanish every night in sleep, come into existence at birth, are always in flux, growing, contracting, and changing throughout life, and they vanish in death. To treat the ego as permanent is like helping your child to overcome their fear of the bogeyman by encouraging him to believe the bogeyman is utterly and completely real!"

"I think I follow," Sandra said, smiling. "But so what?"

Kelly smiled. "Integrate the two. Zen needs therapy. But therapy needs Zen."

As Kelly spent the morning and afternoon soaking in the natural hot springs, he saw that the path to true freedom had to hold both truths as real. There was a small, conditioned ego that could impede every part of your life, *especially* your spiritual insight. Worse, it could deeply distort spiritual insight with its neurosis and pathology. But there was also the Absolute, the ground of being where Kelly had taken his seat. They were both true, in every person — a relative, temporal, and finite ego that would blink out of existence a few decades after it became self-aware, and an immortal, timeless, and utterly imperturbable deeper self that did not come and go, had never been born and would never die, and that saw perfection in the unfolding of every phenomena. Both of these were true, and both of them needed to be integrated for true insight, true wisdom, true freedom.

Therapy, he realized, was important but rooted in a lie — that the egos it served were permanent, or real. And Buddhism too was rooted in a lie — Enlightenment alone would swoop in to save you from yourself. Because of this, therapists often were the *most* trapped in their small selves, even if those small selves were 'healthier' than the other small selves around them. And spiritual teachers, likewise, were often some of the most neurotic people out there. Many at the Dai Bosatsu temple where he trained wanted to simply get away from their small, broken selves, as if becoming Enlightened or Awake or one with Christos or God would somehow magically fix all the broken parts of their small self. As if one *ever* transcended the ego. One did not — insight came through an ego, always, never around one.

As the sun neared the mountains, casting long shadows over the bathers, Kelly saw how he could bring Zen into the twenty-first century, and integrate the insights of the West with the wisdom of the East. He would call it *Stop and Drop*. Stop your reaction to what was happening. Drop into a deeper understanding of your true nature. Work the small mind, the conditioned ego, but be willing and able to drop into a deeper truth of your being, to that place that was beyond duality, beyond emotion, beyond thought, beyond sensing, to pure potentiality at the core of your being, out of which everything arose. People had to wake up from the delusion of impermanence, and they had to grow up into free adults, too.

○

WHILE KELLY HAD BEEN IN PRISON, JOHNNY PURCHASED 80 acres of land in Oregon wilderness. One of the large tributaries feeding the majestic Elk River ran directly through the property, which was so remote there was no electricity, phone lines, or sewer systems. By the 1990s Johnny had grown tired of maintaining the house and the property, and Kelly and Sandra decided to buy it and relocate.

The house was a modestly sized A-frame log cabin, with massive stone fireplaces downstairs and in the upstairs bedroom. There were plenty of windows, an ample and beautifully outfitted kitchen for cooking, and a humongous 3,500-square-foot deck with a redwood tree, nine feet in diameter, coming out of the center. The tree had broken in half during a windstorm, and thereafter the property became known as Broken Tree. The Pacific Ocean was only five miles to the west, and sunny early mornings almost always gave way to fog and drizzle by the afternoons, making everything wet and green and alive for ten months of the year. In the spring the normally placid stream, running just below their deck, would nearly burst its banks, and the noise of madly rushing water would fill the house. Ferns, mushrooms, creeping moss, redwoods, and scores of other trees and plants sprouted in all directions, and Kelly and Sandra shared the land with bear, elk, deer, owls, and other creatures. It was a magical, mystical place deliciously cut off from the world.

Electricity was supplied by a small hydro-generator on the stream, providing just enough power to refrigerate, do laundry, and run basic lighting. There were no computers, cell phones, land phones, email access, or any other connection to the outside world. To stay in touch, Kelly or Sandra would have to drive many miles to the nearest town.

Kelly began to hold retreats and attract a growing number of his own students, and organization became a challenge with such limited access to the outside world. After a few years, he solved this by running several hundred feet of wire into a tree, and setting up a dish at the top of it to boost a cellular phone signal. By bouncing the signal off a nearby mountain, he was able to get intermittent cell phone access. The now-reclusive Kelly and his partner Sandra were deeply in love with the rugged beauty and almost complete seclusion of their lives.

BILL KAUTH, ONE OF THE FOUNDERS OF THE MANKIND Project, came to a Rinzai Zen retreat that Kelly was leading in Wisconsin. The ManKind Project was founded, in part, to help men recapture a healthy masculinity. The group's founders believed that too many men had become confused about the nature of their gender, and out of touch with its innate strengths while all too aware of its weaknesses. The women's movement of the previous fifteen years had done many important things, but one of the causalities of it was that men were less sure than ever before what it actually meant to be a man, if it meant anything at all. Many of the more vocal feminist theorists taught that gender was almost entirely a cultural creation — that is, that there were few *innate* or *natural* strengths in gender beyond obvious physical ones. Men could be tender and sensitive, women could be tough and crass, men and women were equally good at everything, and holding any other opinion meant you were some ignorant, suppressive form of sexist, misogynist, or all of the above.

Kelly and Bill Kauth met and Bill realized that the ManKind Project could use the insights of Zen, and Zen could use some of what the ManKind Project offered. Bill had come to one of Kelly's weekend retreats, so it was now Kelly's turn to be initiated into their order. Kelly and some of his students entered the ManKind Project, and they began attending weekly meetings to get a better understanding of what significance it might hold for them.

A few years later, Kelly was part of a group of leaders who were given twenty minutes to make a presentation to one hundred or so men. Kelly put down a large tarp and asked that the group form a rectangle as a fence around it. An organic farmer, wearing overalls and sporting a thick beard, joined him in the center of the group. In the man's arms was a huge, fully domesticated Rhode Island Red hen.

Kelly looked over the one hundred men. Part of the tradition of the ManKind Project was that men who were initiated into the group took on animal names; these names represented an awakening consciousness, a tie to the larger world, and an embodiment of what they called the "New Warrior" energy. Many had taken the names of birds — Vast Silent Raven, Red Hawk, Fast Eagle, and the like. Kelly asked the men with bird names to step forward, and about forty of the men pushed toward the front row of the rectangle.

"So," Kelly began, looking over the men, "I'm here to talk about the choices we make in our daily lives. Many of you have done great work on yourselves, and had your hearts broken open to feel so much more than you ever did before. You've become more responsible parents, spouses, citizens, and brothers." Kelly paused, taking in the many nodding heads. "But today I'd like to speak to you about the choices you make, and about the integrity of those choices." The farmer began to pass around the trained hen, and she would get set down, walk around a bit, and get picked up now and again.

"So what happens when you buy cheap meat, when you support agribusiness, is two-fold. First off, you're impacting you and your children's heath: the growth hormones and antibiotics with which they inject animals affects our health directly. Cows fed grains only live about a third as long as cows fed grasses — and they produce more Omega 6 fats that clog your arteries and give you heart disease. Cows fed grasses are far lower in unhealthy fats, as are eggs from free-range chickens. In other words, you can eat eggs and beef that are organic and grass-fed and not have the negative impact on your body.

"Second off, you're impacting your children's environment with the carbon and waste output from these massive operations — so you can save a few cents a pound on your meats, and avoid the hassle of driving an extra ten minutes in your car. You're killing our water and our air, leading to massive red tides, and choking out bodies of water like the Chesapeake Bay, so you can save a buck on your dozen of eggs."

"I know what you're saying," Kelly continued. "Organic food is something like twenty percent more expensive than non-organic. And there aren't any stores near your house, which means you have to drive halfway across town to find it. And you've got three children, a wife, alimony, and child support, on top of rent, bills, fifty hours of work a week, and a thousand other things. I hear you, I really do. You're saying to yourself that I must just have more time and more money, right, that I can focus on these things because I have the luxury."

A few heads nodded, vigorously.

"But," Kelly said, his eyes intensely focused, "what you're really doing when you don't buy organic and free-range is that you're paying men to torture animals, to force them to live in stacked chicken-wire battery cages where they can't spread their wings, and they shit on those in the cages below. The men you pay cut their beaks off so they can't peck each other. When chickens hatch, the males are thrown onto a conveyer belt that takes them to a shredder where they get ground up alive and used as animal feed. After about six months of laying eggs, the hens are too bruised from pecking each other with their dulled beaks to be sold as meat in supermarkets, so their meat is sold to the canned food industry."

Kelly surveyed the group. "But you're right — it's *inconvenient* to be asking everyone if their meat is local and sustainable. I get it. And you get to save a few cents a pound on your meat? For that bigger TV — the flat screen. Or that extra case of Budweiser at the end of the month. Because you *deserve* it, you're *entitled* to it, right? For just a little torture and pollution as the cost. No big deal."

Many of the men began to shift uncomfortably.

"To my mind, denial, cynicism, and hypocrisy are not high spiritual ideals. We call ourselves 'New Warriors' and yet most of you are completely out of integrity, right now." The group rustled, and more than a few faces looked at Kelly with what bordered on violence.

"So," Kelly continued, "let's get real, because I'm tired of saying the same shit. I'm tired of people living in denial of this problem. Open your fucking eyes. I'm tired of people cynically telling me that what they do doesn't matter. Bullshit. What matters is your integrity. And I'm tired most of all of the goddamn hypocrisy. This is a group of men who are supposed to be about integrity and being in integrity. So for all of you with bird spirit names, here's what I want you to do."

He then, to everyone's astonishment, pulled out a hammer and a pair of snips.

"If you have an animal spiritual name, and you ate commercial chicken or eggs, or bread or muffins or pancakes today that were not made with cage-free eggs and free-range chicken, what you did was far worse than torture a chicken this morning. You *paid* someone to torture it *for you*. To cut its beak off, to inject it with chemicals that make it grow abnormally and painfully fast, to force it to live in a cage where it can't move at all but spends its entire life inside with other birds shitting all over it. *You* paid for that." His eyes blazed. "*You* paid to force a poor and uneducated man to work in that stinking shithole, that hell realm, to torture those animals *for you* and then to take that stain of shame home to his wife and his children."

"Why do you think slaughterhouse workers have one of the highest suicide rates? Because of what *you* force them to do *for you* to save a few cents on your eggs. So what I ask is for you to be in integrity. Stop being in denial. Stop being a hypocrite. If you're going to *ever* make that decision again, then take this beautiful Rhode Island Red hen here, snip its beak with the pliers and then hit it with the hammer and bruise it the way it would be if it spent its life in a cage. Be in *fucking* integrity for once, and stop paying others to do your dirty work for you."

Kelly now had tears standing out on his face, and his intensity, and his passion caused more than one man to look away. He held up the hammer and snips as the hen clucked and bobbed around the men's ankles. He let the group stew for a full minute in the silence he had created before putting the tools away.

Kelly scanned the crowd before giving up the floor. A dozen men had tears in their eyes. Another dozen looked like they wanted to rip Kelly's head from his neck. The vast majority just seemed in shock, and unhappy with the way they had just been spoken to.

He stepped out of the group and toward the side of the room.

"Hey," one burly man said, approaching Kelly, his face flushed. He was overweight, and his chin was lost in a fold of flesh. "Who do you think you are?" the man accused, jabbing a fat finger at Kelly. "We don't shame others in this group! We have enough fucking shame in our culture and as men without you heaping it on top!"

Kelly looked into the man's fiery brown eyes. "I'm not trying to shame you," Kelly stated, calmly, "brother, I'm trying to let you experience *guilt* by seeing and accepting what you've done. Shame is neurotically beating yourself up and abusing yourself, and in most cases it's not true. How in the world can *I* shame *you*?"

"Don't shame us," the man repeated, his voice quivering with emotion. "Don't you dare. Lot of these men are just barely gettin' by. Don't need no ex-hippie tellin' 'em how to live their lives..."

On the way home that night, Kelly had an insight. How, he wondered, could someone shame another? By definition, you could only shame yourself — someone might say something that would trigger a loop of shame, but ultimately shame had to be an internal reaction to some external event. The men who felt shamed in the ManKind Project group that evening had missed his point entirely; they were so focused on shame they missed the part where they should feel a pang of legitimate guilt. They missed how they were leading lives of denial, cynicism, and hypocrisy, and instead were reacting violently to what Kelly was saying, reacting to the words rather than hearing them, and agreeing or disagreeing from a non-violent and non-reactive place.

There was an important piece to this that Kelly saw, but it would take the disintegration of his own life and his own integrity for him to put all the pieces in place, and for Mondo Zen to be born.

CHAPTER 17

THE GREAT LIBERATORS OF CANCER, BANKRUPTCY, AND GRIEF

KELLY AND SANDRA MOVED FROM BROKEN TREE to Ashland, Oregon, and deepened their roots there. Kelly's life had become stable, predictable, and grounded. He and Sandra ran a successful Buddhist art importing company that allowed him to travel frequently to Nepal, and they lived in a picturesque home. He wasn't making a living underground as an infamous major player in the counterculture movement, wasn't on the run from the DEA or himself, wasn't seeking Enlightenment or insight into his own being. He was simply being, and doing what Swami Gauribala had suggested so many years before: practicing what *is*.

He and Sandra gardened, took long nature hikes, cycled, and traveled. Kelly integrated all the things he had learned along the way into his teachings. He now offered his students seven-day Rinzai Zen retreats combined with a form of psychological work called Stop and Drop. It was his attempt to bring the insights of the West into the wisdom of the East, and he thought he had succeeded in integrating them fully. His forceful personality and deep masculinity attracted hundreds of casual students and dozens of serious ones.

He resisted having his own zendo, though, something like Dai Bosatsu that would keep him in a single place and allow students to come to him. Kelly just wasn't an institutional man, and he didn't like the idea of being bound to a particular place or even to a particular state. So he rented retreat space from other zendos and spiritual centers. Although he had lived happily with Sandra in Oregon for the better part of a decade, the long habit of being ready to hit the road at a moment's notice was deeply ingrained, as were memories of the army and of prison.

Kelly was approaching his middle sixties as a man who had purged himself through the fire of his own mind and his own suffering, and emerged from it stronger and more content than ever before. He lived, day-to-day, with what one might have called an "unreasonable" amount of happiness. He was comfortable as a teacher, but just as happy to become a student of something and someone new. He had come home to himself, and found that there was peace there after all.

And yet Denis Kelly was a complicated man. Shadow lingered still, despite his best efforts to purge it. The tricky thing with shadow is that it, by definition, cannot be seen. It is only visible in one's actions, and in those things we hide from others, and ourselves. Shortly after the turn of the twenty-first century, Kelly's shadow began to creep out over all he had so carefully built.

A woman named Vicara had begun training with Kelly in the 1990s, and they shared an easy and deep chemistry. She was a petite and beautiful woman whose brown hair was close-cropped, and whose quick eyes reflected an effortless intelligence and an open heart. Trained as a medical doctor, she was also a certified therapist and acupuncturist, and her mastery of Eastern and Western modes of healing was deeply attractive to Kelly. In time she and her husband became priests under him, and Kelly and Sandra grew close to them. The two couples were good friends, and socialized a few times a year. Working deeply on spiritual insight, psychological shadow work, and sustaining an ever-growing community meant that Kelly and Vicara were in more and more intimate contact, and after years of working and training together, fell in love.

A teacher falling in love with a student is always a complicated matter, and one that is best managed in the open air of honesty and full disclosure. Kelly and Vicara acknowledged to each other that they had fallen in love, and meant to remain faithful to their spouses until they could sort through the tangle of difficult separations and ended marriages their relationship would have to demand. Yet they crossed a physical barrier in secret, and then lived in shadow and in shame while deepening their deceit — to themselves, their spouses, and the larger community.

Kelly rationalized his actions by telling himself that Sandra couldn't handle the complicated truth, that his community couldn't handle the complicated truth, that the husband of the woman he had fallen in love with couldn't handle the complicated truth. Although Kelly was deeply trained at feeling into his own emotions, when he dropped into that process all he felt was anger at being forced to hide his true feelings and his passions. He and Sandra were in an open relationship, and while he could have approached her before he had crossed a physical boundary, he did not. He feared Sandra would not understand or, worse, would leave him if he chose to pursue a relationship with Vicara, and the very idea filled him with a deep and pervasive anger. Kelly knew he was sitting on a ticking bomb for the simple reason this was no mindless affair.

He was in love, and love did not take prisoners.

He and Vicara saw one another only a few times a year, but after a few years of living their lie they decided they could no longer bear the burden — they had to let their spouses know what was happening. Not long after that decision, though, Kelly received news that commanded all of his attention, and the affair and its repercussions had to be placed aside.

THE GREAT LIBERATORS OF CANCER, BANKRUPTCY, AND GRIEF

He was leading a seven-day retreat in Texas where Vicara was acting as his inji (assistant). The ever-vigilant Vicara noticed a lump in Kelly's neck that looked out of place, and she insisted forcefully that he go and get it checked out as soon as the retreat ended. Kelly followed her recommendation, getting the lump biopsied in Oregon. A week later, his biopsy was thought to be a form of tuberculosis. Then another call came a few days later, saying that there was evidence of cancer, and recommending further tests that eventually showed squamous cell carcinoma of the base of the tongue.

"Mr. Kelly," an oncologist said several weeks later, the results in his hand seeming to pull the corners of his mouth toward them in a kind of grimace. The man sat behind the desk in his office, the diagnosis apparently too serious to be given in the antiseptic austerity of an exam room. "I have bad news, I'm afraid. Your cancer is more advanced than we had hoped."

Kelly took a big breath in and let it slowly out, nodding his head. "How advanced?"

The doctor pursed his lips for a moment. "The cancer is locally advanced. It has spread from the base of your tongue to the lymph nodes on both sides of your neck. The worry is that it may be already in your brain and lungs but in amounts we may not be able to measure."

"Christ," Kelly managed. "*Which stage*?"

"Four," came the response. The doctor, who had told more than his fair share of people terrible news, gave Kelly time.

"Four," Kelly breathed. "At least it's not five." Shock rolled through his system.

The doctor shook his head. "There is no stage five, Mr. Kelly."

"Stage five is dead?"

The doctor nodded.

Kelly gave a hollow laugh. "Does this mean I'm a dead man walking?"

The doctor's face clouded. "No," he said, contradicted by his uncertain tone. "This cancer does respond well to treatment." He paused.

"But?" Kelly asked.

"But, Mr. Kelly, it is in a very difficult location to treat, you see. It may affect or remove your ability to eat, swallow, and speak."

Kelly shook his head. "I've been eating organic foods for forty years, doc," he said, almost defensively, his eyes reflecting the deep pain and uncertainty of a cancer diagnosis. "Have been mostly vegetarian for thirty years. Haven't had a cigarette in forty-five years. I run, swim, or practice yoga six days a week and am a Zen roshi, for God's sake. How the fuck did *I* end up with cancer?"

The doctor shrugged. "Who knows, Mr. Kelly? Genetics, exposure to chemicals perhaps? Did you ever work in an industrial setting?"

Kelly thought of the many years spent in the lab making LSD, with a whole cauldron of carcinogenic compounds. None of them had once worn gloves or ventilation masks.

"Yeah," he said with a sigh, his hand moving up to briefly rub his eyes. "You could say that."

"Well," the doctor said hopefully, "you might be able to sue for compensation."

Kelly smiled wryly. "No blood left in that stone, doc."

The doctor shrugged again. "Okay. One more thing, Mr. Kelly."

Kelly raised his eyebrows.

"Your tongue cancer has spread into your throat and the lymph glands on both sides of your neck, possibly beyond. I recommend full chemotherapy and radiation treatment," the doctor said. "I can set up a team of oncologists and we can begin treatment this week."

Kelly shook his head. "Whoa — I appreciate that. But what I need is my medical records. I'd like to do some investigation on what my full range of options are."

"Mr. Kelly," the doctor said, sternly, "I have to warn you: with stage four throat cancer, time is not on your side. What-ever research you plan on doing, I recommend you do it quickly."

Cancer. Throat cancer. He had quit smoking when he was twenty, and had been living a wholesome life for dozens of years. Organic foods, fruits, yoga, meditation, and emotion-ally cathartic work for over a decade — how was it possible? He had a vigorous and steady daily workout and sitting practice, and had noticed no dip in his energy, any loss of weight, or any other symptoms. How could *he* have cancer? It didn't add up. It didn't make sense. And all of this right after he and Vicara had come clean with their spouses, creating an impos-sible mess in both their homes. First that, and now this.

Over the next month, Vicara and Kelly spoke to half a dozen oncology teams all over the country. Two integrative oncologist physicians, Dr. Raymond Chang (who worked with the Dalai Lama) and Dr. Keith Block helped Kelly and Vicara get a better handle on what alternative treatments had the best options of working.

At the end of his consultation with both doctors, Kelly asked the same question: "Okay, doc. If you were me, what would you do?"

Both men gave the same answer. "Mr. Kelly, you have stage four throat cancer. I would be getting conventional treatment with radiation and chemotherapy. You have thirty days to explore alternate treatments if you want. No more. After that, your treatment will become greatly complicated."

Kelly strongly wanted to avoid the incredibly damaging treatments of conventional chemotherapy and radiation if at all possible, because he knew that for throat cancer some-times the cure was very nearly worse than the disease. Even though he was universally advised to seek conventional treatments given the advanced nature of his cancer, he nevertheless decided alternatives were worth a shot. If he could beat at least some of the cancer back, it would mean exposing himself to less toxic treatments.

Sandra and Kelly flew to Europe to follow up on a treatment Kelly had heard about, one that had a decent track record of treating throat cancer. He was going to take his month. The doctor was a gynecologist, Dr. Nesselhut, who had developed some powerful cancer treatments involving hyper-heating the body along with the simultaneous training of a patient's immune system to go after the specific cancer cells.

The clinic was in a walled, medieval village in Duderstadt in Saxony. In late summer it was simply glorious to behold, and since the doctor's primary practice was gynecology, the village was filled with pregnant women and newborns. Interspersed among them were the cancer patients — thin, gaunt, and often with a touch of fear, resolve, or sadness lingering in their eyes. The contrast was striking to Kelly, and he loved the play of youth, birth, and new beginnings set on top of death, dying, and aging. To him, the sight of the rose-cheeked and smiling mothers did more to put him at ease than anything else, for the wisdom and the beauty of life was impossible to deny there.

Most days found Sandra and Kelly walking or bike riding from their hotel to the treatment center, where Kelly submitted to the daily tests and treatments. After thirty days, tests showed that the tumor on his tongue had not grown, but the cancer in his lymph nodes had. The stage four throat cancer was still progressing — more slowly, it was true, but progressing nevertheless. He was dying, and not in a Sylvia Plath "we're all dying" kind of way. Without treatment, he would be dead in a year.

He and Sandra sat outside of their hotel in Saxony, Germany, and Kelly considered his options.

"I could throw in the towel," he said, exhausted from the intensity of treatments that had heated his body to within a few degrees of death. "Death doesn't worry me, but I'm not really interested in slowly wasting away."

"You've never been one to turn from a challenge," she noted. "Or back down from life. This might be the greatest teaching vehicle of your life." Even though Sandra had been devastated by Kelly's lies about Vicara, she remained as fiercely loving and loyal as she always had been. She was ready to forgive him and to move on, as soon as the illness had been conquered.

"I've died dozens of times on lysergic acid," Kelly noted. "And on my meditation cushion. I know that death is merely a play of perspective." He sighed. "But you're right. It's a hell of a challenge."

"The question seems simple to me," Sandra said quietly. "Do you think your work is done?" The loaded question sat between them.

Kelly looked at the remains of a day quickly disintegrating in the west, the last of the sunlight throwing long shadows into the streets. The sky was a deep, bruised blue, and underneath it land that was almost unbearably green and alive and beautiful. It made his heart ache to think of leaving so much beauty behind.

"I'll fight," he said at last. He took Sandra's hand in his own. "Something I could never do without you." Sandra smiled, slightly, her eyes lost in the deepening sky.

Kelly went to MD Anderson Cancer Center in Houston, to a cancer team that he and Vacara had interviewed extensively. The state-of-the-art complex has one of the best head and neck cancer teams in the world, and the entire structure is dedicated to fighting cancer. At times, the huge and sprawling building seemed more like a cancer treatment factory than a hospital. Kelly found the right floor to meet with the doctors expecting him. A team approach to treatment was necessary because treatment had the potential to cause significant damage to Kelly's speech and ability to swallow. The team consisted of three doctors: a surgeon, medical oncologist, and radiation oncologist. There was also a speech therapist, dentist, social worker, and acupuncturist.

"Mr. Kelly," the lead oncologist, Dr. Kees, said. He was a youthful-looking man, with thin brown hair swept to the side and gentle blue eyes. He looked Kelly over for a few moments, then smiled self-effacingly.

"Well," he said, sounding a little embarrassed. He looked down at Kelly's medical reports for a moment. "I have to be honest here, Mr. Kelly. When we received your records and saw how long you'd waited to seek treatment, and your age, we had prepared palliative care." Palliative care is using just enough chemotherapy and radiation to prevent the cancer from interfering with the body, allowing a patient to die with as little discomfort as possible.

The doctor took in the superbly fit sixty-four-year-old yogi and Zen master sitting in front of him. "You looked very bad on paper." He tapped the folder in front of him. "But when we saw you walk through the door — " he paused. "Mr. Kelly, your overall health is simply remarkable."

"What are you getting at, doc?" Kelly asked.

"The oncology team — Dr. Rosenthal, who does the radiation, Dr. Clayman, the surgeon, and myself are in agreement, Mr. Kelly." He paused. "You look like you can take a punch," Kees said. "I think given the shape you are in, we have a chance to beat this thing. What we'd like to do is treat you like we'd treat a man half your age. It's the only way we can stack the odds far enough in our favor. We're going to have to kill the cancer we can't see to make sure it hasn't spread to your brain and your lungs. You have an aggressive cancer, and you have poor markers in the initial tests we ran. In other words, your cancer may not respond well to chemotherapy, it's pervasive, and it's spreading. So we will need to hit you, and hit you hard."

Kelly smiled. "I've learned to roll with the punches, doc."

"Not like these," he said. "I won't lie to you, Mr. Kelly: It will not be a pleasant experience during or after. There will be serious side effects. We going to recommend you first take two months of chemotherapy, two weeks of rest, and then two months of combined chemo and daily radiation."

Kelly nodded again.

"As you know, the tumors are very close to some very sensitive places in your throat, so we'll need to proceed carefully and watch your progress closely."

The chemotherapy was scheduled to start within a few days. Kelly rented an apartment near a zoo and within walking distance to the hospital. There was a gazebo across the street from the apartment complex, and Kelly went there the first week to practice his yoga. A homeless man was stretched out on the side of the gazebo, and as Kelly began his asanas, the man looked on with a kind of bemused curiosity. When Kelly finished up his practice, he nodded at the man and smiled, who nodded back at him before closing his eyes. They did not speak.

As the weeks went by, Kelly's balance began to falter and his endurance fade. Every day his yoga practice got a little more unstable and difficult to finish, and the homeless addict seemed to understand all too well the hell that Kelly was entering. He would watch Kelly sweating and stumbling, a little thinner with each passing day, and the two men came closer and closer to sharing a common reality. The junkie would look at Kelly and shrug his shoulders sometimes as if to say, "Hey man, the same thing would happen if I tried to do that. What do you expect?"

Every so often Sandra and Vicara would talk on the phone about Kelly and their situation. Vicara traveled to Houston three times to visit, the third time at Sandra's request when Kelly was hospitalized. Kelly was struck by how much both women were willing to tolerate a difficult situation and to put aside their needs for his well-being

AFTER TWO MONTHS OF WEEKLY CHEMOTHERAPY DRIP injections and then two weeks of rest, the first day of radiation treatment began. A mold was made of his upper torso, a kind of plastic screen to keep him from moving at all. The radiation needed to be incredibly precise in order to save some of his salivary glands and tissues so he would be able to swallow and talk after treatment. The slightest miscalibration or movement might mean he would be mute, be reliant on a feeding tube for the rest of his life, or both.

Kelly was brought into an antiseptically clean room, stripped to the waist, and had the plastic screen put over his torso to keep him immobile. He was then bolted to a table, and slid into an IMRT radiation machine. The technicians left and spoke to him through a speaker, and he was eerily alone.

"Okay, Mr. Kelly," a voice crackled through a tiny speaker. "We're set to begin. Just relax."

"Easy for you to say," Kelly said to no one.

The machine moved and whirled ominously around him, offering little noise except innocent-sounding clicks. There was no pain, and not even the sensation of warmth. Kelly, though, had done his homework, and he knew what was happening inside of his throat. After a surprisingly short amount of time the machine moved itself back into its original position and offered a final series of clicks.

"Okay, Mr. Kelly," the disembodied voice said. "We're all through. We're coming in now."

Kelly's brace was unbolted from the table, and the molded screen was then lifted from his torso and head.

This procedure was repeated day after day and, at first, it wasn't so bad. Kelly's throat was a little sore, like he was coming down with a bit of cold. But it gradually and steadily grew worse. After two weeks his throat was blistered, scarred, and peeling in large swaths, and had swollen so much that the screen over his face partially choked him. By week six, swallowing was almost impossible, and the pain in his throat was more intense than anything he had ever experienced.

"It's a burn, Denis," Vicara told him when she came to check on his progress. "A literal burn. Your throat is burned on the inside and out." She left a large supply of herbal tonics and soothing teas, but the truth was that nothing really helped. Painkillers did not stop the pain, and it was only when he tried methadone — used to wean heroin addicts off the drug while minimizing withdrawal — that he found something that worked.

His strength continued to decline as his body atrophied. For a man who had been physically active his entire life, it was a deeply humbling experience to lose command over his body. His treatments, not he, determined what he could and could not do, and Kelly had no choice but to surrender. By the fourth week of combined radiation and chemotherapy, he was doing the "cancer shuffle" down the sidewalks, walking his abused body from the hospital to his apartment, needing to stop to catch his breath along the way. And he always went by the gazebo, and he and the homeless man always nodded at one another, two souls who were transitioning from this world to some other.

By the fifth week of chemotherapy and radiation, his mind began to follow his body into disintegration. His mindfulness, so long a part of his being, faded. That ground of being, that ability to rest in a larger, deeper truth that he had created himself and that had been so hard to realize, vanished. Yet he was the same fierce roshi, not just an old and brittle man dying of cancer, and was able to maintain his sense of humor and his passion even as the world itself — its colors, smells, vibrancy, taste, and sensuality — slid into shadow. The stories of his life, the memories of places he had been and people he had known grew murky and distant and, like trying in vain to spot a familiar marker on a misty northern California beach, he was unable to see them clearly.

Kelly was able to bear this loss only because he saw the truth of the experience, the great gift being offered him. While alive, he was being given a taste of the reality of death, where the bright and colorful world he knew and the bright and colorful man he was would be taken from him. That still, dark Emptiness beyond concept, beyond form, beyond time, beyond death — he had experienced it and spent much of life there, even if he could no longer access it. Like a great love that was no more, he could remember the truth of his experience, and it gave him solace.

Kelly surrendered to whatever his fate might be. The radiation was brutal, even with the methadone. After the first month of radiation he was barely able to swallow, and forty-five pounds slid from his once muscular frame. By the seventh week, his weight had dropped under one-hundred and sixty pounds, and he was admitted to the hospital because of fever, pain, and a low white blood cell count. He was given a simple instruction: drink a ten-ounce shake in two hours, or a feeding tube would have to be inserted. He had to endure only ten more days of treatments, and was determined to continue to feed himself.

Kelly was given a can of a nutritional drink in a hospital bed with Vicara at his side, and the time was duly noted.

"Now, Mr. Kelly," the nurse said, putting her hands on her hips. "I need you to drink every last drop of that. You've got two hours to do it." She tapped her watch. "And I'll be checking on you."

"Funny," Kelly whispered hoarsely, "that drinking a few ounces an hour would come to be a challenge for me."

"It's normal," Vicara comforted. "A lot of people who get your level of throat radiation go through the same thing."

Kelly thought of Patrick, and just shook his head. "This shake," he breathed hoarsely, "doesn't have a chance." He brought the liquid up to his lips. The first swallow tasted like paint, and he gagged and nearly vomited. Rather than swallow, he tried to just pour the liquid down his throat, but it couldn't tell the difference between the larynx and the esophagus. One excruciating swallow at a time it went down. As the nurse came in to check and see if the bottle was finished two hours later, he raised it into the air and emptied the remaining few ounces into his mouth. He collapsed backwards onto the bed, panting.

"Told you," he whispered.

"Mmm hmmm," she said, nodding. She inspected the bottle. "Nice work, Mr. Kelly. That wasn't so bad now, was it?"

Kelly's final week of treatment was spent in a hospital room, with a devastated immune system, skin infection, and radiation burns to his neck. And then the treatments finally ended and he recovered slightly. When he was strong enough, he and Sandra flew back to their home in Oregon where he began a long convalescence.

Follow-up tests showed he was in remission, cancer-free. How long it would last, of course, was anybody's guess. Cancer-free, but at a tremendous cost. Kelly's tear ducts barely worked, so he had to use drops to keep his eyes moist. His sense of taste had been twisted into something dysfunctional — sweet tastes disappeared and acidic things like orange juice tasted like gasoline, while a dizzying array of toxic aftertastes took the joy out of eating anything. Radiation greatly damaged the bone cells of his jaw, weakening the bone. One of four saliva glands had survived, so that his mouth was always dry and he was in danger of losing all his teeth. His sinuses were chronically inflamed and generally aggravated, which was like having a chronic sinus infection, headache and all. Neuropathy, from the chemotherapy, affected his feet, forearms, hands, and calves, and caused the muscles to spasm painfully, and made sleeping through the night difficult. The chemotherapy and radiation had also severely altered his brain chemistry, and Kelly found himself in the grip of a pervasive depression stronger than anything he'd experienced in his life. It was so powerful that he seriously and frequently considered killing himself, and was only stopped by his stubborn desire to come out of the tunnel of his recovery to see what lay on the other side. His memories were intact, but he had trouble getting to them. Entire decades of his life were missing, but sometimes they would be triggered by a thought or a sound, and the memories would come crashing back into his consciousness. He was six-foot two and just over 155 pounds, a shell of his former self. But he was alive, his spirit as unconquerable as it had ever been, and he had some serious decisions to make. Sandra, realizing that Kelly was unwilling to leave her but also unwilling to leave Vicara, moved to the East Coast, and Kelly was left alone with this depression, his badly damaged body, and the repercussions of his actions.

SANDRA AND KELLY HAD BEEN CONVINCED, A FEW YEARS before, to reinvest their significant savings with an investment wizard who promised great returns. Initially skeptical, they had been convinced when a number of their friends explained how much money they'd made in their ten years.

Four months into Kelly's recovery from chemotherapy, the investment wizard's twenty-year Ponzi scheme was exposed. There had never been any investing, for he had been supplying his steady returns only by getting new clients and giving their money directly to his older ones. As is always the case with Ponzi schemes, eventually no new clients came and the house of cards collapsed onto itself. Kelly and Sandra lost hundreds of thousands of dollars in savings, their entire retirement fund. In the middle of his cancer recovery and in a painful separation from Sandra, he was suddenly penniless.

IN THE EARLY SUMMER OF 2007, KELLY TRAVELED TO Denver to meet with a senior student and Zen priest, Doshin M. J. Nelson, who was helping to integrate the contemplative insights of Zen with Ken Wilber's Integral theory. Doshin and Kelly were at an eclectic coffee shop in downtown Denver, with local art hung everywhere, exposed-brick walls, and a well-worn hardwood floor. Tattooed twenty-something baristas moved sullenly behind the counters.

"Hi Jun Po," Doshin said kindly. Although his teacher looked better than he had a few months before, the effects of cancer were still very obvious. Kelly was emaciated and very pale, with hollowed-out cheeks. His eyes reflected the haunted insight of recent cancer survival, where life and death had been pushed too closely together, taking a human being far past what nature had ever intended us to endure.

"Doshin," Kelly responded in a rasp. "Thanks for meeting with me." His hand unconsciously rubbed at the reddened skin of his throat.

"My pleasure, my pleasure," Doshin answered, smiling kindly. Doshin was a brick of a man. A former Judo master, his compact frame and neatly shaved head made for an imposing figure. Behind modest glasses were intense, powerful eyes deeply in touch with their emotions. Doshin had come to Kelly in middle age only a few years before, after his life had begun to fracture in a swirl of uncontrollable anger and purposelessness. He had decades of contemplative practice under his belt, but had been unable to find true happiness or to discipline his strong temper and quick anger. The two middle-aged men immediately took to one another. In only a few years Doshin had become one of Kelly's most senior students and a Zen priest. As Kelly said, Doshin took to Zen like a man falling off a log.

"I've got a problem," Kelly said, his eyes momentarily out the window. They came back to Doshin. "I fucked up," Kelly dropped, with no pretense. "In a big way. Need to get things straight."

Doshin merely raised his eyebrows, knowing that Kelly spoke sparingly and in an unflinchingly honest manner.

"I've fallen in love with Vicara," Kelly stated flatly.

Doshin nodded. He had been on many of the retreats with the two of them, and had noticed a subtle but unmistakable shift in the energy between them. "I figured as much," he said quietly, no judgment in the words.

Kelly sighed. "Damn," he breathed, putting a thin hand up to his face. "But that's not all. I crossed a line with her, physically, before the cancer treatments began, before the bankruptcy. I couldn't live with myself after a few months, so I told Sandra."

"Before the cancer treatments began?"

Kelly nodded.

"How did she take it?"

Kelly, normally composed and disciplined in nature, shook his head, letting tears come freely to his eyes. "She couldn't believe that I had lied to her." His voice dropped to a whisper. "That was what hurt her the most — not that I was with someone else, but that I lied about it."

Doshin felt the sting of the lie in his own chest.

"Chemo brain," Kelly said, tapping his skull. "I can hardly think. Really messes with your memory, and your emotions." He lowered his head for a moment, and when he looked back up the old fires of passion and discipline were alight. "Until the end of my days, Doshin, I'll be on my knees begging for forgiveness for lying to her," he said through clenched teeth. "For deceiving. For deceiving the community, for deceiving Vicara's husband, and most of all for deceiving Sandra." His jaw clenched and his eyes shone so fiercely that Doshin fought the urge to look away. "But I'll never apologize for falling in love. This wasn't some stupid, mindless affair. After a decade of working with Vicara, I fell in love with her. I'm in love with her, right now, more than I can express."

Doshin, suddenly overwhelmed, blinked back tears of his own. A red-haired barista, her left arm tattooed to the shoulder, approached the two men and, seeing the scene in front of her mumbled, "Uh, I'll come back."

Kelly shook his head. "I love Sandra, but I love Vicara too." His hand came up to his eyes. "Jesus, what a mess," he said. "What a fucking mess." A minute of silence passed between them.

Doshin rubbed a hand across his neatly shaved head. "So," he said, gently, "Where do things stand now?"

"Sandra left because she knew I'd never decide," Kelly said. "I was like Buridan's ass, that donkey between two perfect bales of hay, and I was about to starve myself to death. She loved me enough to make that choice, and end this."

Doshin nodded.

Kelly let out a deep sigh.

"I appreciate your honesty," Doshin said quietly.

"Yeah," Kelly said. "I wanted to blame somebody. Anybody. *Anything*. American culture. Puritan culture. Zen culture. Do whatever it took to not have to stand in the truth. What a mess I made."

THE GREAT LIBERATORS OF CANCER, BANKRUPTCY, AND GRIEF

Doshin knew his teacher well, and knew that Kelly had not sat down to solicit advice or to confess his sins. He had come to some kind of understanding, some kind of realization, and was about to share it. So Doshin waited patiently, and listened.

"Vicara and I have already come clean with her ex-husband." Kelly shook his head, and again tears were wiped away. "She and I took six months apart to get our lives straightened out, to make things as good as they could be."

Doshin nodded. "And now?"

"We need to come clean. To our community. This is too big to hide from the group, or to make excuses. Vicara and I have made the choice to stand in front of everyone, and publicly declare our love and admit our mistakes. A truth and reconciliation process, where we will invite all our community to share their opinions."

Doshin shook his head. "That's a big can of worms you're about to open. You could be just like every other spiritual teacher out there, apologize, fade from sight for a few months or years, and then move on." He smiled. "Otherwise, you're opening yourself up to everyone's angry projections. Including my own." His eyes twinkled. He felt anger at Kelly in that moment, for he too had been lied to and deceived.

Kelly reached out and put his hand on Doshin's arm. "I'm sorry, brother. I'm sorry I deceived you. But I need you now to help me make this right. The right thing, the necessary thing, is to come clean, and admit where we were out of line. I would love to take all the heat for this, but Vicara's gonna end up taking way more because she lives in a much more conservative town, and is known as a much more conservative person. The projection will be worse for her." He chewed briefly on his lower lip.

It was Doshin's turn to sigh. He nodded. "Okay," he said at last, the word floating slowly out between them. "What do you need me to do?"

"Help me plan the retreats. I'll send out an email to the community telling everyone what happened, and taking full ownership. I'll invite anyone who would like to speak to attend either a retreat in Colorado, or a retreat in Wisconsin. We'll give everyone a chance to speak their mind, directly to me and to Vicara."

Kelly sat in silence for a moment. "No more playing in the shadows, Doshin. It's time to start dancing in the light."

The retreats were the usual seven-day intensive Rinzai Zen meditation retreats, but then a special truth and reconciliation process was scheduled on the last day. The thirty-five retreat participants formed an outer circle, with the men and women facing inward. Inside of them was another circle, smaller, and made up of the priests and senior students of Kelly's. At the very center of the two circles sat Vicara, Kelly, and a professional facilitator and Zen priest named Tom Pitner, whose dharma name was *Fugen*. And although Sandra and Vicara's ex-husband chose not to be present, two people who knew them well sat inside the circle to represent their points of view. Kelly had already flown to L.A. and done a four-day shadow intensive with Pitner and another psychotherapist to work with conscious and unconscious shadow, guilt, shame, and grief. Kelly and Vicara had also spoken personally and privately to each priest in the order, explaining what had happened so they would not be caught off-guard, and Kelly had also sent a long and personal email to the entire community explaining what had happened.

Kelly and Vicara sat as the inner circle of priests and senior students spoke their experience of the affair, how they felt about the lies given to cover it up, and what they thought about Kelly betraying one of his own priests. It took a long time for the men and women there to speak their minds, and for Kelly and Vicara to respond to what was said. Many were disgusted by Kelly, and felt that he had betrayed the entire community. Others felt that their trust in him was irrevocably damaged. For those who had experienced the sting of infidelity in their own lives, Kelly and Vicara's admission was especially difficult.

Once all of the senior students and priests expressed how they felt personally, they were asked to all speak again, this time as part of a community with the voice of the community. The whole process took several hours, and by the end of it every single person had shed tears — expressed rage, betrayal, and shame. Some had expressed forgiveness, but many had not, and never would.

Vicara and Kelly then flew to Wisconsin and the same thing was repeated with the community there. Vicara then took the additional steps of informing her community in Wisconsin by personally contacting all the priests and lay members, explaining what had happened, how she had been out of integrity, why she had acted the way she had, and what she had done to redress it. She ended by asking anyone who needed to talk to her about it to contact her, and followed with phone calls and handwritten notes to each person. Although the process was incredibly painful and embarrassing, when it was all over she was able to say that while she had acted out of integrity, she had responded to that with *absolute* integrity. Because of this she was, at long last, able to begin laying her own guilt and shame aside so she too can get on with her life. It hadn't been easy, and emotion came readily and easily to the surface at the mere mention of this time in her life.

This wasn't a public lynching, but it was designed so that Vicara and Kelly could face and accept the effects of their actions on those they loved and cared about. It allowed them to look every single person who needed to speak to them in the eye, to hear how their behavior had hurt those around them. It also put the matter into the public sphere, and while it nearly destroyed everything Kelly had built, it was also the only thing that could have saved it.

THE GREAT LIBERATORS OF CANCER, BANKRUPTCY, AND GRIEF

CHAPTER 18

REBIRTH AND RENEWAL

NOT LONG AFTER THE TRUTH AND RECONCILIATION process, Kelly was sailing with some friends off of the West Coast, taking a forty-foot sailboat from Oregon to California. They were sailing after nightfall in rough storm seas, the swells reaching twenty or so feet as they surged beneath the boat. Kelly was on deck, and attached to the boat by a lifeline in case he was thrown overboard. Between the dark sky and the dark water, there was little to be seen save the white foam of the cresting swells. The boat would be overrun by a twenty-foot swell coming from astern, then slide down into the trough. There, for a few tense seconds, they were utterly surrounded by swirling water on all sides, as high as a two-story house. The sailboat would then move to a wave peak, and Kelly could look two stories down into the water around them. Up and down they went, the boat moving steadily in the rough waters.

Such seas are not uncommon in the Pacific, but an experienced crew in a seaworthy boat can survive them. Kelly decided to move from the cockpit forward, and he undid his lifeline to step up on the forward part of the boat. As he did this the boat lurched violently and listed to port, throwing him clear of the boat, lifeline uselessly held in his hand. At the same time the boat dropped into a trough, and for a split second Kelly was in the dizzying place of watching the boat drop out from under him, ten feet behind, and drop under him, twenty feet below. He would, he saw, land in the freezing Pacific water, at night, without a life vest. His body fell through the night air toward the water, and at the last moment the boat, pushed by another wave, swung back under him. He landed squarely in the cockpit in a tangle of legs and arms, and immediately lurched up and secured his lifeline once more.

"You just flew off the boat and back onto it again! I've never seen anything like it," the captain yelled. "Didn't know you had wings."

The boat was lurching violently, and instead of being oriented with the bow to the waves, the boat was abeam, getting rocked violently from side to side.

"What's going on?" Kelly called above the storm.

"Tiller chain broke," the captain yelled back; the boat had lost all ability to steer. He spun the boat's wheel to demonstrate. "That's why you got thrown overboard. I'm trying to control her by trimming the sails, but I don't think I can in this storm."

"Life boats?" Kelly called back.

"Nope. Hate to do it, but we're gonna have to call the Coast Guard and get a tow."

Four hours later a huge Coast Guard vessel appeared out of the darkness, its spotlight cutting neatly through the storm. The crew fired a line via air cannon to the sailboat, and the men were then hauled toward port.

The captain, Kelly, and three other men took shelter below deck.

"I've never seen anything like that," the captain said, passing whiskeys all around. Kelly declined. "A man thrown sideways off a boat who then lands damn near on top of me two seconds later. Someone up there likes you. You okay? Your nerves must be shot." The captain looked a little harder at Kelly. "Except...you're not shaken up by that, are you?"

Kelly smiled. "I'm afraid these days it would take an elephant or better to get my attention."

The captain smiled politely, not understanding the joke.

After everything he had experienced in his life, getting nearly thrown off a sailboat into the roiling Pacific at night seemed a story barely worth remembering. After all, there were no charging elephants, no disappearing swamis and huts, no dancing statues, no dissolution of the fabric of his being, no trips to the edge of sanity and back, no bankruptcy, life-altering affairs, or weeks spent in intensive care. There was just the visceral thrill of being alive, of being bound in his strong and stubborn body, of feeling his heart strain against his ribs and his face ache as he smiled and laughed at the wonder of his life.

WITH THE DISSOLUTION OF HIS RELATIONSHIP WITH SANDRA, Kelly moved to the mountains outside of Boulder, Colorado. He loved the bright skies and clean air of Colorado, and the aesthetic of a town that was at once so genuinely spiritual and so completely self-important. A year had passed since Kelly and Vicara had come clean to the community, and those who remained were beginning to rebuild from the leftover pieces. Kelly was holding a retreat just outside of Boulder, and Doshin was helping him to organize the event. The two men met at a coffee shop in north Boulder, a place situated in the middle of a bustling art deco shopping center. The coffee shop was a quaint place with lime green walls and spectacular views of the mountains, full of bourgeois new mothers and office-less freelance workers sporting goatees and skinny jeans. The baristas, much more clean-cut and with fewer tattoos than their Denver counterparts, sweetly inquired what the two men wanted to drink.

"Would you like soy or rice milk in your latte?" a young woman brightly asked Kelly.

"God no," he laughed. "I'm from Wisconsin. Put whole milk in it. You can throw in a block of cheese if you want."

The girl laughed good-naturedly.

"Doshin?"

"Coffee, black," he said.

"Born for Zen, weren't you?"

Doshin just smiled.

They sat in the window, overlooking a parking lot full of Subarus, Priuses, and hybrid SUVs, watching as fit men and women, many dressed in yoga pants, walked busily outside.

"Didn't we just do this?" Kelly asked.

"Seems like it," Doshin said. "But the last time I saw you, you were barely able to speak above a whisper."

Kelly nodded. His health had recovered, and he was closer to his old self than ever before, at least on the outside. "So I've been thinking since then. About the Stop and Drop process."

Doshin smiled. "I thought you might," he replied, taking a sip of coffee.

"I've been sitting with what happened with me and Sandra. But also looking at all the relationships I've had in my life, all the way back to the violence of my father, and how those have conditioned me. I had an insight why Stop and Drop didn't catch, one that helped me understand things a little deeper."

Doshin nodded.

"When I was caught between Sandra and Vicara, I was so angry at American culture — I blamed it for the dilemma, and was caught in a loop. I couldn't break out of it until I saw a deeper truth. So let me ask you this," Kelly said, raising one of his bushy gray eyebrows, "is anger a feeling?"

Doshin's smile hardened. Anger had been such a powerful part of his life, of his identity, that it was hard for him to get perspective on it. "You're kidding, right?" He laughed.

"No, I'm serious." Kelly leaned toward his friend and student. "*Is anger a feeling*?"

"I would have to say *yes*."

Kelly nodded. "Right. So think of the last time someone made you angry. I mean really, really angry."

Doshin sighed. His inability to control anger had driven him to Kelly in the first place, but he trusted his friend and teacher. So he closed his eyes and called up a recent time when he had felt a powerful, bristling rage within him.

"Got it?" Kelly asked.

"Got it," Doshin responded, and his eyes, when they opened, were vibrating with a visceral intensity.

"Okay. Now, I want you to drop in deeper. What's underneath it?"

Doshin shook his head. "Just intensity."

"Right. No past or future."

Doshin nodded tensely, his jaw muscles bulging.

"Now drop, Doshin," Kelly instructed. "Drop deeper."

Doshin focused, and the pleasurable smells and sounds of the coffee shop faded from his awareness. His strong, set face softened, and the edges of it became more round. The eyes relaxed, and the chest opened to allow a breath of air.

"I'm afraid," he whispered.

Kelly smiled. "Exactly. Fear. You're afraid. Now, what else? Drop deeper."

Doshin's long experience in contemplative practice made it easier for him to let the feeling stay present in his mind while another part of him watched what was arising. Kelly saw Doshin's lower lip begin to tremble, for adjacent to fear is sadness and grief.

"I fucking care," Doshin forced through clenched teeth. "I fucking care *so much*."

"So," Kelly said, "you're afraid." Doshin nodded. "That's what I thought. It was the same with me. And the same with everyone I've asked. So you care, and you feel fear, and you react to it by getting violent." Kelly smiled.

"I don't know," Doshin said, taking a deeper breath and opening his eyes.

"If your wife says something that makes you angry," Kelly said, knowing Patty, Doshin's wife, sometimes did just that, "and you pass a homeless man on the street who says the same thing, would you get mad?"

"Of course not."

"Why not?"

"I don't care what the homeless man thinks of me. I care what Patty thinks."

Kelly nodded. "So is anger a feeling or a violent projection and reaction to a deeper feeling?"

Doshin nodded, and a light came into his eyes. "Yes," he said. "I see what you're getting at."

"Anger is intense clarity, fear, grief, and deep caring. And then we choose either consciously or unconsciously to intervene, to become violent, and kick the dog, yell at the kids, slam the door, to blame American culture, or flip off the other driver. We care and experience intensity, and we choose to react by getting violent. How stupid is that?"

Doshin laughed. "Pretty fucking stupid."

Kelly nodded.

"The unenlightened ego does three things and three things only in reaction to anything life offers: moves toward it, moves away from it, or doesn't care. That's it. Anger, when it becomes violent, is just a strong movement *away* from something. This ain't rocket science."

"But traffic can make me angry, at times," Doshin said, winking. "But I don't *care* about traffic."

"Sure you do," Kelly countered. "You care about being on time. You care about not having your time wasted. You care about yourself, and don't like it when someone doesn't consider your car and your right of way. Do you get angry in traffic on a lazy Sunday afternoon drive when you have nowhere to be?"

Doshin considered. "Good point," he admitted.

"Before I agreed to go into the fire with the community in those two retreats, I had to figure out what was really driving me. I had the insight that anger is a *choice*," he said. "Christ, I was so angry at American culture — in hindsight, it's so stupid. We choose our reaction to the fear, sadness, and the caring, consciously or unconsciously, which most times is experienced as anger, shame, or dissociation. This is because we haven't learned to slow the process down, to see the primary emotions, and then to choose a compassionate and intelligent response. Our hysterical historical story gets in the way."

Doshin laughed. "All right. But what about people who are prone to shaming themselves, saying they're no good, not smart enough, not good-looking enough, whatever the story might be?"

"Same thing," Kelly said. "Shame is just anger directed inward, so instead of exploding violently outward at the world I explode violently inward at myself. Almost always tied to upbringing. Might as well just say, 'Hi mom, hi dad' when you feel shame. I know, because that's how I reacted to things for much of my life."

Doshin considered Kelly, who for so much of his life had been the *rebel*. "Not sure about that last point," he said, "But I take it that we're modifying the Stop and Drop process?"

Kelly laughed. "The Stop and Drop process needs to be fleshed out — it's incomplete. I know, because it didn't work on the most stubborn and arrogant asshole I could find."

"Is he sitting at this table?" Doshin smiled.

"He is. He's taller than you, and a little older, and has made a great deal more mistakes."

"I wouldn't be certain on that last point," Doshin laughed. "But he *is* taller."

"I am the walking example of just how ineffective it is. I think this might be the missing piece."

Doshin nodded. "Not much point to spiritual insight if you don't understand your emotions at a core level."

Kelly nodded. "How many times have awakened teachers screwed up because of something emotional? An affair? A flash of rage? Addiction?"

Doshin nodded again.

"We need to create koans centered around emotions, koans that train us to transform negative emotions within our awakened minds. Therapy and shadow work ain't enough. Meditation ain't enough. The stronger the emotion — depression, anger, anxiety, lust, jealousy — the more fuel there is to drive us to our *true* nature, to wake the fuck up."

"So you have this all worked out?" Doshin asked.

Kelly shook his head, grinning. "Nope. But I want you to start practicing it, and see what kind of feedback we get from the community."

"So," Doshin asked, sipping his coffee again, "you want me to start practicing this, even though I'm not entirely certain what you're talking about, and you haven't explained it fully?"

Kelly nodded, grinning impishly.

Doshin's smile broadened. An intellectual and scholar, his mind quickly ran to a central question. He paused to watch a young woman, in a tight-fitting top, walk by. "I'm curious what you think now about what the Dalai Lama said to you a decade ago. How it relates to this."

"That my realization wasn't deep enough?" Kelly asked, laughing. "He was right."

"But I'm curious what you think about the idea of what he said. That if one's realization is deep enough, it transforms all of his being, and there is no need for psychological shadow work."

Kelly considered. His lips drew in and his eyes momentarily turned inward. "He was right," he said at last. "If your realization is deep enough, it transforms the entirety of the human being."

"But?"

"But there are only a handful of people on the planet who wake up that completely. For the rest of us, it's a process that our shadows interfere with. But completely Awake, Doshin, is completely Awake."

"I'm curious, Jun Po. Have you ever heard of the philosopher Ken Wilber?"

Kelly laughed. "*Ken*? Yeah, me and Sandra used to sell him his Buddhist art back in the early nineties. Knew him as a customer. I've read maybe half a dozen of his books, but nothing in a long while. I tried to read that nine-hundred page tome — what was it?"

"*Sex, Ecology, Spirituality.*" Doshin nodded. "Have you looked at his theory recently?"

"I'm a territory guy, Doshin. I don't have much need for the mapmakers these days."

"I've noticed that," Doshin smiled. "But his new map helps to explain some of the territory you've visited."

"Like what?" Kelly challenged.

"Well," Doshin said, leaning in, "it could, hypothetically, explain how an Enlightened roshi could get into a messy affair with one of his senior students and fuck things up very nearly beyond repair."

Kelly sat back. "Is that so," he said at last. "Is that so?"

WHEN I FIRST MET DENIS KELLY, IT WAS AT A WEEKEND-long discussion in the summer of 2007 about how Ken Wilber's Integral theory can inform our lives and our practices. About thirty "leaders and teachers" showed up for the weekend course at a place called Boulder Integral. After the introductory talks and orientation, we were asked to get into groups of four to answer the question, to each other, about what Ken Wilber's Integral theory meant to us. I was in a group with my friend Jason Lange, a spiritual teacher and sensei named Diane Musho Hamilton, and a tall and imposing man with a shaved head and intense blue eyes. That man went first, and he sat back in his chair, taking a moment to make eye contact with each of us.

"Yeah," he said, his voice low and gravelly. "So they call me Jun Po these days. I'm supposed to be some kind of roshi, I suppose. A few years ago, I started screwing somebody I shouldn't have been screwing," he stated flatly. The three of us all raised our eyebrows. "A priest in my order. And I messed up her marriage, my relationship to my partner, and my entire community. Nearly destroyed everything that I had spent twenty years building. I realized that at 64 I still had more shadow work to do, and so it was back to the therapist. So I'm here to see if Integral can explain just what the hell happened to me."

I could hardly believe my ears. Spiritual teachers were notorious for excusing sexual indiscretion through a lot of doublespeak and bypassing of responsibility. I didn't know who this Jun Po was, but I was determined to find out.

IN THE WINTER OF 2007–2008, I WAS INVOLVED IN A VERY intense and challenging relationship with someone who was as dramatic as she was confrontational, and who brought out the very same behavior in me. Although we cared deeply for each other, we also fought harder and more frequently than in any relationship I'd had before (or since), which was greatly confusing to me. When Kelly was back in Boulder not long after the New Year, I requested that we meet, in part so that I could come to understand my role in my intimate relationship more clearly. He invited me up to a mountain home outside the hills of Boulder, where he was staying. I drove up, parked, and was greeted by Kelly, who was wearing the plain black pants and top common in Zen.

"Come on in," he said casually, and directed me to a place where he had set up two meditation cushions. I took my seat, and Kelly sat down across from me.

We made small talk about our lives; I told him of my recent divorce, my life as a recently published author of fiction, and the turbulence of my current relationship. He shared some stories of his own, and we laughed and connected like two old friends. Between us sat a beautiful Japanese bowl, and with a subtle straightening of his back, Kelly struck it with a wooden handle.

"So," he said, his face growing more serious. "Is there such a thing as pure listening?"

"Pure listening?" I asked, smiling. "Like what?"

"Can you just listen?" he asked, "Simply receive the sound of this bowl ringing?"

I listened, and nodded unsurely. A few minutes passed.

"Mind if I lead you a little," he said, smiling a little.

"Please."

"So just stop the sound," he offered. "Go ahead. Don't let it in."

"Okay," I said, getting the point. "I can't stop hearing the sound."

"I'll ask again: is there such a thing as pure listening, outside of your ego and your story? Is there such a thing as listening without valuation, without form, without thought?"

He struck the bowl forcefully as his eyes, blue and remarkably clear, bore into mine. I heard the sounds coming from the bowl entering my ears and registering in my brain. He struck it again, and I began to feel the ringing in my body, as if I were listening with my heart, not my head.

"Is there such a thing as pure listening," he asked, quietly. I did not respond.

Gradually, as I listened more closely, the beautiful bowl's vibration began to change. I no longer perceived the sound striking my ears and entering my brain; instead, I felt the sound radiating out from my heart to the bowl, and from the bowl through me. He struck the bowl again. I was the sound itself, and the sound was me — there was no listener and nothing to hear, there was only the undulating vibration moving through the room.

I nodded my head very slowly.

"Good," Kelly said, tracking me. "Good. Now, give me your eyes." I looked up.

We sat, a foot apart, for nearly an hour, eyes locked onto each other, Kelly striking the bowl every minute or so.

"What is *this* place?" he asked eventually, his voice reverberating deeply in my chest. "Describe it to me."

"It's vast," I whispered, barely able to speak. "Vast."

He nodded.

"It's peaceful."

He shook his head. "Peace arises from this place. Go deeper."

I did. "It's still. Unmoving. Timeless."

He smiled, and nodded.

"Deathless. Fearless. Immutable."

"Does this place come and go?" he asked.

I smiled. "No," I said, without hesitation. "It's beyond time."

Kelly nodded. "That is your experience now? Right now?"

I nodded.

"Show me. Show me without words."

I smiled, leaned in toward him, and snapped my fingers. He smiled.

"Does this place come and go," he asked again.

REBIRTH AND RENEWAL

"No." I was absolutely certain of my answer.

"Who comes and goes?"

"I do," I said, amazed at my answer. "But this place is beyond just me. It's the space out of which I arise."

"From *this* place," he said, cocking an eyebrow. "Can anyone make you angry?"

I thought of my girlfriend, who made me angry in the most infuriating of ways. The state of consciousness I had just explained to Kelly collapsed completely, and I nodded aggressively. "Of course," I said, eyes narrowing, pulse increasing. "Of course! I mean, that's why I'm here. I told you how she can really get under my skin. Yesterday, for instance..."

Without warning, Kelly took the wooden stick used to ring the bowl, and his arm flashed up and struck me across the temple, turning my head to the side from the force of the blow.

My temple buzzed, and I left my head tilted to the side as thoughts and feelings flooded me. I couldn't believe it. I really couldn't believe it. This old geezer had just *hit* me; *me*, a trained Shaolin Kung Fu master and tournament fighter with almost two decades of training under my belt and thirty years his junior. *He hit me.* My Catholic teachers used to hit me because they too thought they knew better, and I felt rage and indignation boil over in my belly. *Fucker*, I thought. With what bordered on hatred in my eyes, I raised my gaze to him, defiant, forceful, *angry*.

What greeted me froze that story in place: Kelly had tears in his eyes, and had leaned in so close our noses almost touched. I could feel his heart, feel his compassion toward me, feel his deep desire to have me get what he was trying to show me. I felt no smugness, no judgment from him, no patriarchal zeal or arrogance, only love and devotion and complete service.

Speaking very slowly, his voice trembling with emotion, he asked me again. "Brother," he whispered, "this is life and death; *get this*: can *anyone* make you angry?"

In a flash I saw it. I had chosen anger when he had struck me, but he had struck me out of service and love, and because he knew I could take — and needed — a punch. He very, very rarely does this sort of thing. He couldn't make me angry. My girlfriend couldn't make me angry. Only I could make me angry, no matter what came my way. Anger was the choice, the habituated reaction, but he had slowed down that reaction, allowing me to see what was happening in my own mind. As a martial artist, I knew that an angry warrior was a dead warrior, for the simple reason that anger overwhelms training and logic, and causes mistakes in the ring or on the streets. In Kung Fu, anger was channeled into deep clarity and presence. But I didn't see it was the same in my intimate relationships, that the same principle was true with my girlfriend, my parents, my friends, myself. My girlfriend could never, ever make me angry; only I could do that. I understood, for the first time in my life, where Christ was coming from, his state of mind, when he said: "...do good to those who hate you, bless those who curse you, pray for those who mistreat you. If someone strikes you on one cheek, turn to him the other also..."

"What do you really feel?" he asked.

"I *care*. I care *so* much about her," I whispered. "I love her."

"What else?"

"I'm afraid I'll lose her." I was amazed at how close to the surface those insights were, and how much I was fighting back tears.

"So you're afraid and you care deeply, and yet you react with violence? Does that make sense to you?"

I shook my head, slowly. "It doesn't make sense, especially since no one can make me angry but me."

Kelly sat back, and a large smile came to his face. "That's right, Baba," he said. "That's right."

That insight, that feeling of deep love and gratitude at being struck, was only possible because from this vast, empty, quiet, fearless, and timeless place, anger was inconceivable. Not as an idea or a philosophy of peace, but as a lived reality. There simply was no room for anger in such vastness.

Kelly worked with me for another forty-five minutes before we parted company, but I was so shaken from what he had shown me that I forgot to say goodbye, forgot to offer him a donation for his services, forgot to shake his hand or hug him, forgot very nearly how to get back to Boulder. Anger had so long been a part of who I was; I was angry at my upbringing, angry at the Catholic Church of my youth, angry at my bank account, angry at my girlfriend, angry at the world, and often angry at myself. What would it mean to live in a world where anger was inconceivable?

○

WHEN I WAS IN MY MID-TWENTIES, I SUDDENLY AND INEXplicably began to go blind in my right eye. A battery of tests conferred a likely diagnosis of multiple sclerosis, and at twenty-six I was looking at the possibility of blindness, incontinence, impotence, disability, and death. My world came into sharp focus, and through intensive changes in diet, the extensive use of acupuncture and energy work, and a redoubled focus on my life, I regained my eyesight and was symptom-free until the summer of 2009, just before I began work on this book.

I developed numbness in both of my legs at the beginning of the summer, and had to fly out to meet Kelly at a Zen center in Massachusetts to begin interviewing him. Vicara, his partner, treated me with acupuncture, and I made a steady recovery over the course of the summer. That fall we all attended a weekend retreat in Boulder, and afterward four of us went out to dinner.

We were eating in a swanky upstairs restaurant overlooking Pearl Street, one of Kelly's favorite places to eat because it featured local and organic foods. Our companions were in a conversation across the table, and Kelly leaned in close to me.

"How's your body?" he asked, conspiratorially.

"Pretty good," I said, taking a sip of my ale. "Numbness has gone away. I'm feeling like my old self again. Neurologist thinks the numbness might have actually been related to a long motorcycle ride, and not the MS. MRI results were mixed, but..."

Kelly nodded. "That's good, Kogen." (*Kogen*, pronounced like *Logan*, is the spiritual name he gave me half a year before.)

"But look," I said, "If it comes down to it, I'll teach Kung Fu from a wheelchair. I'll come to sesshins with a cane. It won't stop me."

Kelly smiled at me. "I know that. You'd be all the more powerful for it."

"And besides," I said, with a false sense of confidence, "If it gets too bad, I'm not into suffering. I'll take myself out of the picture."

Kelly, wearing his black shirt and pants, leaned in very close to me, and spoke just above a whisper.

"The great gift of death again stares you in your mortal eye, just like it did when you were twenty-six." He touched the scars on his throat from his radiation therapy. "I share this gift of early announcement with you, Kogen. And I will share the smile you will carry as you and I are eaten by the great mother herself. We get to be the ones who know the simple truth: *she eats every one of her children*. That's why you must not hesitate to Awaken."

Kelly paused, and his blue eyes held mine until I had to look away for a moment. When I looked back, he spoke again. "If it comes down to it, I won't let you suffer. We'll have a ceremony, and I'll take care of you myself." He leaned even closer. "You have my word."

For a long moment we held eye contact, and then he sat back. "Of course, I plan on you outliving me by at least several decades, and I expect the same courtesy. Now, more ale?" He topped off my glass from the large bottle in front of me.

KELLY AND I MET AGAIN IN THE FALL OF 2010, AT AN ART opening in Boulder. My former girlfriend Rachael was there, and I introduced her again to Kelly. After the show, I went to dinner with Kelly and Vicara at a nearby restaurant. As we sat down and ordered drinks, Kelly leveled a look at me.

"What the fuck was that about?" he charged.

I paused just as I was raising a glass of water to my lips. "What?"

"Rachael. She's your ex, right?"

"Yeah."

"So why the fuck were you acting that way to her?"

I looked for a twinkle in his eye, some indication he was pulling my leg. All I saw was fierceness.

"What?" I managed.

"You heard me," he said, jaw tight.

"What, am I supposed to be a dick to her? I still care about her!"

Kelly shook his head. "Kogen, that woman is still in love with you. You were being *flirtatious*."

I shook my head. "Respectfully, I wasn't."

Kelly spoke over me. "You need to be her *friend* and control your sexual energy; you need to not be so nice to her, for at least a few months, because your form of niceness is very close to being flirtatious. You need to let her hate you even, if it comes to that, to let her get over you. You need to do that for her."

"What?" I repeated, "Are you *serious*? It's not my fault she's in love with me! I enjoy her company!"

Kelly shook his head again. "You need to get this through your thick skull: It's not about you!"

I sat, somewhat dumbstruck, and felt my cheeks start to burn. "But you told me, just a few months ago, that all one had to do in a relationship was to be honest. That by being truly honest about what I was feeling and what I wanted, I wasn't responsible for what the woman did or how she reacted. That it was her shadows and conditioning and karma and whatever else, and that my responsibility ended with me being completely clear and completely honest."

He nodded. "Yes. That is true."

"And you're telling me now that I need to take responsibility for her, and act with her needs, not mine, in mind?"

"Yes," he said, ignoring the waitress that stood next to us for a moment before realizing it was not a good time. "That too is true."

"But those two things contradict each other!" I nearly shouted. "Either I'm responsible for myself, and being clear and honest, or I'm supposed to manage her!"

He shook his head. "No, Kogen. Never manage. Managing someone is another form of selfishness. Just be kind."

"Jun Po," I said, "So which one is it? Be true and honest to myself and communicate that clearly, and let her be the master of her own fate, or take responsibility for her?"

Kelly's blue eyes glinted. "Yes, Kogen. Yes. They're both true. They're both completely true. If you can't see that, you have no business being in a relationship." His words dropped like steel. Kelly smiled, and nodded at me. "So, what's good to eat here?"

ABOUT A YEAR LATER, KELLY WAS INVITED TO MEET KEN Wilber personally, to explain Mondo Zen and get Ken's thoughts and reactions. Wilber's body of philosophical work, spanning nearly four decades, brought Eastern philosophy and meditative insight into alignment with Western psychological and scientific insight in a unique and stunning way. Wilber is a great synthesizer of information who has created a beautiful overarching theory, a meta theory, that attempts to place the whole of the human experience and understanding in a single map, without resorting to metaphysics. In other words, without having to put God at the beginning or the end of his map. Wilber honors the best of the Western scientific and rational modes of thought while not dismissing or explaining away the incredible contemplative insights of both Eastern and Western mysticism. He was just the person to give Kelly feedback on the merits of Mondo Zen.

Wilber's home is in Denver, at the top of a large apartment building that has an almost gothic configuration. A modern lobby provides access to an elevator that leads directly to Wilber's apartment, some thirty stories above the street in a corner penthouse.

When the elevator door slid open, Kelly saw a beautiful apartment with stunning views south and west, decorated in a minimalist fashion. The main room of the apartment, easily big enough to accommodate thirty people or more, was a large rectangle running east to west. A long couch was arranged in an L shape, and the modernist stainless steel tables and bright red plastic chairs were a striking contrast to large Buddhist statues and other religious iconography.

To the left of the elevator, down a hallway, were Wilber's private rooms.

"Jun Po," a thirty-something man said. "Welcome. My name's Brian." Brian had on designer corduroys, expensive-looking fine leather boots, and a tightly fitted T-shirt that hugged a thin frame. Tattoos covered the better part of his right arm, and he wore a downwardly curving mustache that looked like something out of a seventies detective movie. Brian bowed slightly, and his tall frame remained hunched at the shoulder deferentially. He led Kelly into the main room and to a conference table large enough to seat twelve.

"Can I get you anything?" Brian asked gently, with an erudition that seemed at odds with his facial hair and body art. "Fruit? Water? Coffee or sodas?"

"Water would be great," Kelly responded, smiling. At least Ken wasn't surrounding himself with eggheads. It was a good sign.

Brian opened a bottle of Perrier and set it on the table.

"He'll be right out." Brian sat down nearby, dropping his gaze into a laptop computer screen, legs demurely crossed.

A few moments later, Wilber emerged from the hallway connecting the private rooms. Extremely tall and muscular, Wilber had a shaved head and was wearing eyeglasses with bright red lenses, which gave him a distinctive, other-worldly look. He wore designer jeans that were a faded blue, an open-armed white shirt, and was barefoot. The two men shook hands and sat down at the conference table.

Brian brought Ken a Red Bull and bowl of cherries, and after a few minutes of pleasantries, Wilber settled back into his chair, crossing his legs and bringing his fingers together under his nose.

"So tell me about Mondo Zen," asked Wilber, cutting to the chase.

Kelly nodded, sipping his Perrier. "What we've done is create 12 koans designed to do a couple of things, all in less than two hours. The first thing is to induce a state of clear, empty mindfulness — Dhyana — to give a person going through the process the direct realization, however fleeting, of non-dual, non-separate awareness."

Wilber's brow furrowed. "Not exactly easy," he commented.

"That's the funny part," Kelly said, "Inducing the state temporarily is easier than I thought it would be. It takes practice for people to stay awakened, of course, but what we do is give them a taste of what they've been looking for, on their own, right into their immediate and direct experience. They weren't just hearing about Enlightenment, they were experiencing it for themselves. After all," Kelly said with a smile, "it's right *here*." He snapped his fingers.

Wilber, in addition to having a near-photographic memory of academia, also had decades of intensive contemplative insight and was as comfortable talking about semiotics or ecology as he was about the insights of Nagarjuna. His attention, when it was focused, was like a laser, and his full attention came on Kelly. "How?" was all he asked.

Kelly was in his element. He didn't need to pull punches with Wilber. "Rinzai Zen uses simple concentration meditation to induce the experience of Enlightened mind. We use sound, and get a person to listen as deeply as they can. We then ask them koans around *is there such a thing as pure listening* and the like, and guide them right into their own undifferentiated awareness. It's a question and answer format that uses neurolinguistic programming to help them associate and claim this territory for themselves. In other words, Enlightened mind goes from a concept to a direct experience they're having in this moment."

"Clever," Wilber commented.

"I'd love to set up a demonstration and take someone here through it. Someone," and he looked at Brian, "like *that* guy."

Brian smiled, but didn't look up.

"So," Kelly continued, "We take them to their undifferentiated nature, to the spaciousness that is sitting right under their self-referencing ego awareness. Once they feel this and experience this, we have a series of questions that gets them to claim the experience for themselves — to own it, in other words. We get them to admit and confirm that they can drop into their own true nature easily, and that they are, in this moment with us, experiencing it — that what they've been seeking their whole lives is right under their nose. So a lot of the initial koans play with this and reinforce it."

Kelly smiled. "Tracking me so far?"

"So far so good. And most people get it?" The red lenses of Wilber's eyeglasses made his irises seem nearly black.

"Most," Kelly said. "But sometimes people can't drop. If that's the case, I'll work with their philosophical understanding of enlightenment, which is blocking their insight. But most people drop. From there we shift gears. We move into emotional koans."

"*Emotional* koans?" Ken sat forward.

"Right. The classic koans are cognitive, mental questions — *what is the sound of one hand clapping? Does a dog have Buddha-nature* and the like, right?"

Wilber nodded.

"Well, I found in my life, and in a lot of other lives, that only part of the problem of us staying asleep is philosophical, or mental. The other big problem is emotional. The traditional precept koans tried to address emotional understanding, but they're not really adequate."

"How so?"

Kelly laughed. "Look around at the behavior of a lot of modern Zen roshis."

Wilber smiled, nodding. A great number of spiritual teachers, including Zen ones, had seen some kind of scandal involving sexual or some other form of indiscretion cloud their teachings.

"So after we show them their true nature, we then take them into the most obvious emotions, and ones that everyone can relate to — anger, shame, and dissociation. We get to the root of these emotional reactions with them, at first philosophically."

"Which are...?" Wilber asked. Like a master poker player, his face and eyes gave away little, but it was obvious that his mind was quickly processing the information Kelly was offering.

"Anger only arises when three other emotions are present: fear, grief, and deep caring. Without these three, anger as a violent reaction is impossible. A homeless person calls you a prick on the street, and you keep walking. Your wife calls you a prick, and you hit the ceiling. What's changed? One, you care about your wife and what she thinks, and two, you're afraid she sees you as a prick — for any number of reasons. So I ask people to feel into the truth of anger for themselves."

"And shame?"

"Shame is just anger directly inwardly, an internalized voice of mom or dad or society or whoever."

Wilber said nothing, but his dark eyes were turning and active behind the red lenses.

"Once that's established," Kelly continued, "we ask them to

bring up something in their own life, a personal place where they've become angry or ashamed, and then we work through that scene while getting them to feel the truth and immediacy of their undifferentiated nature — a nature that can't be hurt or offended or angered or shamed — and their new understanding of the true roots of their anger and shame."

"So the idea is to interrupt habitual, emotional reactions," Wilber observed.

"Exactly," Kelly said. "Had a feeling you'd get it quickly. In my experience, it's the emotional things that are most likely to sabotage spiritual insight. By giving people a taste of the Absolute... "

"Where everything is perfect," Wilber interrupted.

"...where everything is perfect, we give them the space, the freedom, to look at their emotional body. Their koan — the question that drives them to wake up for good — comes not from one of the classic 1,400 koans, but right from their own life. Right from their own experience. So that the next time they feel anger or shame arise, they have a neurolinguistic pathway that leads them right back to remembering their awakened nature. So where someone getting angry in traffic was an embarrassing distraction to them before, now it's a method and a path for waking up. Life, not the guru or a retreat, is the most powerful teacher one can have."

Wilber started to ask more detailed questions in his methodical but informal manner. For four hours the two men talked, two old warriors, one of the mind and of ideas, the other of the body and of lived experience. The conversation finally wound down.

"Brian will contact you about coming back to demonstrate Mondo Zen," Wilber said, "I've love to see it in action."

They shook hands.

"Great to meet you," Wilber said.

"Actually, we've met," Kelly replied. "Years ago. You used to buy your Buddhist art from me. I had the finer pieces on consignment at ZiGi's in Boulder."

Wilber's eyes narrowed and his head turned slightly to the side. "Tara and Company?"

Kelly smiled. "That was it. I have to tell you, Ken, I usually don't trust anyone who's written more than three books. Too stuck in their head. And you've written something like twenty-five. But it turns out you're not too much of an asshole after all."

Wilber, used to a certain level of deference when people met him in his own home, roared with laughter.

OUT OF THE FIRES OF BANKRUPTCY, DIVORCE, AND near-terminal cancer a new theory, a new practice, and a new understanding of the world were born. The fires that consumed so much of Kelly's life left insight and clarity in their wake, and gave him the final pieces he needed to create Mondo Zen — the radical invention that brought Zen into the twenty-first century and fully into the West, without losing its power or the essence of its teachings.

Kelly still isn't an institutional man. He settled in Wisconsin with his love and partner, Vicara, and the two of them share a beautiful old Victorian home in the small town of Appleton. When one visits their home, it is obvious how much they love each other. During the day Kelly makes frequent, short calls to Vicara to ask her what she wants for dinner, how her day is going, or to tell her he's thinking of her and loves her. Kelly takes great delight in baking bread and cooking dinners many nights. They have a vibrant social life, a soothing home life, and a tantric intimacy that would be the envy of a couple a quarter their age.

In Kelly's sixty-seventh year he and Vicara started dancing tango together, and even though he is six-foot two and she a whole foot shorter, they make an eye-catching couple on the dance floor. He's taken to calling it "Zen Tango." Their main teacher and favorite tango instructor is Daniel Trenner, and Kelly and Daniel co-led a Zen Tango retreat a couple of years ago in Massachusetts.

Kelly leads up to a dozen weeklong retreats all over the world every year, and spends his spare time practicing yoga, swimming, hiking, hunting for culinary mushrooms in the summer and fall, and cycling, fighting through the physical limitations that remained from his rock-climbing injuries. Nearing his seventieth year, he has been cancer-free since 2006, and is as strong and fit as a man twenty years his junior, although the scars of his battles are still with him. The skin of his throat bears the marks of radiation treatments, the bone cells of his jawbone are damaged, and his tear ducts, saliva glands, and sense of taste have never recovered. Neuropathy, from the chemotherapy, still affects his feet, forearms, hands, and calves, and causes painful spasms that make sleeping through the night difficult. His gate is slightly altered from the fall off the Flatiron Mountains in 1993 and the work done to repair his legs. His mind and his emotions reflect the intensity and wisdom of a man who has seen his fair share of life, death, triumph, and tragedy. The chemotherapy forever altered his ability to process linear logic, forcing Kelly to rely more on intuition and feelings. His spiritual mastery is evident in the depth of his eyes and the power of his speech, and in the way he can open his heart in a moment to touch the person sitting across from him, in places deeper and more profound than they've ever experienced. He is Jun Po Kando Zenji Denis Kelly Roshi, a Roman Catholic boy raised in post-Dust Bowl Wisconsin; a high school dropout, family deserter, survivor of abuse, soldier, wanderer, urban LSD shaman and manufacturer, lover, hippie, convicted felon, federal prisoner, monk, and yogi, an ex-marathon runner, the eighty-third Patriarch of the Rinzai Zen lineage, and a fully empowered Zen master. Far from being above his humanity, he is the most human among us.

FIN

ABOUT THE AUTHOR

KEITH MARTIN-SMITH WAS RAISED in the closed and self-assured world of Catholicism, but by his early teens felt alienated by it and the suburban America that surrounded him. He started out his college career as a mechanical engineering major, but science only led to more questions and an even stronger sense of separation from the world. He ended up with a degree in English and minor in journalism, allowing him to work as a freelance writer not bound to a particular location.

A profound crisis of meaning sent him on an odyssey that spanned ten years and three cities: New York, Philadelphia, and Denver. He searched for answers through post-modern philosophy and bohemia as the esoteric disciplines of Northern Shaolin Kung Fu, Qi Gong, and Buddhism were reshaping his life.

In 2007, Keith met Jun Po Denis Kelly, and in 2010 was given the dharma name *Kogen* (Tiger Eye) and the title of *sensei* (teacher). Keith's first collection of short stories — *The Mysterious Divination of Tea Leaves, and Other Tales* — was published by O-Books in 2009.

In addition to his writing, Zen, and Kung Fu practices, he is also fond of sleeping in, drinking fine ales, and lying about.

He lives in Boulder, Colorado.

You can read more about him, including new works and offerings, at www.KeithMartinSmith.com.

ON THE PRACTICE OF MONDO ZEN

MONDO ZEN

Mondo Zen is based on Japanese Rinzai Zen, updated for the twenty-first century. Mondo Zen transcends the hierarchical/authoritarian, gender-biased and constraining monastic aspects of traditional Zen. It includes a more practical, experiential "in the world" engagement of Zen. Relying only on direct personal experience, as taught by the Buddha himself, it does not allow mythic constructs or mental abstractions to complicate its philosophical orientation. It rejects ideas such as reincarnation, soul as personality, bardo realms, past lives, a creator, and other non-experiential beliefs.

It is important that in the practice of Mondo Zen we consciously choose to set aside all such ideas, at least temporarily. This allows us to experience, test, and evaluate for ourselves a simpler and stronger way of knowing. This is important because our beliefs and concepts about God, karma, or an afterlife can force our immediate experience into a container of predefined understanding. Preconceived ideas rob us of deeper insight. By letting go of our attachment to our beliefs and mythologies — at least while we are actively doing this practice — we remove a barrier to insight caused by our attachment to those views. This attachment to our views is part of why realizing our true nature, in *this* moment, eludes so many of us!

Mondo Zen Koan Dialogue Practice

Mondo is an ancient koan dialogue practice. A koan is a special kind of inquiry, an enigmatic question designed to awaken one to a deeper truth. To answer a koan one must have an actual realization experience, not just an intellectual understanding of it. Koans are designed to break through the neuro-linguistic philosophical language barrier, allowing us to experience the vast empty silence within us, what is called Clear Deep Heart/Mind. They are designed, quite simply, to still the noisy mind and allow the light that is always shining in the silence to *enlighten* us. This is because Enlightenment, as many of us have heard and read, is right here this very moment, permeating all of who we are. It is our conditioning that prevents us from seeing this, and a koan is simply a direct question designed to help break up our habitual way of viewing the world. In an instant flash of insight, we can see the deep truth of our liberated mind. With this two-fold understanding—experiential and philosophical—we can experience and understand the openness and fearless stability within our ordinary mind. We can then choose to articulate, access, recognize, realize, and maintain awareness of Clear Deep Heart/Mind.

Mondo Zen koan dialogue comprises thirteen koans, all requiring a spontaneous answer. The first ten are insight, embodiment, and articulation koans. The last three koans are emotional koans. In traditional Zen, these would be the precepts.

The Emotional Koans

Jun Po Denis Kelly saw that in our culture the traditional view of Enlightenment alone was not enough. We also need emotional maturity. His insight was that emotional koans, taken from our actual lives, provide a process that transforms habitual negative emotional reactions into compassionate intelligent responses. Instead of reacting mindlessly to our emotions, we experience their deeper message, and listen to the information they bring to us. For instance, from Clear Deep Heart/Mind — our Enlightened Self — anger does not mean to act violently; it means to deeply care about something and need to take action. From this new understanding, we can choose a conscious, compassionate response to circumstances instead of reacting unconsciously and violently.

Our modern Mondo Zen dialogue dialectic practice works like this:

1. We help you to deconstruct your current philosophical view, allowing insight that might otherwise be blocked by your philosophy.

2. From this position of deeper insight, you can choose to witness how you have been blocking realization of your true nature by holding a confused, illusory, and ignorant view.

3. This insight and choice transforms your understanding of the nature of your mind and your relationship to circumstances.

4. With this experience confirmed as your foundational perspective, you can choose a new, more liberating philosophy.

5. Then, through engaging an emotional koan practice, you integrate this new understanding into your everyday life.

No one can do this for you! Jun Po encourages "teaching the teacher within," meaning his Mondo Zen dialogue radically undercuts the need for a student to project this "guru" status onto an outside teacher. The Mondo Zen process is a direct transmission of a modern interpretation of this ancient teaching. Ultimately it is you, and you alone, who must claim this realization and understanding for yourself.

We describe this process as "inter-subjective" because the experience exists in a conscious container formed by all present. The truth is that this teaching transmission travels in both directions—from student to teacher as much as from teacher to student.

You can learn more about Mondo Zen
and Jun Po Roshi's practice community
at www.MondoZen.org.

an imprint of MICHAEL WIESE PRODUCTION

DIVINE
A R T S

DIVINE ARTS sprang to life fully formed as an intention to bring spiritual practice into daily living. Human beings are far more than the one-dimensional creatures perceived by most of humanity and held static in consensus reality. There is a deep and vast body of knowledge — both ancient and emerging — that informs and gives us the understanding, through direct experience, that we are magnificent creatures occupying many dimensions with untold powers and connectedness to all that is. Divine Arts books and films explore these realms, powers and teachings through inspiring, informative and empowering works by pioneers, artists and great teachers from all the wisdom traditions.

We invite your participation and look forward to learning how we may better serve you.

Onward and upward,

Michael Wiese

Publisher/Filmmaker

DivineArtsMedia.com